The Unofficial
Harry Potter
Vocabulary Builder

The Unofficial Harry Potter Vocabulary Builder

Learn the 3,000 Hardest Words from All Seven Books and Enjoy the Series More

Sayre Van Young

Ulysses Press

Copyright © 2009 Sayre Van Young. Concept © 2009 Ulysses Press. All rights reserved. No part of this publication may be reproduced, stored in a retrieval system, or transmitted, in any form or by any means without the prior written permission of the publisher, nor be otherwise circulated in any form of binding or cover other than that in which it is published and without a similar condition being imposed on the subsequent purchaser.

Published in the United States by
Ulysses Press
P.O. Box 3440
Berkeley, CA 94703
www.ulyssespress.com

ISBN10: 1-56975-684-8
ISBN13: 978-1-56975-684-3
Library of Congress Control Number 2008904141

Acquisitions Editor: Nick Denton-Brown
Managing Editor: Claire Chun
Editor: Lily Chou
Editorial Associates: Lauren Harrison, Elyce Petker
Design and Production: what!design @ whatweb.com
Illustrations: Miro Salazar

Printed in the U.S. by Bang Printing

10 9 8 7 6 5 4 3 2 1

Distributed by Publishers Group West

IMPORTANT NOTE TO READERS: This book is an independent and unauthorized fan publication. No endorsement or sponsorship by or affiliation with J. K. Rowling, her publishers or other copyright and trademark holders is claimed or suggested. All references in this book to copyrighted or trademarked characters and other elements of the J. K. Rowling books are for the purpose of commentary, criticism, analysis, and literary discussion only. The works of J. K. Rowling referenced in this book are publications of Scholastic Books (U.S.), Raincoast Books (Canada), and Bloomsbury Publishing (U.K.), and readers are encouraged to buy and read these books.

To my wizardly family

Table of Contents

Acknowledgments ✦ viii
How to Use This Book ✦ ix
Dictionary
   A ✦ 1
   B ✦ 12
   C ✦ 27
   D ✦ 46
   E ✦ 61
   F ✦ 70
   G ✦ 80
   H ✦ 89
   I ✦ 98
   J ✦ 109
   K ✦ 111
   L ✦ 113
   M ✦ 121
   N ✦ 134
   O ✦ 138
   P ✦ 143
   Q ✦ 160
   R ✦ 162
   S ✦ 177
   T ✦ 206
   U ✦ 219
   V ✦ 225
   W ✦ 230
   Y ✦ 235
   Z ✦ 236
Epilogue ✦ 238
About the Author ✦ 241

Acknowledgments

Writing can be a lonely job, especially writing a dictionary, so I am especially grateful to friends and family who helped and supported me.

Early on, nephew Brady McCollom brought a youthful perspective to what words to include and, in fact, provided the impetus for *The Unofficial Harry Potter Vocabulary Builder*. As a precocious nine-year-old, he'd already read three of the Potter books, but confided that he wasn't exactly sure what a cauldron was.

Anita Schriver, Resource Specialist and Special Services Department Chair at Bancroft Middle School (San Leandro), provided invaluable editorial advice from an educator's perspective. Her collegial assistance on which words to include and how best to define them was extremely helpful.

At Ulysses Press, special thanks to acquisitions editor Nick Denton-Brown who got me into this, editor Claire Chun who got me through this, and copyeditor Lily Chou who got me out of it without embarrassing myself. All the folks at Ulysses, as always, were wonderful to work with. And special thanks to illustrator Miro Salazar.

Daughter Marin Van Young has always been everything a mother could ask for, and she brought all those sterling qualities to assisting me on this book, including her sensitivity, her imagination, her terrific sense of humor, and, more practically, her speedy typing skills and her magical way with words.

Diane Davenport knew when to say "Finish this!" She was also incredibly patient ("able to endure waiting or delay without becoming annoyed or upset"), caring ("compassionate; looking after another's welfare"), and supportive ("giving support, especially moral or emotional support"). I am grateful way beyond words.

To those of you who appear in this book under other names, you know who you are and how much I appreciate your support. You're all wizards.

Finally, my thanks to J. K. Rowling, creator of a complex, rousing, emotional, and wondrous tale.

How to Use This Book

Seven books. Nearly 16 pounds. Over 4,000 pages. And more than a million words. Whew! Harry Potter's story is a complex one, and author J. K. Rowling uses a complex vocabulary to tell it.

Most of the words and phrases defined here are "life-useful"—you'll encounter them again and again in and out of school. Perhaps you've heard some of them and were unclear on what they meant (like *bury the hatchet* or *decor* or *fluke*). Others may be totally new (*antechamber* or *cosseted* or *niche*).

Plenty of Potter-useful words are also defined. Knowing the difference between *eyeglasses* and *spectacles*, as used by Rowling, or why *stoat* sandwiches are not that tasty, will ease your way into really understanding Harry Potter's world. And since Harry's world is a British one, British words and phrases have been defined and an "American English" equivalent given. Feel free to use *blimey* at appropriate times!

However, only English-language words are defined here. Words like "Muggles" and "Dementors" have been made up by J. K. Rowling and, while wonderful to know, aren't much use in the real world.

The 3,000+ words defined in this illustrated vocabulary builder are arranged alphabetically and accompanied by a straightforward pronunciation—no fancy symbols or systems. Just sound out the word. When you encounter a word part in **bold** type, give that part of the word a little more emphasis. For very short words, a good "rhymes with" will help with pronunciation.

Many of the defined words have multiple meanings, but the definition given matches the use in Potter's story (although sometimes the same word is used in different places in different ways—check the definitions for *bog*, for example). The book and page where the word is used are noted. And the sample sentence, using the word in context, will help you to better understand and use the word.

Those of you who look up more than one or two words will soon realize there's a story going on here, and you may wonder what happens to Brilly, Willow, Annie, Tamika, Ravi, and all the other characters mentioned (especially the evil Blackpool). Check out the Epilogue at the end of the book.

Hardback editions used for this dictionary (all published in the United States by Scholastic Press, Inc.):

Harry Potter and the Sorcerer's Stone, first American edition, October 1998

Harry Potter and the Chamber of Secrets, first American edition, June 1999

Harry Potter and the Prisoner of Azkaban, first American edition, October 1999

Harry Potter and the Goblet of Fire, first American edition, July 2000

Harry Potter and the Order of the Phoenix, first American edition, July 2003

Harry Potter and the Half-Blood Prince, first American edition, July 2005

Harry Potter and the Deathly Hallows, first edition, July 2007

A

abashed (uh-**bashd**)
adjective Somewhat embarrassed and self-conscious. / *Chamber of Secrets*, page 52
An abashed Blackpool had grabbed a stalk of celery, thinking it was his wand.

abate (uh-**bait**)
verb To become less strong. / *Order of the Phoenix*, page 70
Though her anger had abated somewhat, she still thought it unfair to be grounded just for a few unfortunate spells.

abet (uh-**bet**)
verb To help someone do something wrong; often used in the phrase "aid and abet." / *Order of the Phoenix*, page 117
Who would aid and abet Brilly in his latest project—stink bombs in the teachers' lounge?

abject (**ab**-jekt)
adjective Extreme. / *Chamber of Secrets*, page 334
Bella's abject unhappiness after her break-up with Bubba was really painful to see.

abomination (uh-bom-uh-**nay**-shun)
noun Something that causes extreme disgust or hatred. / *Order of the Phoenix*, page 78
"You are a rotten, low-down, no-good abomination!" Willow screamed at the evil Blackpool when he bewitched her puppies.

abruptly (uh-**brupt**-lee)
adverb Suddenly or unexpectedly. / *Prisoner of Azkaban*, page 24
The lecture on charms ended abruptly when Madam Glinch's false teeth fell out and began chattering across the classroom floor.

absentmindedly (ab-sent-**mind**-ud-lee)
adverb Not paying attention, as if your mind were absent. / *Prisoner of Azkaban*, page 47
Dribbles absentmindedly sat on the just-painted park bench and didn't even notice his backside was now both wet and striped.

abstain (ab-**stane** or ub-**stane**)
verb To choose not to do something. / *Order of the Phoenix*, page 400
Fiona usually abstained from eating meat—sometimes she felt it was just too yucky.

abstinence (**ab**-stuh-nunse)
noun The practice of choosing to not have something you enjoy, like a certain food or drink. / *Half-Blood Prince*, page 351
"A little abstinence," suggested Wildwood, "may be good for you."

abstract (**ab**-strakt)
adjective Indefinite and unspecific; not concrete. / *Deathly Hallows*, page 455
The abstract patterns of the clouds shifted and swirled as the thunderstorm approached.

absurdity (ab-**surd**-uh-tee)
noun Something ridiculous, laughably inconsistent, or unreasonable. / *Prisoner of Azkaban*, page 349
Dribbles soon realized the absurdity of it—no one else was sitting in front of the high school on Sunday morning waiting for classes to start.

abysmal (uh-**biz**-mal)
adjective Very, very bad. / *Sorcerer's Stone*, page 307
"Your abysmal grades are extremely disappointing," said the boy's irate mother. "Wait until your father gets home!"

acclimatize (uh-**kly**-muh-tize)
verb To get used to a different situation (weather, place, or circumstances). / *Deathly Hallows*, page 455
Chi-Mun found it hard to acclimatize to using chopsticks after years of eating with a knife and fork.

accommodate (uh-**kom**-uh-date)
verb To provide with a place to stay. / *Half-Blood Prince*, page 634

"We can't accommodate any guests at the castle this weekend," said the queen. "The chambermaids are on strike."

accomplice (uh-**kom**-plus)
noun A helper, usually in doing something wrong. / *Half-Blood Prince*, page 256
Brilly and his accomplice Dribbles spread the slimy goo across the floor of the school gym.

accordance (uh-**kor**-dunce)
noun An agreement; used in the phrase "in accordance with…." / *Order of the Phoenix*, page 352
Another boring announcement from the principal: "In accordance with school policy, anyone wearing anything striped or polka-dotted will be immediately sent home."

accost (uh-**cost**)
verb To approach someone, often in an annoying or threatening way. / *Goblet of Fire*, page 424
The pushy panhandler accosted Blackpool and demanded change, so Blackpool changed him into a hedgehog.

accusation (ak-yoo-**zay**-shun)
noun A statement that someone is guilty of wrongdoing. / *Goblet of Fire*, page 153
The principal's latest accusation was that Brilly had put Foaming Burbles in all the school toilets.

accusatory (ak-**kyoo**-zuh-tor-ee)
adjective Accusing or blaming. / *Order of the Phoenix*, page 230
The queen's accusatory look was entirely justified—the king had once again forgotten her birthday.

acquit (uh-**kwit**)
verb To conduct oneself in a positive manner (honorably, well, etc.). / *Order of the Phoenix*, page 838
Butch Thuggins, famed soccer player, acquitted himself far beyond the coach's expectations in the league championships.

acrid (**ak**-rid)
adjective Sharp, bitter, and irritating; usually said of smell. / *Chamber of Secrets*, page 180
The acrid smell of the truck exhaust made Fiona's nose itch and her stomach turn somersaults.

activate (**ak**-tuh-vate)
verb To make active; to turn on or start up. / *Order of the Phoenix*, page 616
To activate the hex, just say "Plunk your magic twanger, Froggie!"

adamant (**ad**-uh-munt)
adjective Not giving in easily. / *Goblet of Fire*, page 316
An adamant Wildwood refused to wear a top hat and tails to the dress-up party.

Adam's apple (**ad**-ums **ap**-ul)
noun The lump at the front of the throat, most noticeable in older boys and men. / *Order of the Phoenix*, page 136
His Adam's apple bobbed up and down every time he swallowed.

adder
See **snake** elsewhere in this dictionary.

addle (**ad**-dul)
verb To confuse or mix up. / *Goblet of Fire*, page 706
Worrying about the botany test addled Elrod so much that he put his backpack on upside down.

addled (**ad**-duld)
adjective Mentally confused. / *Order of the Phoenix*, page 486
The addled wizard waved the porcupine, trying to enchant his wand.

adept (uh-**dept**)
adjective Skilled; able to do something really well. / *Goblet of Fire*, page 319
Madam Glinch was particularly adept at spells and wand work, but she was remarkably unskilled in potion preparation.

adjacent (uh-**jay**-sent)
adjective Nearby or next to. / *Deathly Hallows*, page 627
The adjacent houses looked exactly alike…except for the mysterious red blotches on the sidewalk in front of one of them.

admonition (ad-muh-**nish**-un)

noun A mild criticism or friendly warning. / *Order of the Phoenix*, page 660
His mother's latest admonition was "Do not push the menus off the table to get the waiter's attention."

admonitory (ad-**mon**-uh-tor-ee)

adjective Serving as a warning. / *Order of the Phoenix*, page 284
Luckily, the admonitory honking of the bus driver warned the jaywalking elf in time.

adrenaline (uh-**dren**-uh-lin)

noun A chemical the body produces in frightening or really exciting situations, making for an alert and energy-filled feeling. / *Goblet of Fire*, page 358
The burst of adrenaline Rupert felt as the door mysteriously creaked open set his heart to pounding and his legs to running.

adversary (ad-vur-**sare**-ee)

noun An opponent or foe. / *Half-Blood Prince*, page 178
Wildwood didn't consider Blackpool his adversary, but he wasn't exactly his friend, either.

advert (ad-**vurt**)

noun In British usage, short for "advertisement," a public notice, usually in a newspaper, offering something for sale or announcing something wanted. / *Order of the Phoenix*, page 104
Winston noticed an advert in the Daily Planet offering to give away used cauldrons, but only to good homes.

advise (ad-**vize**)

verb To give advice to someone. Watch out: *Advice* is what you give, *advise* is what you do. / *Sorcerer's Stone*, page 241
Blackpool advised the angry shouter to calm down, sit down, and quiet down, but the man paid no attention to the advice and kept on shouting.

aerial (**air**-ee-ul)

noun An antenna that receives TV or radio signals. / *Goblet of Fire*, page 342
The TV aerial on the castle tower looked oddly out of place, but the king insisted it improved reception of his favorite programs.

aerodynamic (air-oh-die-**nam**-ik)

adjective Designed to move quickly and easily through the air. / *Prisoner of Azkaban*, page 51
Captain Hummingbird's sleek, aerodynamic design meant he could fly as fast as 70 miles an hour.

affinity (uh-**fin**-ih-tee)

noun A natural connection or attraction. / *Deathly Hallows*, page 494
"I seem to have an affinity for trouble," said Elrod. "I'm just drawn to it, I guess."

affliction (uh-**flik**-shun)

noun Something that causes suffering, pain, or distress. / *Deathly Hallows*, page 213
Harold, the miniature dragon, had never suffered the affliction of mumps—swollen dragon cheeks are very painful.

Dragon with the affliction of mumps

affronted (uh-**frun**-tid)

adjective Offended or insulted. / *Chamber of Secrets*, page 219
Madam Glinch looked affronted when the principal suggested she use better denture glue.

aftermath (**af**-tur-math)

noun Not something that happens after math class, but a result or consequence,

generally an unpleasant one. / *Chamber of Secrets*, page 192
The aftermath of the sisters' argument was the drawing of a line down the center of their bedroom; Bella was to stay on one side and her sister on the other.

agapanthus (ag-uh-**pan**-thus)
noun A flowering outdoor plant with tall stems and blue, purple, or white funnel-shaped flowers. / *Half-Blood Prince*, page 46
A border of blue and white agapanthus edged the castle flower garden.

agape (uh-**gayp**)
adjective Wide open. / *Half-Blood Prince*, page 574
Brilly stared, his mouth agape, as Blackpool demonstrated his latest card trick.

aggravate (**ag**-ruh-vate)
verb To make something—a situation, illness, or injury—even worse. / *Goblet of Fire*, page 631
Tiny Tinkles, the fairy, aggravated her rheumatism by flying in the chilly rainstorm.

aggravated (**ag**-ruh-vay-tid)
adjective Annoyed or irritated. / *Chamber of Secrets*, page 151
He was so aggravated by her off-key singing that he was ready to stuff tea towels in her mouth.

aggrieved (uh-**greevd**)
adjective Distressed or troubled. / *Half-Blood Prince*, page 64
"Hey, I was trying to teach that wasp to do tricks, and you just swatted him dead!" said Elrod in an aggrieved voice.

aghast (uh-**gast**)
adjective Shocked or horrified. / *Chamber of Secrets*, page 254
Madam Glinch was aghast when Brilly's homework started to smoke and bounce across the desk.

agility (uh-**jil**-uh-tee)
noun Alertness and quickness. / *Order of the Phoenix*, page 707
The levitation contest called for both physical and mental agility.

agitated (**adj**-uh-tay-tid)
adjective Nervous or worried. / *Goblet of Fire*, page 518
Annie was really agitated as the principal slowly handed out next year's teacher assignments. What if she got cranky Mrs. Snodgrape?

agitation (adj-uh-**tay**-shun)
noun Emotional disturbance or excitement. / *Chamber of Secrets*, page 208
Blackpool, in his agitation over the troll raid, tripped on his cloak and fell on his face.

agog (uh-**gog**)
adjective Really surprised and excited. / *Half-Blood Prince*, page 313
Everyone was simply agog when soccer star Butch Thuggins walked into the classroom.

aid and abet
See **abet** elsewhere in this dictionary.

airing cupboard (**air**-ing **kuh**-burd)
noun In British usage, this can be either a linen closet (for storing towels, sheets, etc.), or a small, warm room with the water heater and a drying rack for damp clothes. / *Order of the Phoenix*, page 505
Winston spread out his damp cloak to dry in the airing cupboard.

ajar (uh-**jar**)
adjective Slightly open. / *Sorcerer's Stone*, page 182
The front door was ajar. Peering inside, she caught a glimpse of a bloody glove on the floor.

albeit (all-**bee**-it)
conjunction Although. / *Half-Blood Prince*, page 391
The young giantess was very graceful albeit 12 feet tall.

albino (al-**by**-no)
adjective Whitish or pinkish, like an albino, a person or animal with a genetic condition that gives their skin, hair, or feathers no coloration at all. / *Deathly Hallows*, page 455
The albino wolf, stalking his prey across the snowy hills, was almost impossible to see.

alchemist (al-kem-ist)

noun Someone who studies and practices alchemy. / *Sorcerer's Stone*, page 220
The alchemist suggested that he change Wildwood's tuba into gold, a well-meant offer but ultimately quite unsuccessful.

alchemy (al-kem-ee)

noun The ancient science of trying to change ordinary metal into gold; alchemy also involved finding the "elixir of life," which could make someone live forever. / *Sorcerer's Stone*, page 103
Alchemy is much harder than it looks—no matter what she tried, Katie's bowlful of pennies refused to turn into gold.

algae (al-jee)

noun Small plants—without roots, stems, or leaves—that grow in water or on very damp surfaces. / *Goblet of Fire*, page 497
The mysterious green algae was slowly spreading across the brick path ahead of the travelers, faster than they could walk.

alibi (al-uh-by)

noun An excuse, particularly one that puts a person somewhere else other than where something was happening. / *Sorcerer's Stone*, page 242
"Someone's sneaking into the cemetery and knocking over tombstones. I suppose you have a good alibi for where you were last night?" asked the cemetery caretaker.

Alice band (al-us band)

noun A headband, much like Alice in Wonderland might wear, with a bow on the top. / *Order of the Phoenix*, page 203
Willow adjusted her Alice band before going into the principal's office—she wanted to look as innocent as possible.

all of a dither

See **dither** elsewhere in this dictionary.

all of a flutter

See **flutter** elsewhere in this dictionary.

alleged (uh-ledgd)

adjective Suggested as true but not proven. / *Order of the Phoenix*, page 308
The alleged burglar turned out to be Elrod, who'd snuck in to take a nap.

allegiance (uh-lee-juns)

noun Loyalty or devotion. / *Goblet of Fire*, page 648
The principal recited the "Allegiance to Wizardry" pledge over the school's public address system, but most students weren't paying much attention.

alleviate (uh-lee-vee-ate)

verb To relieve or lessen; to make more bearable. / *Goblet of Fire*, page 229
To alleviate her rheumatism, Tinkles massaged warm newt oil on her painful fairy joints.

allotted (uh-lot-tid)

adjective Assigned or set aside for someone. / *Deathly Hallows*, page 3
The allotted seats for the potions class were at the back of the auditorium.

allusion (uh-loo-zhun)

noun A reference to. / *Half-Blood Prince*, page 370
The spell teacher made no allusion to Bella's earlier—and not very successful—efforts to turn a brick into a kitten.

ally (al-eye)

noun A person working with you for a common purpose. Plural: allies. / *Half-Blood Prince*, page 28
The king's ally in getting the castle bathrooms renovated was the Master of the Knights—it's a long, cold walk to the castle outhouse when you're in armor.

altitude (al-tih-tood)

noun The height or distance above the ground. / *Chamber of Secrets*, page 74
From an altitude of almost 100 feet, Captain Hummingbird sighted the blossoms and prepared for a lunch dive.

amber (am-bur)

adjective Yellowish-brown. / *Sorcerer's Stone*, page 48

The bubbling amber liquid looked a lot like a banana-and-snail milkshake.

amble (**am**-bul)
verb To walk slowly. / *Sorcerer's Stone*, page 44
The gigantic lizard ambled across the parking lot, slowly smacking one car after another with its huge tail.

amend (uh-**mend**)
verb To clarify and improve. / *Order of the Phoenix*, page 691
"I meant to say you're really bubbly, not ugly," amended the embarrassed boy.

amendment (uh-**mend**-munt)
noun An addition to a policy or law. / *Order of the Phoenix*, page 416
Brilly proposed an amendment to the team's rules—it's okay to miss a practice, but only if you bring doughnuts to the next practice.

amethyst-colored (**am**-uh-thyst-kul-ord)
adjective Light purple or violet. / *Deathly Hallows*, page 144
Bella's lovely amethyst-colored dress clashed with her latest hair color.

amicably (**am**-uh-kuh-blee)
adverb In a friendly way. / *Goblet of Fire*, page 417
The two parted amicably after a lengthy metaphysical debate on whether the goblet was half full or half empty.

amok (uh-**muk**)
adverb In a violent and uncontrolled way; usually used with "ran." / *Goblet of Fire*, page 141
Someone ran amok in the school garden, pulling up plants and stomping on the tomatoes.

amulet (**am**-yuh-lit)
noun Something worn on the body because of its magical protective powers; a charm or talisman. / *Chamber of Secrets*, page 142
Though some people wear magic bracelets or necklaces, Dribbles' sneakers were his special amulet.

anecdote (**an**-ek-dote)
noun A brief—often funny—retelling of an incident or experience. / *Half-Blood Prince*, page 147
Hassan's anecdote about the drooling giraffe had everyone laughing.

anguished (**ang**-gwishd)
adjective Distressed or worried. / *Prisoner of Azkaban*, page 178
The anguished sounds from the baby ostrich meant only one thing—he was done napping and was ready for a snack.

angular (**ang**-gyoo-lur)
adjective Bony and lean, often lacking grace or smoothness. / *Order of the Phoenix*, page 643
The angular professor thought he looked like Abraham Lincoln, but actually he looked more like Ichabod Crane.

animatedly (**an**-uh-**may**-tid-lee)
adverb In an energetic and enthusiastic way. / *Goblet of Fire*, page 500
"I think there really is an Island of Jelly Beans," said the little boy animatedly, "and I want to go there."

animosity (an-uh-**mos**-uh-tee)
noun Open dislike or even hatred. / *Goblet of Fire*, page 209
The animosity between the river spirits and the lake demons made for a rough boat ride to the island.

annotation (an-uh-**tay**-shun)
noun An explanatory note in a book or document. / *Half-Blood Prince*, page 189
The previous textbook owner had made many helpful annotations, unfortunately all in disappearing ink.

anomaly (uh-**nom**-uh-lee)
noun Something different from the usual or expected. / *Deathly Hallows*, page 223
It's an interesting anomaly that the world's meanest creature—the Raging Riptar—can only be found on the Golden Isle of Love.

antechamber (**an**-tee-chaym-bur)
noun A smaller room at the entrance to another, larger, room. / *Half-Blood Prince*, page 558
Brilly sat in the antechamber to the principal's office, gloomily waiting for his parents to come out.

anticlimax (an-tee-kly-max)

noun Something that's less dramatic or important than expected. / *Deathly Hallows*, page 126
"Gee, finally meeting Butch Thuggins was an anticlimax," said Rupert. "He's shorter than me, and he giggles like a gecko."

antics (an-tiks)

noun Odd or unusual behavior; sometimes pranks or goofing off. Usually used in the plural. / *Goblet of Fire*, page 203
Blackpool's antics often mystified his neighbors.

antidote (an-tuh-dote)

noun Something that stops a poison from working. / *Chamber of Secrets*, page 92
Quick, get the antidote—someone's poisoned the trombone player with Splendiferous Flux!

anvil (an-vil)

noun A heavy iron block on which hot metal is shaped by hammering. / *Deathly Hallows*, page 536
The blacksmith sweated next to his furnace, forging the king's battle swords and shields on his anvil.

apathetic (ap-uh-thet-ik)

adjective Having little or no interest in anything. / *Order of the Phoenix*, page 44
The apathetic crowd perked up when the Rolling Bones finally came onstage.

apoplectic (ap-uh-plek-tik)

adjective Extremely mad, upset, and furious. / *Chamber of Secrets*, page 185
Brilly's father was apoplectic with rage—practicing fire-juggling in the library was simply not acceptable.

apothecary (uh-poth-uh-kare-ee)

noun An old-fashioned word for a drugstore or pharmacy. / *Sorcerer's Stone*, page 71
The coughing wizard hoped the apothecary would have some Urping Elmer's Cough Syrup.

apparition (ap-uh-rish-un)

noun A ghost or phantom. / *Goblet of Fire*, page 577
The ghostly apparition seemed to glide down the stairs toward the kitchen.

appeal (uh-peel)

noun The transferring of a legal case to another—higher—court for review or rehearing. / *Prisoner of Azkaban*, page 292
Blackpool realized an appeal of his broomstick speeding ticket was hopeless—he *had* been going 83mph in a school zone.

appointment (uh-poynt-munt)

noun The naming or selecting of someone for a specific position. / *Chamber of Secrets*, page 263
His appointment as chief bottle washer made the man very proud even though the pay was lousy.

apportion (uh-pore-shun)

verb To divide up and hand out. / *Half-Blood Prince*, page 29
Mrs. Snodgrape apportioned the classroom tasks so everyone would have something to do while she snuck a chocolate frisblot.

appraisal (uh-pray-zul)

noun An act of appraising, or judging, the worth and value of something. / *Deathly Hallows*, page 100
The villagers' appraisal of the new Garden of Secrets was evenly divided—some folks thought there were too many secrets and not enough garden, and others thought there was too much garden and not enough secrets.

appraising (uh-prayz-ing)

adjective Evaluating how successful, effective, or valuable something is. / *Goblet of Fire*, page 394
The girl's appraising look at the soccer captain suggested she thought him quite attractive.

apprehend (ap-rih-hend)

verb To catch. / *Goblet of Fire*, page 589
The police apprehended the masked burglar four blocks from the scene of the crime. He probably shouldn't have left his mask on.

apprehensively (ap-rih-**hen**-siv-lee)
adverb In an anxious or fearful way. / *Chamber of Secrets*, page 62
Katie apprehensively awaited her next dentist appointment; all that toffee hadn't been such a good idea.

aptitude (**ap**-tuh-tude)
noun Natural ability or talent. / *Order of the Phoenix*, page 664
Elrod's aptitude for bungling was almost as well-known as Brilly's aptitude for troublemaking.

aquamarine (auk-wah-muh-reen)
adjective Bluish-green. / *Chamber of Secrets*, page 77
The aquamarine fish was almost invisible in the lake's aquamarine water.

arachnid (uh-**rak**-nid)
noun A small animal with eight legs, a body divided into two parts, and no wings—think spider or scorpion. / *Half-Blood Prince*, page 484
Studying arachnids was Tamika's least favorite subject—too many legs…though not as bad as centipede study had been.

archenemy (arch-**en**-uh-mee)
noun Someone's main and worst enemy. / *Chamber of Secrets*, page 8
Blackpool's arch-enemy, Blistock, stared across the crowded room at him.

archway (**arch**-way)
noun An entrance or passageway with a curved roof. / *Sorcerer's Stone*, page 71
The lovely troll bridesmaid walked through the church archway, merrily tossing rose petals from her mossy basket.

ardently (**ar**-dunt-lee)
adverb Eagerly and enthusiastically. / *Order of the Phoenix*, page 298
Willow ardently hoped that her new boyfriend would remember their six-day anniversary.

arithmancy (**air**-ith-man-see)
noun A branch of magic that does divination with numbers, especially based on the letters in one's name; it's sometimes called numerology. / *Prisoner of Azkaban*, page 251
When Wildwood studied arithmancy in school, he discovered he was independent, imaginative, talented, stable, loyal, perceptive, and determined. But then, so was his dog.

arrant (**air**-ant)
adjective Total, downright, or complete. / *Chamber of Secrets*, page 151
Brilly was an arrant mischief-maker, and everyone in school knew it.

arrogance (**air**-uh-guntz)
noun Excessive pride or self-importance. / *Order of the Phoenix*, page 756
"The arrogance of that wizard," complained Mrs. Birch. "He thinks because he has a new broomstick that he's better than the rest of us."

arrogant (**air**-ruh-gunt)
adjective Conceited and way too proud. / *Prisoner of Azkaban*, page 284
The arrogant rat insisted his whiskers were more sensitive and his tail longer than anyone else's.

articulate (ar-**tik**-yoo-late)
verb To speak distinctly. / *Order of the Phoenix*, page 802
The wizard's sore throat meant he could barely articulate his name let alone a spell for laryngitis.

artifact (**ar**-tuh-fakt)
noun Something handmade, especially a primitive tool or simple object. / *Chamber of Secrets*, page 30
The artifacts found deeply buried just outside the castle walls were clearly from an ancient civilization.

ascend (uh-**send**)
verb To rise or go upward. / *Half-Blood Prince*, page 620
As the huge balloon began to ascend, Milton leaned out of the passenger basket and shouted, "I'm not sure this is such a good idea!"

ascertain (as-sur-**tane**)
verb To find out or determine. / *Order of the Phoenix*, page 35

"I'd like to ascertain exactly who put glue in the tapioca," said the cafeteria manager calmly.

ashen-faced (**ash**-en-fayst)
adjective Pale, like the color of ashes. / *Sorcerer's Stone*, page 52
The ashen-faced policeman slowly turned over the still body of the enormous sea slug.

askew (uh-**skyoo**)
adjective Not straight; on one side. / *Sorcerer's Stone*, page 172
After the brawl with the giant spider, Parker's glasses were askew and both of his eyes were slowly turning purplish-green.

Glasses askew

aspect (**as**-pekt)
noun The way one looks or appears. / *Chamber of Secrets*, page 299
The aspect of Tinkles, the fairy, changed completely when she got eyeglasses—not only did her appearance change, but she became much more confident.

asperity (uh-**spare**-ih-tee)
noun Irritability, impatience, and annoyance. / *Order of the Phoenix*, page 223
The tone of asperity in the king's voice was clear—washing the armor in the moat had been a bad idea.

aspersion (uh-**spur**-shun)
noun A damaging or slanderous remark. / *Order of the Phoenix*, page 653
Blackpool frequently cast aspersions on anyone else's abilities to concoct a minimizing potion.

aspidistra (as-pih-**dis**-truh)
noun A house plant with tall, pointed, glossy leaves. / *Deathly Hallows*, page 65
The castle's Great Hall was decorated with dozens of aspidistra, all planted in large planter boxes.

aspiring (uh-**spy**-ring)
adjective Hoping to be successful in a particular job or activity. / *Goblet of Fire*, page 255
Bella considered herself an aspiring actress; unfortunately, the play's director did not.

assiduously (uh-**sidj**-yoo-us-lee)
adverb Diligently and industriously. / *Order of the Phoenix*, page 840
Even though he worked assiduously on his potions homework, it usually came back covered with negative comments from the teacher.

assuage (uh-**swayj**)
verb To lessen or calm the intensity of something. / *Deathly Hallows*, page 86
"To assuage your doubts about my skills," said the job-hunting wizard, "I shall change your coffee cup into a golden cauldron."

astride (uh-**stride**)
adverb With one leg on each side. / *Sorcerer's Stone*, page 14
Butch Thuggins sat astride his new motorcycle and flirted with all the girls.

astute (uh-**stoot**)
adjective Shrewd, with keen judgment. / *Half-Blood Prince*, page 278
The astute lawyer suggested Father Goose forget the idea of starting a feather pillow factory.

asunder (uh-**sun**-dur)
adverb Into separate parts or pieces; usually used with "torn." / *Goblet of Fire*, page 724
The ancient oak on the village green was torn asunder in the Great Storm of '09.

asylum (uh-**sy**-lem)
noun A hospital for those with mental disorders. / *Half-Blood Prince*, page 270

The local asylum was currently overcrowded with people who thought they were centaurs and centaurs who thought they were people.

at loggerheads
See **loggerhead** elsewhere in this dictionary.

atmosphere (at-mus-feer)
noun The general feeling or mood of a place. / *Chamber of Secrets*, page 266
An atmosphere of dread filled the classroom as Madam Glinch handed back the graded quiz.

atrium (ay-tree-um)
noun A skylit central room or court. / *Order of the Phoenix*, page 126
"I think the castle renovation should include an atrium," suggested the queen. "Just because it's not traditional is no reason not to try it."

atrocity (uh-tros-ih-tee)
noun An act of extreme and really nasty cruelty. / *Half-Blood Prince*, page 12
"It's an atrocity to enchant puppies," Willow shouted. "I'm reporting you to the Pet Police!"

attendant (uh-ten-dunt)
adjective Accompanying or following as a result. / *Half-Blood Prince*, page 262
The attendant hopelessness and shock—as the ferryboat slowly sank beneath the waves—was almost paralyzing.

attentively (uh-ten-tiv-lee)
adverb In a careful and interested way. / *Deathly Hallows*, page 158
Fiona listened attentively, but she still couldn't figure out what the potions teacher was complaining about.

auburn (aw-burn)
adjective Reddish-brown; often said of hair. / *Chamber of Secrets*, page 245
Bella's dad used to have auburn hair, but what's left was mostly gray now.

audacious (aw-day-shus)
adjective Daring and bold. / *Order of the Phoenix*, page 191
It was an audacious plan—sneaking across the meadow to break into the Fortress of Solitude in the middle of the day.

audible (aw-duh-bul)
adjective Loud or clear enough to hear. / *Chamber of Secrets*, page 262
The audible moans echoed up and down the school corridor as the students learned of their Saturday detention.

augury (oh-gur-ee)
noun An omen. / *Half-Blood Prince*, page 449
The augury wasn't good—his cereal had formed an "X" in the bottom of the bowl.

aura (or-uh)
noun An energy field that surrounds a person. / *Prisoner of Azkaban*, page 107
The aura of the princess could best be described as pink and white, with bright bolts of light flashing skyward.

austere (aw-steer)
adjective Forbidding, cold, and solemn. / *Order of the Phoenix*, page 138
The austere look on the principal's face meant only one thing—a stay after school.

authenticity (aw-then-tis-ih-tee)
noun The condition of being authentic and genuine. / *Deathly Hallows*, page 497
The authenticity of the artifacts found buried just outside the castle walls was obvious—they must have been thousands of years old…and they looked it.

autobiography (aw-toh-by-og-ruh-fee)
noun One's life story, written by that person. If someone else writes that life story, it's a biography. / *Chamber of Secrets*, page 58
Lucinda loved rereading her autobiography—especially the part she'd written about being born in a log cabin.

averse (uh-vurs)
adjective Having strong feelings of opposition or resistance to something. / *Order of the Phoenix*, page 845
Dylan was averse to going to the circus—the smell of popcorn made him want to throw up.

avert (uh-vert)
verb To look away from something. / *Prisoner of Azkaban*, page 273

"Ladies and gentlemen," announced the stage magician, "please avert your eyes while I saw this lovely lady in half."

averted (uh-**ver**-tid)
adjective Turned away from something. / *Prisoner of Azkaban,* page 245
Mrs. Snodgrape's averted eyes missed the drama of Brilly crossing the cafeteria with his lunch tray balanced on his head.

avid (**av**-id)
adjective Eager and enthusiastic. / *Order of the Phoenix,* page 645
Ethelbell, one of the Sisters of Sorcery, was an avid collector of masks.

awestruck (**aw**-struk)
adjective Filled with awe, a mixture of reverence and wonder. / *Chamber of Secrets,* page 85
The awestruck crowd cheered themselves hoarse when Butch Thuggins scored his third goal.

awkward (**awk**-wurd)
adjective Uncomfortable. / *Sorcerer's Stone,* page 172
An awkward silence fell over the classroom when the teacher burped…and a golden butterfly flew out of his mouth.

awry (uh-**rye**)
adverb Wrong or amiss; usually used with "go." / *Order of the Phoenix,* page 625
Things began to go awry at the Flufftones Ball when the band's instruments mysteriously flew out the door.

Axminster (**aks**-min-stur)
noun A type of woven carpet made in Axminster, England. / *Goblet of Fire,* page 91
Wildwood's flying Axminster was so worn and bare in spots, he had to be careful whenever he took it out for a spin; mostly it just floated around in the hallway.

B

babble (bab-ul)

noun Idle or foolish talk, or indistinct sounds that can't quite be heard clearly. / *Sorcerer's Stone*, page 70
The crowd's babble gradually grew louder, but the boy couldn't make out what they were shouting. Was it "School is out!"? Or was it "Drooling snout!"?

badge (badj)

noun A small piece of plastic, metal, or cloth showing membership in a group or society. In British usage, a badge is more like a political button and less like a sheriff's badge. / *Goblet of Fire*, page 224
The witch proudly wore her membership badge from the OHG, the Old Hags Choir.

badger (badj-ur)

verb To nag, or to pester with questions. / *Goblet of Fire*, page 717
Brilly loved to badger his younger brother with dumb questions.

balaclava (bal-uh-klah-vuh)

noun A knit head and neck covering with an opening for the eyes and nose, somewhat like a ski mask. / *Chamber of Secrets*, page 201
Wearing his balaclava meant a bad hair day, but at least he was warm walking to school.

balderdash (bol-dur-dash)

noun Senseless nonsense. / *Goblet of Fire*, page 191
The balderdash spread around town by Rilda, who was practically a professional rumormonger, was just amazing.

baleful (bale-ful)

adjective Expressing anger and hate. / *Deathly Hallows*, page 389
The cat gave the mouse a baleful look—once more it had stolen her cat crunchies from under her nose.

ballistic

See **go ballistic** elsewhere in this dictionary.

balm (rhymes with **calm**)

noun Something that soothes and comforts. / *Deathly Hallows*, page 747
The soothing eel balm helped his aching muscles.

balmy (bah-mee)

adjective Mild and pleasant; usually said of weather. / *Order of the Phoenix*, page 751
Balmy summer days are great for picnics, lousy for skiing.

balustrade (bal-uh-strayd)

noun A handrail and a row of posts supporting it. Indoors, it often separates two sections or levels of a room, like a courtroom; outdoors, it's more like a balcony, with vase-shaped stone posts. / *Deathly Hallows*, page 258
Blackpool's lawyer leaned over the balustrade to talk to the judge.

bamboozle (bam-boo-zul)

verb To deceive by trickery. / *Goblet of Fire*, page 279
"You're not going to bamboozle me, Klinkster," said the wandmaker. "You substituted horse hair for unicorn hair."

bandy (ban-dee)

adjective Bent or curved; often said of legs. / *Prisoner of Azkaban*, page 146
The dwarf's bandy legs made for slow going down the steep tower steps.

bandy (ban-dee)

verb To say or discuss casually, often to sound impressive; usually used with "about." / *Chamber of Secrets*, page 198
Rilda liked to bandy about the latest gossip as soon as she heard it.

bang on course

phrase In British slang, exactly and correctly on course. / *Goblet of Fire*, page 630

"You're bang on course to get top marks this term," said Winston's proud father to his son.

bang out of order

phrase In British slang, totally unacceptable and out of order. / *Order of the Phoenix*, page 319
"Winston, that behavior is bang out of order, so quiet down, please," said Mrs. Snodgrape.

banister (ban-uh-stur)

noun A stair railing and its supporting posts; often used in the plural. / *Goblet of Fire*, page 405
The blind elf gripped the banisters tightly as he made his way up the curving stairs.

banked (rhymes with **tanked**)

adjective Arranged in rows. / *Order of the Phoenix*, page 405
The banked gym bleachers were filled with cheering basketball fans.

banshee (ban-shee)

noun In folklore, a female spirit that wails loudly, warning of a death; more generally, if someone "screams like a banshee," he or she is screaming really loudly. / *Chamber of Secrets*, page 20
"She screamed like a banshee," said Brilly, "when I put the ice cubes down her back."

bare (rhymes with **dare**; sounds exactly like **bear**)

verb To reveal, expose, or show. / *Chamber of Secrets*, page 190
Ruffles, the Royal Ripsnorter, was baring his teeth and refusing to let the duke's envoy cross the castle drawbridge to meet with the king.

barge (rhymes with **large**)

verb To rudely interrupt or intrude. / *Chamber of Secrets*, page 237
"You can't barge in on us like that," said Fiona. "We're having a very private discussion."

barking mad

phrase In British slang, acting crazy or at least very strangely; usually used in a humorous way. / *Goblet of Fire*, page 359 / Note: In *Sorcerer's Stone* (page 90), if someone is acting really crazy, they're "barking howling mad." Also sometimes shortened to just "barking," like in *Order of the Phoenix* (page 580).
"She's so barking mad over this new guy I can hardly believe it, said Winston.

barmy (bar-mee)

adjective In British slang, crazy. / *Goblet of Fire*, page 380
"Are you barmy? There's no way I'm going to climb that tree—the bark has fangs!" said Winston.

barrier (bare-ee-ur)

noun An obstruction, like a wall or fence. / *Sorcerer's Stone*, page 92 / Note: See also **ticket barrier** elsewhere in this dictionary.
The construction barrier across the village's main street was causing quite a bit of consternation.

basilisk (bas-uh-lisk)

noun A mythological snake-like monster able to kill with one look. / *Chamber of Secrets*, page 290
Ravi was afraid to even look at the picture of the basilisk—what if it looked back at him?

Basilisk

bask (rhymes with **mask**)

verb To warm oneself in the sun or by a fire. / *Sorcerer's Stone*, page 263

The exhausted python basked lazily in the afternoon sun.

bated breath (bay-tid breth)

noun A holding off of breathing because of suspense, great fear, or wonder. / *Sorcerer's Stone*, page 234

Julio waited with bated breath to hear who won the grand prize—84 jars of pickled mushrooms, his favorite.

bathing costume (bay-thing kos-tum)

noun In British usage, an old-fashioned word for bathing suit. / *Half-Blood Prince*, page 199

Winston was really embarrassed when his bathing costume turned transparent in the enchanted swimming pool.

battalion (buh-tal-yun)

noun A large group. / *Half-Blood Prince*, page 109

A battalion of irate parents was shouting suggestions at the softball coach, but the team lost anyway.

battering ram (bat-ur-ing ram)

noun A heavy wooden beam used to ram down the gates or walls of an enemy's castle. / *Chamber of Secrets*, page 75

The king's soldiers lifted the heavy battering ram and slammed it against the walls of the duke's manor.

battlement (bat-ul-munt)

noun The low wall around a castle tower with notched spaces to shoot weapons through. / *Half-Blood Prince*, page 596

The soldiers patrolled the castle's battlements, watching for approaching danger.

batty (bat-ee)

adjective Eccentric and a little crazy. / *Order of the Phoenix*, page 2

The batty math teacher came up with the weirdest problems, like "If four ghostly hounds ran at ten miles an hour, and the little girl could only run three miles an hour but she had a ten-minute start, would she get from the village center to the Haunted Forest first, or would the hounds get from the Forest to the village center first, and what would she have for lunch?"

bay window (bay win-doh)

noun A window projecting out from a wall so that a small alcove is inside. / *Order of the Phoenix*, page 335

The prince stood in the throne room alcove, staring out the bay window at the endless rain.

beakerful (bee-kur-ful)

noun A beaker is a cylindrical plastic or glass container with a pouring spout; a beakerful is a full beaker. / *Chamber of Secrets*, page 174

Brilly gleefully poured a beakerful of frog slime on Willow's backpack.

beam (rhymes with **dream**)

verb To smile with great enthusiasm. / *Sorcerer's Stone*, page 123

Chuckles, the usually lousy clown, beamed at the crowd of laughing children—he'd actually made them happy.

beat a tattoo

phrase To beat or tap rhythmically. / *Order of the Phoenix*, page 136

Willow's heart seemed to beat a tattoo in her throat as the new boy smiled at her across the cafeteria.

bedeck (bee-dek)

verb To decorate or adorn. / *Goblet of Fire*, page 83

The king's throne was bedecked with several colorful pillows, including one for his bad back.

bedlam (bed-lum)

noun Confusion, disorder, and a noisy uproar. / *Prisoner of Azkaban*, page 53

The bedlam in Madam Glinch's classroom was easily explained—there was a substitute teacher who knew nothing about wand work.

bedpan (bed-pan)

noun A container used as a toilet for someone bedridden. / *Prisoner of Azkaban*, page 173

"Are you kidding? Do I have to use a bedpan?" asked poor sick Dylan.

bedraggled (bih-drag-uld)

adjective Wet and dirty. / *Chamber of Secrets*, page 87

The bedraggled traveler stopped at the inn after his boat trip across the dangerous Sea of Slippery Rocks.

befoul (bih-**fowl**)
verb **To soil or make dirty.** / *Chamber of Secrets*, page 126
The very sick troll had befouled his under-bridge home.

befuddled (bih-**fud**-uld)
adjective **Confused and perplexed.** / *Prisoner of Azkaban*, page 91
A befuddled Lucinda found the new postage rates totally confusing, and the village post office wasn't much help.

begonia (bih-**go**-nya)
noun **An outdoor tropical plant with bright, showy flowers.** / *Chamber of Secrets*, page 93
Seventy-six blooming begonias brightened the pathway to the King's Royal Tennis Court.

beleaguered (bih-**lee**-gurd)
adjective **Harassed or beset with difficulties.** / *Deathly Hallows*, page 82
The beleaguered cafeteria manager couldn't understand why so many students had started bringing their lunches—didn't they like fried possum?

bell jar (**bell** jar)
noun **A large bell-shaped glass container used to protect something delicate.** / *Order of the Phoenix*, page 776
The bell jar on Mrs. Snodgrape's bedside table protected her beloved childhood toy—her precious stuffed chicken.

belligerent (buh-**lij**-ur-unt)
adjective **Unfriendly and wanting to argue or fight.** / *Half-Blood Prince*, page 449
Blackpool was in a belligerent mood, so everyone was staying out of his way.

bellpull (**bell**-pull)
noun **A handle or cord that when pulled rings a doorbell (or, if inside, a servant's bell). Not the sort of thing you'd normally see on a tent, for example.** / *Goblet of Fire*, page 78
"Pull the bellpull, dear. Otherwise they won't know we're here on their doorstep," said Winston's mum.

bemused (bih-**myoozd**)
adjective **Confused and bewildered.** / *Chamber of Secrets*, page 322
Elrod's bemused expression meant the discussion of the geography of Forgotten Places was not making any sense to him.

bemusement (bih-**myooz**-munt)
noun **Confusion and bewilderment.** / *Deathly Hallows*, page 41
The cafeteria manager experienced some bemusement when the delivery truck pulled up—who had ordered 70 boxes of popsicles for the cafeteria?

benign (bih-**nine**)
adjective **Gentle and kind.** / *Goblet of Fire*, page 679
"You know, Brilly, I once was a benign, calm person, but then you came to this school, and my life was changed forever," said the principal, grimacing.

bequeath (bih-**kweeth**)
verb **To pass on or hand down.** / *Prisoner of Azkaban*, page 191
Wildwood bequeathed all his duplicate gardening tools to Mr. Glinch.

bequest (bih-**kwest**)
noun **Money or property that is bequeathed by will, to be given after a person's death.** / *Deathly Hallows*, page 124
Katie's grandfather left her a large bequest, enough to buy a horse.

berate (bih-**rate**)
verb **To scold severely.** / *Prisoner of Azkaban*, page 219
The art teacher berated Brilly for his outrageous behavior in art class—that whole business with the paint and the glue just wasn't acceptable.

bereavement (bih-**reev**-munt)
noun **The losing of someone close when they die.** / *Deathly Hallows*, page 759
"Everyone experiences bereavement and grief sometime, but that doesn't make it any easier—especially when it's your very own monster chicken," Wildwood said sadly.

beribboned (bih-**rib**-und)
adjective Adorned with ribbons. / *Deathly Hallows*, page 251
The beribboned baby goat—all clean and fluffy and just back from the Goaty Groomers—frolicked around the yard.

berk (rhymes with **lurk**)
noun In British slang, a really stupid person. / *Order of the Phoenix*, page 426
"You berk! Nobody dunks doughnuts in orange juice!" shouted Winston.

berserk (**bur**-surk)
adjective To be very mad, violently angry, or even a little insane. / *Sorcerer's Stone*, page 176
The usually calm elf suddenly became a very berserk elf the second time the waiter spilled hot soup in his lap.

berth
See **wide berth** elsewhere in this dictionary.

beseech (bih-**seech**)
verb To ask earnestly; to implore. / *Deathly Hallows*, page 469
Madam Glinch beseeched Brilly to mend his troublesome ways and start behaving.

besiege (bih-**seej**)
verb To harass or overwhelm with requests or questions. / *Half-Blood Prince*, page 356
Madam Glinch's students besieged her with requests to get into her advanced wand class.

besmirch (bih-**smurch**)
verb To soil or tarnish. / *Order of the Phoenix*, page 784
"How dare you say that! You have besmirched my reputation!"

besom (**bee**-zum)
noun Literally, an old-fashioned broom made with twigs tied to the handle. More generally, if someone were calling a witch names, this might be a word they'd use. / *Deathly Hallows*, page 591
"You old besom, get out of my way," said a rude and impatient Blackpool as the elderly witch crossed the street.

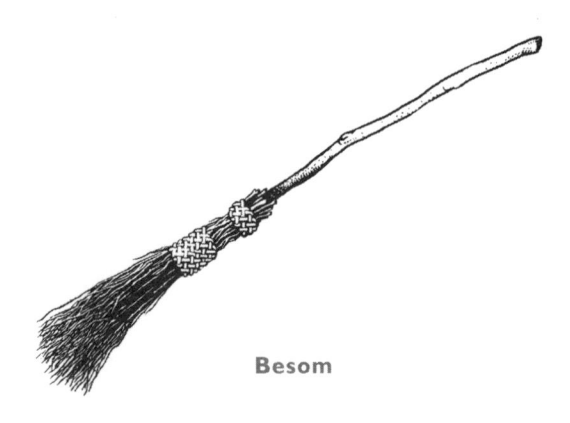

Besom

besotted (bih-**sot**-tid)
adjective Infatuated; so in love with something or someone that you can't think of anything else. / *Half-Blood Prince*, page 214
The besotted Willow stared dreamily at her new boyfriend.

bespectacled (bih-**spek**-tuh-kuld)
adjective Wearing eyeglasses. / *Deathly Hallows*, page 52
The bespectacled fairy Tinkles loved her new glasses, though she did misplace them frequently.

bestial (**bees**-chul)
adjective Like a beast. / *Half-Blood Prince*, page 271
"That is such bestial behavior, Brilly," said his mother. "Sometimes I think you're half pig."

betrayal (bih-**tray**-ul)
noun The act of being disloyal or unfaithful to those who trust you. / *Order of the Phoenix*, page 602
"Telling mean stories about your friends is a betrayal of their trust in you," suggested the wise old woman, but the evil Blackpool just snickered.

bewitch (bih-**witch**)
verb To put under a magic spell. / *Sorcerer's Stone*, page 110
Bella loved to bewitch her brother's pet centipede—it was hilarious when it turned into a hundred-legged meatloaf.

bezoar (bee-zor)

noun A hard clump of swallowed foreign material (usually hair, fiber, fruits, etc.) that collects in the stomach of an animal, thought by many to have magical qualities, especially as a poison antidote. A hair ball thrown up by a cat is an example (except for the magical part). / *Sorcerer's Stone*, page 137 / Note: In Potter's world, a bezoar is from the stomach of a goat and is more stone-like.

"I know bezoars can be useful," said Madam Glinch, "but personally I find them icky."

biased (bye-uhst)

adjective Showing bias or prejudice; favoring one side too much. / *Sorcerer's Stone*, page 221

"You're so handsome," said Blackpool's mother to her grown son. "But then, I'm biased."

bigotry (big-uh-tree)

noun Intolerance of people who are different. / *Goblet of Fire*, page 434

"There is no room for bigotry in my classroom. Wizards, non-wizards…it just doesn't matter."

bile (rhymes with **file**)

noun A fluid produced by the liver to help digest foods. / *Goblet of Fire*, page 518

"I'd suggest adding the bile of a billy goat to that potion, young man," said the potions master.

bilge (bilj)

noun Stupid talk or nonsense. / *Order of the Phoenix*, page 146

"That's the silliest bilge I've ever heard—mermaids don't water ski!"

billow (bil-oh)

verb To rise or surge out. / *Chamber of Secrets*, page 74

Smoke was already billowing out of the apothecary window when the fire engines finally pulled up.

billycan (bil-ee-kan)

noun A traditional Australian utensil for cooking liquids over a campfire. / *Deathly Hallows*, page 277

There's nothing quite like hot choco-lotta-latté, boiled up in a billycan when you're camping out.

bin (rhymes with **din**)

noun In British usage, a household trash container, although there are also vegetable bins, recycling bins, etc. / *Sorcerer's Stone*, page 151 / Note: See also **dustbin** elsewhere in this dictionary.

The bin was so full, Dylan couldn't even cram the last few ostrich eggshells in it.

bin (rhymes with **din**)

verb To put something in the trash. / *Order of the Phoenix*, page 67

"Just bin it, Dylan. Stuff it in," urged Ravi.

biography (by-og-ruh-fee)

noun One's life story, written by someone else. If someone writes their own life story, it's an autobiography. / *Deathly Hallows*, page 153

Lucinda couldn't understand why no one seemed interested in writing her biography.

birds of prey (burds of pray)

noun Birds (owls, eagles, and hawks) that hunt other animals for food. / *Order of the Phoenix*, page 57

The birds of prey that inhabited the brush near the Haunted Forest were ready for lunch—time to swoop over the meadow and find something tasty.

birthright (burth-rite)

noun Something you're entitled to because of your birth or origin. / *Deathly Hallows*, page 500

"It is my birthright," announced the king to his gathered subjects, "to live in this castle as long as I remain your king. I do, however, welcome visitors."

biscuit, biscuit tin (bis-kit, bis-kit tin)

nouns In British usage, a cookie; a biscuit tin is a can holding cookies. / *Order of the Phoenix*, pages 248 and 414

The biscuits in the biscuit tin were Bella's favorites—chocolate chip frisblots and yak butter twackoids.

bit keen
See **keen** elsewhere in this dictionary.

bit of a damper
See **damper** elsewhere in this dictionary.

bit of a lie-in
See **lie-in** elsewhere in this dictionary.

bite off more than you can chew
phrase To decide to do or agree to do more than you can actually handle. / *Chamber of Secrets*, page 56
Katie had bitten off more than she could chew when she promised to weed the entire herb garden in one afternoon.

bizarre (bih-zar)
adjective Really strange or odd. / *Prisoner of Azkaban*, page 7
The bizarre behavior of tiny Tinkles, the fairy, was easily explained—she'd gotten caught in a spider's web.

blackmail (blak-mail)
verb To extort money (or certain actions) from someone by threatening to tell their secrets; any money extorted is also called "blackmail." / *Chamber of Secrets*, page 263
Blackpool blackmailed Brilly into exercising his racing worms for an entire week—otherwise he'd tell Brilly's mother about the bubblegum in the aquarium.

black-market (blak-mar-kit)
adjective Bought or sold in defiance of government marketing controls or rules. / *Order of the Phoenix*, page 738
"Wow, how many black-market cloaks did you buy? Are you going to resell them or what?"

black pudding (blak puh-ding)
noun In British usage, "pudding" usually refers to a dessert, but "black pudding" is definitely not dessert—it's a thick, dark sausage made with animal blood and fat, and is sometimes called blood sausage. / *Goblet of Fire*, page 251
"Pass your uncle the black pudding. It's his favorite, you know," said Winston's mum.

bladder (bla-dur)
noun The organ in the body that holds urine. / *Goblet of Fire*, page 418 / Note: See the related noun **bladder** below.
Dribbles' bladder was ready to burst—he never should have had that fourth soda.

bladder (bla-dur)
noun A bag of leather or rubber inside a football or basketball that can be filled with air. / *Order of the Phoenix*, page 256 / Note: See the related noun **bladder** above.
Someone had either bewitched the football's bladder or they'd pounded a nail in it—it was flat as a crumpet.

blanch (rhymes with **ranch**)
verb To become pale. / *Chamber of Secrets*, page 146
Blackpool blanched when his elderly mother threatened to break his wand in two unless he stopped practicing card tricks and started on the yard work.

blancmange (bluh-manhj)
noun A sweet dessert made from gelatin, milk, and flavoring. / *Goblet of Fire*, page 253
Dylan loved blancmange, especially when he had a sore throat.

blandly (bland-lee)
adverb In a pleasant, unexciting way. / *Order of the Phoenix*, page 611
The bank manager blandly told the confused robber to put down the potato gun and step away from the counter.

blasé (blah-zay)
adjective Unconcerned and disinterested. / *Half-Blood Prince*, page 501
Nathan tried to act blasé as he unwrapped the large package, but he really hoped it was a new skateboard.

blatant (blay-tent)
adjective Completely obvious, especially in a brazen way. / *Goblet of Fire*, page 93
"Your blatant disregard for every school rule is going to get you expelled, Brilly!" shouted the principal.

bleak (rhymes with **sneak**)

adjective Gloomy and desolate. / *Goblet of Fire*, page 586

The bleak, windswept streets were empty of every sign of life.

bleary (**bleer**-ee)

adjective Blurred by lack of sleep or weariness. / *Prisoner of Azkaban*, page 7

The old hag's bleary eyes looked over the wreckage of her late-night party; what a wonderful night it had been!

bleat (rhymes with **cleat**)

verb To make a sound like a sheep or goat; to whine. / *Order of the Phoenix*, page 747

The little boy bleated "I wanna!" once too often.

bleeding (**blee**-ding)

adjective In British slang, an offensive word used to emphasize something when you're really angry. / *Half-Blood Prince*, page 204

"Get your bleeding hands off my homework," threatened Winston.

blight (rhymes with **light**)

verb To frustrate, spoil, damage, or even destroy something. / *Half-Blood Prince*, page 139

"Class," said the substitute teacher, "I believe your behavior today has blighted my entire teaching career."

blighter (**bly**-tur)

noun In British slang, a rascal or unpleasant person; it can also just mean a man or a guy. / *Chamber of Secrets*, page 101 / Note: In Potter's world, even a Cornish pixie is called a blighter.

"Is that blighter really stealing cookies from the Squirrel Scouts?" wondered Winston.

blimey (**bly**-mee)

interjection In British slang, an expression of surprise, roughly meaning "Yikes!" / *Sorcerer's Stone*, page 54

"Blimey, Ted, you forgot to zip up your pants," laughed Winston.

blinker (**blink**-ur)

verb Literally, to put blinkers on a horse's eyes, a technique of putting two leather flaps on a bridle to keep a horse from seeing to the side; more generally, to focus on one thing, unable to pay attention to the surroundings. / *Order of the Phoenix*, page 603 / Note: In British usage, blinkers are used; in American usage, blinders are used.

"Who blinkered Winston? I've never seen him so focused on a project."

blithely (**blythe**-lee)

adverb In a carefree, cheerful way. / *Half-Blood Prince*, page 294

Rupert blithely announced his new career choice to his family—lion tamer.

bloke (rhymes with **broke**)

noun In British slang, a man or guy. / *Sorcerer's Stone*, page 70

"Who's that bloke banging on the front door?" asked Winston's dad.

bloodcurdling (**blud**-curd-ling)

adjective So terrifyingly horrible it would curdle (thicken) the blood. / *Sorcerer's Stone*, page 206

Bloodcurdling screams echoed down the dark hallway—who was in the mansion, and why were they screaming?

bloodshot (**blud**-shot)

adjective Inflamed, with tiny enlarged blood vessels; usually said of eyes. / *Prisoner of Azkaban*, page 28

Katie's bloodshot eyes were puffy and bleary after a late night studying for her potions test.

bloodthirsty (**blud**-thur-stee)

adjective Eager to hurt or kill; murderous and cruel. / *Deathly Hallows*, page 509

The bloodthirsty monster rampaged through the village; luckily, everyone stayed inside.

bloomers (**bloo**-merz)

noun In British usage, old-fashioned women's underwear, loose-fitting and ending at the knees. / *Order of the Phoenix*, page 505

"Oh Mum, those bloomers are the baggiest, ugliest, and funniest I've ever seen," laughed her daughter.

blot (rhymes with **not**)

verb To spot or stain with ink, a particular problem with quill or ink pens. / *Chamber of Secrets*, page 158
One more time, her quill blotted right in the middle of the page—at this rate she'd never finish her essay on barn ghouls.

blotchy (blot-chee)

adjective Spotted and discolored. / *Prisoner of Azkaban*, page 69
Her nasty case of blotchy skin could be fixed, suggested the dermotolo-witch, with repeated applications of essence of rhino horn.

bludgeon (bludj-un)

verb To beat or strike, usually with a heavy stick. / *Prisoner of Azkaban*, page 141
Rupert tried to bludgeon the escaped giant slug, but every time he got near it, it squirmed away.

blurt (rhymes with **hurt**)

verb To say something suddenly or thoughtlessly. / *Sorcerer's Stone*, page 266
He wanted to blurt out the truth—the mermaid had really bad breath.

bluster (blus-tur)

verb To make loud empty threats or protests. / *Goblet of Fire*, page 533
"If you ever say that again," blustered the red-faced bank clerk, "I'll…I'll…bounce all your checks!"

blustery (blus-tur-ee)

adjective Windy and cold. / *Deathly Hallows*, page 510
The blustery winter weather reminded Mrs. Snodgrape of her childhood home in Alaska.

boa constrictor

See **snake** elsewhere in this dictionary.

boar (rhymes with **sore**; sounds exactly like **bore**)

noun A wild pig. / *Goblet of Fire*, page 171
The angry boar stared across the field at the picnicking girls; they were in his field and he didn't like it.

board duster (bord dus-tur)

noun Blackboard (or whiteboard) eraser. / *Goblet of Fire*, page 297
"Elrod, please clean the board dusters," said Madam Glinch. "And don't get dust everywhere."

boarhound (bore-hound)

noun Not a boring dog, but a kind of large dog once known for hunting boars; most likely a Great Dane. / *Sorcerer's Stone*, page 140
Max, the boarhound, felt his talents were being wasted carrying groceries home.

boat (rhymes with **goat**)

noun A serving dish that resembles a boat. / *Sorcerer's Stone*, page 203
At the king's lavish dinner, most of the gravy boats were filled with delicious beef gravy, but a few were filled with mushroom gravy for the vegetarian guests.

bob (rhymes with **sob**)

verb To make short, quick motions up and down. / *Order of the Phoenix*, page 738
The light bobbed up and down across the dark field as the lantern-carrying giant took one enormous step after another.

bode (rhymes with **toad**)

verb To be a sign or omen of something; usually used in phrases like "bodes well" or "bodes ill." / *Half-Blood Prince*, page 4
"It doesn't bode well that Brilly has been behaving—what do you think he's up to?" worried the principal.

bog (rhymes with **fog**)

noun A wet, spongy area of decaying plants, much like a marsh. / *Prisoner of Azkaban*, page 186 / Note: See also the noun **bog** below.
Stepping into the Big Bog was a little like stepping into a gigantic sponge—except it smelled worse.

bog (rhymes with **fog**)

noun In British slang, a vulgar word for toilet. / *Deathly Hallows*, page 242 / Note: See also the noun **bog** above.
"Done in the bog yet?" Winston rudely asked his younger brother.

boggart (boh-gart)

noun In British folklore, a mischief-making household spirit, able to take whatever shape it wants and usually causing things

to disappear or go wrong. / *Goblet of Fire*, page 211 / Note: In Potter's world, a boggart is a shape-shifter, able to take on the shape of one's worst fear.
Winston's father was certain a boggart had taken his pipe and hidden it in the refrigerator.

boil (rhymes with **oil**)

noun A really painful, infected sore, usually with pus surrounding a hard center (yuck). / *Sorcerer's Stone*, page 138
The nasty boils on Elrod's back developed soon after he fell into the poisonous hedge.

bolstered (bol-sturd)

adjective Supported or heartened. / *Half-Blood Prince*, page 237
Bella felt bolstered by her parents cheering on her performance as "Glenda the Good Witch."

bolt (rhymes with **jolt**)

verb To swallow quickly without chewing. / *Sorcerer's Stone*, page 166
Daniel bolted lunch—he was late to the match between the Terrible Trolls and the Horrible Hordes.

bomber jacket (bom-ur jak-et)

noun A short jacket, made of leather and often lined with sheepskin; similar to jackets worn by World War II bomber crews. / *Order of the Phoenix*, page 122
Rupert's grandfather promised to give Rupert his old bomber jacket from the war when Rupert went off to college.

bonbon (bon-bon)

noun A type of candy, usually a small piece of chocolate-covered fruit or nuts. / *Prisoner of Azkaban*, page 197
Mrs. Snodgrape's candy dish was filled with chocolate bonbons. Actually, it was more of a candy bowl. All right, it was a candy platter piled high with bonbons.

book (rhymes with **hook**)

verb To reserve or schedule. / *Chamber of Secrets*, page 110
Katie booked the softball field for a Sunday-afternoon practice.

boot (rhymes with **hoot**)

noun In British usage, a car trunk. / *Deathly Hallows*, page 31
"Put the picnic hamper in the boot and let's drive to the park," said Winston's mum.

bosom (buh-zum)

noun A woman's chest. / *Goblet of Fire*, page 275
The librarian's bosom heaved with delight—14 cartons of new books had just arrived.

bosom friend (buh-zum frend)

noun A best friend. / *Half-Blood Prince*, page 332
Emily and Katie were bosom friends; so were Rupert and Hassan.

bough (rhymes with **wow**; sounds exactly like **bow**)

noun A large tree branch. / *Chamber of Secrets*, page 75
The evergreen boughs in the Haunted Forest seemed to be dancing in the blustery wind.

bouillabaisse (boo-yah-bays)

noun A thick fish stew, with plenty of fish, shellfish, tomatoes, etc. / *Goblet of Fire*, page 251
Tonight's meal was Fiona's favorite—a delicious bouillabaisse with fresh homemade prune bread and yak butter.

boulderish (bowl-dur-ish)

adjective Like a boulder or large rock—stony, gray, lumpy, and not moving much. / *Order of the Phoenix*, page 697
The giant's boulderish face peered out from between the topmost tree branches.

bound and gagged

phrase Tied up (bound) with a gag in the mouth, preventing any kind of crying out for help. / *Prisoner of Azkaban*, page 376
The bungling burglar bound and gagged the bank manager, then realized no one else could open the bank vault.

bowlegged (boh-leg-ud)

adjective Having bent or curved legs. / *Prisoner of Azkaban*, page 60
Butch Thuggins feared he'd be bowlegged for life after he'd been riding his motorcycle for eight hours straight.

bowler (boh-lur)

noun A dignified hat, usually black and usually worn by older British businessmen; sometimes called a derby. / *Sorcerer's Stone*, page 117

Winston's father carefully adjusted his bowler—he looked like he had a small, black flying saucer on his head.

Bowler hat

Boxing Day (box-ing day)

noun A British holiday, the first weekday after Christmas. / *Goblet of Fire*, page 433

Winston spent Boxing Day recycling gift boxes, gift wrappings, and gift ribbons.

bracingly (bray-sing-lee)

adverb In a supporting or invigorating way. / *Prisoner of Azkaban*, page 97

"Buck up, Winston, not everyone gets that potion right the first time," said Mrs. Snodgrape bracingly.

bracken (brak-un)

noun A large fern, found in woods and meadows, that turns reddish-brown in the fall. / *Order of the Phoenix*, page 693

The fawn was exactly the color of bracken.

bracket (brak-et)

noun A fixture protruding from a wall or column to hold a lamp, candle, torch, or sign. / *Chamber of Secrets*, page 139

After the castle's candle brackets were all rewired, the king put in energy-saving light bulbs.

braggart (brag-urt)

noun A boastful person who brags a lot. / *Prisoner of Azkaban*, page 100

Duke Fresser had always been a braggart—he claimed he'd walked and talked by the time he was six months old.

brainwashed (brayn-washd)

adjective Being made to believe something that isn't true, by force, confusion, or constant repetition. / *Goblet of Fire*, page 239

The brainwashed fairies had been convinced they'd explode if they disobeyed.

brainwave (brayn-wave)

noun A sudden inspiration. / *Goblet of Fire*, page 618 / Note: Brainwave can also be spelled as two words—**brain wave**—like in *Half-Blood Prince* (page 456).

"Hey, I just got a brainwave—let's go shopping for new cauldrons today."

bramble (bram-bul)

noun A prickly shrub or vine, like wild blackberry. / *Deathly Hallows*, page 389

The brambles had completely overgrown the long-abandoned cottage.

brandish (bran-dish)

verb To wave or shake something in a threatening way. / *Sorcerer's Stone*, page 198

The little boy brandished his wooden sword at the giant gecko; she just laughed at him.

brandy (bran-dee)

noun An alcoholic liquor. / *Sorcerer's Stone*, page 29

"Brandy sounds really good right now," said Wildwood, stomping and shaking the snow off his boots.

bravado (brah-vah-doh)

noun Pretended or defiant courage. / *Half-Blood Prince*, page 302

As the hungry hawk swooped around him, Captain Hummingbird tried a show of bravado, bravely flying his own swoops and loops.

brawl (rhymes with **tall**)

verb To fight or quarrel noisily. / *Chamber of*

Secrets, page 63
Brilly and Flintlock brawled in potions class, then they brawled on the soccer field, and finally they brawled sitting in the principal's office.

breach (rhymes with **teach**)

noun An action that breaks a law or rule. / *Half-Blood Prince*, page 204
"There has been a serious breach of school rules," announced the principal. "Several students are wearing polka-dotted socks."

breach (rhymes with **teach**)

verb To break through or make an opening in. / *Deathly Hallows*, page 487
The walls around the Fortress of Solitude had been breached, and wisps of loneliness were leaking out.

breadwinner (bred-win-ur)

noun Someone who earns money to support the rest of the family. / *Deathly Hallows*, page 18
Madam Glinch had always been the breadwinner in her family—her husband preferred to stay home to garden and read trashy novels.

break ranks

phrase To leave an assigned place in a formation or grouping. / *Order of the Phoenix*, page 55
The tuba players in the school marching band began to break ranks as their bewitched tubas suddenly sprouted giant fountains of Foaming Burbles.

breakneck (brake-nek)

adjective Dangerously fast. / *Chamber of Secrets*, page 57
The breakneck ride down the mountain on the back of Brilly's broom was the scariest thing Willow had ever experienced.

brilliance (bril-yunce)

noun Smartness and talent. / *Goblet of Fire*, page 630
She couldn't believe her own brilliance—she'd solved the sudoku puzzle in five minutes.

brink (rhymes with **think**)

noun The edge, or a critical point in something. / *Deathly Hallows*, page 655
"I am on the brink of a great discovery," said Mrs. Snodgrape. "I believe my new charm will keep the class awake for an entire school day."

bristle (briss-ul)

noun Short, stiff, coarse hairs. / *Chamber of Secrets*, page 214
The bristles of the magical paint brush were made from the hair of an enchanted wild boar.

bristling (briss-ling)

adjective Bristle-like and prickly. / *Chamber of Secrets*, page 54 / Note: A related adjective in *Prisoner of Azkaban* (page 80), **bristly** also means "bristle-like and prickly."
Blackpool's bristling beard was so wiry that he could have used it for sandpaper.

broach (rhymes with **roach**)

verb To write about or discuss something for the first time. / *Order of the Phoenix*, page 330
Rupert broached the topic of an allowance increase but, given his father's bad mood, it didn't go over well.

brood (rhymes with **food**)

verb To worry and think constantly about something. / *Prisoner of Azkaban*, page 66
The king brooded on the fate of his court jester, who was in the hospital with laughing gastritis.

brusque (rhymes with **tusk**)

adjective Rudely abrupt, curt, and blunt. / *Order of the Phoenix*, page 114
The principal's brusque voice echoed up and down the school corridor—"Get OUT of your locker, Dribbles!"

brusquely (brusk-lee)

adverb In an abrupt, blunt way. / *Goblet of Fire*, page 312
"You are *not* wearing that out of this house," said Bella's father brusquely.

brutal (broo-tul)

adjective Cruel and violent. / *Goblet of Fire*, page 439
The brutal attack of the mountain gremlins on Wildwood's baby goats upset everyone in the village.

brutality (broo-tal-uh-tee)

noun Violent behavior. / *Half-Blood Prince*, page 229
"The brutality of American football is quite

astounding," said the king, watching the Super Bowl on his widescreen TV.

brute (rhymes with **newt**)
noun A nonhuman creature, and generally a savage and cruel one. / *Prisoner of Azkaban*, page 118
The vicious brute stormed across the valley and headed toward the small cottage, hungry for lunch and someone tasty.

brutish (broo-tish)
adjective Coarse, stupid, and cruel, like a brute. / *Deathly Hallows*, page 267
The brutish ogres were trying to stomp on the old witch's baby pigs.

buck (rhymes with **muck**)
verb To throw off a rider—or try to—by jumping in the air with the back arched. / *Sorcerer's Stone*, page 189
The pony bucked 14 times in a row, but Katie held on tight.

buckle (buk-ul)
verb To bend suddenly. / *Sorcerer's Stone*, page 69
When introduced to the famous Butch Thuggins, Rupert was so excited and nervous his knees almost buckled.

buck-toothed (buk-toothd)
adjective Having prominent front teeth, especially the two middle upper teeth. / *Order of the Phoenix*, page 258
The buck-toothed boy really wanted braces. He was tired of being called Bunny Boy.

budge up
phrase In British slang, to move over or move along. / *Sorcerer's Stone*, page 47
"Budge up, budge up, more passengers are trying to get on the bus," barked the driver.

budgerigar, budgie (budj-uh-ree-gar, bud-jee)
nouns A small parakeet, popular as a caged bird. "Budgerigar" is the formal name, "budgie" the shortened form. / *Order of the Phoenix*, page 4
The old hag's budgie actually learned to repeat spells, a trick that sometimes caused problems.

Budgie

buffer (buf-er)
noun In British usage, an incompetent or foolish man. / *Half-Blood Prince*, page 68
"The king's just a barmy old buffer, but he does try his best," said Winston's dad.

buffet (buf-it)
verb To be moved first one way than another with some force. / *Prisoner of Azkaban*, page 431
The wind buffeted the boat, but thanks to his magic Retchable pills, Milton didn't get seasick.

buffoon (buh-foon)
noun A fool or someone behaving foolishly. / *Order of the Phoenix*, page 696
Brilly never thought of himself as a bumbling buffoon; he felt he was more of a creative jokester.

build (rhymes with **filled**)
noun Body type. / *Sorcerer's Stone*, page 151
The gnome's build—short and stocky like a fire hydrant—made him a better football player than a basketball player.

bulbous (bul-bus)
adjective Fat and round, and not very attractive. / *Chamber of Secrets*, page 126
The old man's bulbous nose twitched as he smelled the popcorn inside the movie theater.

bulge (rhymes with **indulge**)

verb To swell beyond the usual size. / *Prisoner of Azkaban*, page 29

Mrs. Snodgrape's eyes bulged with delight as she entered the Hurly Burly Emporium; she'd waited all year for this sale.

bulrushes (bool-rush-es)

noun A swamp or wetlands plant, with tall, erect, and arching stems. Drawings or outlines of bulrushes are sometimes used as designs or symbols. / *Deathly Hallows*, page 88 / Note: In Potter's world, golden bulrushes were a design on a pair of Quidditch socks.

Bella went down to the lakeside and gathered bulrushes to use as decorations at her "Swamp Days Are Here Again" party.

bulwark (bul-wurk)

noun A strong structure, like a wall, that provides defense against some danger. / *Deathly Hallows*, page 631

The bulwark of closely planted trees helped protect the wizard's garden against strong winds.

bung (rhymes with **dung**)

verb In British slang, to toss something in a careless and offhand way. / *Goblet of Fire*, page 155

"Just bung those in the dustbin," the recycling truck driver suggested to Winston.

bungle (bung-gul)

verb To botch or mess things up. / *Chamber of Secrets*, page 294

"Let's hope Elrod doesn't bungle it," said Hassan. "We'll need those practice potions for the next assignment."

bungler (bung-lur)

noun Someone who does something in an unskillful way, generally messing things up. / *Sorcerer's Stone*, page 65

Elrod was an expert bungler—he could botch up anything.

buoy (rhymes with **toy**; sounds exactly like **boy**; can also be pronounced **boo-ee**)

verb To cheer up someone. / *Order of the Phoenix*, page 351

The wonderful letter from his grandmother—and the money she enclosed—buoyed Rupert's spirits.

buoyant (boy-yent)

adjective Happy and confident. / *Goblet of Fire*, page 126

Merlin was feeling particularly buoyant: his breakfast crumpet had been delicious, he'd just paid all his wizarding taxes, and his new cloak looked very elegant.

burgeon (bur-jun)

verb To grow or flourish. / *Order of the Phoenix*, page 29

Hope burgeoned in Willow's heart as the new boy walked toward her—perhaps he'd ask her to the Flufftones Ball.

burgeoning (bur-jun-ing)

adjective Growing or developing quickly. / *Deathly Hallows*, page 140

The farmer's burgeoning fields of corn would soon be converted to biodiesel fuel.

burly (bur-lee)

adjective Heavy, strong, and muscular. / *Sorcerer's Stone*, page 150

Even with five burly moving men, it was a struggle to get the piano to the top room in the castle tower.

burnish (bur-nish)

verb To polish something until it's smooth and bright. / *Deathly Hallows*, page 225

Mrs. Fracket burnished the pan until she could see her reflection in the bottom.

bury the hatchet

phrase To end a quarrel or fight. / *Prisoner of Azkaban*, page 264

Blackpool and Wildwood finally buried the hatchet after three days of refusing to speak to each other.

bust (rhymes with **dust**; sounds exactly like **bussed**)

noun A sculpture of someone's head, shoulders, and upper chest. / *Order of the Phoenix*, page 281

The bust of Merlin looked a lot like him, except it missed the twinkle in his eyes.

bustle (bus-sul)

verb To act or move with a great show of

energy. / *Goblet of Fire*, page 257
Words to live by: "Hustle more, bustle less."

buttocks (but-uks)

noun The rounded fleshy part of the rump. If you're sitting while reading this, you're sitting on your buttocks. / *Order of the Phoenix*, page 48
Uh-oh, one of the king's archers seems to have missed the target and to have hit the royal buttocks instead.

bypass (by-pass)

verb To avoid or to go past something. / *Order of the Phoenix*, page 600
Every Friday, Chi-Mun bypassed the cafeteria line—he hated fried possum.

by-the-by now

phrase Something incidental. / *Half-Blood Prince*, page 12
"Oh, that's just by-the-by now; don't worry about it anymore."

C

cache (rhymes with **rash**; sounds exactly like **cash**)
noun Something hidden or concealed. / *Half-Blood Prince*, page 274
The cache of gold wouldn't be found for a thousand years.

cackle (kak-ul)
verb To make a shrill broken sound, like a chicken happy with its new-laid egg; poltergeists, hags, crones, and some old witches tend to cackle a lot. / *Sorcerer's Stone*, page 159
The old hag cackled as she mixed the perfect potion to turn her obnoxious neighbor's hair into ivy.

cackling (kak-ling)
noun A shrill broken sound. / *Prisoner of Azkaban*, page 417
The mysterious cackling heard throughout the Haunted Forest meant only one thing—it was the witching hour.

cacophony (kah-kof-uh-nee)
noun A harsh, unpleasant sound. / *Order of the Phoenix*, page 102
That blaring cacophony was the school marching band tuning their instruments.

cadge (rhymes with **badge**)
verb To try to get something by wheedling, begging, or mooching. / *Goblet of Fire*, page 100
Brilly tried to cadge money off Dribbles for lunch, but Dribbles didn't have any—lucky for him, since Brilly often forgot his debts.

cajolingly (kuh-johl-ing-lee)
adverb In a persuasive, wheedling way. / *Chamber of Secrets*, page 73
"But Mom," said Bella cajolingly, "everyone else has their ears pierced. Sometimes twice."

calamity (kuh-lam-ih-tee)
noun A disaster. / *Deathly Hallows*, page 693
The calamity began when Brilly built a campfire for roasting marshmallows inside the garden shed.

caliber (kal-uh-bur)
noun Degree of worth or quality. / *Half-Blood Prince*, page 498
"I like to think our school attracts young wizards of a certain caliber…a high caliber, that is," said the president of the PWA (the Parent-Wizards Association).

callous (kal-us)
adjective Unfeeling or unsympathetic. / *Order of the Phoenix*, page 610
Blackpool seemed to take some sort of callous pleasure in seeing the baby goats fall on their faces.

callus (kal-us)
noun A hardened or thickened part of the skin, usually on the hands or feet. Plural: calluses. / *Goblet of Fire*, page 52
The gravedigger had some impressive calluses on his hands (and blisters, too) after digging 12 graves in a week.

camouflage (kam-uh-flahj)
verb To conceal or hide by a disguise or protective coloring. / *Deathly Hallows*, page 137
The thick ivy camouflaged the green meersnouts from the hungry owls flying overhead.

canapé (kan-uh-pee *or* kan-uh-pay)
noun An appetizer; usually a cracker topped with meat, cheese, etc. / *Deathly Hallows*, page 89
The canapés at the Royal Tea Party were especially tasty—fancy crackers with teeny slices of ostrich egg or melted chudbutt on top.

candelabra (kan-duh-lah-bra)
noun A large, decorative candlestick with several branches or arms for holding candles. / *Order of the Phoenix*, page 61
Her candelabra lighting the way, the princess walked

from her royal bedroom to the castle kitchen—time for a midnight snack.

Candelabra

candyfloss (kan-dee-flos)
adjective Light and airy like cotton candy, the spun-sugar treat at carnivals. / *Deathly Hallows*, page 399
Willow's candyfloss hair spread out around her head like a cloud.

cane (rhymes with **pain**)
noun In British usage, and in some British private schools, getting whipped with a cane was sometimes an acceptable punishment. The cane wasn't a walking-stick type of cane, but a birch or rattan switch, applied to the palms or the backside. So "Do they use the cane?" means "Do they use corporal punishment?" / *Prisoner of Azkaban*, page 24
"Brilly, you are so lucky they don't use the cane in this school—you'd be in such trouble."

canker (kang-kur)
noun Literally, an ulcer-like sore or some sort of diseased tissue; more generally, something nasty that corrupts or destroys. / *Deathly Hallows*, page 11
The preacher thundered: "Pride…selfishness…vanity…all these are cankers on our souls!" Blackpool, the evil wizard, who might have benefited from these words of wisdom, was not in church that day.

canopy (kan-uh-pee)
noun A cloth covering hung above a bed; also any similar covering overhead—a canopy of thunderclouds, for example. / *Chamber of Secrets*, pages 121 (bed) and 72 (overhead)
The bed's canopy was dark green, and Chi-Mun would often lie on his bed pretending a canopy of forest leaves was spread out above him.

canter (kan-tur)
verb To move at a speed that's slower than a gallop and faster than a walk; usually said of horses. / *Sorcerer's Stone*, page 259
The galloping stallion slowed and cantered when he saw the speed zone sign.

capacious (kuh-pay-shus)
adjective Roomy. / *Deathly Hallows*, page 228
The capacious horse-drawn carriage could hold six humans or one very young giant.

capitalize (kap-ih-til-ize)
verb To profit by. / *Deathly Hallows*, page 754
Rupert capitalized on the brief time Madam Glinch was writing on the blackboard to stuff an entire chocolate frisblot in his mouth.

capitulation (kuh-pitch-uh-lay-shun)
noun Surrender. / *Deathly Hallows*, page 461
Thrilled by the capitulation of his enemies, the army general announced a pay raise for all his troops.

carapace (kare-uh-pace)
noun Literally, the shell or bony covering of an animal, like a turtle, armadillo, lobster, or crab; more generally, it refers to something very much like an animal's hard shell—like a thick layer of ice. / *Deathly Hallows*, page 367
The carapace on certain animals is one of many reasons they're not cuddly pets.

cardigan (kar-duh-gun)
noun A knitted sweater with buttons down

the front. / *Chamber of Secrets*, page 179
As Bella buttoned her pink cardigan, she hoped everyone would notice it exactly matched her toenail polish.

careen (kuh-**reen**)
verb To lurch or swerve. / *Chamber of Secrets*, page 171
Nathan's skateboard careened into the street, but luckily he hopped off at the curb.

carpetbag (**kar**-pit-bag)
noun An old-fashioned traveling bag, made from carpet fabric. / *Order of the Phoenix*, page 852
Mrs. Fracket's carpetbag was carefully packed with several pairs of bloomers, her dressing gown, her nightdress, and a supply of lemon drops.

carriage clock (**kare**-ij clok)
noun A mantel clock with a decorative handle on top. / *Deathly Hallows*, page 36
The carriage clock sitting on the fireplace mantel struck midnight.

cartomancy (**kar**-toh-man-see)
noun Fortune-telling or divination using a deck of cards. / *Half-Blood Prince*, page 544
Cartomancy was a total mystery to Willow—how could a card tell your future? She preferred her mother's crystal ball.

cascade (kas-**kade**)
verb To fall in a cascade, like a waterfall. / *Chamber of Secrets*, page 54
The gummy bears cascaded out of the shop's dispenser and onto the floor.

casing (**kay**-sing)
noun An outer layer or case that protects something. / *Deathly Hallows*, page 197
The casing of the princess's royal locket had become tarnished and dented.

casket (**kas**-kit)
noun A small case or chest to hold jewels or other valuables. / *Goblet of Fire*, page 253
"Bring me my casket of royal jewels," commanded the queen.

caster (**kas**-tur)
noun A small wheel on the bottom of a chair leg; usually used in the plural: four chair legs = four casters. / *Chamber of Secrets*, page 194
The casters spun wildly as Ravi used the office chair as a makeshift skateboard.

catapult (**kat**-uh-pult)
noun In British usage, a slingshot. More generally, a catapult is an ancient fighting device for hurling huge stones or other missiles at an enemy—sort of a giant slingshot. / *Half-Blood Prince*, page 526
Winston and his pocket catapult had not proved very successful in driving the vultures out of the fangbark tree—what he needed was a real catapult to lob some giant rocks at them.

cataract (**kat**-uh-rakt)
noun A clouded eye lens, causing partial or complete blindness. / *Deathly Hallows*, page 335
Brilly's grandfather's cataracts made it difficult for him to see the mischievous gleam in his grandson's eyes.

catcall (**kat**-kall)
verb Not to call a cat, but to shout or whistle to indicate disapproval. / *Goblet of Fire*, page 494
The disgruntled audience began to catcall and stomp their feet midway through the performing seal's first trick.

categorically (kat-ih-**gore**-ih-kuh-lee)
adverb Absolutely, positively, and without a doubt. / *Half-Blood Prince*, page 231
Brilly categorically denied having anything to do with the stopped-up school toilets.

caterwauling (kat-ur-**wall**-ing)
adjective Shrill and screechy. / *Deathly Hallows*, page 558 / Note: In Potter's world, a Caterwauling Charm, set off in Hogsmeade, made a horrible screeching sound.
The caterwauling howls of the old lady's 12 hungry cats could be heard up and down the street.

cauldron (**kol**-drun)
noun A large kettle or pot used for preparing

magical potions. / *Sorcerer's Stone*, page 67
The three witches stood around the huge cauldron, stirring the bubbling potion, and worrying if they'd added enough eye of newt.

cavalcade (kav-ul-kade)
noun A procession or parade. / *Deathly Hallows*, page 634
The cavalcade of carriages and marching bands slowly passed by the grandstand.

cavernous (kah-vur-nus)
adjective Huge and hollow, like a cave. / *Prisoner of Azkaban*, page 88
Somewhere inside the cavernous temple the treasure was hidden, but how would they ever find it?

cavort (kuh-vort)
verb To romp or frolic. / *Goblet of Fire*, page 675
The baby goat cavorted playfully in the back yard.

celestial (sel-les-chul)
adjective Related to the sky or heavens. / *Goblet of Fire*, page 200
The celestial sounds of a hundred harps filled the auditorium, as if an angels' orchestra were performing.

centaur (sen-taur)
noun A mythical creature, part man (head, chest, and arms), and part horse (body and legs). / *Sorcerer's Stone*, page 252
Lunchtime—and the centaur couldn't decide between a grilled cheese sandwich or some nice, fresh hay.

chamber music (chaym-bur mew-sik)
noun Classical music performed by a small group, often a trio or quartet. / *Sorcerer's Stone*, page 103
Wildwood's favorite chamber music was anything written in the 17th century.

chamber pot (chaym-bur pot)
noun A portable container—often with a lid—used as a toilet. / *Order of the Phoenix*, page 387
"Oh dear, who'll empty the chamber pots now that the castle chambermaids are all on strike?" worried the queen.

Centaur

chameleon (kuh-meel-yun)
noun A small lizard that easily changes the color of its skin to match its background. / *Order of the Phoenix*, page 54
The chameleon could handle a green or a brown background, but if he wandered onto a picnicker's tartan blanket, he was in real trouble.

chandelier (shan-duh-leer)
noun A lighting fixture suspended from the ceiling, with many bulbs or candles on separate branches. / *Chamber of Secrets*, page 102
"Light the chandelier, please. I can hardly see to read anymore," said Winston's father.

channel (chan-uhl)
verb To enter a meditative, trancelike state to convey messages from a spirit guide. / *Order of the Phoenix*, page 264
"I can't believe it—I think Brilly is channeling his Great Great Uncle Brilltoe—either that or he's having a bad dream."

chaos (kay-os)
noun A confused, disorganized, and out-of-

control situation. / *Chamber of Secrets*, page 203
The usual chaos of the first day of school was only made worse when someone enchanted the chairs, and they all walked outside.

charred (rhymes with **guard**; sounds exactly like **chard**)

adjective Scorched. / *Goblet of Fire*, page 269
The letters from Uncle Clem must have accidentally fallen into the fireplace—they were certainly charred and blackened.

chasm (**kaz**-um)

noun Literally, a very deep, wide hole, like a gorge or an abyss; more generally, an emptiness or feeling of being distantly disconnected from someone or something. / *Order of the Phoenix*, page 828
The chasm between Wildwood and Blackpool was growing wider by the day—they didn't even begin to understand each other.

cheek (rhymes with **beak**)

noun In British usage, disrespectful and impertinent behavior. Often used in the phrase "you've got a lot of cheek," roughly meaning "you've got a lot of attitude." / *Sorcerer's Stone*, page 138
"Brilly, you've got a lot of cheek to think you can get away with imitating Madam Glinch's lisp—you're toast!" said Winston.

cherub (**chair**-ub)

noun A small, chubby, winged, child-like angel, often seen in paintings or statues. / *Order of the Phoenix*, page 559
Pictures of cherubs decorated every spare inch in Mrs. Fracket's kitchen—she even had a cherub sculpture sitting on a refrigerator shelf.

chestnut (**chess**-nut)

adjective Reddish-brown. / *Sorcerer's Stone*, page 252
The chestnut horse galloped down the road to his lunchtime conference with the donkey.

chimaera (kih-**meer**-uh)

noun In Greek mythology, an imaginary and very grotesque creature that breathes fire; it has the head of a lion, the body of a goat, and the tail of a serpent. / *Order of the Phoenix*, page 442
"Chimaeras seem to have a very mixed family background," said Dribbles seriously.

Chimaera

chink (rhymes with **link**)

noun A clinking sound. / *Chamber of Secrets*, page 16 / Note: See also the related noun **chink** below.
Dribbles heard the chink of his allowance falling out of his pocket as he clambered over the fence.

chink (rhymes with **link**)

noun A small crack or opening. / *Order of the Phoenix*, page 593 / Note: See also the related noun **chink** above.
Peering through the narrow chink in the rock, the green-frilled frogette spied the hunters finally giving up and wandering away.

chintz (rhymes with **hints**)

adjective Made of printed shiny fabric, usually of bright or pastel colors, used to upholster furniture or for curtains. / *Prisoner of Azkaban*, page 102
Aunt Margaret's chintz armchairs looked like they'd been covered in real flowers.

chips (rhymes with **pips**)

noun In British usage, french fries. / *Half Blood Prince*, page 163

The mermaid was embarrassed to admit that her favorite meal was fish and chips.

chisel (chis-ul)
noun A sharp tool for woodcarving and carpentry. / *Goblet of Fire*, page 184
The woodworker's chisel lay on her workbench, ready for the next project.

chivalrous (shiv-ul-rus)
adjective Kind, honorable, generous, courteous—all the things that knights of the Middle Ages were supposed to be. / *Deathly Hallows*, page 369
"Chivalrous behavior would be to help your date onto your broom first," suggested Rupert's father. "Not to get on and wait for her impatiently."

chivalry (shiv-ul-ree)
noun Behavior reminiscent of the ideal knight: kind, honorable, generous, courteous. / *Sorcerer's Stone*, page 118
"Chivalry is not dead," smiled Willow, as her boyfriend presented her with a bouquet of roses.

chivvy (chiv-ee)
verb To try to make someone do something faster, especially in an annoying way. / *Goblet of Fire*, page 164
"Come on, get in line, get in line, get in line," chivvied the impatient teacher.

chortle (chore-til)
verb To make a gleeful sound. / *Sorcerer's Stone*, page 166
The burglar chortled when the vault door swung open—at last, the treasure was his.

chuck (rhymes with **muck**)
verb To throw or toss. / *Chamber of Secrets*, page 9
Rupert chucked his half-eaten sandwich in the bin—roasted chudbutts were not his favorite.

chuffed (rhymes with **muffed**)
adjective In British slang, pleased and happy. / *Order of the Phoenix*, page 345 / Note: And if someone is really pleased, they're **dead chuffed**, like in *Goblet of Fire* (page 455).
Winston was chuffed about getting out of washing the dinner dishes.

chunter (chun-tur)
verb To mutter or grumble. / *Order of the Phoenix*, page 349
The king chuntered to himself all the way to the Royal Garden; everything and everyone was bugging him today.

churlish (chur-lish)
adjective Ungracious, uncivil, and boorish. / *Order of the Phoenix*, page 343
The churlish behavior of ogres makes them unpopular guests at dinner parties.

churn (rhymes with **turn**)
verb To move or swirl about violently. / *Chamber of Secrets*, page 49
His insides churned as poor Dylan headed for the bathroom—maybe it was the sardine candies that had upset his stomach.

chute (rhymes with **hoot**; sounds exactly like **shoot**)
noun A slide or tube for moving from one place to another. / *Deathly Hallows*, page 241
The water chute was the most popular ride at the Dungeons of Doom Amusement Park.

circlet (sir-klit)
noun A little circle; especially a headband, armband, crown, or ring of gold, silver, or jewels. / *Deathly Hallows*, page 587
The dainty circlet on Madam Glinch's arm had been a gift from her first wizardry coach.

circuit (sir-cut)
noun A circular or at least continuous path around an area. / *Goblet of Fire*, page 104
Willow and Bella made a circuit of the mall, stopping at every clothing shop along the way.

circular (sir-kyu-lur)
adjective Rounded; shaped like a circle. / *Chamber of Secrets*, page 84
Was that circular stain on the wall a splash of dragon's blood or just where the baby had thrown his mashed potatoes and gravy?

cistern (sis-turn)
noun In British usage, the tank at the back

of the toilet; more generally, any tank that holds water. / *Half-Blood Prince*, page 522
The cisterns in the girls' bathroom provided endless troublemaking opportunities for Brilly.

civil (**siv**-ul)

adjective Polite and courteous. / *Prisoner of Azkaban*, page 19
"Now, now, let's try for a civil discussion," the mayor urged, as the laughing dwarf and Blackpool began to argue.

clairvoyant (klare-**voy**-unt)

adjective Having powers of clairvoyance, to see objects and events that can't be perceived by the senses. / *Goblet of Fire*, page 578
The clairvoyant wizard suggested that Wildwood stay away from the Haunted Forest for the next few days.

clamber (**klam**-bur)

verb To climb clumsily, usually using both hands and feet. / *Sorcerer's Stone*, page 97
The miniature dragon clambered up the kitchen cabinet to reach the cookie jar; he was still too young to fly.

clammy (**klam**-ee)

adjective Damp, cold, and uncomfortable. / *Goblet of Fire*, page 349
Fiona's hands were clammy and her knees were shaking as she stepped out on stage to sing the school song for the entire school.

clamor (**klam**-ur)

noun A loud uproar. / *Deathly Hallows*, page 613
The clamor of the soccer crowd grew louder and louder—they were probably doing The Wave.

clamor (**klam**-ur)

verb To make insistent demands, or to make a hubbub of noise. / *Chamber of Secrets*, page 58
Elrod's allowance was clamoring to be spent—he almost felt like he could hear the money in his pocket suggesting things he could buy.

clamp (rhymes with **damp**)

verb To close tightly. / *Sorcerer's Stone*, page 52
Tamika clamped her mouth shut as Blackpool approached—last time he'd bewitched her braces and turned them into vines.

claptrap (**klap**-trap)

noun Dumb, showy talk. / *Deathly Hallows*, page 31
"Blah blah blah. The claptrap on TV today is terrible," said the king, relaxing on his throne and idly changing TV channels.

claustrophobic (klaws-truh-**foh**-bik)

adjective Tending to induce claustrophobia, a fear of being in small or enclosed spaces. / *Deathly Hallows*, page 258
Even the queen got claustrophobic shivers sometimes, especially in the tiny tower rooms.

claw-footed (**klaw**-foot-id)

adjective Having feet like claws; usually said of old-fashioned furniture or bathtubs. / *Chamber of Secrets*, page 205
The princess stepped into the claw-footed bathtub and snuggled down into the bubbly hot water to read her new book by candlelight.

Claw-footed bathtub

cleave (rhymes with **heave**)

verb To split or to divide. / *Order of the Phoenix*, page 17
He managed to cleave the log with one giant swing of the ax.

clench (rhymes with **wrench**)

verb To tighten up; said of stomachs, fists,

teeth, etc. / *Sorcerer's Stone*, page 56
Bella's stomach clenched as the play's director began to announce the results of the audition.

climate (kly-mit)

noun Not weather—but the general attitudes or situation of a place or group. / *Prisoner of Azkaban*, page 45
"Under the current climate of educational reform, we need to institute more potions and charms tests—remember, no wizard left behind," said the principal.

cloister (kloy-stur)

verb To be secluded, protected, or hidden, as if in a cloister (a monastery). / *Half-Blood Prince*, page 136
The forest elves had been totally cloistered from the rest of the world.

close ranks

phrase Armies close ranks when they're ready to fight a foe; more generally, the phrase means to become united to meet a challenge. / *Goblet of Fire*, page 285
The teachers closed ranks when the students threatened to go on strike.

closure (kloh-zure)

noun The act of closing permanently. / *Half-Blood Prince*, page 628
The closure of the local Star Ducks came as a complete surprise to the villagers.

clotted cream (klot-tid kreem)

noun A British treat; very thick cream made by slowly heating whole milk and skimming the cream off as it rises. Also called Devonshire cream. / *Prisoner of Azkaban*, page 77
"Would you like clotted cream and fresh strawberries, or just plain strawberries?" asked Winston's mum.

clout (rhymes with **out**)

verb To hit hard, usually with your hand. / *Sorcerer's Stone*, page 57
He clouted the monster chicken in the beak, but it still kept fighting.

clutch of eggs

phrase A nest of eggs. / *Goblet of Fire*, page 354
The clutch of peacock eggs would make an immense omelet.

cobble (kob-ul)

verb To quickly make something useful but perhaps not perfect; usually used with "together." / *Order of the Phoenix*, page 270
The fans had cobbled together a new cheer for the soccer star, but it needed work: Go Butch Go Butch Go Butch.

cobbled (kob-uld)

adjective Made of cobble stones, the slightly rounded stones once used to pave streets. / *Sorcerer's Stone*, page 71
The cobbled street was so bumpy that it was difficult for Nungie, the one-legged elf, to roll his wheelchair along.

cobra

See **snake** elsewhere in this dictionary.

cock-and-bull story (kok-and-bull stor-ee)

noun A made-up story meant to deceive or fool someone. / *Order of the Phoenix*, page 567
Blackpool's cock-and-bull story about finding the Lost Gold Mine of the Golden Miner wasn't believed by anyone.

cockatrice (kok-uh-tris)

noun A legendary monster with a deadly glance, hatched by a serpent from the egg of a cock; it has the head, legs, and wings of a cock and the body and tail of a dragon. / *Goblet of Fire*, page 238
Dribbles worried: "The cockatrice can kill you just by looking at you—do you think that's where the phrase 'If looks could kill' came from?"

cockroach (kok-rohch)

noun An unappealing brownish insect, with a flat body and long wiggly antennae. / *Prisoner of Azkaban*, page 139
The giant cockroach wiggled his cockroachy behind in glee—he'd just discovered a kitchen with a greasy stove and tasty stale crumbs all over the floor.

codger (kod-jur)

noun An odd or eccentric old man. / *Goblet of Fire*, page 380

The strange, old codger shook his walking stick at Dribbles and shouted, "Out of my way, whippersnapper."

codswallop (kods-swal-up)

noun Foolish nonsense. / *Sorcerer's Stone*, page 57

"That's just codswallop," said Winston. "There's no way the Loch Ness monster is looking over my shoulder."

coerce (koh-urse)

verb To compel someone to do something by threats, force, or intimidation. / *Half-Blood Prince*, page 372

Blackpool tried to coerce Flintlock into exercising his racing worms, but Flintlock refused to do it.

coercion (koh-ur-zhun)

noun The use of threats or force to make someone do something. / *Half-Blood Prince*, page 68

Coercion does not work well on vampires.

cog (rhymes with **dog**)

noun Literally, small machinery parts, like gearwheels and cog wheels; more generally, the "wheels turning" in a person's mind. / *Order of the Phoenix*, page 826 (machinery); *Goblet of Fire*, page 34 (head)

The cogs began to turn in Dribbles' head—it must be the cogs in the old grandfather clock making that loud ticking sound.

coherent (koh-here-unt)

adjective Understandable and making sense. / *Deathly Hallows*, page 197

Willow's coherent report on "Innovative Uses of Blood-sucking Leeches" got an "Excellent" from the teacher.

coil (rhymes with **oil**)

noun A spiral or loop. / *Sorcerer's Stone*, page 27

The coils of Mother Serpent were tight little snaky circles.

collage (koh-lahj)

noun A picture made by overlapping many other pictures, photographs, notices, etc. / *Deathly Hallows*, page 187

Blackpool decorated his living room wall with a collage of hundreds of spooky pictures.

colleague (kol-eeg)

noun A fellow member of a group or organization. / *Order of the Phoenix*, page 437

Merlin and his wizarding colleagues never missed the monthly meetings of the Chamber of Wizards.

collecting tin (kuh-lect-ting tin)

noun A container to collect donations; in British usage, a tin is a container or can. / *Sorcerer's Stone*, page 4

The members of the Old Hags Choir sang their favorite tune—"How Much Is That Froggie in the Window?"—but no one dropped a single coin into their collecting tin.

collude (kuh-lewd)

verb To work together secretly, especially when doing something dishonest or illegal. / *Goblet of Fire*, page 238

Young Flintlock and Blackpool—the evil wizard—colluded in a plan to enchant the elephants in the visiting circus.

collywobbles (kol-ee-wob-uls)

noun In British usage, a term for that uncomfortable feeling when something makes you nervous. / *Prisoner of Azkaban*, page 40

Even the king got the collywobbles sometimes, walking along the castle's silent, empty corridors.

combatant (kum-bat-nt)

noun A person engaged in fighting or combat. / *Deathly Hallows*, page 638

The two combatants slowly circled each other—who would be the first to draw his wand?

combative (kum-bah-tive)

adjective Ready to fight; belligerent. / *Chamber of Secrets*, page 190

His sword at the ready, the knight assumed a combative position, ready to fight to the death.

comeuppance (kom-**up**-unce)

noun Well-deserved punishment or retribution. / *Chamber of Secrets*, page 213

Brilly finally got his comeuppance—grounded a month for burning down the garden shed.

coming up to scratch

See **up to scratch** elsewhere in this dictionary.

commence (kuh-**mentz**)

verb To begin. / *Deathly Hallows*, page 580

Work finally commenced on the castle renovations last year and they're still not finished.

commentary (kom-un-**tare**-ee)

noun A series of explanations or descriptions. / *Sorcerer's Stone*, page 186

The newspaper commentary on the bank robbery never mentioned the guard had been turned into a hamster.

commentator (kom-un-**tay**-tur)

noun Someone who provides commentary. / *Half-Blood Prince*, page 166

The sports commentator, hexed by the losing team, kept burping up entire pieces of french toast whenever he mentioned a missed goal.

commiserate (kuh-**miz**-uh-rate)

verb To feel or express sympathy or compassion. / *Half-Blood Prince*, page 533

The Sisters of Sorcery commiserated with Ethelbell over the sad loss of all her enchanted lizards.

common room (kom-mun **room**)

noun In British usage, a room at school for students to socialize (usually) or study (sometimes) in. / *Sorcerer's Stone*, page 114

Sitting in the common room after class and gossiping was almost as much fun as stomping full milk cartons at lunchtime.

commotion (kuh-**moh**-shun)

noun Sudden activity usually accompanied by noise. / *Chamber of Secrets*, page 238

The wizard stilled the noisy commotion in the room with one wave of his wand.

commune (kuh-**myoon**)

verb To talk together. / *Deathly Hallows*, page 303

"I go now to commune with the spirits from the other world," intoned Mrs. Sprocket, the village seer and fortune-teller.

compartment (kum-**part**-munt)

noun In a train car, one of several separate, small rooms with two long seats facing each other and a sliding door to the train car's hallway. / *Sorcerer's Stone*, page 94

Every compartment on the train seemed full, most with mysterious cloaked men or gruesome dwarfish women—it was a trainful of weirdness.

compensation (kom-pun-**say**-shun)

noun Payment for injury or loss. / *Goblet of Fire*, page 151

When his silver motorcycle was stolen, Butch Thuggins demanded compensation from his insurance company.

compere (kom-**pare**)

noun In British usage, a TV emcee; more generally, someone who acts as host and keeps things going. / *Half-Blood Prince*, page 145

The king acted the compere at his birthday party, introducing everyone grandly and passing appetizers.

complacency (kom-**play**-sen-see)

noun Contentment or self-satisfaction. / *Deathly Hallows*, page 48

With an air of complacency, the queen waved her royal wave as she rode in her carriage past the crowd.

complacent (kom-**play**-sunt)

adjective Self-satisfied and smarmy. / *Order of the Phoenix*, page 743

After several years as the star of the Horrible Hordes, Butch Thuggins had become complacent about his soccer skills.

complexion (kum-**plek**-shun)

noun The natural color of the skin. / *Order of the Phoenix*, page 405

Dylan's complexion was ashen by the time he staggered off the roller coaster.

complexity (kum-**plek**-sih-tee)
noun The quality of being complex, complicated, hard to understand, or with many different parts. / *Deathly Hallows*, page 247
The complexity of the math problems Bella could do was astounding; it was like she could speak algebra!

component (kum-**poh**-nunt)
noun One of the parts of a whole. / *Half-Blood Prince*, page 375
"Every component brings something vital to the final potion," intoned the potions master.

comport (kum-**port**)
verb To behave in a certain way. / *Half-Blood Prince*, page 164
"Brilly, I expect you to comport yourself in a well-behaved, mature way on this field trip," urged Madam Glinch.

compost, compost heap (**kom**-post, **kom**-post heep)
nouns Decaying organic matter (leaves, grasses, kitchen waste, etc.) used to enrich the soil; a compost heap is a pile of that decaying matter. / *Chamber of Secrets*, pages 93 and 268
Auntie Baba's fruitcake often ended up in the compost, usually at the very bottom of the compost pile.

comprise (kum-**prize**)
verb To be composed of or made up of. / *Goblet of Fire*, page 264
Blackpool's emergency wand-o-pak comprised his favorite potions, a backup wand, a booklet of charms, and a portable cauldron for enduring calamities, earthquakes, disasters, and mysterious enchantments.

compulsory (kum-**pul**-suh-ree)
adjective Required. / *Deathly Hallows*, page 210
P.E. (Personal Experience) was compulsory for all wizards-in-training.

concealment (kun-**seel**-munt)
noun The hiding of something. / *Prisoner of Azkaban*, page 205
The concealment of the queen's jewels was much easier once the Royal Wizard was called in to provide a little magical assistance.

concede (kun-**seed**)
verb To admit or acknowledge grudgingly. / *Deathly Hallows*, page 142
Brilly conceded that he had been a little obnoxious on the field trip to the Museum of Magic.

conclusive (kun-**kloo**-siv)
adjective Decisive and without a doubt. / *Order of the Phoenix*, page 203
"I have conclusive proof of the defendant's guilt," thundered the lawyer.

concoct (kun-**kokt**)
verb To make something to eat or drink by mixing together ingredients, especially ones not usually combined. / *Order of the Phoenix*, page 660
The girls decided to concoct something special for their dinner party that night.

concussed (kon-**kust**)
adjective Bonked on the head and likely having a concussion. / *Order of the Phoenix*, page 188
The concussed boxer staggered to the corner of the boxing ring and blearily asked his manager, "Is it over yet?"

condensation (kon-den-**say**-shun)
noun The moisture that forms on a cold surface (window, mirror, etc.) when warm air touches it. / *Goblet of Fire*, page 435
Brilly wrote "Wash me!" in the condensation on the Introductory Spells classroom window—so it washed him.

condescend (kon-duh-**send**)
verb To do something in a way showing that it is beneath you. / *Deathly Hallows*, page 392
Rupert condescended to help his fourth-grade brother with his homework.

confection (kun-**fek**-shun)
noun An object that's very delicate and elaborate and even a little fussy or flamboyant. / *Goblet of Fire*, page 79
Bella's dress for the Flufftones Ball was a confection of spun gold and silver with little tinkling bells and flashing neon sequins sewn on.

confidential (kon-fuh-**den**-shul)

adjective Secret, and meant to be kept that way. / *Half-Blood Prince*, page 234
She kept all her confidential papers—including her prized recipe for chilled nettle soup—in the magical wardrobe in the attic.

confines (kon-**fines**)

noun The limits or borders of a place. / *Goblet of Fire*, page 314
"Class, please stay within the confines of the playing field—no sneaking off under the bleachers," instructed the gym teacher.

confirmation (kon-fur-**may**-shun)

noun Something that confirms, supports, or verifies. / *Half-Blood Prince*, page 243
Brilly felt that the sudden appearance of a bag of fireworks on his doorstep was confirmation of his current plans; his neighbor Rupert, however, had just wanted to get the fireworks out of the house before his mother discovered them.

confiscate (kon-fuh-**skate**)

verb To seize or take something away. / *Sorcerer's Stone*, page 296
Mrs. Snodgrape confiscated Rupert's backpack after he swung it at poor Dribbles.

conga (**kong**-guh)

noun A type of dance, done in single file. / *Half-Blood Prince*, page 514
"It's the conga!" shouted the deejay. "Hold on to the waist of the person in front of you, make a line, and let's one-two-three-kick!"

congealed (kun-**jeeld**)

adjective Thickened. / *Order of the Phoenix*, page 421 / Note: **Congealing**, a related adjective in *Order of the Phoenix* (page 364), means thickening.
"Ewwww, what is that congealed green stuff on your head?

congregate (**kong**-grih-gate)

verb To gather together in a group. / *Goblet of Fire*, page 235
The Sisters of Sorcery congregated monthly in Ethelbell's drawing room to practice a few old-time spells.

Conga line

conjure (kun-**joor** or **kon**-jure)

verb To practice magic. / *Sorcerer's Stone*, page 181
With one wave of his wand, Blackpool conjured the bloodcurdling image of a drooling ogre.

conscience (**kon**-shuns)

noun An inner sense of right and wrong. / *Deathly Hallows*, page 461
"I try to let my conscience be my guide," said Brilly. "But sometimes it doesn't guide me very well."

conservatory (kun-**sur**-vuh-tor-ee)

noun A greenhouse for plant growing. / *Half-Blood Prince*, page 434
The conservatory overflowed with hungry Venus flytraps, snapping at any fly that got near.

consignment (kun-**sign**-munt)

noun Items sent for sale. / *Goblet of Fire*, page 425
The consignment of dragon's teeth finally arrived at the Hurly Burly Emporium.

consort (kun-**sort**)

verb To associate or keep company with. / *Chamber of Secrets*, page 329
The mules like to consort with the donkeys, but the donkeys want to avoid the mules…trouble in the pasture!

conspicuous (kun-**spik**-yoo-us)

adjective Obvious and easily seen. / *Goblet of Fire*, page 163

Mrs. Sprocket's fortune-telling office was very conspicuous—it was shaped like a giant crystal ball.

conspiratorially (kun-spir-uh-**tor**-ree-uh-lee)
adverb In a secretive way, as if conspiring or plotting something. / *Goblet of Fire*, page 351
The guppies gathered conspiratorially behind a clump of seaweed, hatching a plot to go body surfing.

consternation (kon-stur-**nay**-shun)
noun Astonishment or dismay. / *Deathly Hallows*, page 285
With a great deal of embarrassed consternation, Willow realized she'd forgotten her term paper on the Ghoul Bus that morning.

constitute (**kon**-stih-toot)
verb To establish or create. / *Goblet of Fire*, page 256
The Radish Nose Spell was unsightly, but it didn't constitute a reason to stay home from school, at least according to the boy's mom.

constrained (**kun**-straind)
adjective Restrained, holding back. / *Goblet of Fire*, page 727
Deep in her yoga pose, Bella's constrained voice was barely audible: "I'm stuck…my head is jammed behind my knee…help me…."

constrict (**kun**-strikt)
verb To tighten or make narrower. / *Order of the Phoenix*, page 782
Fiona's throat constricted as she stood up at the front of the assembly to sing the school song.

constricted (kun-**strik**-tid)
adjective Tight or squeezed. / *Order of the Phoenix*, page 415
In a constricted voice, the pet shop owner promised his snake a tasty snack if he'd just let go of his neck.

consummate (**kon**-suh-mut)
adjective Skilled or expert. / *Deathly Hallows*, page 78
Blackpool was the consummate evil wizard—ever ready to perform a spell or concoct a potion that would ruin someone's day.

contagious (kun-**tay**-jus)
adjective Easily passed to another person; usually refers to sickness, disease, or germs. / *Goblet of Fire*, page 236
"Do you think he's contagious?" Julio asked as the green-faced boy was led off to the infirmary.

contaminate (kun-**tam**-uh-nate)
verb To make impure or unclean; to pollute by contact. / *Order of the Phoenix*, page 162
"Don't even touch my notebook," growled Bella. "You'll contaminate it with your grubby hands."

contaminated (kun-**tam**-uh-nay-tid)
adjective Tainted, infected, impure, soiled, stained. All in all, yucky. / *Order of the Phoenix*, page 492
Instead of a smooth, green liquid, the contaminated potion had become a bubbling and smoking orange mess—plus it was making odd yodeling sounds.

contemplate (**kon**-tum-plate)
verb To think about. / *Deathly Hallows*, page 36
"Am I the only one who ever contemplates leaving the teaching profession?" asked a very tired Madam Glinch in the teachers' lounge.

contemplation (kon-tum-**play**-shun)
noun The thoughtful looking at or consideration of something. / *Half-Blood Prince*, page 539
"Contemplation of the hardworking honey bee provides perspective on life's journey," said the wizard sagely…but Blackpool just sneered.

contemptuous (kun-**temp**-choo-us)
adjective Feeling or showing that someone is worthless and inferior and deserves no respect. / *Prisoner of Azkaban*, page 97
With a contemptuous look at them all, Blackpool stormed out of the village meeting.

contort (kun-**tort**)
verb To twist or bend out of normal shape. / *Chamber of Secrets*, page 317
Dribbles' face contorted with his efforts to levitate his pencil.

contraband (**kon**-truh-band)
noun Items smuggled or snuck in. / *Deathly Hallows*, page 632
The pirates rowed ashore with cases of stolen contraband hidden in their small boat.

contract (kon-trakt)

noun A formal agreement between two people. / *Goblet of Fire*, page 256
Blackpool and Mrs. Fracket shook hands and signed the contract.

controversial (kon-truh-vur-shul)

adjective Involving debate, argument, or controversy. / *Order of the Phoenix*, page 308
In a controversial decision, the principal decided to shorten lunch period and lengthen math period.

convalescent (kon-vuh-les-unt)

adjective Ailing but recovering. / *Order of the Phoenix*, page 547
The convalescent pole vaulter—sidelined with a broken arm—was still able to compete in the levitation contest.

converge (kun-verj)

verb To come together in one place. / *Order of the Phoenix*, page 292
The Sisters of Sorcery regularly converged in Ethelbell's drawing room for an evening of Crazy Fates.

convey (kun-vay)

verb To communicate; to explain or get something across to someone. / *Half-Blood Prince*, page 4
"Please convey my best wishes to your mother," said the wandmaker to the little girl.

convoy (kon-voy)

noun A group of moving vehicles traveling together. / *Half-Blood Prince*, page 156
The mice convoy passed right in front of the dozing cat.

convulsive (kun-vul-siv)

adjective Sudden and uncontrolled. / *Order of the Phoenix*, page 471
With a convulsive shiver, the dwarf mouse rolled over dead—scared to death by a tiger on *Wild Kingdom*.

coop (rhymes with **poop**)

noun A small building or pen, usually for chickens. / *Chamber of Secrets*, page 201
Wildwood's chicken coop wasn't large enough for his entire flock, so he kept a few hens in his camping tent.

coop (rhymes with **poop**)

verb To confine or cage, as if in a coop; usually used with "up." / *Chamber of Secrets*, page 249
"I have been cooped up in this moldy old castle all week," complained the princess, "and I want to go shopping!"

copious (koh-pee-us)

adjective Large and abundant in quantity. / *Order of the Phoenix*, page 847
Copious amounts of frog slime covered poor Willow's backpack.

copse (rhymes with **hops**; sounds exactly like **cops**)

noun A thicket of trees or bushes. / *Half-Blood Prince*, page 201
The copse provided an excellent hiding place for the green-frilled frogette.

cordially (kor-jul-lee)

adverb Pleasantly; in a warm and sincere way. / *Goblet of Fire*, page 85
The sorceress cordially welcomed the evening's guests—what a delight to have the Sisters of Sorcery together again.

corking (kor-king)

adjective Terrific; sometimes used a bit sarcastically. / *Prisoner of Azkaban*, page 62
"It'd be, like, corking if you'd make sausages-and-mash for dinner, mum," Winston suggested brightly.

Cornish pasty

See **pasty** elsewhere in this dictionary.

corporeal (kor-pore-ee-ul)

adjective Related to the body; having tangible form. / *Order of the Phoenix*, page 141
"At least corporeal things aren't a worry anymore," said the ghost. "Like runny noses, or rashes, or ear aches, or…oh, never mind."

corpulent (kor-pyoo-lunt)

adjective Fat or overweight. / *Order of the Phoenix*, page 473
The corpulent cop couldn't run fast enough to catch a bus let alone an escaped monster chicken.

corrosive (kuh-**row**-siv)

adjective Destructive, caustic, corroding. / *Deathly Hallows*, page 309
"Your corrosive remarks have hurt my feelings terribly," she sobbed, running from the room.

corset (**kor**-sut)

noun An old-fashioned stiffened garment worn to give shape to a woman's hips and waist. / *Half-Blood Prince*, page 436
"Let me adjust my corset a bit," said the queen's elderly mother. "I want to look good for the Royal Tea Party."

cosseted (**kos**-ih-tid)

adjective Pampered. / *Half-Blood Prince*, page 72
The princess had always lived a very cosseted life in the castle.

cotton (**kot**-tun)

verb To get it, or to become aware of something; usually used with "on." / *Goblet of Fire*, page 54
"Did you cotton on to the fact that Madam Glinch thinks there's school this Friday?" asked Emily.

countenance (**kown**-tun-uns)

noun Face or appearance. / *Half-Blood Prince*, page 307
The frog's countenance turned pale and his legs twitched as he considered the possibility of being someone's gourmet meal.

counter-

This prefix adds the concept of *against* or *opposite* to many ordinary words:

argument/counterargument
noun / *Deathly Hallows*, page 100

attack/counterattack
noun / *Prisoner of Azkaban*, page 136

charm/countercharm
noun / *Chamber of Secrets*, page 317

clockwise/counterclockwise
adjective / *Order of the Phoenix*, page 233

curse/countercurse
noun / *Order of the Phoenix*, page 648

enchantment/counter-enchantment
noun / *Deathly Hallows*, page 188

jinx/counterjinx
noun / *Order of the Phoenix*, page 613

sign/countersign
verb / *Order of the Phoenix*, page 595

spell/counterspell
noun / *Order of the Phoenix*, page 810

coup (rhymes with **poo**; sounds exactly like **coo**)

noun A takeover. / *Deathly Hallows*, page 207
The students planned a cafeteria coup—everyone was tired of the same food, day after day, and something needed to be done.

course (rhymes with **horse**; sounds exactly like **coarse**)

verb To run down or flow through. / *Chamber of Secrets*, page 328
Tears coursed down the king's cheeks as his favorite contestant was voted off Survivor: The Molten Swamp.

covert (**koh**-vurt)

adjective Concealed or hidden. / *Half-Blood Prince*, page 330
Rupert was quite interested in the new girl but, not wanting to stare, he just kept sneaking covert glances at her.

covet (**kuv**-et)

verb To enviously want or crave something someone else has. / *Deathly Hallows*, page 615
The princess coveted the priceless jewels of her great aunt, the elderly Empress of Nars.

covetous (**kuv**-uh-tus)

adjective Greedy; desiring something belonging to someone else. / *Order of the Phoenix*, page 105
His covetous looks were obvious to everyone—he really wished he'd won that beautiful silver bowling ball.

cower (**kow**-ur)

verb To cringe. / *Sorcerer's Stone*, page 49
Rupert cowered behind the large rock as the gruesome Flying Fiends flew high overhead.

cozy
See **tea cozy** elsewhere in this dictionary.

cracker (krak-ur)
noun A small tube of colored paper that two people pull apart—it makes a loud pop or "crack" when pulled open and usually contains a small toy, a bad joke, and a silly hat; a British holiday tradition. / *Sorcerer's Stone*, page 203
Winston handed out crackers to his holiday guests, and then the fun began.

crackpot (krak-pot)
adjective Crazy or eccentric. / *Sorcerer's Stone*, page 59
"Where do you get these crackpot ideas? Make-up for mermaids? It'll just wash off!"

crane (rhymes with **brain**)
verb To stretch the neck—sort of like a crane—to see something. / *Sorcerer's Stone*, page 1
Father Goose craned his long neck around the edge of the morning paper and reminded his young son to put marmalade on his toast, not on his feathers.

cravat (kruh-vat)
noun A necktie. / *Half-Blood Prince*, page 483
Adjusting his cravat as he looked in the mirror, Blackpool smiled knowingly—he would clearly be the best-dressed wizard at the party.

creditable (kred-ih-tuh-bul)
adjective Deserving credit or praise, though perhaps not wildly enthusiastic credit or praise. / *Order of the Phoenix*, page 266
The teacher told Willow she'd written a creditable term paper on "Rhyming Incantations," though it offered no fresh insights.

creed (rhymes with **seed**)
noun A belief system, or a statement of beliefs or principles. / *Order of the Phoenix*, page 842
The creed of the truly evil Draconia Deveel was "Destroy now, ask questions later."

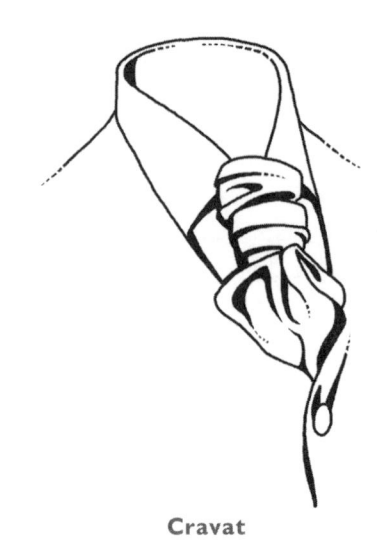

Cravat

crenellated (kren-uhl-ay-tid)
adjective Having square notches in the outer walls on top of a castle tower. / *Half-Blood Prince*, page 583
After climbing all the way to the top, the exhausted king sat down in one of the notches of the tower's crenellated wall and reconsidered his prohibition against elevators in the castle.

crescendo (kruh-shen-doh)
noun A gradual increase; usually said in relation to sound or activity. / *Goblet of Fire*, page 353
The Old Hags Choir ended their performance with a crescendo of disharmony.

crest (rhymes with **best**)
noun The top or highest point of a hill. / *Goblet of Fire*, page 71 / Note: See also the related noun **crest** below.
The frolicking boarhound puppies had just reached the crest of the hill when they realized how very far they were from their mother—and they came racing back down the hillside.

crest (rhymes with **best**)
noun A family crest; a picture or design used on a shield or helmet as the sign of a family. / *Order of the Phoenix*, page 117 / Note: See also the

related noun **crest** above.
The Dribbles family crest featured a prancing stag, a field of wheat, and the motto "Faithful though unfortunate."

crestfallen (krest-faw-lun)

adjective Disappointed and upset. / *Prisoner of Azkaban*, page 112
Brilly was crestfallen when the teacher said he couldn't bring his worm farm to class.

crevice (krev-is)

noun A narrow crack or opening, especially in a rock. / *Half-Blood Prince*, page 578
Peering through the crevice in the rocks, the giant watched the activity on the road below.

crick (rhymes with **brick**)

verb To turn or wrench your head so quickly that you get a painful cramp or muscle spasm. / *Order of the Phoenix*, page 139
The old gremlin cricked his neck while watching the lightball tennis match.

cricket ball (krik-it ball)

noun A red ball, about the size of a baseball or tennis ball, used in the British game of cricket. / *Order of the Phoenix*, page 695
The giant had eyes the size and color of cricket balls.

crikey (kry-key)

interjection In British slang, an expression showing surprise or annoyance, roughly meaning "Gosh" or "Good grief!" / *Sorcerer's Stone*, page 65
"Crikey, Teddy, I can't believe it—you forgot to zip your pants up again!" giggled Winston.

crinoline (krin-ih-lin)

noun A hoop skirt, an old-fashioned, very full skirt with hoops underneath that make the skirt stand out in a bell shape. / *Prisoner of Azkaban*, page 101
Blackpool's elderly mother still had an old crinoline she'd pull out of the closet for special parties.

crisp (rhymes with **lisp**)

noun In British usage, a potato chip. / *Goblet of Fire*, page 403 / Note: In at least one instance in Potter's world, such as in *Sorcerer's Stone* (page 48), "chip bags" are mentioned; most likely, this should have been "crisp bags."
Roasted toadbutts and crisps were Elrod's favorite afternoon snack.

croak (rhymes with **broke**)

verb To speak in a low, hoarse voice, like a frog or crow. / *Chamber of Secrets*, page 54
He croaked out a reply to the doctor's question: "Yes, I have a terrible sore throat."

croaky (krow-kee)

adjective Deep and hoarse. / *Chamber of Secrets*, page 288
"Mom," groaned the teenage frog, "I'm not sick, I'm just croaky. I always sound this way."

crocheted (krow-shayd)

adjective Done in needlework using one needle, not two (which would be knitting). / *Goblet of Fire*, page 80
Madam Glinch enjoyed making crocheted wand sacks for the students in her Advanced Wandwork class.

crone (rhymes with **bone**)

noun A witchlike old woman. / *Prisoner of Azkaban*, page 193
The old crone cackled excitedly when Gretel finished cleaning the oven.

crony (krow-nee)

noun A buddy or friend. Plural: cronies. / *Chamber of Secrets*, page 97
The Sisters of Sorcery and their old cronies from Cauldron College got together to play Witch Poker once a year.

cropped (rhymes with **dropped**)

adjective Cut short. / *Goblet of Fire*, page 435
Dribbles' cropped hair was the result of his falling asleep while the barber's magical scissors snipped away.

crossbow (kros-boh)

noun Not a grouchy bow, but a weapon, somewhat like a very heavy bow and arrow device, but held crosswise, not up and down. / *Sorcerer's Stone*, page 140

The crossbow is best against larger targets—it's not very useful against mice.

crumpet (krum-pit)

noun A British treat resembling a small, thick pancake, eaten with butter and jam. / *Sorcerer's Stone*, page 204

"The worst thing about vacationing in a cave," thought Merlin, "is there's no toaster—I do miss my morning crumpets."

cryptic (krip-tik)

adjective Mysterious or puzzling. / *Order of the Phoenix*, page 830

The cryptic note made little sense until the boy realized it was written upside down and backwards.

crystalline (kris-tih-lin)

adjective Crystal-like. / *Goblet of Fire*, page 372

Mama's Crystal Ball Cleaner is best for putting a crystalline shine on your crystal ball.

cubicle (kyoo-bih-kul)

noun A small room or compartment; there are office cubicles, toilet cubicles, etc. / *Order of the Phoenix*, page 131

"Not your ordinary cubicle, is it?" said Mr. Snodgrape, showing off his workspace designed to look like the inside of a whale's stomach.

cudgel his brain

phrase To try to remember or understand something. / *Deathly Hallows*, page 313

No matter how hard he cudgeled his tiny brain, the mouse could not remember where he'd hidden the cheese.

cue (rhymes with **due**)

noun A signal for action. / *Order of the Phoenix*, page 118

"Okay, on my cue, we make a lot of noise," said the crow. "Maybe they'll think there's going to be an earthquake."

cuff (rhymes with **buff**)

verb To hit someone lightly, in a friendly way. / *Chamber of Secrets*, page 194

"She cuffed me on the shoulder," said Rupert. "Do you think that means she likes me?"

culminate (kul-muh-nate)

verb To end dramatically. / *Goblet of Fire*, page 407

The Rolling Bones performance culminated with the musicians levitating their guitars over the crowd.

cupboard (kuh-burd)

noun In British usage, a small closet, often under the stairs. / *Sorcerer's Stone*, page 19

The cupboard was large enough for Parker to hide in, but it was also large enough for 17 slightly damp overcoats, 23 pairs of shoes, 4 suitcases, and 73 empty coat hangers.

cuppa (kup-uh)

noun In British usage, a shortened way to say "cup of tea." / *Goblet of Fire*, page 3

"Ready for a cuppa?" asked Winston's mum, holding the teapot.

cur (rhymes with **fur**)

noun A mongrel dog. / *Prisoner of Azkaban*, page 175

Saying "You mangy cur!" is a lot like saying "You dirty dog!"

cured ham (kyurd ham)

noun A ham (a cut of meat from a pig) that's been salted or smoked to preserve it. / *Goblet of Fire*, page 264

The old witch had several cured hams hanging from her scullery ceiling, waiting to be made into her favorite ham-and-dregs sandwiches.

curio (kyur-ee-oh)

noun An unusual or rare object, valued as a curiosity. / *Deathly Hallows*, page 681

Mrs. Snodgrape kept all her curios—the water balls, the flannel snake cozy, the antique teledrone—in her locked curio cabinet.

curse (rhymes with **purse**)

noun An appeal for evil or harm to happen to someone. / *Sorcerer's Stone*, page 55

The witch raised her fist to the sky and shouted an evil curse on all little turnip-eating pigs—they had ruined her garden.

cursory (kur-suh-ree)
adjective Not thorough; superficial. / *Deathly Hallows*, page 619
The policewoman's cursory inspection suggested that the burglar must have entered through the broken window.

curtsy (kurt-see)
verb To bend one knee with one foot in front. Women curtsy, men bow, both as a sign of respect. / *Goblet of Fire*, page 376
The chambermaids curtsied as the princess grandly descended the castle staircase.

cutlery (kut-lur-ee)
noun Generally, silverware—knives, forks, and spoons. In some cases, only knives for chopping and cutting are meant. / *Goblet of Fire*, page 59
"Put the cutlery out, please. I can't cook and set the table too," said Winston's harried mum.

cuttlebone (kut-tul-bone)
noun A chalky fishbone, given to cage birds to chew on so they get enough calcium. / *Deathly Hallows*, page 683
Jake the budgie loved to gnaw on the hunk of cuttlebone in his birdcage.

CV (see-vee)
noun Like a resume, a document listing one's education and previous jobs. CV is an abbreviation for the Latin *curriculum vitae*, roughly meaning "the course of life." / *Deathly Hallows*, page 34
When applying for a wizarding job, be sure your CV lists all the spells and charms you know.

cylindrical (sih-lin-drih-kul)
adjective Shaped like a cylinder; a soda can is a cylinder. / *Order of the Phoenix*, page 578
The cylindrical instrument case was bewitched to look like it contained just a flute, but it actually held a giant cello.

D

dab (rhymes with **cab**)
verb To apply or wipe with short, light strokes. / *Chamber of Secrets*, page 15
The school nurse dabbed at Dribbles' bloody nose after he ran into someone's fist.

dab hand (**dab** hand)
noun Someone skilled in an activity. / *Half-Blood Prince*, page 191
Butch Thuggins considered himself a dab hand at repairing motorcycles.

daggers
See **look daggers** elsewhere in this dictionary.

dais (**day**-us or **die**-us)
noun A raised platform for a throne, a speaker, etc. / *Order of the Phoenix*, page 773
The throne room had a dais at one end for the king's throne and a dais at the other end for his widescreen TV.

damper (**dam**-pur)
noun Someone or something that dampens or depresses spirits. Often used in the phrase "bit of a damper." / *Deathly Hallows*, page 136
The unexplained fire in the Royal Kitchen was a bit of a damper as far as the king and his birthday guests were concerned.

dank (rhymes with **tank**)
adjective Damp and chilly. / *Prisoner of Azkaban*, page 279
The dank, mossy dungeon smelled faintly of old mushrooms.

dappled (**dap**-uld)
adjective Spotted or mottled. / *Sorcerer's Stone*, page 258
The dappled pattern of the moonlight, filtering through the leaves onto the tombstones, was peacefully beautiful.

daresay (dare-say)
verb To suggest something is likely or certain. / *Prisoner of Azkaban*, page 417
"I daresay the gravediggers will finish by noon," said the cemetery caretaker.

darn (rhymes with **barn**)
verb To mend or repair cloth by weaving new thread or yarn across a hole. / *Goblet of Fire*, page 152
Dribbles' mother darned his favorite socks—though they were more holes than sock.

daub (dawb)
verb To spread or smear something (usually messy or sticky) with quick strokes. / *Chamber of Secrets*, page 138
Brilly angrily daubed most of his chudbutt stew on the cafeteria table—it was the fourth time this week it had been served.

dead… (rhymes with **red**)
adverb Completely or really. Used in phrases like "dead chuffed" (*Goblet of Fire*, page 455) or "dead clumsy" (*Order of the Phoenix*, page 52), or "dead depressing." (*Chamber of Secrets*, page 130).
"You're dead wrong! Dead wrong and dead stupid!" taunted Blackpool.

deadpan (**ded**-pan)
adjective Showing no emotion. / *Deathly Hallows*, page 10
The deadpan reaction of the audience suggested they were not finding the play very funny.

debris (duh-**bree**)
noun Scattered wreckage or rubbish. / *Prisoner of Azkaban*, page 266
Debris—mostly rotten eggs and worm chunks—fell on the party guests when the possessed piñata exploded.

decant (dih-**kant**)
verb To pour a liquid from one container to

another without disturbing the sediment at the bottom. / *Half-Blood Prince,* page 376
Rilda spent detention decanting beakers of gunky ogre saliva.

decanter (dih-**kan**-tur)
noun A decorative glass bottle with a stopper, used to hold liquids, usually wine. / *Half-Blood Prince,* page 66
A lovely decanter of Bite Wine sat on the table, awaiting the vampire's birthday celebration.

Decanter

decapitation (dih-kap-ih-**tay**-shun)
noun A beheading. / *Goblet of Fire,* page 223
Decapitation was the monster chicken's worst fear—even the sight of the ax sent her into terrified clucking.

decipher (dih-**sy**-fur)
verb To decode or figure out something. / *Goblet of Fire,* page 200
"I can't decipher your mother's note, Brilly. Does it really say 'My mother says Brilly is excused today'?"

decontaminate (dee-kun-**tam**-uh-nate)
verb To remove a dangerous or harmful substance. / *Order of the Phoenix,* page 68
Rupert decontaminated his broom with vinegar before flying his girlfriend to the party; they both arrived smelling like salad.

decor (**day**-kor *or* **dah**-kor)
noun The decorative style of a room. / *Goblet of Fire,* page 730
Inspired by the decor of the Master Spider, the decorator decided, "From now on, all my clients shall have webbed walls embedded with mummified bugs. It'll be fabulous!"

decoy (**dee**-koy *or* **duh**-koy)
noun Something that lures someone away or to something else (think about a duck decoy and hunters). / *Deathly Hallows,* page 50
Dribbles was the decoy, asking Mrs. Snodgrape endless questions while Brilly snuck toward her magical storage cabinet.

decree (duh-**kree**)
noun Official orders. / *Chamber of Secrets,* page 21
The latest decree from the principal's office said no bringing pets to school, and especially no pet cockroaches or pet wasps.

decrepit-looking (dih-**krep**-it-**look**-ing)
adjective Looking worn-out or broken down. / *Chamber of Secrets,* page 206
The free couch was a little decrepit-looking, but it'd be perfect in her bedroom, thought Willow—but how would she get it home and up the stairs without her parents seeing?

deduce (dih-**doose**)
verb To reach a conclusion by reasoning. / *Order of the Phoenix,* page 533
"I can deduce what happened easily enough," said the pompous police inspector. "One tied-up bank manager, and no money—I believe there must have been a bank robbery."

deduction (dih-**duk**-shun)
noun The process of figuring out something, using whatever knowledge or information you have. / *Goblet of Fire,* page 255
Using his powers of deduction, Brady determined it

was the butcher's son who'd turned his dirt bike into a pork loin.

deem (rhymes with **seem**)
verb To judge, consider, or believe. / *Deathly Hallows*, page 106
He hadn't deemed the invitation to the Sea Prom dangerous until the pretty mermaid dragged him 50 feet underwater.

deferentially (def-uh-**ren**-shul-ee)
adverb In a respectful and courteous way. / *Order of the Phoenix*, page 710
The cat deferentially placed the dead mouse on her owner's pillow, and was surprised when screams rather than applause greeted her gift.

deftly (**deft**-lee)
adverb In a quick and skillful way. / *Prisoner of Azkaban*, page 343
The prince deftly rode his horse across the castle drawbridge, avoiding the holes, and into the Royal Stables.

deign (rhymes with **main**; sounds exactly like **Dane**)
verb To do something you think you're really too important to do; to condescend to do something. / *Deathly Hallows*, page 393
"I do not deign to clean my own glasses or make my own bed," announced the queen grandly.

delapidated
See **dilapidated** elsewhere in this dictionary. / Note: There are over one million words in Potter's story, and this is one of the few misspelled words. It's "dilapidated," not "delapidated." / *Prisoner of Azkaban*, page 88

delegation (del-uh-**gay**-shun)
noun Persons representing others. / *Goblet of Fire*, page 242
The delegation from the Castle Workers Union asked to meet with the king to discuss vacations for the chambermaids.

deliberate (dih-**lib**-ur-ate)
verb To think carefully and slowly. / *Half-Blood Prince*, page 344
Chi-Mun deliberated over his Father's Day gift—should he get his dad a pair of enchanted socks or some Wilson's Wand Wax?

delicacy (**del**-ih-kuh-see)
noun Consideration and tactfulness. / *Half-Blood Prince*, page 649
With her usual tact and delicacy, Willow whispered to Bella that there was toilet paper stuck to her shoe.

delinquent (dih-**ling**-kwent)
noun A young person guilty of antisocial or criminal behavior. / *Goblet of Fire*, page 390
"Brilly, you're going to turn into a delinquent unless you mend your ways," warned the principal.

delirious (dih-**leer**-ee-us)
adjective Talking continuously and without making much sense, especially because of illness or high fever. / *Deathly Hallows*, page 681
Dylan was so sick he was delirious, asking over and over where his pet orangutan was.

delude (dih-**lewd**)
verb To make someone else believe something that isn't true; to purposely confuse someone. / *Order of the Phoenix*, page 697
"You deliberately deluded me into buying that useless moat-sweeper," ranted the king to the salesman.

deluge (**del**-yooj)
noun Huge flood or downpour. / *Deathly Hallows*, page 534
Last week's deluge flooded every basement in the village.

deluge (**del**-yooj)
verb To flood with an overwhelming amount of something. / *Order of the Phoenix*, page 696
Madam Glinch was deluged with student requests to go on the Museum of Magic field trip.

delusional (dih-**loo**-jhyun-ul)
adjective Having a false belief about yourself or the situation you're in. / *Order of the Phoenix*, page 567
"Are you delusional, Blackpool? You are definitely not the world's greatest wizard—nor the handsomest."

delve (rhymes with **twelve**)
verb To really search or dig into something. /

Order of the Phoenix, page 531
Rilda delved into the reference books in the library, seeking a remedy for poison snoak.

demeanor (dih-**mee**-nur)

noun The way someone acts, dresses, looks, etc., that shows what kind of a person they are. / *Order of the Phoenix,* page 665
The king's demeanor was usually quite regal—standing tall, with crown in place—but today he had a terrible toothache and his demeanor was much less regal.

demented (dih-**men**-tid)

adjective Insane; having a serious mental disorder. / *Half-Blood Prince,* page 138
The demented elf fluffed his pink tutu and prepared to practice his tippy toes routine.

demise (dee-**mize**)

noun Death. / *Goblet of Fire,* page 511
The demise of the village mascot—a giant horned toad—plunged the entire village into mourning.

demonic (dih-**mon**-ik)

adjective Demon-like or fiendish. / *Chamber of Secrets,* page 20
With a demonic grin, Blackpool waved his wand and turned Willow's puppies into rats.

demur (dih-**myur**)

verb To object. / *Prisoner of Azkaban,* page 203
"I must demur," said the elderly wizard at the village meeting. "I do not believe we want nor need new taxes on wands."

denizen (**den**-uh-zun)

noun Inhabitant or occupant. / *Goblet of Fire,* page 488
The denizens of the Haunted Forest get together annually to celebrate New Fear's Eve.

depict (dih-**pikt**)

verb To represent in words or pictures. / *Half-Blood Prince,* page 3
The epic "Battle of Echo Island (Echo Island)" was depicted in the oil painting that hung over the library's fireplace.

deplore (dih-**plor**)

verb To lament or regard as unfortunate. / *Deathly Hallows,* page 528
The king deplored the castle workers' use of the castle moat as a garbage dump—no wonder there was so much slime in it.

derailment (dee-**rail**-munt)

noun The act of a train going off the rails. / *Deathly Hallows,* page 34
The derailment of the Whine Train was all over the TV news that night.

deranged (dih-**raynjd**)

adjective Unbalanced or insane. / *Prisoner of Azkaban,* page 360
The deranged blue-footed booby kept stamping its blue feet and refusing to fly.

derelict (**dare**-uh-likt)

adjective Abandoned and neglected. / *Goblet of Fire,* page 1
The derelict building stood empty, the windows broken and ivy growing through holes in the roof.

dereliction of duty

phrase Abandonment of one's duty. / *Order of the Phoenix,* page 473
"Sergeant, you're guilty of dereliction of duty. You just can't leave for a month to go find out who serves the biggest hamburger."

derisive (dih-**rye**-siv)

adjective Mocking or ridiculing. / *Chamber of Secrets,* page 220
Esmerelda's loud, derisive laughter, when Blackpool asked her out for coffee, filtered out the window and up and down the street.

derivation (dare-uh-**vay**-shun)

noun The origin or source. / *Order of the Phoenix,* page 316
"What's the derivation of the spell *Absoluto Inducio*?" asked the teacher.

descendant (dih-**sen**-dunt)

noun Someone descended from specific ancestors. / *Chamber of Secrets,* page 158
"I am a descendant of ancient Mayan rulers," proudly asserted the king.

desecrated (**des**-ih-kray-tid)

adjective Spoiled, damaged, or violated,

especially of something deserving respect. / *Half-Blood Prince*, page 308
The desecrated tomb stood empty, the body once inside having mysteriously disappeared.

desiccated (des-ih-kay-tid)
adjective Really dried out. / *Deathly Hallows*, page 14
The desiccated body of a red-breasted tripsover bird lay by the side of the road.

desist (dih-sist)
verb To stop doing something. / *Goblet of Fire*, page 309
"I insist you desist!" shouted the substitute spell master as the students began to cast spells on anything in the room that wasn't moving.

despicable (des-pih-kuh-bul)
adjective Deserving scorn or contempt; hateful. / *Goblet of Fire*, page 593
"You are a despicable, mean, awful wizard, Blackpool, and I hate you!" shouted Willow.

despoiled (dih-spoyld)
adjective Plundered, pillaged, and robbed. / *Half-Blood Prince*, page 308
The despoiled manor must have been ransacked by angry ogres.

destabilization (dee-stay-buh-lih-zay-shun)
noun The act of upsetting the smooth functioning of something. / *Deathly Hallows*, page 315
The destabilization of the village government began when the mayor broke his leg, the village clerk got the flu, and the village treasurer unbalanced the budget.

desultory (des-ul-tor-ee)
adjective Ho hum; done with no particular purpose or plan. / *Order of the Phoenix*, page 715
Dribbles took his usually desultory afternoon walk—here, there, over there, back here, down there, over here, and then home.

deteriorate (dih-tir-ee-uh-rate)
verb To worsen. / *Deathly Hallows*, page 626
"His condition deteriorated sharply this morning,"
said the nurse sadly. The giant horned toad was dying.

detrimental (deh-truh-men-til)
adjective Harmful or injurious. / *Half-Blood Prince*, page 501
It's probably detrimental to your health to eat too many frozen crayfish-icles.

detritus (dih-try-tus)
noun Trash and waste; debris. / *Order of the Phoenix*, page 279
The detritus from the party littered the beach—damp towels, broken sunglasses, empty sunscreen containers, and one abandoned pair of swim trunks.

deviate (dee-vee-ate)
verb To stray or depart from an expected path or plan. / *Half-Blood Prince*, page 194
Don't deviate from the safe path in the Haunted Forest or the ghostly hounds may get you.

devise (dih-vize)
verb To plan or figure out a plan. / *Chamber of Secrets*, page 108
"Let's devise a way to sneak out of potions class early," suggested Brilly.

devoid (dih-voyd)
adjective Empty or lacking. / *Prisoner of Azkaban*, page 230
"Are you totally devoid of any sense at all?" asked a frustrated Madam Glinch.

dewy (doo-ee)
adjective Like the freshness or purity (and dampness) of dew. / *Prisoner of Azkaban*, page 299
Willow's dewy smile immediately caught the attention of the new boy in school.

diadem (die-uh-dem)
noun A royal crown. / *Deathly Hallows*, page 513
The queen carefully adjusted her golden diadem and prepared to make her grand entrance into the Royal Tea Party.

diagonally (die-ag-un-uh-lee)
adverb At an angle. / *Sorcerer's Stone*, page 282
Parker jumped diagonally, then jumped again, and again, and won! Gee, outdoor checkers was fun.

diaphragm (die-uh-fram)
noun The body area between the chest and stomach. / *Deathly Hallows*, page 447
"Unpff!" Butch Thuggins had blocked the penalty kick with his diaphragm.

diatribe (die-uh-tribe)
noun Bitter and abusive words denouncing something or someone. / *Goblet of Fire*, page 40
Blackpool's angry diatribe against the new tax plan was the highlight of the village meeting.

dictate (dik-tate)
verb To set, impose, or establish. / *Half-Blood Prince*, page 442
"I'm the king and I'll dictate the rules," said the king as the jousting tournament was about to begin.

diffused (dih-fyoozd)
adjective Spread out or scattered. / *Deathly Hallows*, page 275
The diffused light, shining through the castle's stained-glass windows, was astonishingly beautiful.

digest (duh-jest *or* die-jest)
verb To take in or absorb mentally. / *Half-Blood Prince*, page 616
"I can't begin to digest all these new spells," wailed Tamika.

dilapidated (dih-lap-ih-day-tid)
adjective Deteriorated or falling apart from neglect. / Note: There are over one million words in Potter's story, and this is one of the few misspelled words. It's "dilapidated," not "delapidated," as seen in *Prisoner of Azkaban* (page 88).
The dilapidated cottage looked like no one had lived there for years.

dilate (die-late)
verb To become wider; generally used in reference to body parts like eye pupils and nostrils. / *Goblet of Fire*, page 473
The principal's nostrils dilated as he took a deep breath—his meeting with Brilly's parents was about to begin.

diligently (dil-uh-jent-lee)
adverb In a careful and thorough way. / *Half-Blood Prince*, page 634
Fiona diligently wrote her grandmother every week, though the letters were sometimes rather short.

din (rhymes with **in**)
noun A jumble of loud sounds. / *Deathly Hallows*, page 145
The din from the fairies' party next door kept Mrs. Fracket awake all night.

dingbat (ding-bat)
noun An eccentric or silly person. / *Goblet of Fire*, page 307
"You dingbat—you're supposed to put both socks on, then both shoes—not sock, shoe, sock, shoe."

dingy (din-jee)
adjective Grimy, dirty, discolored. / *Chamber of Secrets*, page 53
Brilly's dingy jeans looked like they hadn't been washed in a year.

disabuse (dis-uh-byooz)
verb To free someone from a misconception or an error. / *Half-Blood Prince*, page 115
"Allow me to disabuse you of that notion, class. We are not turning mice into mouseburgers today."

disarm (dis-arm)
verb To win over someone. / *Half-Blood Prince*, page 181
Rupert disarmed Tamika with his charm…his politeness…his vintage broomstick.

disarray (dis-uh-ray)
noun Disorder and confusion. / *Prisoner of Azkaban*, page 262
The disarray in Ravi's backpack made finding anything a real challenge.

disband (dis-band)
verb To cause an organization to be dissolved or to break up. / *Goblet of Fire*, page 20
The Moosekateers disbanded—it turned out it wasn't really that much fun to wear moose antlers and to practice moose calls.

discern (dih-surn)
verb To perceive or detect. / *Half-Blood Prince*, page 201

The shadowy outlines of a man's face could barely be discerned in the stones in the castle wall.

discernible (dih-**sir**-nuh-bul)
adjective Visible if you looked carefully. / *Half-Blood Prince*, page 641
Blackpool's magic tattoo was discernible only in moonlight.

disciplinarian (dis-uh-pluh-**nare**-ee-un)
noun Someone who enforces or believes in strict discipline. / *Order of the Phoenix*, page 238
Mrs. Snodgrape's reputation as a strict disciplinarian was well-earned.

discomfited (dis-**kum**-fih-tid)
adjective Uneasy, disconcerted. / *Half-Blood Prince*, page 26
Hassan was discomfited by Brilly's plan to duct-tape the cafeteria manager to the cafeteria refrigerator.

discomforted (dis-**kum**-for-tid)
adjective Uncomfortable, annoyed, embarrassed, distressed. / *Goblet of Fire*, page 136
The knight looked seriously discomforted—he'd just gotten all his armor on and now he had to go to the bathroom.

discompose (dis-kum-**pose**)
verb To bother or perturb. / *Half-Blood Prince*, page 24
Nungie wasn't discomposed by the library steps—his wheelchair could easily levitate.

disconcerted (dis-kun-**sur**-tid)
adjective Confused and embarrassed. / *Deathly Hallows*, page 89 / Note: **Disconcerting**, a related adjective in *Goblet of Fire* (page 20), means "confusing and embarrassing."
The disconcerted duck-billed platypus suddenly realized how difficult it was to eat a banana.

disconsolate (dis-**kon**-suh-lit)
adjective Very sad and hopeless. / *Order of the Phoenix*, page 133
Wildwood was disconsolate—the Squirrel Scouts had sold all their cookies, so no more Fin Hints cookies until next year.

discord (**dis**-kord *or* dis-**kord**)
noun Lack of agreement; disharmony. / *Goblet of Fire*, page 723
There was often plenty of discord at village meetings if the discussion turned to wand or cauldron taxation.

discordant (dis-**kor**-dunt)
adjective Disagreeable, harsh, and conflicting; usually said of sounds or music. / *Goblet of Fire*, page 102
The discordant sound of Rupert's violin playing was driving his sister crazy.

discourse (**dis**-korse *or* dis-**korse**)
verb To speak formally and at length. / *Deathly Hallows*, page 754
Wildwood discoursed on "Hells, Bells, and Spells" at the Chamber of Wizards meeting.

discredit (dis-**kred**-it)
verb To damage someone's reputation or to cast doubts on it. / *Order of the Phoenix*, page 95
Blackpool—the evil wizard—discredited Madam Glinch and her wand techniques by suggesting she was a little awkward in her wand use.

discreet (dih-**skreet**)
adjective Prudent and careful in what is said or done. / *Goblet of Fire*, page 711
Her discreet silence suggested she realized the problem but didn't want to rush in with a solution.

disdainful (dis-**dane**-ful)
adjective Aloof and scornful. / *Goblet of Fire*, page 278
Blackpool's disdainful attitude didn't make him many friends.

disembark (dis-um-**bark**)
verb To get off a train, plane, or ship. / *Goblet of Fire*, page 732
The entire Fracket family disembarked from the excursion train, thrilled that the long ride was over.

disembodied (dis-um-**bod**-eed)
adjective Separated from the body. / *Chamber of Secrets*, page 209
The disembodied voice of the principal blared out of the speakers: "Everyone to be in his or her classroom....Now!"

disembowelment (dis-um-**bow**-ul-munt)
noun The removal of the bowels (intestines).

/ *Prisoner of Azkaban*, page 192
The disembowelment of the Hopeless Shapeless Things wasn't a pretty sight, but it had to be done.

disenchanted (dis-en-**chan**-tid)
adjective Disillusioned; no longer enchanted with. / *Deathly Hallows*, page 186
Willow was a little disenchanted with her new boyfriend—he'd given her a pet rock for her birthday.

disengage (dis-en-**gayj**)
verb To become free or detached; to disconnect. / *Order of the Phoenix*, page 229
Bella couldn't easily disengage from her relationship with Bubba, her boyfriend since second grade.

disentangle (dis-en-**tang**-gul)
verb To free from tangles or confusion. / *Order of the Phoenix*, page 395
Wildwood disentangled the charmed seaweed tendrils clogging the pumps in the village aquarium.

disfigurement (dis-**fig**-yur-munt)
noun A spoiled, deformed, or misshapen appearance. / *Order of the Phoenix*, page 484
The disfigurement of Dribbles' face happened in potions class and it was ugly, but Mrs. Snodgrape quickly repaired it.

disgorge (dis-**gorj**)
verb To pour forth; to spew. / *Order of the Phoenix*, page 798
The overloaded washing machine disgorged its contents—five heavy cloaks, twenty pairs of Madam Glinch's drawers, and two dressing gowns.

disgruntled (dis-**grun**-tld)
adjective Discontented or grumbling. / *Sorcerer's Stone*, page 94
The disgruntled river spirits were upset when their peaceful waters were used for scuba diving practice.

disheveled (dih-**shev**-uld)
adjective Untidy or disorderly looking. / *Chamber of Secrets*, page 334
Dribbles' disheveled appearance was easily explained. He'd waved his wand to the left rather than to the right, and then his pants had exploded.

disillusionment (dis-ih-**loo**-shun-munt)
noun The realization that something once thought true was actually not true. / *Deathly Hallows*, page 362
Disillusionment began to set in when the team was down 0-6—no soccer tournament this year.

disinherit (dis-in-**hare**-it)
verb To take away the right to inherit. / *Deathly Hallows*, page 755
Great Grandfather Brill angrily disinherited Brilly after the arrival of a packet of exploding sugar tentacles at the Home for Elderly Sages.

disinterred (dis-in-**turd**)
adjective Dug up. / *Deathly Hallows*, page 579
The disinterred body of the wild boar was attracting a lot of attention from the local fly community.

dismantle (dis-**man**-tul)
verb To take apart. / *Prisoner of Azkaban*, page 67
Butch Thuggins dismantled his silver motorcycle to fix the engine, but then he couldn't get it back together again.

disorientated (dis-or-ee-en-**tay**-tid)
adjective Confused, disoriented. / *Goblet of Fire*, page 145
A disorientated Dribbles worried: Was he on the corner of First and Main or the corner of Main and First?

disparaging (dih-**spare**-ih-jing)
adjective Belittling, disrespectful, and rude. / *Deathly Hallows*, page 671
The princess made several disparaging remarks about her mother's party outfit.

disparate (**dis**-pur-it)
adjective Completely different. / *Half-Blood Prince*, page 375
"Our disparate interests will never make this friendship work," said the mouse to the owl.

dispassionately (dis-**pash**-uh-nit-lee)
adverb In an impartial and calm way; not having any personal feeling. / *Half-Blood Prince*, page 317
The bank manager dispassionately explained the bank's policy to the apprentice thief—"No ID, no withdrawals."

dispel (dih-**spel**)
verb To scatter or drive away. / *Deathly Hallows*,

page 79
Madam Glinch dispelled the evil spirits in the attic with that old standby—the *Adios Spiritus* spell.

dispensable (dih-**spen**-suh-bul)
adjective Not essential. / *Deathly Hallows*, page 568
"If I were to choose, I'd say chudbutt stew is totally and completely dispensable," said Brilly.

disperse (dih-**spurse**)
verb To break up and send off in different directions. / *Chamber of Secrets*, page 238
The police dispersed the rowdy soccer fans by spraying them with crudstopper spray.

dispirited (dih-**speer**-ih-tid)
adjective Discouraged and low in spirit. / *Goblet of Fire*, page 114 / Note: Dispiriting, a related adjective in *Half-Blood Prince* (page 155), means "discouraging."
The dispirited knight angrily threw his armor in the corner—first he'd lost the jousting tournament, then the king reprimanded him for unpolished armor.

disposed (dih-**spozd**)
adjective Having a certain willingness or inclination. / *Order of the Phoenix*, page 444
The principal was not disposed to overlook Brilly's latest efforts at chaos.

disproportionate (dis-pruh-**por**-shuh-nut)
adjective Out of proportion; too much or too little. / *Deathly Hallows*, page 143
"It's not that I'm overweight," said the plump little witch. "It's just that my height is disproportionate to my weight."

disrepair (dis-rih-**pair**)
noun Often used in the phrase "a state of disrepair," meaning the condition of needing repair or being abandoned or neglected. / *Goblet of Fire*, page 4
After the warehouse fire, the building remained in a state of disrepair for years.

disrepute (dis-rih-**pyoot**)
noun Disgrace; loss of admiration or trust. / *Chamber of Secrets*, page 222
One of the village's pubs—the Trolls' Hole—had fallen into disrepute after it was discovered serving underage wizards.

dissent (dih-**sent**)
noun Disagreement with an accepted opinion. / *Goblet of Fire*, page 588
Signs of dissent—hushed murmurs, raised eyebrows, dirty looks—spread through the village meeting. Perhaps the proposed tax on cloaks wasn't such a good idea.

disservice (dih-**sur**-vus)
noun An action that isn't helpful. / *Half-Blood Prince*, page 78
"You do your brother a disservice by not helping him out when he needs it," suggested Rupert's father.

dissuade (dih-**swayd**)
verb To convince or persuade someone not to do something. / *Order of the Phoenix*, page 660
None of Brilly's friends could dissuade him from his "lizards in the lunchroom" plan.

distaste (dis-**tayst**)
noun A dislike or strong objection about something. / *Deathly Hallows*, page 209
Wildwood's distaste for conflict meant he sometimes agreed to do something he didn't really want to do.

distended (dih-**sten**-ded)
adjective Swollen, especially from pressure inside. / *Deathly Hallows*, page 451
Teddy's big toe was stepped on by the rhino in the zoo's baby animals exhibit, and it—the toe—was painfully distended.

distractedly (dih-**strak**-tid-lee)
adverb Anxiously; unable to think clearly. / *Goblet of Fire*, page 124
"I think the ghostly hounds have escaped the Haunted Forest and are headed this way," he said distractedly.

distraught (dih-**strot**)
adjective Anxious, worried, and agitated. / *Chamber of Secrets*, page 185
Mother Serpent was distraught—Slick wasn't home yet and it was after midnight.

dither (dih-thur)

verb To be nervously unable to make a decision or be certain about something. / *Half-Blood Prince*, page 114

Winston's mum dithered about the guest list for the family's annual Day of the Dead party—all wizards? Or not?

dither, as in **I'm all of a dither**

phrase In a flutter or a tizzy. / *Order of the Phoenix*, page 164

"Oh, I'm all of a dither about the party," worried Winston's mum. "What shall I do about the dinner menu?"

dittany (dit-un-ee)

noun A mint plant, thought to have medicinal benefits. / *Deathly Hallows*, page 346

Dribbles wondered: "Do you think mint gum has any dittany in it?"

diversion (dih-vur-shun)

noun Something that diverts or distracts the attention from something else. / *Sorcerer's Stone*, page 183

As a diversion, Brilly exploded a small stink bomb, but the math teacher still gave the test.

diversionary (dih-vur-shun-air-ee)

adjective Diverting or drawing attention somewhere else. / *Goblet of Fire*, page 354

The diversionary tactics of the giant seagull were unsuccessful—the sunbathers did not abandon their sandwiches to see what he was doing.

divert (dih-**vert** or **die**-vert)

verb To change the direction of something. / *Half-Blood Prince*, page 13

The mayor's scheme to divert the Weeping Highway through the village center was very unpopular among the villagers.

divest (dih-**vest**)

verb To free yourself of something. / *Deathly Hallows*, page 756

"It's time to divest yourself of all your rowdy friends, Brilly, and grow up!" admonished his father.

divination (div-uh-**nay**-shun)

noun The foretelling of the future by omens or magic powers. / *Order of the Phoenix*, page 236 / Note: In Potter's world, Divination is a class taught by Professor Trelawney.

"Using my powers of divination, I shall predict whether you will get any cavities in the next six months," said the wizard dentist.

divine (dih-**vine**)

verb To guess or figure out. / *Deathly Hallows*, page 134

"I just cannot divine what the baby wants," worried the concerned mother of the little crying gecko.

divulge (dih-**vulj**)

verb To reveal or tell. / *Prisoner of Azkaban*, page 205

"Do not divulge my secrets to anyone," whispered the mysterious hooded figure.

do her nut

phrase In British slang, to become very angry. / *Order of the Phoenix*, page 312

"She'll do her nut if she has to clean up after that spoiled brat one more time," said Winston.

do me a brew

phrase In British slang, asking someone to make tea. / *Goblet of Fire*, page 89

"It's tea time, dear. Do me a brew, would you?" Winston's dad asked his wife.

docile (**doss**-ul)

adjective Submissive and easy to handle. / *Chamber of Secrets*, page 194

The docile boarhound puppy was not always going to remain docile, nor was it going to remain puppy-sized for long.

dock (rhymes with **lock**)

verb To penalize by deducting. / *Order of the Phoenix*, page 625

The team was docked five points for "conduct unbecoming of players who should know better."

doddery (dod-uh-ree)

adjective Old and weak; shaking and tottering. / *Prisoner of Azkaban*, page 292

Her doddery uncle came for a visit and brought along his cane, his walker, his wheelchair, and his nurse.

dodgy (doj-ee)
adjective In British slang, sneaky, dishonest, or, at the very least, evasive. / *Goblet of Fire*, page 533
Blackpool's dodgy way of behaving made most people think he was up to something.

doff (rhymes with **off**)
verb To remove or take off. / *Half-Blood Prince*, page 56
Mr. Glinch politely doffed his hat as he passed the lovely sorceress in the street.

dog (rhymes with **bog**)
verb To trail or follow persistently. / *Half-Blood Prince*, page 409
The little boy dogged the steps of his older brother, trying to do everything his idol did.

dogmatically (dawg-mat-ik-lee)
adverb In an opinionated, arrogant way. / *Deathly Hallows*, page 401
Blackpool, the evil wizard, dogmatically denied ever—ever!—turning puppies into rats.

doily (doy-lee)
noun A fancy, small, round mat (lace or paper) used to protect a surface. Plural: doilies. / *Order of the Phoenix*, page 265
"Dearie, put doilies on the table, please," said Auntie Baba, "one under each dish of pinecone sherbet."

doleful (dole-ful)
adjective Very sad and mournful. / *Order of the Phoenix*, page 22
The doleful look of the lonely owl was clear—where were his buddies?

dollop (doll-up)
noun A lump, clump, or small quantity of a substance. / *Chamber of Secrets*, page 215
Emily spooned large dollops of ice cream into her hot chocolate—tasty, but an unusual method for making a chocolate ice cream sundae.

domain (doh-mayn)
noun A territory or area of control. / *Goblet of Fire*, page 417
The water demons' domain had been invaded by the school waterskiing club.

done a bunk or **done a runner**
phrases In British slang, both phrases mean to flee or run away. / *Deathly Hallows*, page 609 (done a bunk); *Goblet of Fire*, page 564 (done a runner)
Whether he'd done a bunk or done a runner, he was gone.

doppelganger (dop-ul-gang-ur)
noun Someone who looks exactly like someone else. / *Deathly Hallows*, page 52
Everyone secretly hopes they have a doppelganger somewhere in the world, but preferably not in the same village.

dormant (door-munt)
adjective In an inactive state. / *Order of the Phoenix*, page 828
The secrets of Nightmare Alley had lain dormant for centuries, but now they were about to be revealed.

dormice (door-mice)
noun Plural of dormouse, a small rodent that looks like a squirrel. / *Sorcerer's Stone*, page 60
The hungry dormice spied on the dog, eager to steal his dinner.

dormitory (dor-muh-tor-ee)
noun A building where many students live, usually run by the school. / *Sorcerer's Stone*, page 114
The boy went back to his dormitory after class for a quick nap.

dosage (doh-sij)
noun The amount administered or applied at one time. / *Order of the Phoenix*, page 253
The suggested dosage written on the small bottle was "Four cups every hour," but that couldn't be right.

doss (rhymes with **toss**)
noun In British slang, something that doesn't need much effort. / *Half-Blood Prince*, page 172
"A day at the beach—now that's a real doss," said Winston.

dote (rhymes with **goat**)
verb To show excessive love and affection for someone. / *Deathly Hallows*, page 180

Blackpool—the evil wizard—just dotes on his racing worms. Get a life.

dottiness (dot-ee-ness)

noun Weirdness, oddness, eccentricity. / *Order of the Phoenix*, page 185
The dottiness of Auntie Baba was well-known in the family—she'd once given everyone framed recycling instructions for Christmas.

double agent (dub-bul ay-jent)

noun Someone who serves as a spy for someone while really working for someone else. / *Prisoner of Azkaban*, page 206
Marmaduke was a double agent—he spied for the king but was also working for the king's archenemy, Duke Fresser.

doublet (dub-lit)

noun A man's tight, sleeveless jacket, worn in the 1600s and 1700s. / *Goblet of Fire*, page 173
Dribbles' new parka vest was a lot like an old-fashioned doublet…well, except for the zipper.

doughy (doh-ee)

adjective Like dough—pasty, white, and soft. / *Order of the Phoenix*, page 580
The man's doughy complexion plus his rather large size made him look like a giant slug.

dour (rhymes with **sour**)

adjective Stern, forbidding, gloomy. / *Deathly Hallows*, page 287
The dour school secretary had never been known to smile.

douse (rhymes with **mouse**)

verb To drench with water. / *Order of the Phoenix*, page 15
The firefighters doused the blaze in the castle kitchen—the royal doughnuts had caught fire.

downcast (down-kast)

adjective Blue, depressed, low in spirits. / *Prisoner of Azkaban*, page 113
The downcast prince missed his girlfriend who'd gone to her parents' home to celebrate Old Year's Eve.

downright (down-rite)

adverb Completely and utterly. / *Sorcerer's Stone*, page 177

"You wish you had legs?" said the mermaid's mom. "That's downright disgusting!"

downtrodden (down-trod-un)

adjective Oppressed and harshly treated. / *Prisoner of Azkaban*, page 2
The downtrodden castle workers were ready to go on strike.

draft (rhymes with **raft**)

noun A current of cold air that can be felt. / *Chamber of Secrets*, page 202 / Note: See the related noun **draft** below.
"Feel that draft? That means someone's just walked over your grave."

draft (rhymes with **raft**)

noun A swallow of a liquid. / *Order of the Phoenix*, page 426 / Note: See the related nouns **draft** above and **draught** below.
"Don't just sip it—take a long draft. You'll enjoy it."

dratted (drat-id)

adjective Stupid, dumb, annoying, or unfair. / *Sorcerer's Stone*, page 53
The giant lizard's dratted brother gave him a pain… in his tail.

draught (rhymes with **raft**; sounds exactly like **draft**)

noun A British spelling of "draft," a swallow of a liquid. / *Goblet of Fire*, page 186 / Note: See the related noun **draught** below.
Winston paused for a long draught of the cold soda, and then went back to work on the troll fence.

draught (rhymes with **raft**; sounds exactly like **draft**)

noun A British spelling of "draft," an old-fashioned word for a liquid medicine. / *Chamber of Secrets*, page 213 / Note: See the related nouns **draught** and **draft** above.
Winston swallowed the sleeping draught, and was soon sound asleep.

drawers (dror-urs)

noun Old-fashioned women's underpants. / *Goblet of Fire*, page 120
Winston realized there were some things you just don't say, like "Keep your drawers on, Mum!"

drawing room (draw-ing room)
noun A large room for entertaining guests. / *Order of the Phoenix*, page 101
Ethelbell seated her guests in the drawing room, then brought in tea and crumpets.

drawling (drawl-ing)
adjective Slow and dragged out; usually said of a voice or an accent. / *Sorcerer's Stone*, page 77
His drawling way of speaking often made his listeners think he'd forgotten the first part of a word by the time he got to the second part.

dreadlocks (dred-loks)
noun A hairstyle in which the hair is twisted into ropelike braids. / *Sorcerer's Stone*, page 94
Wildwood had always wanted dreadlocks, but now that he was balding, it seemed unlikely he'd ever have enough hair for them.

Dreadlocks

dredge (rhymes with **edge**)
verb To unearth or come up with. / *Order of the Phoenix*, page 844
"Where did you dredge up those old photos of the village?" asked the librarian.

dregs (rhymes with **begs**)
noun The last little yucky bits (also called sediment) in a liquid. Usually used in the plural. / *Prisoner of Azkaban*, page 104 / Note: See the related noun **dregs** below.
As the party wound up, all that was left was the last few dregs of the Bite Wine.

dregs (rhymes with **begs**)
noun An offensive way to refer to people considered the least important or useful. / *Chamber of Secrets*, page 178 / Note: See the related noun **dregs** above.
The queen archly suggested, "Give that last bit of wine to those dregs working in the kitchen…they might like something a little classy."

dresser (dress-ur)
noun In British usage, a kitchen or dining room cabinet, with drawers on the bottom and open display shelves on the top. It's where plates are kept, not socks. / *Order of the Phoenix*, page 80
"Please get the dishes from the dresser and finish setting the table," said Winston's mum.

dressing gown (dress-ing gown)
noun A fancy term for a bathrobe. / *Chamber of Secrets*, page 179
The king's dressing gown was embroidered with tiny golden crowns that magically twirled whenever he wore it.

drone (rhymes with **stone**)
noun A low, dull humming sound. / *Sorcerer's Stone*, page 113
The refrigerator's drone covered up the annoying mumbling of the enchanted cuckoo clock.

drought (rhymes with **out**)
noun A long period of little—if any—rainfall. / *Order of the Phoenix*, page 1
Because of the drought, the water level in the castle moat was steadily decreasing.

dry rot (dry rot)
noun A disease of cut lumber in which it gets…dry and rotten. / *Goblet of Fire*, page 19
The castle catapult had a bad case of dry rot.

dubious (doo-bee-us)
adjective Questionable, suspicious, uncertain, doubtful. / *Goblet of Fire*, page 477

The dubious honor of Most Disruptive Student was awarded to Brilly at the end-of-year school assembly.

due course

See **in due course** elsewhere in this dictionary.

duffer (**duf**-ur)

noun Someone who isn't very good at something and who's a bit plodding and clumsy. / *Sorcerer's Stone*, page 80

"You are such a duffer at this," said the swimming coach to the dogpaddling boy.

dulcet (**dul**-sut)

adjective Soothing and agreeable, usually said of music or sounds. / *Order of the Phoenix*, page 68

Both Mr. and Mrs. Fracket preferred the dulcet sounds of the Tomb Tones to the raucous music of the Rolling Bones.

dumb (rhymes with **thumb**)

adjective Speechless, because of anger, fear, surprise, etc.; often used with "struck." / *Half-Blood Prince*, page 55

The usually talkative woman was struck dumb when the toilet in the upstairs bathroom started calling her name.

dumbfounded (**dum**-fown-did)

adjective Bewildered or speechless with amazement or confusion. / *Sorcerer's Stone*, page 107

Fiona was dumbfounded to discover her mother could actually float seven inches off the floor.

dumbstruck (**dum**-struk)

adjective Shocked, surprised, speechless. / *Chamber of Secrets*, page 28

Madam Glinch was dumbstruck—every single student had successfully changed owl droppings into hockey pucks.

dumpy (**dum**-pee)

adjective Plump and squat. / *Goblet of Fire*, page 32

The dumpy witch vowed to go on a diet…after the holidays.

dun-colored (**dun**-kul-ord)

adjective A dull grayish-brown. / *Order of the Phoenix*, page 757

Poison snoak leaves are dun-colored and should be easy to identify, but every year Rilda managed to walk right into a patch of it.

dunderhead (**dun**-dur-hed)

noun A stupid or foolish person. / *Sorcerer's Stone*, page 137

The new teacher dreaded getting a class of dunderheads, but they seemed okay—except for the boy who kept trying to write with the eraser end of his pencil.

dung (rhymes with **sung**)

noun Animal feces (poop). / *Chamber of Secrets*, page 29 / Note: See also **eat dung** elsewhere in this dictionary.

Cleaning the Temple of Dung—also known as the cat box—was Brady's responsibility.

dung beetle (**duhng bee**-tul)

noun A kind of beetle that eats or lays its eggs in dung. / *Chamber of Secrets*, page 8

The dung beetle wasn't a very popular guest at bug parties.

dungeon (**dun**-jun)

noun An underground prison. / *Sorcerer's Stone*, page 132

The castle's old dungeon still echoed with the ghostly moans of long-dead prisoners.

dunghill (**duhng**-hill)

noun Literally, a hill of dung; more generally, any filthy, foul, and yucky place. / *Half-Blood Prince*, page 20

"Ewww, your locker is a dunghill—don't you ever clean it out?!"

duplicity (doo-**plis**-ih-tee)

noun An act of deceit and double-dealing. / *Half-Blood Prince*, page 617

Blackpool's latest act of duplicity was offering to pick up Willow's birthday cake for her at the bakery, and then serving it to his own guests that night.

dusky (**dus**-kee)

adjective Darkish. / *Order of the Phoenix*, page 766

Bella's dusky purple gown looked particularly attractive with her lilac-colored hair.

dustbin (dust-bin)
noun In British usage, an outdoor garbage can. / *Goblet of Fire*, page 159
"Please take the trash out to the dustbin," said Winston's mum.

dustpan (dust-pan)
noun A short-handled flattish container to sweep floor dust into. / *Goblet of Fire*, page 58
"That's a dustpan, not a flag—just finish sweeping the floor and stop waving the dustpan out the window."

dwarf (rhymes with **wharf**)
verb To make small by comparison. / *Goblet of Fire*, page 420
His teammates all dwarfed Butch Thuggins, the good but short soccer star.

dwindle (dwin-dul)
verb To gradually decrease until nothing is left. / *Goblet of Fire*, page 180
Hassan's secret supply of Swirling Sardine Candy Loops was rapidly dwindling.

E

ear trumpet (ear trum-pit)

noun An old-fashioned hearing device—a longish funnel/tube to funnel sounds into the ear of someone who can't hear well. / *Deathly Hallows*, page 403 / Note: Also called a **hearing trumpet**, as used in *Order of the Phoenix* (page 486).
The ear trumpet had never been very successful for Great Grandfather Brill—he used it faithfully but still couldn't hear a word.

Ear trumpet

eardrum (ear-drum)

noun A delicate membrane inside the ear that vibrates when sound is made. / *Goblet of Fire*, page 356

Tamika could almost feel her eardrums vibrating as the annual fireworks show drew to a close.

earmuffs (ear-mufs)

noun Ear coverings to keep ears warm in cold weather. / *Sorcerer's Stone*, page 11
Bella's new earmuffs kept her ears warm, but they also made her look like she had a furry doughnut on each ear.

earshot (ear-shot)

noun Within range of hearing. / *Sorcerer's Stone*, page 147
As soon as her mother was out of earshot, Fiona began to strum her new guitar and loudly sing "The Lament of the Lovesick Lizard."

earsplitting (ear-split-ing)

adjective Deafening; loud enough to really hurt the ears. / *Chamber of Secrets*, page 17
The earsplitting sound of the village dragon-warning siren, tested every Wednesday at noon, gave most villagers weekly headaches.

eat dung

phrase An expression of extreme annoyance and anger, roughly equivalent to "eat s—." / *Goblet of Fire*, page 168
"Dude, eat dung!" shouted the angry castle guard to the surly intruder.

eau de cologne (oh duh ka-lone)

noun Lightly perfumed cologne. / *Goblet of Fire*, page 266
Bella dotted a bit of her new eau de cologne, "Haunted Nights," on her wrists and behind her ears.

ebb (rhymes with web)

noun The tide flowing away from the shore. / *Goblet of Fire*, page 499
The ocean's ebb left dozens of purple-and-pink-striped seashells behind.

ebb (rhymes with web)

verb To recede or flow away. / *Chamber of Secrets*, page 177
Rupert's attention gradually ebbed as Mrs. Snodgrape went over the same potion ingredients again…and again.

eccentric (ik-**sen**-trik)
adjective Odd, unusual, strange, peculiar. / *Goblet of Fire*, page 437
The eccentric visitor got up at 3 a.m., went to bed at 6 p.m., and ate all his meals standing up.

éclair (a-**klair**)
noun A sweet pastry, shaped like a flattened hot dog bun, with custard inside and chocolate on top. / *Sorcerer's Stone*, page 125 / Note: **Eclair** can be spelled with or without the accent mark.
Wildwood stopped by Star Ducks every morning for an éclair and a cappuccino.

eclipse (ih-**klips**)
verb To overshadow or obscure. / *Half-Blood Prince*, page 11
"Your beauty is only eclipsed by your kindness," said the prince to his new girlfriend. "Or is it the other way around?"

Edam (**ee**-dum)
noun A mild cheese, usually with a shiny, red, waxy coating. / *Goblet of Fire*, page 102
The Edam cheese practically glowed as it sat on the cheeseboard, ready for the evening's guests.

eddy (rhymes with **ready**)
noun A circular movement of water, dust, snow, or fog—like a whirlpool. / *Deathly Hallows*, page 331
The eddy of water swirled tiny Tinkles, the fairy, around and around as the water drained out of the bathtub.

efficacious (ef-uh-**kay**-shus)
adjective Effective; producing the desired result. / *Order of the Phoenix*, page 384
"The most efficacious way to resolve the village's budget crisis would be to tax crumpets," suggested the slightly dotty old professor.

effigy (**ef**-ih-jee)
noun A sculpture or other image of a famous person; sometimes a roughly made model of someone you hate. / *Deathly Hallows*, page 620
The effigy of the principal appeared mysteriously in the school corridor one day; it was soon decorated with an eye patch, lipstick, and a smelly cowboy hat.

effusion (ih-**fyoo**-zhun)
noun An outpouring of feelings. / *Deathly Hallows*, page 359
With great effusion, Ethelbell welcomed her guests to the monthly gathering of the Sisters of Sorcery.

egg (rhymes with **leg**)
verb To encourage or urge. / *Chamber of Secrets*, page 196
Her friends egged her on: "Go on, Willow, just ask him out!"

eggcup (**eg**-kup)
noun A small cup just big enough to hold a boiled egg. / *Goblet of Fire*, page 398
Winston's eggcup had a picture of a blue-eyed chicken on the side.

ejaculate (ee-**jak**-yoo-late)
verb To exclaim or speak suddenly. / *Order of the Phoenix*, page 242
"You did *what*?!" ejaculated Brilly's father.

elastic band (ee-**las**-tik **band**)
noun A rubber band. / *Sorcerer's Stone*, page 34
By carefully stretching the elastic band between his thumb and index finger, then bending his thumb, he could easily hit the target—the back of his brother's head.

elation (ih-**lay**-shun)
noun Great happiness and joy. / *Half-Blood Prince*, page 478
With elation (and some relief), Mr. and Madam Glinch announced the upcoming wedding of their oldest daughter, the somewhat bow-legged and slightly cross-eyed Glenda.

elephantine (el-uh-**fan**-teen *or* el-uh-**fuhn**-teen)
adjective Enormous in size and strength (or sound), like an elephant. / *Goblet of Fire*, page 263
The troll's elephantine feet would never fit in regular shoes…but then, he never wore shoes.

Troll with elephantine feet

elite (ih-**leet** or a-**leet**)
noun Best of the best; superior. / *Order of the Phoenix*, page 228
Only the elite of village society were invited to the castle for the annual Royal Tea Party.

elixir (ee-**lik**-ser)
noun A substance that supposedly can make one live longer—even forever; also called the elixir of life. / *Sorcerer's Stone*, page 293
The alchemist was thrilled that his experimental elixir seemed successful—at least, the giant cockroach in his kitchen seemed to be living forever.

elongate (ee-**long**-gate)
verb To lengthen. / *Goblet of Fire*, page 111
"Eeee-longg-gaate and emphasize the sounds when uttering a *Mumblicious* spell," advised Madam Glinch.

elope (ih-**lope**)
verb To run away to get married. / *Goblet of Fire*, page 447
Willow hoped to elope with her new boyfriend, but so far they'd only gone on one date.

eloquent (**el**-uh-kwint)
adjective Moving and expressive. / *Half-Blood Prince*, page 32
The eloquent speaker retold her terrible experiences on the Island of Chance, moving many in the audience to tears.

elude (ih-**lewd**)
verb To avoid or escape from. / *Prisoner of Azkaban*, page 37
The green-frilled frogette eluded the frogette hunters, even though they had froggy twangers with them.

elusive (ih-**loo**-siv)
adjective Difficult to find or locate. / *Deathly Hallows*, page 224
The elusive elf had 14 different hiding places just in the kitchen alone.

emaciated (ih-**may**-shee-ay-tid)
adjective Extremely thin and starved-looking. / *Half-Blood Prince*, page 316
The emaciated stable boy decided his fried toad diet had worked all too well.

emanate (**em**-uh-nate)
verb To send forth or flow out. / *Order of the Phoenix*, page 813
The mysterious traveler emanated a faint odor of sawdust and straw.

embargo (em-**bar**-go)
noun An official government ban on trade of certain items with another country. / *Goblet of Fire*, page 91
The embargo on Boil & Bubble charms was proving to be a headache for potion teachers everywhere.

embedded (em-**bed**-ded)
adjective Stuck in firmly. / *Order of the Phoenix*, page 485
The embedded sliver in Blackpool's finger really hurt until his magical tweezers zoomed in and pulled it out.

embellish (em-**bel**-ish)
verb To decorate or add details to. / *Order of the Phoenix*, page 643
Willow embellished her signature with a small heart over the letter "i" and a smiley face in the letter "o."

ember (em-bur)

noun A small piece of glowing wood in the ashes of a fire. / *Sorcerer's Stone*, page 155

The last embers in the fireplace were still visible at 3 a.m. when Fiona got up to go to the bathroom.

emblazon (im-blay-zun)

verb To adorn a surface boldly. / *Deathly Hallows*, page 252

The stadium wall was emblazoned with magical fire that read: "Coming Soon—The Rolling Bones in Their Farewell Concert!"

embodiment (em-bod-ee-munt)

noun Representative of an ideal. / *Deathly Hallows*, page 360

Blackpool seemed the embodiment of evil, but he did have a softer side—he was devoted to his racing worms.

embossed (em-bosd)

adjective With a raised design. / *Deathly Hallows*, page 126

The embossed pattern on his shield indicated the knight was one of the king's special forces: The Green Hurrays.

embroider (em-broy-dur)

verb To decorate with needlework. / *Half-Blood Prince*, page 580 / Note: See the related verb **embroider** below.

The queen's fancy riding pants were embroidered with little horses, ponies, and unicorns.

embroider (em-broy-dur)

verb To add imaginary details to make a story more interesting or exciting. / *Goblet of Fire*, page 1 / Note: See the related verb **embroider** above.

Parker embroidered his story of his night in the Haunted Forest—he'd actually fallen asleep under a tree, but by the seventh retelling, he'd fought off a pack of ghostly hounds and hunted down and killed two giant spiders.

emit (ih-mit)

verb To send out something—like sound, light, gas, or liquid. / *Chamber of Secrets*, page 324

The church organ emitted a ghostly tune that fateful Sunday, right before the explosion.

emphatically (em-fat-ih-kul-lee)

adverb In a forceful and definite way. / *Order of the Phoenix*, page 434

The king emphatically denied underpaying the castle chambermaids.

emporium (em-poor-ee-um)

noun An old-fashioned word for a large shop selling many different things. / *Sorcerer's Stone*, page 72

On sale this week at the Hurly Burly Emporium: Boil & Bubble Charms, Mama's Crystal Ball Cleaner, Wilson's Wand Wax, and Dancing Eagle Elixir.

emulate (em-yuh-late)

verb To try to equal or imitate. / *Deathly Hallows*, page 440

"Please try to emulate someone kind and good, not someone who sets off stink bombs every day," pleaded Brilly's dad.

encase (en-kase)

verb To enclose in a case or something like a case. / *Half-Blood Prince*, page 23

The hideous giant leech was encased in a protective shield of gluco-ment—the leech was visible, but it couldn't escape.

enchant (en-chant)

verb To cast a magic spell. / *Chamber of Secrets*, page 38

Tiny Tinkles could only enchant beings smaller than herself, so she mostly dealt with small insects and rodents.

enchantment (en-chant-munt)

noun A magic spell. / *Sorcerer's Stone*, page 64

"Magical enchantments just aren't what they used to be," said the elderly wizard. "Now, in my day...."

enclosure (en-kloh-zhur)

noun Land surrounded by a fence, usually to contain animals. / *Goblet of Fire*, page 327

The enclosure for Blackpool's warty pigs was near his back door so that he could hear if anyone tried to kidnap them.

encompass (en-**kum**-pus)

verb To include comprehensively. / *Half-Blood Prince*, page 5

The principal's job encompassed dealing with teachers, staff, parents, and students…including the impossible Brilly.

encumber (en-**kum**-bur)

verb To be burdened and bothered. / *Half-Blood Prince*, page 56

Jenn was so encumbered by her fear of snakes that she rarely ventured into the meadow.

end of her tether

See **tether** elsewhere in this dictionary.

endeavor (en-**dev**-ur)

noun An effort or attempt. / *Half-Blood Prince*, page 187

His endeavors to find the fog-shrouded castle were not going well—so far, he'd only stumbled into the manure-filled sheep pasture.

endeavor (en-**dev**-ur)

verb To try, or to make an effort. / *Half-Blood Prince*, page 346

Willow endeavored to keep her temper when Blackpool started blabbering on and on about the uselessness of puppies.

engender (en-**jen**-dur)

verb To produce or bring with it. / *Half-Blood Prince*, page 443

"Your antics engender an appropriate response, Brilly. And what do you suggest that response should be, now that you've blown up the janitor's closet?"

engraving (en-**gray**-ving)

noun A picture made by cutting a design into metal or some other hard substance. / *Chamber of Secrets*, page 300

The engraving scratched on the flagpole appeared to be someone's initials and the outline of a firecracker.

engross (en-**gross**)

verb To totally occupy or absorb someone's attention. / *Order of the Phoenix*, page 222

Their conversation engrossed the girls so completely they held up the entire cafeteria line with their chatting.

Engraving on flagpole

engulf (en-**gulf**)

verb To overwhelm or swallow up. / *Sorcerer's Stone*, page 203

Fear engulfed Nathan when the zombie rudely demanded his skateboard.

enhance (en-**hans**)

verb To improve or increase. / *Half-Blood Prince*, page 499

Your chances of surviving the Wild Cave Trek are enhanced if you take along a map and a big ball of string.

enigmatic (en-ig-**mat**-ik)

adjective Mysterious, puzzling. / *Half-Blood Prince*, page 278

The enigmatic message dropped on Willow's desk puzzled her—was someone asking her to lunch or threatening to rip her head off?

enlighten (en-**lie**-ten)

verb To make the facts clear to someone. / *Half-Blood Prince*, page 427

Brilly enlightened his little sister about the birds and the bees—birds have baby birds, bees have baby bees.

enmity (en-**mih**-tee)

noun A deep-seated and often mutual

hatred. / *Prisoner of Azkaban*, page 301
The enmity between the two wizards would not soon disappear—especially as they were barely speaking to each other.

ensconce (en-skonse)
verb To settle in comfortably. / *Half-Blood Prince*, page 192
Ensconced on a stool at the Trolls' Hole pub, Blackpool told story after story of his evil exploits to the assembled drinkers.

enslavement (en-slayve-munt)
noun The condition of being a slave, or of being subjugated and dominated by another. / *Chamber of Secrets*, page 177
Spending eight hours a day in a classroom seemed a modern form of enslavement to Brilly.

ensnare (en-snare)
verb Literally, to catch in a trap or snare; more generally, to be caught or trapped as if ensnared in a trap. / *Sorcerer's Stone*, page 137
Poor Brilly was ensnared by his own rotten behavior—and now he'd have to pay the price.

en suite (ohn sweet)
adjective Literally, French for "in a series"; more generally, refers to accommodations arranged together, such as a bedroom with an adjoining bathroom. / *Goblet of Fire*, page 151
The hotel accommodations for the visiting wizards were quite plush; every wizard got his or her own large bedroom with a wandpool en suite.

ensue (en-soo)
verb To result or follow from an action. / *Half-Blood Prince*, page 179
Chaos ensued after the monsters had marched through the village; even though no one was hurt, everyone was in an uproar that it even happened.

enthrall (en-thrawl)
verb To captivate or charm. / *Deathly Hallows*, page 497
The new boyfriend had so enthralled Willow that she could talk of little else.

entomb (en-toom)
verb To bury. / *Goblet of Fire*, page 650
The body of dear old Wizard Spurkin was entombed in the Crypts 'R Us cemetery.

entourage (ahn-too-rahj)
noun The friends or associates accompanying someone. / *Half-Blood Prince*, page 640
Soccer star Butch Thuggins and his entourage—a manager, agent, barber, manicurist, trainer, bodyguard, massage therapist, doctor, and two gofers—arrived at the stadium for the soccer match.

entrails (en-traylz)
noun The internal organs of the body; usually used in the plural. / *Prisoner of Azkaban*, page 53
Supposedly studying the entrails of an animal can tell a lot about the future—and it may make you decide to be a vegetarian, too.

entrant (en-trant)
noun Someone who enters a competition. / *Goblet of Fire*, page 265
"Will all the entrants for the jousting tournament please ride past the grandstand and the royal viewing area?" blared the announcer.

entwined (en-twhynd)
adjective Twined around or coiled together. / *Chamber of Secrets*, page 304
The two entwined figures on the couch—Willow and her new boyfriend—rapidly unentwined when her dad walked in.

enumerate (ih-noo-mur-rate)
verb To name or list, one by one. / *Goblet of Fire*, page 440
"Please enumerate all the qualities of a skilled wizard, Hassan," requested the teacher.

envisage (en-viz-ij)
verb To form a picture in one's mind; to visualize. / *Half-Blood Prince*, page 432
The aspiring wizard could easily envisage his future—but sadly it did not include a starring role on TV.

envoy (en-voy *or* on-voy)
noun A messenger, often a diplomatic representative of a government. / *Goblet of Fire*,

page 708
Duke Fresser's envoy demanded a meeting with the king.

epitaph (ep-ih-taf)
noun An inscription on a tombstone in memory of the person buried there. / *Deathly Hallows*, page 683
Dribbles had always thought the epitaph RIP on a tombstone meant "Really Interesting Person," not "Rest in Peace."

eradication (ih-rad-ih-kay-shun)
noun The destruction or elimination of something. / *Chamber of Secrets*, page 163
The complete eradication of moat slime at the castle was the Royal Plumber's goal.

erode (ih-rode)
verb To eat into, undermine, or wear away. / *Deathly Hallows*, page 435
The heavy rains eroded the dirt under the road, and soon a large sinkhole developed.

erratic (ih-rat-ik)
adjective Uneven and irregular. / *Order of the Phoenix*, page 394
Tiny Tinkles, the fairy, was taking an erratic flight path across the garden—apparently she was dodging a wasp.

erstwhile (urst-wile)
adjective Former, or from times past. / *Order of the Phoenix*, page 785
Blackpool's erstwhile friends refused to talk to him anymore, not since the scandal.

eschew (es-choo)
verb To deliberately avoid or shun something. / *Deathly Hallows*, page 6
"I eschew snails," said Madam Glinch. "Gesundheit," said her slightly deaf husband.

essence (es-uns)
noun A concentrated extract of a substance, mixed in a solution of alcohol. / *Order of the Phoenix*, page 325
The wizard's potion for scabiferous acnoids called for essence of eel liver.

esteem (ih-steem)
noun Great regard and respect; often used in the phrase "hold you in great esteem." / *Order of the Phoenix*, page 822
"You know I hold you in great esteem, Madam Glinch," said the principal. "But you really must ensure your dentures never fall out again during class."

estrangement (ih-straynj-munt)
noun A separation of two people because of an argument or difference. / *Order of the Phoenix*, page 172
The estrangement of the king and his cousin, Duke Fresser, had gone on for over 20 years.

etch (rhymes with **retch**)
verb To cut words or a picture into metal, usually using acid, but also just to scratch them on. / *Deathly Hallows*, page 451
Brilly etched his own initials on the school flagpole, which made it pretty easy to figure out who had done it.

ethereal (ih-theer-ee-ul)
adjective Light and airy in an almost unreal way. / *Order of the Phoenix*, page 315
Her ethereal voice seemed to float across the room as the little boys listened to her read the fairy tale about the "Three Pasture Poltergeists."

euphoria (yoo-for-ee-uh)
noun A feeling of happiness and well-being. / *Prisoner of Azkaban*, page 314
Willow's euphoria about being asked out by the new boy was clear—she couldn't stop smiling.

evasively (ih-vay-siv-lee)
adverb In a vague, evading way. / *Deathly Hallows*, page 89
"I didn't exactly set off the firecrackers," said Brilly evasively. "I just lit a match sort of near them."

exacerbate (ig-zas-ur-bate)
verb To make worse or to aggravate. / *Goblet of Fire*, page 293
The king's loneliness was exacerbated by the fact that not only was the queen away, but so were the prince and princess, the Royal Electrician, the Royal

Plumber, the Royal Executioner, the Keeper of the Closet, and the Keeper of the Hounds.

exasperated (ig-**zhas**-puh-ray-tid)
adjective Irritated, annoyed, and impatient. / *Chamber of Secrets*, page 270
The exasperated teacher wondered if anyone in his rowdy classroom was even listening to him.

exclamation (ek-skluh-**may**-shun)
noun Something said suddenly and forcefully. / *Half-Blood Prince*, page 390
Her exclamation of surprise was really more of a scream—she hated cockroaches.

excruciating (ik-**skroo**-shee-ay-ting)
adjective Extremely painful. / *Goblet of Fire*, page 579
Dribbles worried: "Won't it be excruciating to have my wisdom teeth pulled? Why are they called that, anyway?"

excursion (ik-**skur**-shun)
noun A short journey or trip. / *Half-Blood Prince*, page 634
The Fracket family's excursion to MysticLand was much better than last year's trip to DisneyGalaxy.

executioner (ek-suh-**kyoo**-shuh-nur)
noun Someone who puts a condemned person (or animal) to death. / *Prisoner of Azkaban*, page 316
The Royal Executioner was retiring—business had been slow for years.

exemplary (ig-**zem**-pluh-ree)
adjective Commendable; excellent. / *Order of the Phoenix*, page 261
"You've made exemplary progress in wand work this year, class," said Madam Glinch. "Except for that time with the rabbits."

exemplify (ig-**zem**-pluh-fie)
verb To illustrate or be an example of. / *Goblet of Fire*, page 721
Wildwood exemplified all the qualities of a good wizard; Blackpool exemplified all the qualities of an evil one.

exhort (ig-**zort**)
verb To urge on. / *Deathly Hallows*, page 437
The crowd exhorted the king's archers with chants of "Bull's-eye! Bull's-eye!"

exiled (**eg**-zayld *or* **ek**-siled)
adjective Banished, driven away from one's home country. / *Goblet of Fire*, page 595
The exiled wizard began a list of all the things he missed most, but after putting down "Friends" and "Home," he burst into tears and could write no more.

expectancy (ik-**spek**-tun-see)
noun A feeling of anticipation. / *Half-Blood Prince*, page 443
With great expectancy, the villagers awaited the TV crew—the local pub was to be featured on Wizards Gizzards on the Food Network.

expedient (ik-**spee**-dee-unt)
noun A resource or method. / *Deathly Hallows*, page 521
By the simple expedient of adding a few rainbow-colored feathers, Bella dressed up her plain black cloak.

expertise (ek-spur-**teez**)
noun Expert skill or knowledge. / *Chamber of Secrets*, page 163
Daniel showed great expertise in calming the Whirling Derbies dance troupe when their luggage got lost.

explicable (eg-**splih**-kuh-bul)
adjective Understandable or explainable. / *Half-Blood Prince*, page 502
His explicable behavior was much easier to deal with than his inexplicable behavior.

explicit (ik-**splis**-it)
adjective Clear, with nothing left out. / *Deathly Hallows*, page 102
The explicit—but not very helpful—instructions on the king's new moat-sweeper were "Turn on. Sweep moat. Turn off."

expound (ik-**spownd**)
verb To set forth or present. / *Order of the Phoenix*, page 550
Madam Glinch could expound for days on the intricacies of effective wand work.

extent (ik-**stent**)
noun The length, size, or height of

something. / *Goblet of Fire*, page 409
The queen pulled her fancy white gloves up to their highest extent—way past her elbows.

extinct (ik-**stingkt**)
adjective No longer burning; extinguished. / *Order of the Phoenix*, page 279
The extinct campfire was going to be of little use in warming the cold hikers.

extract (ek-**strakt**)
noun An excerpt or selection. / *Order of the Phoenix*, page 582
The assigned extract from the History of Magic textbook had been not-so-magically torn out.

extract (ik-**strakt**)
verb To draw out, pull out, or take out. / *Goblet of Fire*, page 602
The wizard carefully extracted the fire diamond from the secret drawer in the jewel box.

extremities (ik-**strem**-ih-teez)
noun Arms, legs, hands, and feet. Singular: extremity. / *Half-Blood Prince*, page 397
As the clumsy Elrod tumbled down the small hill, his extremities seemed to fly in all directions.

extricate (ek-**strih**-kate)
verb To set free from a difficulty; to disengage. / *Prisoner of Azkaban*, page 263
Brilly tried to extricate himself from his latest prank—but explaining away smelly clouds of crudstopper spray in the teachers' lounge was going to be tricky.

exuberantly (ig-**zoo**-bur-unt-lee)
adverb In a joyful, unrestrained way. / *Order of the Phoenix*, page 509
The students exuberantly left the potions classroom, having worked the paralyzing charm to perfection on the student teacher.

exude (ig-**zood**)
verb To ooze or discharge. / *Half-Blood Prince*, page 190
The golden figs exuded so much sticky juice that they were stuck in the serving bowl.

exultant (ig-**zul**-tunt)
adjective Very happy, especially for having done or accomplished something. / *Order of the Phoenix*, page 749
The pesky poltergeist was exultant—he'd already managed to annoy everyone in the house and it was only 8 a.m.

eyeglass (**eye**-glas)
noun In British usage (and especially in Potter's world), "eyeglass" refers to a magnifying lens, not to a pair of spectacles. / *Sorcerer's Stone*, page 73
The jeweler used his eyeglass to closely examine the fire diamond the old witch claimed to have discovered in her underwear drawer.

eyesore (**eye**-sore)
noun Literally, something so ugly or unpleasant looking that seeing it would make one's eyes sore; more generally, anything really ugly or out of place. / *Half-Blood Prince*, page 209
The miserable abandoned shack, right in the middle of the village, was an embarrassing eyesore.

F

false pretenses (fahls pree-ten-sis)
noun A misrepresentation of facts; usually used with "under." / *Goblet of Fire*, page 561
Bertha enrolled in the Young Flyers Club under false pretenses—she looked 13 but was really 144 years old.

falter (fall-tur)
verb To speak or act in an unsteady way. / *Sorcerer's Stone*, page 12
The teacher's voice faltered as the giant greenish moth—as big as a desk—flew in the door.

faltering (fall-tur-ing)
adjective Stumbling or hesitant. / *Deathly Hallows*, page 39
In a faltering voice, Winston asked the new girl to the Flufftones Ball.

fanatic (fuh-nah-tick)
noun Someone who gets carried away with unreasonable enthusiasm or devotion to beliefs, feelings, or things. / *Sorcerer's Stone*, page 216
Nico didn't think he was a fanatic about collecting model dragons—but he did have 347 in his collection.

fancy (fan-see)
verb To be attracted to someone. / *Chamber of Secrets*, page 36 / Note: See the related verb **fancy** below.
Willow fancies the new boy that moved in across the street.

fancy (fan-see)
verb In British usage, to like or want something; used in phrases like "fancy a flutter (a bet)?" or "fancy a kip (a nap)?" / *Goblet of Fire*, pages 87 and 368 / Note: See the related verb **fancy** above.
"Fancy a mouseburger?" asked Mother Serpent.

fang (rhymes with **bang**)
noun A long, pointed tooth. / *Sorcerer's Stone*, page 238
The village dentist, Dr. Greenteeth, needed to talk with Mother Serpent about her son Slick—his fangs just weren't growing in straight.

far-fetched (far-fecht)
adjective Hard to believe. / *Prisoner of Azkaban*, page 369
The village dentist had several far-fetched ideas about utilizing molar power to solve the energy crisis.

fashion (fash-un)
verb To make, shape, or form. / *Chamber of Secrets*, page 314
At the beach, Rupert fashioned a fish out of sand and was astonished when it suddenly wiggled its way to the water and swam away.

fathom (fath-um)
verb To understand or comprehend. / *Prisoner of Azkaban*, page 361
"I can *not* fathom why you'd keep a boa constrictor in the closet!" Annie's mother shouted.

fathomless (fath-um-less)
adjective Literally, bottomless and too deep to measure; more generally, impossible to understand. / *Prisoner of Azkaban*, page 367
As the leftover steak disappeared into the fathomless depths of the garbage disposal, the dog whined with disappointment.

fat's in the fire
phrase An old-fashioned phrase meaning something already done that can't be undone—like when fat falls into a fire and quickly burns up. / *Goblet of Fire*, page 153
"Well, the fat's in the fire now," said the wandmaker. "I've signed a lease for that building next door—time to expand the Wandatorium Shop!"

fawn (rhymes with **dawn**)
adjective Pale, grayish-yellow. / *Deathly Hallows*, page 30

Ready for a change, Bella asked the hairdresser to dye her normally fawn locks a subtle green.

fawn (rhymes with **dawn**)

verb To flatter someone a bit too much. / *Goblet of Fire*, page 249
The vampire fawned over the young woman, hoping endless compliments would distract her from the empty coffin in the corner.

feedback (**feed**-bak)

noun A response or reaction. / *Order of the Phoenix*, page 307
When the swimmer asked the mermaid for feedback on his backstroke, he wasn't expecting hysterical laughter.

feign (rhymes with **mane**)

verb To pretend. / *Order of the Phoenix*, page 472
Brady feigned indifference when the new girl went to the dance with his best friend, but inside, he was *so* disappointed.

feint (rhymes with **paint**; sounds exactly like **faint**)

verb To make a deceiving move or attack. / *Order of the Phoenix*, page 704
Facing the drooling cat, the mouse feinted left and then ran right as fast as he could.

fen (rhymes with **den**)

noun Low, swampy ground; fen country in England is in eastern England. / *Goblet of Fire*, page 177
The damp fen was home to millions of bugs, making it the perfect place for the Critter Club's annual picnic.

ferment (fur-**ment**)

verb To cause excitement or agitation. / *Half-Blood Prince*, page 472
His Mother's Day ideas had been fermenting in his mind for months, but he finally settled on a puppy as the best possible gift.

ferocity (fuh-ross-ih-tee)

noun The state of being ferocious or really fierce. / *Goblet of Fire*, page 111
Clearly, from the ferocity of their buzzing, the bees had no intention of giving up their honey.

ferret (**fair**-it)

noun A small, furry, domesticated mammal that can be trained to hunt rats or rabbits. / *Chamber of Secrets*, page 38
The ferret was supposed to rid the house of rats, but being both lazy and friendly, he preferred napping with his new rat buddies.

ferret (**fair**-it)

verb To hunt for something. / *Prisoner of Azkaban*, page 413
Birds know the best time to ferret out plump, juicy worms is right after a rainstorm.

fertilizer (**fur**-tul-eye-zur)

noun Manure or compost added to the soil to help plants grow. / *Chamber of Secrets*, page 90
The Royal Gardener applied concentrated dragon dung fertilizer to the castle flower garden.

fervent (**fur**-vunt)

adjective Enthusiastic, passionate, ardent; showing great emotion or zeal. / *Prisoner of Azkaban*, page 254
Rupert's fervent (and off-key) violin playing was less musical passion than it was a desire to torment his sister.

festoon (fess-**toon**)

noun A string of small branches, lights, ribbons, or similar items hanging between two points. / *Sorcerer's Stone*, page 196
Festoons of dead tree branches, artichoke leaves, and spiny nettles added holiday cheer to the dwarf's cottage.

fetch (rhymes with **retch**)

verb To go and get something. / *Half-Blood Prince*, page 551 / Note: See the related verb **fetch** below.
"Fetch your wands, class, we're going on a charms walk," said Madam Glinch.

fetch (rhymes with **retch**)

verb To sell for or to bring a particular price. / *Goblet of Fire*, page 101 / Note: See the related verb **fetch** above.
Annie hoped the famous goblin's used handkerchief would fetch a fortune at the magic shop.

The Unofficial Harry Potter Vocabulary Builder • 71

fetid (fet-id)
adjective Having an awful, offensive odor. / *Deathly Hallows*, page 339
The smell of hamburgers may be mouth-watering to humans, but it's a fetid stench to vampires.

fetter (fet-ur)
verb Literally, to put chains or shackles on the feet, a technique to keep horses from moving; more generally, to restrict or restrain. / *Order of the Phoenix*, page 603
Blackpool was fettered in his ambitions to be mayor because of his lousy attitude, few friends, and evil ways.

feverishly (fee-vur-ish-lee)
adverb In an excited, restless, agitated way. / *Chamber of Secrets*, page 188
Brilly feverishly added one potion ingredient after another, eager to finish the assignment.

fez (rhymes with **pez**)
noun A felt hat, shaped like a chopped-off cone; often red, it has a black tassel hanging from the top and is worn by men in the eastern Mediterranean area. / *Prisoner of Azkaban*, page 10
Wildwood wore a fez, a poncho, and a kilt for Halloween and called himself the United Nations.

Fez

fiasco (fee-as-koh)
noun A complete and utter failure; a real mess-up. / *Chamber of Secrets*, page 28
Mistaking salt for sugar turned her chocolate cake recipe into an inedible fiasco.

fiddly (fid-lee)
adjective In British usage, difficult to do, especially because something has many steps or ingredients. / *Order of the Phoenix*, page 233
The fiddly potion was bound to backfire with so many opportunities to make a mistake.

figment (fig-munt)
noun Something imagined or existing only in your mind; often used in the phrase "figment of your imagination." / *Order of the Phoenix*, page 147
The boy's mother insisted the monster under his bed was just a figment of his imagination—until it turned up in her closet.

filigree (fill-uh-gree)
adjective Lacy, delicate, intricate design, usually of jewelry. / *Half-Blood Prince*, page 437
The queen's filigree necklace was so airy and delicate, she always imagined it would someday just float away.

finality (fie-nal-ih-tee)
noun The fact or condition of being final and unchangeable. / *Goblet of Fire*, page 604
"Wands down…*now*!" said Madam Glinch with finality.

fissure (fish-ur; sounds exactly like **fisher**)
noun A long, narrow opening in a rock. / *Goblet of Fire*, page 521
Bella very carefully reached into the fissure to retrieve her stuck shoe—who knew how many spiders were down there?

fixation (fik-say-shun)
noun An obsessive preoccupation. / *Goblet of Fire*, page 580
Blackpool didn't consider it a fixation, but he did spend hours and hours with his racing worms.

flabbergasted (flab-ur-gas-tid)
adjective Astounded and astonished. /

Chamber of Secrets, page 329
A flabbergasted Hassan could only stare at the quiz paper—he'd gotten a perfect score.

flagged stone (flagd stone)

adjective Not a stone with lots of flags, but in British usage, paved with flagstone—large, flat pieces of rock used as flooring in old castles and new walkways. / *Sorcerer's Stone*, page 113 / Note: The adjective **stone-flagged** is used in *Goblet of Fire* (page 204), also meaning "covered with flagstones."
The flagged stone path passed between the two creepiest houses in the neighborhood.

flagon (flag-un)

noun A large container to drink liquids from, with a handle, spout, and hinged lid. / *Prisoner of Azkaban*, page 230
Flagons aren't particularly easy to carry (another reason why bottled water is so popular today), but they do make great containers for mulled wine.

flail (rhymes with wail)

verb To beat or strike; to wave or swing at. / *Sorcerer's Stone*, page 176
Elrod flailed at the ball with the bat but only managed to hit himself in the back.

flamboyantly (flam-boy-unt-lee)

adverb In an exaggerated, showy way. / *Order of the Phoenix*, page 148
The famous author of *A Witch's Stitches—Sewing Spells for Today's Wicked Seamstresses* waved flamboyantly to her fans, who all oohed and aahed as autographed books appeared magically in their hands.

flank (rhymes with tank)

noun The side, between the ribs and hips. / *Sorcerer's Stone*, page 257
The horse's flanks were so sweaty he looked like he'd gotten stuck in a car wash.

flank (rhymes with tank)

verb To be on either side of. / *Sorcerer's Stone*, page 153
Parker was flanked on his left by his brother and on his right by his trusty dirt bike.

flap (rhymes with whap)

noun A situation in which people are excited or worried. / *Prisoner of Azkaban*, page 43
Blackpool was in a flap because his racing worms had done so poorly in the weekend races.

flare (rhymes with mare; sounds exactly like **flair**)

verb To burst out or erupt. / *Goblet of Fire*, page 152
Rupert flared up when his little brother made fun of his bow tie.

flask (rhymes with mask)

noun A small, flattened bottle for liquids, perfect to slip into a pocket; sometimes called a hip flask because it would fit perfectly into a hip pocket. / *Goblet of Fire*, page 186
Brilly carefully poured the leftover mini-max potion into his father's borrowed hip flask—you never know when you might need a sip to change your size.

flat (rhymes with splat)

noun In British usage, an apartment. / *Half-Blood Prince*, page 87
Willow and Fiona dreamed of getting a flat together after high school.

flay (rhymes with slay)

verb Literally to whip, or to strip the skin off; more generally, used in expressions like "flay you alive" or "flay you within an inch of your life," meaning "punish you extremely severely." / *Chamber of Secrets*, page 20
When the comic threatened to flay the audience alive if they didn't laugh at his jokes, he was fired on the spot.

fleck (rhymes with deck)

noun A small bit—a drop or speck. / *Goblet of Fire*, page 113
Flecks of paint chipped off the kitchen table—time to repaint.

fleck (rhymes with deck)

verb To be marked with flecks. / *Prisoner of Azkaban*, page 23
Paint chips flecked the kitchen floor, but the giant cockroach knew they weren't edible.

flex (rhymes with **hex**; sounds exactly like **flecks**)
verb To bend or contract. / *Prisoner of Azkaban*, page 216
The miniature dragon flexed his wing muscles and stepped off the edge of the table. His first flight did not go well.

flibbertigibbet (flib-ur-tee-jib-it)
noun A silly, scatterbrained person. / *Prisoner of Azkaban*, page 295
Willow had gotten a reputation as a flibbertigibbet, but she really was a very serious, focused, hardworking student.

flighty (fly-tee)
adjective Given to unsteady or fickle behavior. / *Half-Blood Prince*, page 56
Tiny Tinkles was considered by many to be a bit flighty, but she just had a hard time making up her mind.

flit (rhymes with **sit**)
verb To move quickly. / *Sorcerer's Stone*, page 84
Captain Hummingbird flitted from flower to flower, seeking lunch.

flock (rhymes with **rock**)
verb To move all together, in a crowd or group. / *Sorcerer's Stone*, page 263
Customers flocked to the Hurly Burly Emporium every Friday, the best day for sales on cloaks and robes.

floodlit (flud-lit)
adjective Brightly lit by artificial lights. / *Chamber of Secrets*, page 275
The spell-a-thon took place in the floodlit auditorium.

flourish (flur-ish)
noun A showy display. / *Half-Blood Prince*, page 532
With a dramatic flourish, the mayor cut the ribbon across the newly completed Garden of Secrets and welcomed the villagers to come inside.

flounce (rhymes with **bounce**)
verb To walk away with a show of impatience or anger. / *Order of the Phoenix*, page 262
The dog flounced to her bed with a sigh of irritation when her owner left for a walk without her.

flout (rhymes with **out**)
verb To show contempt or scorn for something or someone. / *Chamber of Secrets*, page 81
The fairies flouted the ban on fairy picnics by inviting all their friends to the park for lunch and a rousing game of softball.

fluently (floo-unt-lee)
adverb Smoothly and effortlessly; often said of someone's speaking or language abilities. / *Goblet of Fire*, page 555
The elf child was raised speaking Elfin, but he could also converse fluently in English.

fluke (rhymes with **puke**)
noun Something that happens by chance. / *Order of the Phoenix*, page 327
It was just a fluke that Brady was sitting in the village diner when Butch Thuggins, soccer star, walked in.

flummoxed (flum-uksd)
adjective Confused and perplexed. / *Order of the Phoenix*, page 133
The flummoxed man couldn't believe his eyes—he'd just returned from vacation to find macaroni and cheese growing in his vegetable garden.

flushed (rhymes with **hushed**)
adjective Red-faced or blushing. / *Sorcerer's Stone*, page 161
The miniature dragon looked flushed; he'd probably been practicing fire breathing in the mirror.

flustered (flus-turd)
adjective Nervous, excited, confused. / *Order of the Phoenix*, page 214
The garden gnome always got flustered and wet his trousers whenever he saw a snake.

flutter (flut-ur)
noun In British slang, a bet on something; often used in the phrase "fancy a flutter?" / *Goblet of Fire*, page 87 / Note: See also the related noun **flutter** below.
"Fancy a flutter on who gets the highest grade on the test?" asked Winston.

flutter (flut-ur)
noun A feeling of excitement, nervousness, or confusion; often used in the phrase "I'm

all of a flutter." / *Sorcerer's Stone*, page 69 / Note: See also the related noun **flutter** above.
Bella was all of a flutter after getting an autograph from the famous witch.

foal (rhymes with **goal**)

noun A very young horse or unicorn. / *Order of the Phoenix*, page 699
The unicorn foal stood on trembling legs and stabbed his very first apple with his horn.

foil (rhymes with **boil**)

verb To frustrate or thwart. / *Deathly Hallows*, page 109
"Aha!" shouted the wandmaker. "I have foiled your attempts to steal my wandmaking secrets. Out, out, and never come back!"

foist (rhymes with **moist**)

verb To force something upon another, either unjustifiably or fraudulently. / *Order of the Phoenix*, page 344
Klinkster tried to foist off the swamp goo as authentic water from the home of the Loch Ness monster, but he was having a hard time finding gullible customers.

followed suit

phrase To do the same as someone else has done. / *Chamber of Secrets*, page 158
When the school marching band mistakenly marched into the swamp, the pompom girls blindly followed suit.

football (fut-ball)

noun What soccer is called in Britain. / *Goblet of Fire*, page 191
Butch Thuggins played soccer in the United States and football in England, but in neither place had the phrase "bend it like Thuggins" caught on.

footfall (fut-fall)

noun The sound of a footstep; usually used in the plural. / *Deathly Hallows*, page 446
Brady hid under the porch, listening in terror to the approaching footfalls of the zombie.

forage (for-ij)

verb To search or hunt for. / *Goblet of Fire*, page 376
Hungry for a midnight snack, Blackpool foraged through the refrigerator but could only find some leftover chudbutts and three rotting apples.

foray (for-ay)

noun An attempt at an activity, and generally a new one. / *Order of the Phoenix*, page 542
The Cyclops' foray into the world of designer eyeglasses ended in failure.

forebears (for-bares)

noun Ancestors. / *Deathly Hallows*, page 302
Interestingly, the forebears of bears are bears.

foreboding (for-boh-ding)

noun A strong feeling that something bad is about to happen. / *Prisoner of Azkaban*, page 88
Rupert had a foreboding of trouble when the door of the abandoned cottage creaked open and ghostly groaning filled the air.

forefinger (for-fing-gur)

noun The finger next to the thumb; also called an index finger; excellent for both shaking or pointing. / *Goblet of Fire*, page 73
Madam Glinch angrily shook her forefinger at Brilly and said, "Young man, I expect you never, ever to try that again."

forerunner (for-run-ur)

noun Someone or something who came before, or that is a sign of what's to follow. / *Order of the Phoenix*, page 653
The forerunner of the cafeteria's armadillo/possum stew had been the wonderful armadillo/possum soup the cafeteria manager remembered his dear mother making.

forestall (for-stawl)

verb To prevent, delay, or hinder by acting in advance. / *Half-Blood Prince*, page 26
"As you return to class after this assembly, I'd like to forestall any possible problems in the halls by suggesting that troublemakers will spend spring vacation weeding my garden," warned the principal.

foretold (for-told)

verb To say or predict what will happen in the future. / *Order of the Phoenix*, page 601
The fortune-teller had foretold that this very moment would happen.

forewarn (for-**warn**)
verb To be warned or alerted ahead of time. / *Goblet of Fire*, page 223
"I have forewarned you all," intoned the fortune-teller. "Never accept potions from strangers."

forge (rhymes with **gorge**)
verb To make or develop a new bond, especially between people or groups. / *Half-Blood Prince*, page 75 / Note: See the related verb **forge** below.
The cocktail party was a chance for gargoyles and elves to forge new relationships while enjoying tasty appetizers.

forge (rhymes with **gorge**)
verb To make something from metal by heating and shaping it. / *Deathly Hallows*, page 298 / Note: See the related verb **forge** above.
Brady tried unsuccessfully to forge a makeshift sword in the heat of the campfire.

forgo (for-**goh**)
verb To give up or do without. / *Half-Blood Prince*, page 634
The campers had to forgo making s'mores in order to contend with the tent demons.

forlorn (for-**lorn**)
adjective Sad, lonely, wretched, pitiful. / *Goblet of Fire*, page 114
The forlorn wood nymph sat on the tree stump, worrying. Why were her friends so late?

formulate (for-**myoo**-late)
verb To work out or form in your own mind; to devise or develop. / *Goblet of Fire*, page 717
The potion master encouraged his students to do their practice assignments, but also to formulate their own concoctions.

forsaken (for-**say**-kun)
adjective Deserted, abandoned, forlorn. / *Chamber of Secrets*, page 321
A forsaken Willow felt like her friends had forgotten her—actually, they were just avoiding her because they didn't want to blurt out something about the surprise party.

fortifying (for-tuh-**fie**-ing)
adjective Invigorating and strengthening. / *Order of the Phoenix*, page 424
After a fortifying cup of breakfast cocoa, Winston was ready for the school spell-a-thon.

fortnight (**fort**-nite)
noun A two-week period of time. / *Goblet of Fire*, page 20
"You only have a fortnight to study for your levitation exams," warned Madam Glinch. "Better start floating."

foul play (fowl play)
noun An unfair or treacherous action, usually involving violence. / *Goblet of Fire*, page 579
Catching a whiff of fried chicken coming from the restaurant, the rooster crowed "I suspect foul play!"

four-poster (для-**post**-ur)
noun A bed with tall posts at each corner, often with hanging curtains or drapes around all four sides and a canopy over the top. Often "four-poster bed" but sometimes just "four-poster." / *Sorcerer's Stone*, page 130
Willow's four-poster bed had lovely pink curtains hanging on the sides; Brilly's four-poster had black-and-red curtains with lightning bolts and skeletons on them.

fraction (**frak**-shun)
noun A very small amount. / *Prisoner of Azkaban*, page 165
The leprechaun's gold was only a fraction of what Blackpool needed.

frail (rhymes with **trail**)
adjective Physically weak or not strong. / *Half-Blood Prince*, page 382
Sick with a very nasty flu, the frail giant was unable to wreak havoc on the village.

frankly (**frank**-lee)
adverb In a frank, straightforward way; sincerely. / *Goblet of Fire*, page 532
The Bee Queen spoke frankly to her troops, emphasizing it was in their best interests to steer clear of birds.

fraternization (frah-tur-nih-**zay**-shun)

noun Association with others in a brotherly or friendly way. / *Order of the Phoenix*, page 297
The fraternization between the gerbil and the ferret could only lead to problems—their parents would never approve of their friendship.

fraud (rhymes with **broad**)

noun An imposter, swindler, or otherwise deceptive person. / *Prisoner of Azkaban*, page 321
Klinkster was a fraud who enjoyed selling faulty wands to young wizards, as Rupert realized when his new wand turned into a candlestick.

fraught (rhymes with **bought**)

adjective Full of problems. / *Deathly Hallows*, page 517
The relationship between Wildwood and Blackpool was fraught from the start, but it hit a new low when Blackpool bulldozed a huge gap in Wildwood's just-completed troll fence.

fray (rhymes with **stay**)

noun A scuffle or brawl. / *Half-Blood Prince*, page 598
Dylan wanted to break up the fray, but the fighting dogs were a dangerous tumble of fangs and claws.

frayed (rhymes with **stayed**)

adjective Worn and tattered. / *Sorcerer's Stone*, page 117
When Bella tried on the frayed jacket in the used clothing shop, she suddenly had a vision of the previous owner's life.

freak (rhymes with **sneak**)

adjective Unusual, abnormal, and different from the normal. / *Chamber of Secrets*, page 9
"Cauldron College? I wouldn't go to that freak school if you paid me," said Rilda.

free rein

See **rein** elsewhere in this dictionary.

frenzied (**fren**-zeed)

adjective Frantic. / *Order of the Phoenix*, page 802
The audience applauded Annie's frenzied tap dance, unaware that her spirited performance was the result of Blackpool's latest hex.

fret (rhymes with **net**)

verb To worry or be troubled. / *Sorcerer's Stone*, page 263
"Now don't you fret, little caterpillar. We'll find your home."

frilly (**fril**-ee)

adjective Overly fancy, with frills, trimming, ruffles, etc. / *Order of the Phoenix*, page 562
Julio hated the frilly new shirt his mother expected him to wear to the dance.

Julio in frilly shirt

fringe (rhymes with **cringe**)

noun In British usage, bangs (hair hanging down on the forehead). / *Order of the Phoenix*, page 129
The humidity wasn't kind to Bella's fringe—she looked like she'd stuck her finger in an electric socket.

frisk (rhymes with **brisk**)

verb To search someone for something hidden. / *Order of the Phoenix*, page 657
Underage wizards entering the castle were frisked for unauthorized wands and hidden potions.

frisson (free-soh)

noun A shudder or shiver of excitement, fear, or pleasure. / *Order of the Phoenix*, page 87

A frisson of delight went through Fiona as the world's most-famous witch entered the deli.

frock coat (**frok** kote)

noun An old-fashioned formal coat for men, coming down to the knees and double-breasted (lapping over, with two rows of buttons). / *Half-Blood Prince*, page 199
To play the role of an old wizard in the school play, Rupert had to wear an unflattering frockcoat—he looked like a short Abraham Lincoln.

frog-march (**frog**-march)

verb To grab someone by the arm and force them to walk along with you. / *Sorcerer's Stone*, page 203
Bella and Tamika frog-marched Milton out of their very private clubhouse.

froth (rhymes with **moth**)

verb To give off froth or foam. / *Chamber of Secrets*, page 188
The mermaid tried to warn the humans about the Loch Ness monster, but when her voice met the air it just frothed and drifted away in the breeze.

fruitcake (**froot**-kake)

noun A hard, dense cake filled with raisins, currants, nuts, and odd little green and orange bits. / *Sorcerer's Stone*, page 40
Auntie Baba always sent a holiday fruitcake—uneaten, it would eventually be tucked at the bottom of the compost pile.

fruitless (**froot**-less)

adjective Unproductive and unsuccessful. / *Prisoner of Azkaban*, page 100
After his fruitless attempts to design a troll alert system, Dr. Greenteeth gave up and went back to work on his molar power invention.

fry-up (**fry**-up)

noun In British usage, a quick meal—likes eggs and bacon. / *Prisoner of Azkaban*, page 27
There's nothing as satisfying as a good old-fashioned fry-up after a long night spent fighting evil.

fug (rhymes with **bug**)

noun Heavy humid air in a closed stuffy room. / *Half-Blood Prince*, page 38 / Note: A slight problem in Potter's world—it's possible that Rowling meant "fog" instead of "fug," since it's Potter's misty breath leaving the "fug" on the window.
The fug in the Trolls' Hole pub was so hot and close, you could write your name in the moisture on the windows.

full-pelt (**full**-pelt)

adverb As fast as possible. / *Order of the Phoenix*, page 722
Caught skinny-dipping in the castle moat, the knight grabbed his suit of armor and ran full-pelt back into the castle.

full-rein

See **rein** elsewhere in this dictionary.

fume (fyoom)

noun Smoke and vapor. / *Order of the Phoenix*, page 603
The knight defeated his dragon foe in a blaze of fume and fire.

fungi (**fun**-ji or **fun**-guy)

noun Organisms that are neither plant nor animal—like mold or mildew. Singular: fungus. / *Sorcerer's Stone*, page 66
Furry gray fungi were slowly spreading across the stone floor and up the dungeon walls.

furl (rhymes with **swirl**)

verb To roll up or fold up (especially in the case of a winged creature). / *Goblet of Fire*, page 355
The paper boy furled the morning newspaper and tossed it on the Frackets' front porch.

furor (**fyur**-or)

noun An uproar and commotion. / *Deathly Hallows*, page 627
A furor erupted at the hospital when a blood drive was announced—what if a vampire came?

furrowed (**fur**-rohd)

adjective Wrinkled; usually said of someone's brow (forehead) and usually implying confusion or worry. / *Prisoner of Azkaban*, page 69
Madam Glinch's furrowed brow meant she'd forgotten where she'd stored her backup wand.

furtive (fur-tiv)
adjective Stealthy and sneaky. / *Prisoner of Azkaban,* page 108
Members of the Thieves Guild held a furtive meeting to discuss upcoming thievery projects.

fuse (rhymes with **use**)
verb To mix or unite as if melted together. / *Order of the Phoenix,* page 37
When she awoke abruptly, her dream and real life strangely fused into one reality…except she didn't know where she was.

fussed (rhymes with **bust**)
adjective In British usage, worried or upset. / *Half-Blood Prince,* page 386
The boy escaped but the demon wasn't fussed—he knew there'd be plenty more dinner options.

G

gabble (gab-ul)
verb To speak so quickly that people can't understand you. / *Goblet of Fire*, page 218
"Stop gabbling and just tell me what happened," said the impatient policeman.

gable (gay-bul)
noun The upper end of a house where it joins the sloping roof and makes a triangle shape. / *Deathly Hallows*, page 232
Many of the houses in the older part of the village had fancy gables edged with intricate gingerbread trim.

gag (rhymes with **hag**)
verb To choke or retch. / *Half-Blood Prince*, page 457 / Note: See the related verb **gag** below.
Rupert gagged when his mother asked how he liked the roasted eel stew.

gag (rhymes with **hag**)
verb To prevent someone from speaking or crying out by putting a cloth in or over their mouth. / *Order of the Phoenix*, page 742 / Note: See the related verb **gag** above.
The apprentice bank robber gagged the bank manager, but then forgot to tie up his hands and feet.

gaga (gah-gah)
adjective An insulting word describing someone's who's confused because they're old. / *Deathly Hallows*, page 158
"Great Grandfather Brill has gone a little gaga," said Brilly, "so my parents moved him to the Home for Elderly Sages."

gaggle (gag-ul)
noun A noisy group of people. / *Prisoner of Azkaban*, page 262
A gaggle of eager shoppers impatiently waited for the Hurly Burly Emporium to open and the half-price sale on cauldrons to start.

gait (rhymes with **plate**; sounds exactly like **gate**)
noun The way someone walks. / *Half-Blood Prince*, page 203
The giant's gait could best be described as a lumbering waddle.

gale (rhymes with **tale**)
noun A very windy storm. / *Prisoner of Azkaban*, page 169 / Note: See the related phrase **gale of laughter** below.
A gale was blowing outside but inside the Witching Hour pub, all was calm.

gale of laughter
phrase A noisy outburst of laughter. / *Order of the Phoenix*, page 86
Gales of laughter met Wildwood's stories about the king's struggles with the unworkable moat-sweeper.

gallantry (gal-un-tree)
noun Chivalrous attention toward women. / *Deathly Hallows*, page 176
The gallantry of the knight was remarkable—he whipped off his cloak and spread it across the puddle so the feet of the princess wouldn't get wet.

galling (gol-ing)
adjective Irritating or exasperating. / *Order of the Phoenix*, page 9
The king's galling new moat-sweeper not only didn't work, it had also been ridiculously expensive.

galoshes (gul-osh-us)
noun Waterproof overshoes or rain boots worn to keep regular shoes dry; used in the plural. / *Sorcerer's Stone*, page 140
Galoshes are excellent for puddle stomping and fish punting.

galvanize (gal-vuh-nize)
verb To stir into action or awareness. / *Deathly Hallows*, page 437
The villagers were galvanized into immediate action when the evil developer suggested building hundreds of new condos in the meadow.

gambol (gam-bul; sounds exactly like **gamble**)
verb To frolic or run about playfully. / *Order*

of the Phoenix, page 181
The boarhound puppies gamboled around the dog kennel.

gamekeeper (game-keep-ur)
noun A person who takes care of game (animals). / *Sorcerer's Stone*, page 59
Butch Thuggins, famed soccer player, had always wanted to be a gamekeeper, but his initial attempts at raising stinging nurch babies convinced him that soccer was a safer career.

gangling (gang-gling)
adjective Tall and awkward. / *Sorcerer's Stone*, page 93
The gangling giant loved to play basketball, even though his waist was higher than the basket and he often tripped over his feet.

gape (rhymes with **tape**)
verb To stare open-mouthed; to gawk or gawp. / *Sorcerer's Stone*, page 152
The giant gecko gaped at the giant—now he was *really* big.

garbled (gar-buld)
adjective Unclear and confusing. / *Order of the Phoenix*, page 89
Brilly's clever repairs on the school's public address system meant every announcement was now so garbled no one could understand it.

gargantuan (gar-gan-choo-un)
adjective Immense. / *Half-Blood Prince*, page 231
The gargantuan cockroach knocked over the kitchen chair as it scurried over to look closely at the cake on the counter.

gargoyle (gar-goyl)
noun Literally, a water spout carved in the shape of a grotesque animal or fantastic creature, projecting from a building or gutter; more generally, anything or anyone that looks like a gargoyle. / *Half-Blood Prince*, page 465
Ever wonder if gargoyles come down off their buildings to sit around and play Crazy Fates?

Gargoyle

garish (gare-ish)
adjective Gaudy and way too bright. / *Order of the Phoenix*, page 739
Bella wore a garish red and orange dress to the Halloween dance.

garland (gar-lund)
noun Flowers or leaves (or holly and tinsel) tied together and draped as a decoration. / *Half-Blood Prince*, page 303
Garlands of ivy and blackberries decorated Blackpool's mantelpiece.

gateau (gah-toh)
noun A very light sponge cake with rich filling or icing...or both. / *Half-Blood Prince*, page 163
Tamika wanted a strawberry gateau with sparklers on top for her birthday.

gaudy (gaw-dee)
adjective Very showy. / *Order of the Phoenix*, page 798
"Don't you think that outfit is a trifle gaudy?" asked Bella's father as she got ready for the Halloween dance.

gauge (rhymes with **rage**)

verb To measure or evaluate. / *Half-Blood Prince*, page 412

It was difficult to accurately gauge the temperature during the heat wave since all the thermometers in the village broke.

gaunt (rhymes with **haunt**)

adjective Thin and bony. / *Sorcerer's Stone*, page 124

The gaunt hawk hadn't had a good mouse meal in days.

gauzy (gaw-zee)

adjective Thin and almost transparent, like gauze bandages; usually said of clothing. / *Prisoner of Azkaban*, page 102

The woman's gauzy scarf fluttered behind her in the breeze as she flew on her broomstick through the valley.

gawk (rhymes with **hawk**)

verb To stare stupidly. / *Sorcerer's Stone*, page 95

The lizard gawked at the giant gecko—she sure was one pretty reptile.

gawp (rhymes with **top**)

verb To stare open-mouthed in wonder and astonishment. / *Goblet of Fire*, page 290

Mrs. Snodgrape's guests gawped at the array of treasures in her curio cabinet—especially the elegant snake cozy.

generation (jen-uh-**ray**-shun)

noun About 30 years, the time between the birth of parents and the birth of their children. Nine generations, for example, would be about 270 years. / *Chamber of Secrets*, page 200

"My family came to the village generations ago in an enchanted covered wagon," said Madam Glinch.

genial (**jee**-nee-ul)

adjective Pleasant and friendly. / *Half-Blood Prince*, page 379

The genial wandmaker welcomed school visits to his Wandatorium Shop.

genteel (jen-**teel**)

adjective Polite and well-bred. / *Deathly Hallows*, page 591

With a genteel curtsy, Winston's mother approached the queen.

geranium (juh-**ray**-nee-um)

adjective Reddish/pinkish, like the color of many geranium blooms. / *Half-Blood Prince*, page 146

Bella's geranium pink coat clashed with her red and orange Halloween dress.

gerbil (**jur**-bul)

noun A small mouse-like rodent with a long tail and long back legs. / *Half-Blood Prince*, page 6

Brady's pet gerbil ran away with the cute mouse from the attic.

gesticulate (jeh-**stik**-yuh-late)

verb To make gestures to emphasize what you're saying. / *Order of the Phoenix*, page 319

Parker gesticulated wildly as he retold the story of his terrifying night in the Haunted Forest.

get a grip

phrase Roughly the same as saying "get a hold of yourself." / *Half-Blood Prince*, page 380

"Get a grip, will you? It's not the end of the world."

get wind of

phrase To learn of. / *Half-Blood Prince*, page 5

The potions class first got wind of the test when Mrs. Snodgrape brought in 17 mysterious containers and lined them up on her desk.

getaway (**get**-a-way)

noun An escape. / *Deathly Hallows*, page 162

Brilly made a fast getaway after plugging up the sinks in the girls' bathroom…and turning on all the faucets.

ghastly (**gast**-lee)

adjective Terrible and frightful. / *Deathly Hallows*, page 419

Rupert was convinced some ghastly creature haunted the book stacks in the school library.

ghoul (rhymes with **fool**)

noun In folklore, an evil spirit that steals bodies from graves…and eats them. / *Chamber of Secrets*, page 29 / Note: In Potter's

world, ghouls are ugly dim-witted creatures that live in wizards' attics. They're relatively harmless, though they can make a lot of noise.
Once Parker heard what ghouls do, he never walked home through the cemetery again.

gibber (jib-ur)
verb To chatter on and on, not making any sense at all. / *Sorcerer's Stone*, page 29
The girl gibbered wildly when she saw the giant cockroach calmly sitting—its legs crossed—at the kitchen table.

giddy (gid-ee)
adjective Lighthearted and happy (and sometimes even lightheaded and dizzy). / *Order of the Phoenix*, page 157
The giddy boy couldn't believe it—he'd actually won the school lottery and would get to take home the school's best broomstick over spring vacation.

gild (rhymes with **build**; sounds exactly like **gilled**)
verb Literally, to cover with a thin layer of gold; more generally, to look as if something is covered in gold. / *Order of the Phoenix*, page 719
The sun gilded the heads of the two little blond boys as they ran through the meadow.

gilt (rhymes with **built**; sounds exactly like **guilt**)
adjective Covered with thin layers of gold called gilt. / *Goblet of Fire*, page 96
The librarian hired Wildwood to clean the gilt decoration on the huge picture frame hanging over the library fireplace.

gimlet-eyed (gim-lit-eyed)
adjective Having a sharp or piercing glance. / *Order of the Phoenix*, page 473
With a gimlet-eyed glare, Madam Glinch suggested Brilly immediately put down his wand and clean up the frog slime.

ginger (jin-jur)
adjective Reddish-orange; often said of hair or fur. / *Prisoner of Azkaban*, page 213 / Note: "Ginger" is also sometimes used as a mildly belittling name for someone with ginger-colored hair, as in *Deathly Hallows* (page 448).

Blinky, the overweight ginger cat, looked like a gigantic furry caterpillar.

gingerly (jin-jur-lee)
adverb In a careful and cautious way. / *Goblet of Fire*, page 574
The old wizard stood up gingerly—it doesn't pay to move too fast when you're 173.

gist (jist; rhymes with **mist**)
noun A central or main idea. / *Goblet of Fire*, page 300
"I get the gist of what you're saying," said the lawyer. "But the details are unclear."

git (rhymes with **fit**)
noun In British slang, an offensive word for an annoying, unpleasant person. / *Chamber of Secrets*, page 163
"You selfish git," said Winston's brother, "share some of Mum's sausage-and-mash."

glazed (rhymes with **blazed**)
adjective Glassy or unfocused; dazed. / *Prisoner of Azkaban*, page 26
His glazed eyes suggested that the class was either very boring or that he was already half-asleep.

glean (rhymes with **mean**)
verb To gather bit by bit. / *Order of the Phoenix*, page 118
Fiona gleaned a lot of useful information from the article on barn ghouls.

glee (rhymes with **flee**)
noun Delight or joy. / *Sorcerer's Stone*, page 164
Mother Serpent couldn't hide her glee when baby Tweedee first learned to slither.

glen (rhymes with **pen**)
noun A secluded small valley. / *Goblet of Fire*, page 176
The mysterious fog crept slowly across the meadow and down into the grassy glen.

gloss (rhymes with **loss**)
verb To cover up by misrepresenting facts; to hide the real nature of something. / *Chamber of Secrets*, page 20
Brilly tried to gloss things over: "Gosh, who knew a single tiny firecracker would cause such problems?"

glower (gloh-ur)

noun A look of discontent or anger. / *Deathly Hallows*, page 280

The king's glower should have warned the moat-sweeper salesman that he had a very dissatisfied customer on his hands.

glum (rhymes with **dumb**)

adjective Gloomy and dejected, and not in a mood to talk about it. / *Order of the Phoenix*, page 127

The glum boy couldn't remember another day that had gone as badly.

glutinous (gloot-un-us)

adjective Like glue: sticky and gluey. / *Chamber of Secrets*, page 215

The school vote for the most glutinous cafeteria dessert was a tie between tapioca and rice pudding.

gnarled (narld)

adjective Bent and twisted; often said of trees, fingers, and feet. / *Chamber of Secrets*, page 36

The gnarled trees of the Haunted Forest looked like old wizards, bowing and turning in their dark cloaks.

gnash his teeth

phrase Literally, to grind the teeth in anger; more generally, to be really angry (whether actually gnashing or not). / *Chamber of Secrets*, page 94

Blackpool gnashed his teeth when his ace racing worm got a cramp and fell far behind the others in the annual worm derby.

gnome (rhymes with **home**; sounds exactly like **nome**)

noun In folklore, a shriveled old man who guards the earth's interior and its treasure. / *Chamber of Secrets*, page 29 / Note: In Potter's world, garden gnomes—shaped like potatoes with legs—are rather dim garden pests, digging up roots and causing a mess.

The gnome under the library building had just discovered manga comics; they were much more interesting than guarding treasure.

Gnome

go ballistic

phrase To become exceedingly angry or irrational. / *Prisoner of Azkaban*, page 255

Wildwood would go ballistic every time Blackpool enchanted his tuba—playing a tuba while soap suds pour out of it isn't much fun.

go round the twist

phrase In British slang, similar to saying "he's gone round the bend" or "he's gone crazy." / *Order of the Phoenix*, page 83

The old witch had gone round the twist—she sat all day and muttered partial spells and waved a green bean like it was her wand.

go spare

phrase In British slang, to lose your temper completely. / *Order of the Phoenix*, page 63

The class was sure Madam Glinch would go spare when she discovered the storage cabinet had been emptied out by several of her students.

go starkers

phrase In British slang, to go naked (as in "stark naked"). / *Goblet of Fire*, page 156

"I don't care what you wear for Halloween—go starkers for all I care," huffed an impatient Winston.

go to town

phrase To get busy on a project. / *Order of the Phoenix*, page 75

"Let's go to town on this troll fence and finish it today," urged Wildwood.

goad (rhymes with **toad**)

verb To make someone do something by annoying, provoking, or really urging them on. / *Order of the Phoenix*, page 833

Brilly goaded Dribbles into smearing frog slime on the principal's desk.

goatee (goh-**tee**)

noun A small pointed beard, usually ending right below the chin. / *Goblet of Fire*, page 247

Blackpool trimmed his full beard to just a goatee, then dyed it red for the party; he looked like the devil.

goblet (**gob**-let)

noun A drinking glass with a base and a stem, usually made of glass or pewter; fancier and heavier than an ordinary wine glass. / *Sorcerer's Stone*, page 116

The king hoped to serve his guests a special wine in his fanciest goblets, but they were all in the goblet-washer.

goblin (**gob**-lun)

noun In folklore, a mischievous ugly evil creature, known for tricking people. / *Sorcerer's Stone*, page 63 / Note: In Potter's world, goblins are very intelligent creatures, living side by side with wizards but not respected or treated well by most wizards.

Eldira the goblin lived for Halloween, the best day of the year because she could trick people with no consequences. Pretty much.

godfather (**god**-fah-thur)

noun Traditionally, a man at a child's baptism who takes responsibility for the child's religious upbringing; more generally, a man who serves as guardian or protector. / *Prisoner of Azkaban*, page 379

When Brilly realized he didn't have a traditional godfather, he hoped Wildwood would step in if something happened to his parents.

Goblin holding a goblet

goggle (gog-ul)

verb To stare at, often in amazement. / *Sorcerer's Stone*, page 97

Elrod's mother simply goggled at him when he broke his toothbrush—that boy was so clumsy.

going...

See **go...** elsewhere in this dictionary.

gooseberry (**goos**-bare-ee)

adjective Like a gooseberry, a small grape-like fruit. / *Half-Blood Prince*, page 67

The elf had a gooseberry face—round, watery, and pale green.

gore (rhymes with **tore**)

verb To stab with a horn. / *Goblet of Fire*, page 309

The rhino accidentally gored the gamekeeper in the thigh, then sat down and begged his forgiveness.

gorge (rhymes with **forge**)

verb To stuff yourself; to eat and eat until you can't eat any more. / *Order of the Phoenix*, page 445

Having gorged himself all afternoon on crisps and

chocolate frisblots, Brilly found the prospect of a huge dinner unappealing.

gorgon (gor-gun)

noun In mythology, any of three sister monsters (with snakes for hair, and other unappealing features). / *Sorcerer's Stone*, page 52
Dribbles wondered: Would he rather run into a gorgon or a gargoyle?

Gorgon

gormless (gorm-less)

adjective In British slang, stupid and clueless. / *Order of the Phoenix*, page 86
"You're the most gormless git I've ever known," muttered Winston to his brother.

gossamer (gos-uh-mur)

adjective Delicate, light, flimsy. / *Order of the Phoenix*, page 533
The gossamer threads of the dancers' gowns glowed in the stage lights.

goulash (goo-losh)

noun A Hungarian beef and vegetable stew, seasoned with paprika. / *Goblet of Fire*, page 418
Willow's brother loved goulash so much he could eat it for breakfast, lunch, and dinner.

gramophone (gram-uh-fone)

noun An old-fashioned word for a record player or phonograph. / *Half-Blood Prince*, page 463
Willow loved playing records—especially the early Rolling Bones—on her mother's old gramophone.

grandeur (gran-joor)

noun Grandness and magnificence. / *Half-Blood Prince*, page 212
The grandeur of the castle was most evident in the Royal Bathroom—gold faucets, a marble toilet, a huge sunken bathtub, and a widescreen TV so the king wouldn't miss a minute of his favorite soap operas.

granite (gran-it)

noun A very hard stone often used for tombstones. / *Deathly Hallows*, page 325
The granite in a far corner of the cemetery was a tombstone marking the grave of the village's founder.

grapple (grap-ul)

verb To struggle. / *Deathly Hallows*, page 40
Brilly grappled with thoughts of mayhem, but in the end, he decided to just go ahead and take the test.

grate (rhymes with **fate**; sounds exactly like **great**)

noun An iron frame that holds logs in a fireplace. / *Sorcerer's Stone*, page 48
The fireplace grate was covered with sticky ashes from last night's marshmallow-and-jello roast.

gravitate (grav-ih-tate)

verb To move toward; to be attracted by an irresistible force. / *Half-Blood Prince*, page 362
The lizard gravitated toward the sunniest spot on the deck.

greengrocer (green-groh-sur)

noun A grocer (or grocery) who sells primarily fruits and vegetables. / *Deathly Hallows*, page 261
The greengrocer was having a big sale on nettles—time to make soup!

greenhouse (green-hows)

noun A building with glass walls and roof to grow plants in. / *Chamber of Secrets*, page 89
The ugly thick vines—with their strange black flowers—slowly crept up the walls of the greenhouse.

grievously (gree-vus-lee)

adverb In a really serious way, causing great

pain and suffering. / *Chamber of Secrets*, page 14
Blackpool's feelings were grievously hurt when no one—except Blackpool himself—voted for him in the village election.

griffin (**grif**-un)
noun A mythical beast with the head and wings of an eagle and the body of a lion; often seen in statues or sculptures. / *Sorcerer's Stone*, page 173
What did that tiny carved griffin really mean, the one she always wore on a gold chain around her neck?

Griffin

grille (rhymes with **drill**)
noun A decorative metal grating on an elevator, the front of a car, etc. / *Order of the Phoenix*, page 129
The elevator grille closed slowly, quietly, with an ominous soft swishhhh.

grindylow (**grin**-dee-loh)
noun A bogeyman-type mythological creature from English folklore that lives in the water and grabs children who get too close to the edge. / *Prisoner of Azkaban*, page 425 / Note: In Potter's world, a grindylow is a more pleasant underwater creature that co-exists with merpeople.

Ever since his mother told him about grindylows grabbing people, Elrod refused to go on picnics to the lake.

grisly (**griz**-lee)
adjective Gruesome or terrifying. / *Goblet of Fire*, page 129
The bare bones of dozens of dead cows were a grisly sign that something terrible had happened in the meadow.

grit (rhymes with **pit**)
noun Courage or pluck. / *Half-Blood Prince*, page 225
Soccer captain Butch Thuggins knew he should show more grit, but he was exhausted and they were losing 0-6—he just wanted to go home and have a hot bath.

grit (rhymes with **pit**)
verb To clench or grind your teeth in anger or determination. / *Sorcerer's Stone*, page 276
Nungie, the one-legged elf, gritted his teeth in anger when Blackpool suggested a jump rope contest.

grizzled (**griz**-uld)
adjective Partly gray; sometimes called "salt and pepper" gray. / *Goblet of Fire*, page 210
The principal's hair seemed to be getting more grizzled every day.

grope (rhymes with **rope**)
verb To make your way by reaching about uncertainly. / *Goblet of Fire*, page 6
Parker groped his way out of the Haunted Forest as enchanted tree roots tried to trip him and tree stumps moved into his path.

grotesque (groh-**tesk**)
adjective Fantastically ugly, bizarre, and strange. / *Goblet of Fire*, page 119
The grotesque stone mask on the wall slowly began to smile as something...red...dripped from its mouth.

grotto (**grot**-oh)
noun A cave-like structure or shrine. / *Goblet of Fire*, page 413
The Royal Grotto lay deep beneath the castle walls, lit by dozens of burning torches.

grovel (grov-ul)
verb To cringe or humble yourself, in great fear or humility. / *Prisoner of Azkaban*, page 372
"Please, I am just so very sorry for borrowing your ever-so-clever ideas, sir, please forgive me," groveled Klingster to the wandmaker.

grub (rhymes with **rub**)
noun The fat, wormlike larva of some beetles and other insects. / *Half-Blood Prince*, page 230
Blackpool's giant grubs began to twitch and writhe in the warm light of his Bug-arium.

grub (rhymes with **rub**)
verb To look for something on or just under the ground. / *Half-Blood Prince*, page 205
The hungry monster chicken grubbed in the dirt for mega-worms.

grudge (rhymes with **trudge**)
noun A deep-seated feeling of resentment. / *Chamber of Secrets*, page 29
It was never clear what the grudge was between the king and the duke, but over the years it had caused many problems.

grudging (grudj-ing)
adjective Reluctant or unwilling. / *Prisoner of Azkaban*, page 401
The team broke into a grudging trot as the coach shouted, "Let's go! Just 12 laps—that's all!"

grueling (grew-ling)
adjective Mentally and physically exhausting. / *Half-Blood Prince*, page 7
The king actually thought the village boys would enjoy the grueling work of cleaning the castle moat.

guardian (gar-dee-un)
noun Someone or something that guards or protects. / *Prisoner of Azkaban*, page 237 / Note: See a related use of the noun **guardian** below.
"Sometimes, Elrod, I think you need a full-time guardian just to make sure you don't get into any trouble."

guardian (gar-dee-un)
noun A person legally responsible for the care of someone's child, especially after the death of the child's parents. / *Prisoner of Azkaban*, page 379 / Note: See a related use of the noun **guardian** above.
No one had ever asked Wildwood to be a guardian, at least not until Brilly popped the question.

guff (rhymes with **buff**)
noun Nonsense, foolish, stupid, or untrue talk. / *Order of the Phoenix*, page 286
"I've had enough of your guff, Blackpool," shouted Willow. "You keep yourself, your wand, and your mean hexes away from my puppies!"

guffaw (guh-faw)
verb To laugh heartily, boisterously, and in an unrestrained way. / *Goblet of Fire*, page 168
The king slapped his thigh and guffawed loudly as the court jester shared his latest jokes.

gullible (gul-uh-bul)
noun Those who are easily deceived and fooled. / *Chamber of Secrets*, page 151
The gullible will always fall for something that sounds good even if it isn't likely—like "free fireworks in the library today!"

gully (guh-lee)
noun A ditch in the ground formed by running water, especially after a deluge. / *Order of the Phoenix*, page 432
The muddy rainwater rushed down the gully as more storm clouds gathered overhead.

guttering (guh-tur-ing)
adjective Burning low and flickering. / *Order of the Phoenix*, page 475
The guttering torches cast dancing shadows in the dark corners of the Royal Grotto.

guttural (gut-ur-ul)
adjective Harsh and throaty. / *Deathly Hallows*, page 294
The troll's guttural voice sounded especially spooky echoing out from under the bridge.

guy rope (guy rope)
noun A rope used to hold down a tent. / *Deathly Hallows*, page 273
As they were putting up the tent, Dribbles wondered: Why it was called a "guy rope" and not a "gal rope"?

H

habitat (hab-ih-tat)
noun The environment an animal normally lives in. / *Order of the Phoenix*, page 443
The habitat of the giant cockroach is really just about anywhere he wants to be, as long as there is food around.

hack (rhymes with **crack**)
verb To cut or chop at with crude blows. / *Deathly Hallows*, page 465
The knight hacked at the rope holding the castle's huge catapult, but his sword was dreadfully dull.

hacked off
phrase In British slang, to be extremely annoyed about something. / *Goblet of Fire*, page 181
Winston was so hacked off about being grounded that he slammed his fist in the wall, causing, unfortunately, two broken fingers and one large hole in the wall.

hacking (hak-ing)
adjective Dry, rough, and coarse; usually said of coughs. / *Goblet of Fire*, page 201
The giant's hacking cough could be heard for miles.

hackles (hak-uls)
noun The hair on the back of a dog's neck that bristles or stand ups when the dog is angry or frightened. / *Goblet of Fire*, page 705
The dog's hackles raised at the odd mooing sound from the horse barn

haddock (had-uk)
noun An ocean fish. / *Goblet of Fire*, page 385
The cafeteria ladies served up fried haddock for lunch…the third time in a week!

hag (rhymes with **bag**)
noun A witch or sorceress; sometimes an ugly, vicious, old, witch-like woman. / *Sorcerer's Stone*, page 71
The toothless old hag waved her wand and turned Katie's backpack into a flying squirrel.

haggis (hag-iss)
noun A Scottish dish: the heart, lungs, and innards of a sheep or a calf, mixed with suet, oatmeal, and seasoning, then boiled in the animal's stomach. / *Chamber of Secrets*, page 133
They say haggis is an acquired taste, but it was one Fiona hoped never to acquire.

haggle (hag-ul)
verb To argue over the price of something. / *Chamber of Secrets*, page 52
"Brilly, you can't haggle over prices in the grocery store."

hairpin (hair-pin)
adjective Shaped like a hairpin, a small, skinny piece of U-shaped metal designed to hold hair in place. / *Deathly Hallows*, page 534
The hairpin turn on the hill road had been nicknamed "Scarepin Turn" because so many people had had scary accidents there.

half-
This prefix adds the concept of *half*-ness to many ordinary words:
  half-furled
  adjective / *Goblet of Fire*, page 353
  halfheartedly
  adverb / *Prisoner of Azkaban*, page 151
  half-octave
  noun / *Goblet of Fire*, page 98
  half-plucked
  adjective / *Chamber of Secrets*, page 115

hallmark (hol-mark)
noun A distinguishing characteristic, idea, method, or quality. / *Order of the Phoenix*, page 826
The hallmark of the soccer team was "big"—big wins, big losses, big players. Except for Butch Thuggins, who wasn't big…but had big ideas about himself.

hallucination (hah-loo-suh-**nay**-shun)

noun Something imagined to be real, but isn't really there at all. / *Prisoner of Azkaban*, page 283

"I think the prince is having hallucinations," said the queen. "He keeps saying every suit of armor stored in the Royal Atrium has someone inside it."

hamper (**ham**-pur)

noun In British usage, a large basket with a lid, filled with food and wine and sent to someone as a gift; also used as a picnic basket. / *Half-Blood Prince*, page 71

Winston's mum shopped at the Hurly Burly Emporium for a holiday hamper for her mother-in-law, then stopped by the village market for some treats to tuck inside.

hamper (**ham**-pur)

verb To prevent or make difficult. / *Chamber of Secrets*, page 266

Brilly was hampered in his revenge on the cafeteria manager by the high expenses involved in his latest plan.

hangdog (**hang**-dog)

adjective Looking shamefaced, guilty, or browbeaten. / *Deathly Hallows*, page 46

"That hangdog look means just one thing," said the boy's mother. "You're in trouble again at school, aren't you?"

hank (rhymes with **dank**)

noun A coil, knot, or loop; usually said of hair. / *Deathly Hallows*, page 50

Blackpool's long hair really annoyed his elderly mother, who was always threatening "to cut a hank of that stuff off!"

hanker (**hang**-kur)

verb To yearn or long for. / *Half-Blood Prince*, page 210

Bella really hankered after the red dress in the window of the Hurly Burly Emporium, but it was *so* expensive.

hanky (**hang**-key)

noun A shortened form of "handkerchief." Plural: hankies. Sometimes used in a taunting way, suggesting that only big tough guys use handkerchiefs, while wimps use hankies. / *Goblet of Fire*, page 315

"Uh-oh, you dropped your sweet little hanky, Brilly," taunted Blackpool, the evil wizard.

haphazardly (hap-**haz**-urd-lee)

adverb In a random, casual, unplanned way. / *Chamber of Secrets*, page 34

Fiona never did things haphazardly—she even read the dictionary from A to Z.

harassed-looking (huh-**rasd**-look-ing)

adjective Irritated and worn out. / Note: There are over one million words in Potter's story, and this is one of the few misspelled words. It's "harassed-looking," not "harrassed-looking," as seen in *Chamber of Secrets* (page 59).

The harassed-looking librarian had sent out dozens of overdue notices, and no one—not one person—had returned a single overdue book.

hare (rhymes with **snare**; sounds exactly like **hair**)

verb In British usage, to run fast. / *Prisoner of Azkaban*, page 308

Winston went haring down the street, trying to catch up with the bookmobile.

harebrained (hair-**braynd**)

adjective Silly, reckless, and not likely to succeed. / *Goblet of Fire*, page 325

"That's your most harebrained idea yet, Brilly. Lizards in the lunchroom? How do you plan on finding enough lizards?"

harelip (**hair**-lip)

noun An offensive word for having a divided top lip that failed to develop correctly before birth. / *Chamber of Secrets*, page 297

Nungie, the one-legged elf, was born with a harelip, but at least that could be easily fixed.

harrassed-looking

See **harassed-looking** elsewhere in this dictionary. / Note: There are over one million words in Potter's story, and this is one of the few misspelled words. It's "harassed-looking," not "harrassed-looking."

harried (**hair**-eed)
adjective Bothered, disturbed, distressed, and annoyed, especially by small problems. / *Half-Blood Prince*, page 111
The harried bartender was trying to mix a Foaming Dragon's Blood Martini, wipe off the bar, and dry glasses, all at the same time.

hastily (**hay**-stuh-lee)
adverb Quickly and speedily; with haste. / *Order of the Phoenix*, page 28
After seeing the huge creepy snake peering out of the pond at him, Rupert hastily decided to forego fishing for the day.

hat stand (**hat** stand)
noun A tall pole with hooks at the top to hang hats and coats on. / *Prisoner of Azkaban*, page 23
Wildwood had invited just a few friends over, but already the hat stand in the hall was buried under six cloaks, two shawls, two top hats, a beret, and three witch's hats.

haughty (**haw**-tee)
adjective Stuck-up, too proud, and snobbish. / *Goblet of Fire*, page 321
Blackpool looked especially haughty after everyone congratulated him on his speech against any new taxes on wands or cauldrons.

haunt (rhymes with **gaunt**)
noun A favored place to hang out. / *Order of the Phoenix*, page 7
Wildwood's usual haunts were Star Ducks, the library, and the Witching Hour pub.

haven (**hay**-vun)
noun A place of safety and comfort. / *Goblet of Fire*, page 319
Brilly's personal haven was the garden shed, at least until he accidentally burned it down.

haversack (**hav**-ur-sak)
noun An old-fashioned word for a bag similar to a backpack, but with just one strap. / *Order of the Phoenix*, page 421
The wizard carefully packed his haversack for his overnight visit—he didn't want any time-shifter potion to spill on his pajamas.

havoc (**hav**-uk)
noun A really messed-up situation that isn't easy to fix. / *Chamber of Secrets*, page 126
The havoc created when the janitor's closet mysteriously blew up threw the entire school in an uproar.

haywire (**hay**-wire)
adjective Out of control, crazy, or erratic; things usually "go haywire." / *Goblet of Fire*, page 548
"My TV's gone haywire!" raged the king. "I can't get anything on it other than *Court TV*."

head boy, head girl (**hed** boy, **hed** girl)
noun In British usage, a student that heads the oldest class of students in a school, somewhat like a student president or a head prefect. / *Sorcerer's Stone*, page 55
At the beginning of the school year, the head boy spoke at the all-school assembly about the importance of recycling.

headlock (**hed**-lok)
noun A way to hold someone's head so they can't move. / *Chamber of Secrets*, page 192
The headlock is a very effective technique, unless you're wrestling the Headless Horseman.

headmaster, headmistress (**hed**-mas-tur, **hed**-mis-tres)
noun A man (headmaster) or woman (headmistress) in charge of a private school, like a principal. / *Sorcerer's Stone*, pages 51 (headmaster) and 25 (headmistress)
Everyone groaned when the headmaster announced there would be school all day on Saturday.

headstone (**hed**-stone)
noun A gravestone marking a burial place. / *Goblet of Fire*, page 637
The headstones of the village's oldest wizarding family floated about three inches above each grave.

hearing trumpet
See **ear trumpet** elsewhere in this dictionary.

hearth rug (**harth**-rug)
noun A small rug in front of the fireplace to protect the floor from sparks, and much favored by sleeping dogs and cats. / *Goblet of*

Fire, page 15 / Note: **Hearth rug** can also be spelled as one word—hearthrug—as seen in *Order of the Phoenix* (page 457).
The cat, peacefully curled up on the hearth rug, was actually having nightmares about the terrifying rat gang in the barn.

heave (rhymes with **leave**)
verb To lift or raise up, especially something heavy. / *Sorcerer's Stone*, page 240
Wildwood heaved the last stone into place. Finally, the troll fence was finished.

heckle (**hek**-ul)
verb To interrupt and try to embarrass someone, especially if they're speaking or performing in public. / *Half-Blood Prince*, page 224
Several disappointed members of the audience heckled the lousy performing seal, who was only trying to do his best.

hedge (rhymes with **ledge**)
noun A row of small bushes or trees. / *Chamber of Secrets*, page 7
Every Saturday morning, Mr. Glinch trimmed the hedge around his front yard, whether it needed it or not.

hedgehog (**hedj**-hog)
noun A small European mammal, with a round body covered with sharp prickly spines. / *Goblet of Fire*, page 100
"Everyone thinks hedgehogs are so cute," thought the dog. "You try eating one."

hedgerow (**hedj**-row)
noun A line of hedges, or bushes, growing along the edge of a field or road. / *Half-Blood Prince*, page 199
The lonely country road had looming hedgerows on either side, making the road seem even more narrow and gloomy.

heinous (**hay**-nus)
adjective Hateful, abominable, really really awful. / *Goblet of Fire*, page 594
The heinous behavior of Blackpool, the evil wizard, had enraged Willow's father, who threatened to hex Blackpool's racing worms unless he started being nicer to Willow.

heir (rhymes with **care**; sounds exactly like **air**)
noun Someone who will inherit the property or title of another when they die. / *Chamber of Secrets*, page 151
The prince, heir to the kingdom, had no interest in being king. He wanted to be a rock musician.

heirloom (**air**-loom)
noun A valuable object handed down from one generation to the next. / *Half-Blood Prince*, page 367
The castle was overflowing with heirlooms—oak furniture and old vases and gold lamps—from the king's parents and grandparents.

heliotrope (**hee**-lee-uh-trope)
adjective Pale purple, like the flowers on the heliotrope plant. / *Deathly Hallows*, page 238
"No, it's not light maroon…and it's not purple….and it's not lilac…I think it's heliotrope," said Fiona, trying to describe Bella's new hair color.

henceforth (**hens**-forth)
adverb From now on. / *Prisoner of Azkaban*, page 205
Henceforth, the king vowed always to test appliances before he bought them—at least any moat-sweepers.

henchman (**hench**-man)
noun A faithful supporter willing to do things illegal or violent in support of a leader. Plural: henchmen. / *Half-Blood Prince*, page 445
The duke's henchmen rode toward the castle, eager to steal the king's sheep and terrorize the villagers.

herbology (ur-**bol**-uh-jee)
noun The study of herbs. / *Chamber of Secrets*, page 89 / Note: In Potter's world, herbology is the study of magical plants and fungi. In Britain, this is pronounced "**Her**-bology, the study of **h**erbs," but in the U.S., the "h" is silent: "urbology, the study of urbs." Someone who studies herbs is an herbologist.
Blackpool got a book on herbology from the library—he wanted to find an herb that would improve the performance of his racing worms.

hew (rhymes with **brew**)
verb To cut or carve. Past tense: hewn. / *Order of the Phoenix*, page 695

Hewn in the tree was a giant "B," but Brilly insisted his Great Grandfather Brill must have done it years ago.

Hippogriff

hewn

See **hew** above.

hex (rhymes with **Tex**)

noun An evil curse. / *Chamber of Secrets*, page 38
Blackpool put a hex on Willow's puppies again, this time turning them into stinging nurch babies.

hex (rhymes with **Tex**)

verb To put an evil curse on someone or something. / *Goblet of Fire*, page 367
After Blackpool hexed Willow's puppies, turning them into stinging nurch babies, three of them stung him so badly he turned them back into puppies.

higgledy-piggledy (**hig**-ul-dee-**pig**-ul-dee)

adverb Jumbled together in a messy, confused way. / *Half-Blood Prince*, page 38
Dribbles' clean socks lay higgledy-piggledy in the drawer; no wonder he always seemed to be wearing two different-colored socks.

highflier (**hye**-fly-ur)

noun A person who is really successful at something. / *Half-Blood Prince*, page 84
Wildwood felt like a real highflier after rousing applause greeted his speech to the Chamber of Wizards meeting.

hilarity (hih-**lar**-ih-tee)

noun Exuberant cheerfulness and merriment. / *Half-Blood Prince*, page 303
There was great hilarity in the Haunted Forest—the horned owl was telling shaggy werewolf jokes.

hillock (**hil**-uk)

noun A little hill or mound. / *Goblet of Fire*, page 82
The mayor suggested a golf course for the meadow, taking advantage of the hillocks already there.

hilt (rhymes with **built**)

noun The handle of a knife or sword, where the blade is attached; sometimes used in the phrase "to the hilt," meaning completely. / *Chamber of Secrets*, page 320 (hilt); *Half-Blood Prince*, page 480 (to the hilt).
The hilt of the king's ceremonial sword was encrusted with rubies and emeralds, making it beautiful to look at but difficult to hold. So the king asked the Royal Swordmaker, whom he trusted to the hilt, to pry off the many jewels so the king could more easily hold the sword.

hindquarters (hynd-**kwawr**-turs)

noun The rear part of an animal with four legs. / *Prisoner of Azkaban*, page 117
It was difficult for the centaur to scratch his hindquarters—thank goodness for tree bark.

hinkypunk (**hing**-kee-punk)

noun In British folklore, a will o' the wisp, a ghostly flickering light sometimes seen at night over bogs. / *Goblet of Fire*, page 211 / Note: In Potter's world, a hinkypunk is a translucent creature that carries a lantern in one hand and hops on a single foot. Humans who follow this light may find themselves immersed in a marsh.
Elrod was certain he'd seen a hinkypunk down by the lake, but it's likely it was just lights reflecting off the water.

hip flask

See **flask** elsewhere in this dictionary.

hippogriff (**hip**-uh-grif)

noun A mythological flying creature with the wings, claws, and head of a griffin, and the

body and hindquarters of a horse. / *Prisoner of Azkaban*, page 114
Dribbles wondered: Why don't hippogriffs look more like hippopotamuses?

hitch (rhymes with **ditch**)

noun A snag or problem. / *Sorcerer's Stone*, page 238
Willow discovered a hitch in her latest plan—being invisible was great for sneaking around but not great for flirting.

hitch (rhymes with **ditch**)

verb To pull up or hike up, often said in relation to pants. / *Prisoner of Azkaban*, page 43
Elrod hitched up his pants, which were sagging almost to his knees.

hitherto (hith-ur-too)

adverb Up to now. / *Chamber of Secrets*, page 209
"Hitherto, I have put up with your antics, Brilly, but from now on…it's behave or be gone," warned the principal.

hives (rhymes with **dives**)

noun A condition in which the skin becomes very red and itchy. / *Half-Blood Prince*, page 208
The inept wizard broke out in terrible hives after practicing the *Maximus Hivo* spell in front of the mirror.

hobble (hob-ul)

verb To limp or to walk with difficulty because of painful feet or legs. / *Goblet of Fire*, page 232
The old witch slowly hobbled up the library steps—she was tired, but she really needed a good mystery to read.

hobnailed boots (hob-neyld boots)

noun Boots with short, heavy nails (hobnails) in the soles, to make them last longer and provide better traction; usually worn by workers and the military. / *Deathly Hallows*, page 449
The clicking sound in the market's aisles was Wildwood in his hobnailed boots, dashing in to get some drinks for his hardworking fence builders.

hoist (rhymes with **moist**)

verb To lift or raise up something heavy, usually with a piece of equipment—like a crane. / *Sorcerer's Stone*, page 251
The wizard was tempted to use his wand and a bit of magic to hoist the piano into his bedroom, but the piano movers wanted to earn their money.

hold in great esteem

See **esteem** elsewhere in this dictionary.

hollow (hol-oh)

noun A small, sheltered valley. / *Chamber of Secrets*, page 276
The hollow at the far end of the meadow was the usual place for the village's annual picnic.

hone (rhymes with **bone**)

verb To improve or make more effective; to perfect. / *Prisoner of Azkaban*, page 51
Brilly began to hone his skills as a troublemaker years ago, when he first discovered his kindergarten teacher was afraid of spiders.

hone in

phrase To move or advance toward something, or to focus on something. / *Deathly Hallows*, page 546
The ghostly hound moved closer and closer, honing in on its prey.

honeysuckle (hun-ee-suk-ul)

noun An outdoor climbing plant with fragrant yellow, pink, or white flowers. / *Goblet of Fire*, page 63
The honeysuckle had grown up the side of the greenhouse, and its blooms filled the air with the most lovely of smells.

hoodwink (hood-wink)

verb To trick or fool someone. / *Chamber of Secrets*, page 330
Brilly hoodwinked the mailman into believing there was a moaning ghost in the mailbox.

hoof

See **hooves** elsewhere in this dictionary

hooligan (hoo-lih-gun)

noun A noisy violent person; a hoodlum. /

Order of the Phoenix, page 11
"But Mom, I'm not a hooligan. I'm a fool-again!" joked Brilly.

hooves (rhymes with **moves**)
noun Plural of hoof, the tough, horny part on a horse's foot (also on the feet of cows, pigs, deer, etc.). / *Sorcerer's Stone*, page 254
"Wheee, my hooves hurt after a long day pulling the milk cart," said the old horse.

horde (rhymes with **board**; sounds exactly like **hoard**)
noun A large group. / *Goblet of Fire*, page 657
A horde of giant spiders marched up the basement wall, across the ceiling, and down the other side.

horizontal (hor-uh-**zon**-tul)
adjective Going sideways, level with the ground. / *Goblet of Fire*, page 86
The horizontal design on Bella's shirt made her look chunky.

hornbeam (**horn**-beem)
noun A tree producing a very hard, heavy wood. / *Goblet of Fire*, page 309
"I'm really disappointed," said Willow. "I thought 'hornbeam' sounded so magical but it's just a tree."

horned toad (hornd tohd)
noun Not a toad, but a lizard with hornlike spines on its head and a broad, flat body covered with scales. / *Goblet of Fire*, page 210
The giant horned toad, the village mascot, was feeling so poorly his scales ached.

horoscope (**hor**-uh-skope)
noun A detailed description of one's character and future, based on calculating the position of the stars and planets by one's date and time of birth. Very general horoscopes are printed in daily newspapers. / *Goblet of Fire*, page 212
The newspaper said Rupert's horoscope for today was, "You are a trusting sort, but don't believe everything you read."

horrific (hoh-**rih**-fik *or* haw-**rif**-ik)
adjective Causing horror. / *Goblet of Fire*, page 300
"I don't like camping out—there are horrific things out there in the woods!" worried Brady.

hosepipe (**hose**-pipe)
noun In British usage, a garden hose. / *Order of the Phoenix*, page 1
Being a wizard made it much easier to coil the hosepipe after watering the lawn.

hostilities (hos-**til**-uh-tees)
noun Literally, acts of war or warlike activities; more generally, a hostile situation varying from unfriendliness to ill will to actual fighting; used in the plural. / *Deathly Hallows*, page 123
Hostilities had broken out between Willow's father and Blackpool, the evil wizard.

hourglass (**our**-glass)
noun A glass container for measuring time; sand moves slowly from the top section to the bottom, taking exactly an hour to do so. / *Order of the Phoenix*, page 626 / Note: In Potter's world, hourglasses are used to time tests, and also to record House points; each of these is filled with jewels rather than sand.
The king turned over his hourglass—just an hour to go until *The Young and the Rustless* was on TV.

housecoat (**hows**-koht)
noun A woman's robe-like garment, long and loose, for wearing about the house. / *Half-Blood Prince*, page 46
Mrs. Fracket's housecoat had 15 safety pins pinned on the front, pockets filled with old handkerchiefs, and a hem that was finally—after many years—beginning to unravel.

hovel (**huv**-ul)
noun A small, wretched, humble dwelling. / *Order of the Phoenix*, page 412
The dwarf's miserable hovel was disgustingly filthy—time for the Fairy Maids to come and clean up the place.

hover (**huh**-vur)
verb To float or stay suspended in the air. / *Sorcerer's Stone*, page 148

The ghost of the former principal hovered near the classroom ceiling, pelting dozing children with erasers.

Ghost hovering near ceiling

hovercraft (huh-vur-kraft)
noun A vehicle that travels just above the surface of land or water on the cushion of air its engines produce beneath it. / *Chamber of Secrets*, page 204
The mayor's latest suggestion for village improvement was a fleet of hovercraft to take passengers across the lake.

hubbub (hub-ub)
noun An uproar caused by excitement and characterized by loud voices. / *Chamber of Secrets*, page 285
The hubbub gradually grew louder as the villagers debated what to do about the latest mysterious happenings in the meadow.

humbly (hum-blee)
adverb Respectfully, modestly, and feeling a little sorry for a situation. / *Deathly Hallows*, page 109
"I'm really sorry about the frog slime," said Dribbles humbly. "It wasn't my idea, but I didn't exactly stop Brilly from doing it, either."

humbug (hum-bug)
noun A British hard candy. / *Sorcerer's Stone*, page 62
Winston loved peppermint humbugs almost as much as chocolate ice cream.

humiliated (hyoo-**mil**-ee-ate-ud)
adjective Having lost some pride or dignity; being shamed. / *Deathly Hallows*, page 54
The cat felt a little humiliated when she accidentally tipped over the Temple of Dung (her cat box).

humiliation (hyoo-mil-ee-**ay**-shun)
noun The feeling of being embarrassed or mortified. / *Chamber of Secrets*, page 98
Oh the humiliation—the knight's dull sword couldn't even cut a cantaloupe in half.

humongous (hyoo-**mung**-gus or hyoo-**mong**-gus)
adjective Huge. / *Prisoner of Azkaban*, page 63
The humongous crowd poured out of the stadium after the Rolling Bones concert—it took hours before everyone got home.

humor (**hyoo**-mur)
verb To go along with someone else's mood or plans so as not to upset them. / *Half-Blood Prince*, page 135
Brilly's friends thought it best to humor him when he started plotting things like "lizards in the lunchroom." Sometimes he just gave up on his grand plans if you didn't argue with him.

hunch (rhymes with **bunch**)
verb To pull your head down between your shoulders and lean forward. / *Sorcerer's Stone*, page 294
Tamika hunched over her plate of chocolate-covered grasshoppers—they were her favorite dessert and no one else was going to get any.

hunchback (hunch-bak)
noun A person whose back is humped because their spine is abnormally curved. / *Goblet of Fire*, page 90
The rumor in the village was that a hunchback in the church tower rang the bells every hour, but most villagers thought it unlikely.

husbandry (huz-bun-dree)

noun The science of raising crops or animals. / *Half-Blood Prince*, page 486

Wildwood had incredible skills in animal husbandry; his friends joked he didn't have a green thumb, he had a furry and feathered one.

huskily (husk-uh-lee)

adverb In a somewhat hoarse and whispered way, from stress or strong emotion. / *Prisoner of Azkaban*, page 402

"Here, take this and run," said the thief huskily, handing his accomplice the prized golden statue from the museum's display case.

hygienic (hye-jee-**en**-ik)

adjective Sanitary or healthful. / *Sorcerer's Stone*, page 296

"Oh yuck, Elrod—you know the five-second rule—it's not hygienic to eat anything that's been on the floor more than five seconds. And that's been there for minutes, not seconds."

hypocrite (hip-uh-krit)

noun A person who pretends to have morals and beliefs that they don't actually have. / *Half-Blood Prince*, page 300

"You hypocrite, Blackpool. Don't pretend you care about little puppies after what you did last week," accused Willow.

hypothetical (hye-puh-**thet**-uh-kul)

adjective Not real, but possible or supposed. / *Half-Blood Prince*, page 499

"In a hypothetical situation, it would be possible to avoid having condos built on the meadow—but this is real, not hypothetical, and I'm not sure we can prevent it."

hysteria (hih-**stare**-ee-uh)

noun Extreme uncontrollable emotion, characterized by weeping, laughter, irrationality, etc. / *Half-Blood Prince*, page 21 / Note: In *Goblet of Fire* (page 236), a related noun, **hysterics**, means "a fit of uncontrollable laughter or weeping."

A wave of hysteria swept over the four girls when they realized they were stranded inside the Museum of Magic for the night.

hysterical (hih-**stare**-uh-kul)

adjective Uncontrolled emotionally. / *Order of the Phoenix*, page 582

Her hysterical sobbing during the sad parts of the movie drove everyone in the theater crazy.

I

idly (eyed-lee)
adverb In an idle way; casually or lazily. / *Chamber of Secrets*, page 308
The evil sorceress stood idly by as her pet boa constrictor slithered toward the frightened mouse.

ignite (ig-nite)
verb To set on fire. / *Deathly Hallows*, page 222
The spell was intended to ignite the campfire, but it burned the marshmallows instead—what a waste.

ignition (ig-nish-un)
noun The switch that starts the electrical system that ignites the fuel that—finally—starts the vehicle. / *Chamber of Secrets*, page 70
Annie, somewhat new to the principles of flying, frantically searched for the ignition on her broomstick.

ignominy (ig-nuh-min-ee)
noun Humiliation and disgrace. / *Deathly Hallows*, page 550
The ignominy of detention was bad enough, but when Mrs. Snodgrape was in charge, detention also involved singing the school song in front of all the other kids in detention.

ill-disposed (il-dih-spozd)
adjective Unsympathetic or having a negative attitude. / *Half-Blood Prince*, page 544
Hassan was ill-disposed toward potions class but he excelled in botany.

illicit (ih-lis-it)
adjective Unauthorized, illegal, or not permitted. / *Goblet of Fire*, page 471
The illicit practice of black magic was not worth the punishment.

illuminate (ih-loo-muh-nate)
verb To light up. / *Goblet of Fire*, page 119
One hundred carved pumpkins, each with a flickering candle, illuminated the village green every Halloween.

illustrious (ih-lus-tree-us)
adjective Distinguished and/or famous. / *Half-Blood Prince*, page 147
Although the illustrious botany teacher was widely known for his botanico-potion work, his students found him mind-numbingly boring.

imbibe (im-bybe)
verb To take in or absorb. / *Deathly Hallows*, page 304
No matter how much was poured into the enchanted glass, it never filled, as though the glass itself was imbibing the liquid.

imbue (im-byoo)
verb To impregnate, saturate, or fill. / *Deathly Hallows*, page 410
Imbued with focus and newfound strength (her boyfriend was watching), Annie surged ahead to win the broomstick race.

immaculate (ih-mak-yuh-lit)
adjective Spotlessly clean. / *Chamber of Secrets*, page 89
After the Fairy Maids cleaned the dwarf's home, it was so immaculate it actually glowed.

immaterial (im-uh-teer-ee-ul)
adjective Unimportant and not pertinent. / *Deathly Hallows*, page 488
"Brilly, lousy food in the cafeteria is immaterial; you're going to school to learn wizardry, not just to eat," reminded his father.

immerse (ih-murse)
verb To be involved deeply. / *Chamber of Secrets*, page 58
Blackpool was immersed in a book on the ancient secrets when the doorbell rang.

imminent (im-uh-nunt)
adjective Likely to happen at any moment. / *Order of the Phoenix*, page 414
The imminent arrival of the new potions master plunged his waiting students into an expectant silence.

immobilize (ih-moh-buh-lize)
verb To make immobile or incapable of

movement. / *Chamber of Secrets*, page 103
The jellyfish immobilized the swimmer with one light touch of its tentacles.

immortal (ih-**mor**-tul)
adjective Not mortal; living forever and never dying. / *Sorcerer's Stone*, page 220
The immortal alchemist worried that maybe this would be the year when the hundreds of candles on his birthday cake would set off the smoke alarm.

immortality (ih-mor-**tal**-uh-tee)
noun Unending life. / *Half-Blood Prince*, page 502
The vampire may have achieved immortality, but he could never enjoy a sunny day at the beach.

impacted (im-**pak**-tid)
adjective Tightly packed or packed down. / *Deathly Hallows*, page 323
The impacted ant hill had been crushed flat by the giant stomping across the meadow.

impale (im-**pale**)
verb Literally to pierce through; more generally, to be harmed or embarrassed by something you thought would harm another. / *Chamber of Secrets*, page 331
The wooden stake was meant for his rival, but the vampire tripped and was impaled on his own weapon.

impartial (im-**par**-shul)
adjective Fair; not partial or biased. / *Goblet of Fire*, page 187
It was difficult to find an impartial jury for the trial because everyone in the village knew of Blackpool's evil deeds.

impassive (im-**pas**-iv)
adjective Unmoving; calm and unemotional. / *Prisoner of Azkaban*, page 286
When the normally impassive Cyclops was invited to the dance, his one big eye filled with tears.

impeccably (im-**pek**-uh-blee)
adverb Flawlessly, perfectly. / *Goblet of Fire*, page 90
The fashionable mermaid was impeccably dressed for the Sea Prom in a glistening gown of seaweed and sea shells.

impede (im-**peed**)
verb To obstruct, hinder, or stop. / *Goblet of Fire*, page 140
The progress of the picnickers across the meadow was impeded by a swarm of very angry wasps.

impenetrable (im-**pen**-ih-truh-bul)
adjective Not penetrable; incapable of being understood. / *Prisoner of Azkaban*, page 427
Annie read the Beauty Spell over and over, but the impenetrable instructions were way too complicated.

imperceptibly (im-pur-**sep**-tuh-blee)
adverb So slightly it might not even be perceptible. / *Deathly Hallows*, page 10
The stage magician imperceptibly flipped the trap door switch to make the rabbit disappear.

imperiously (im-**peer**-ee-us-lee)
adverb In an imperious way: overbearingly and arrogantly. / *Goblet of Fire*, page 275
The queen imperiously ordered the Keeper of the Hounds to pay more attention to his hounds and less attention to the princess.

impersonate (im-**pur**-suh-nate)
verb To assume the characteristics or appearance of someone else, especially fraudulently. / *Half-Blood Prince*, page 87
Brilly was impersonating Madam Glinch and her droning lectures…when she appeared in the classroom doorway.

impertinent (im-**pur**-tin-unt)
adjective Rude, insolent, and presumptuous. / *Order of the Phoenix*, page 495
"That's an impertinent question, young lady," said Mrs. Snodgrape. "I am a happily married woman and, no, I'm not running off with a handsome stranger."

impervious (im-**pur**-vee-us)
adjective Incapable of being affected by something. / *Half-Blood Prince*, page 535
The Whale King was impervious to insults about his size.

impetus (im-**pih**-tus)
noun An impelling force or momentum. / *Deathly Hallows*, page 58

The sudden impetus of the skateboard plunging down the hill practically gave Nathan whiplash.

implode (im-plohd)

verb To burst inward (the opposite of explode). / *Half-Blood Prince*, page 417
The windows imploded when the blast caused all the air to be sucked out of the room.

imploringly (im-plor-ing-lee)

adverb In a begging, piteous way. / *Chamber of Secrets*, page 96
The Princess of the Deep imploringly asked the Prince of Tides to bring her a new seashell necklace—her last one had drifted away and gotten lost.

imposter (im-pos-tur)

noun A person who assumes the name, identity, or character of someone else. / *Goblet of Fire*, page 630
Clearly the pizza-delivery man was an imposter—the pizza box was full of anchovies but no pizza.

imprecation (im-prih-kay-shun)

noun A curse or insult. / *Order of the Phoenix*, page 349
Brilly's loud and rude imprecation, directed at the cafeteria manager, momentarily made him feel better, but it also got him suspended from school for a week.

imprecise (im-pree-sise)

adjective Not precise or clear. / *Sorcerer's Stone*, page 260
"Preparing potions," the wizard lectured, "is an imprecise art, sometimes depending more on instinct than exact measurements."

impregnable (im-preg-nuh-bul)

adjective Unconquerable; strong enough to be safe from attack. / *Goblet of Fire*, page 396
The impregnable castle was protected by hundreds of knights, huge kettles of boiling oil ready to be poured down on attackers, and the slime-filled moat.

imprint (im-print)

noun Literally, a mark or impression left by pressure; more generally, an influence or effect. / *Order of the Phoenix*, page 861 / Note: In Potter's world, wizards—at death—could leave behind an imprint of themselves as a ghost, like Nearly Headless Nick.
Brilly's award for Most Disruptive Student had an imprint of a broken broomstick on it.

improvise (im-pruh-vize)

verb To invent something to say off the top of your head; to make something up quickly. / *Deathly Hallows*, page 149
Asked to name seven famous wizards, Brilly improvised: Sleepy, Dopey, Grumpy....

impulse (im-puls)

noun A sudden urge or inclination to do something. / *Order of the Phoenix*, page 11
After an extensive play session with her catnip mouse, the cat had a sudden impulse to jump on her own shadow, to kiss the kitchen sponge, and then to turn several somersaults.

impunity (im-pyoo-nih-tee)

noun Exemption from any detrimental effects, including punishment, laughter, etc. / *Deathly Hallows*, page 52
Rupert's impressive double somersault off the diving board provided some impunity from taunts about his hot pink swimming trunks.

in convoy

See **convoy** elsewhere in this dictionary.

in due course

phrase To happen in the proper and natural order of things. / *Half-Blood Prince*, page 440
"In due course, Brilly, you'll more fully understand why we have rules about certain things, like jellyfish in the pool or compost in the drinking fountains."

in high dudgeon

phrase To experience a feeling of anger, resentment, or sullenness. / *Half-Blood Prince*, page 290
In high dudgeon, the queen stalked away from the table—the king had actually suggested she cut her own meat.

in league with

phrase To work together with someone, often secretly or sneakily. / *Prisoner of Azkaban*, page 342

Blackpool was in league with Klingster in planning the enchantment of the May Fete queen.

in the same league
> See **not in the same league** elsewhere in this dictionary.

in unison
> *phrase* All together; saying or doing the same thing at the same time. / *Goblet of Fire*, page 595
> In unison, the entire potions class poured the last ingredient into their cauldrons and the entire room was suddenly filled with a pulsating purple haze.

Pouring in unison

inadequacy (in-**ad**-ih-kwuh-see)
> *noun* The condition of being not adequate; a failing or a lack. / *Deathly Hallows*, page 454
> The impoverished leprechaun, who had no gold at all, somewhat made up for his inadequacy with a charming Irish accent.

inadvertent (in-ud-**vur**-tunt)
> *adjective* Not intentional. / *Deathly Hallows*, page 359
> It was totally inadvertent—he hadn't meant to hex the library book and have it turn to dust.

inadvisable (in-ud-**vie**-zuh-bul)
> *adjective* Not advised; unwise. / *Order of the Phoenix*, page 531
> It's inadvisable to get anywhere near the Sucking Quicksand Quagmire.

inarticulate (in-are-**tik**-yuh-lit)
> *adjective* Not articulate (clear and understandable) or said without ordinary words (like a yell of rage). / *Half-Blood Prince*, page 603
> Bella's inarticulate sobbing over her breakup with Bubba could be heard all over school.

inattentively (in-uh-**ten**-tiv-lee)
> *adverb* Not attentive; not paying attention. / *Goblet of Fire*, page 337
> While inattentively flying through the garden, tiny Tinkles, the fairy, smashed head-on into a butterfly.

inaudible (in-**od**-uh-bul)
> *adjective* Not audible; incapable of being heard. / *Half-Blood Prince*, page 205
> If the mutterings of Blackpool, the evil wizard, were inaudible, it usually meant he was just practicing a new enchantment.

incandescent (in-kun-**des**-unt)
> *adjective* Lit up and glowing; the phrase "incandescent with rage" means almost glowing with anger. / *Order of the Phoenix*, page 581
> The principal was incandescent with rage over Brilly's latest mayhem.

incantation (in-kan-**tay**-shun)
> *noun* A magical spell or charm. / *Prisoner of Azkaban*, page 237
> The incantation for getting rid of meddlesome spirits is *Adios Spiritus*.

incense (in-**sens**)
> *verb* To make someone angry or enraged. / *Order of the Phoenix*, page 812
> Brilly incensed just about everyone when he thawed frozen cockroaches in the school microwave.

incentive (in-**sen**-tiv)
> *noun* Something that encourages you to do something. / *Order of the Phoenix*, page 828
> The thrill of knowledge just wasn't enough incentive to make Rupert study for his geography of Forgotten Places quiz.

incline (in-**kline**)
noun A sloped or slanted surface. / *Deathly Hallows*, page 300
The village skateboard park had one steep incline that Nungie was trying to master in his wheelchair.

inclusion (in-**kloo**-zhun)
noun The condition of being included. / *Deathly Hallows*, page 179
The inclusion of Blackpool, the evil wizard, in the Day of the Dead festivities was probably a mistake.

incoherent (in-koh-**heer**-unt)
adjective Not coherent or not making any sense. / *Order of the Phoenix*, page 448
The boy shouted a warning about the giant sea urchin, but he was shaking so hard he was practically incoherent.

incomprehensible (in-kom-prih-**hen**-suh-bul)
adjective Not comprehensible or understandable. / *Goblet of Fire*, page 457
The incomprehensible instructions for his new Big Bug Trappah were useless, so Blackpool just plugged it in and waited for the giant cockroach to walk into the kitchen.

incomprehension (in-kom-prih-**hen**-shun)
noun A lack of comprehension or understanding. / *Half-Blood Prince*, page 334
Dribbles' look of incomprehension wasn't unusual—math was neither his best subject nor his favorite.

inconsequentially (in-kon-sih-**kwen**-shul-ee)
adverb In an insignificant, trivial, not very important way. / *Half-Blood Prince*, page 219
In the middle of the outdoor botany lecture, Willow looked skyward and said inconsequentially, "Don't those clouds look like big, white, floppy caterpillars?"

incontrovertible (in-kon-truh-**vur**-tuh-bul)
adjective Not open to question or dispute. / *Deathly Hallows*, page 693
It's an incontrovertible truth—dull guillotine blades are remarkably ineffective and terribly messy.

incredulity (in-krih-**doo**-lih-tee *or* in-krih-**dyoo**-lih-tee)
noun An inability or unwillingness to believe. / *Order of the Phoenix*, page 575
When Oscar said he could make himself invisible, his friends regarded him with incredulity—until he disappeared.

incredulous (in-**kredj**-uh-lus)
adjective Not credulous; skeptical and inclined not to believe something. / *Order of the Phoenix*, page 323
The mayor's incredulous look said it all—no, the village would not celebrate International Women's Day by holding a bathing suit contest.

incumbent (in-**kum**-bunt)
adjective Resting upon as a duty or obligation. / *Order of the Phoenix*, page 523
With his parents out for the evening, it was incumbent upon Rupert to assure his little brother that there was no monster under the bed.

incurably (in-**kyoor**-uh-blee)
adverb Hopelessly; incapable of changing. / *Prisoner of Azkaban*, page 19 / Note: In Potter's world, Uncle Vernon told Aunt Marge that Harry was attending St. Brutus's Secure Center for Incurably Criminal Boys.
Many of the villagers considered Brilly incurably impossible, but he wasn't really a bad guy at heart.

incursion (in-**kur**-zhun)
noun An invasion. / *Order of the Phoenix*, page 532
The Ant Army made a strategic incursion into the kitchen, sending one battalion left to the spilled sugar and another under the table and toward the sink.

indecisively (in-dih-**sye**-siv-lee)
adverb Not decisive; in an irresolute and undecided way. / *Deathly Hallows*, page 100
The bee flew indecisively around the garden, tempted by blossoms in every direction and unsure just where to begin.

indignation (in-dig-**nay**-shun)
noun Righteous anger at something considered unjust or unfair. / *Prisoner of Azkaban*, page 185
Ethelbell's indignation seemed entirely justified—when was someone else going to volunteer to host the monthly Sisters of Sorcery meeting?

indignity (in-**dig**-nih-tee)
noun A humiliating insult or injury to one's dignity. / *Order of the Phoenix,* page 864
"The indignity of it," moaned Madam Glinch. "My false teeth fell out right in the middle of class."

indigo (**in**-dih-go)
adjective Deep blue-violet. / *Order of the Phoenix,* page 16
The peacock proudly spread his fan of feathers—iridescent indigo blue, glistening green, and fiery orange.

indisposed (in-dih-**spohzd**)
adjective Mildly ill. / *Goblet of Fire,* page 435
Brilly told his mom he was indisposed and couldn't go to school, but she impatiently suggested he get himself un-indisposed immediately.

indistinguishable (in-dih-**sting**-gwish-uh-bul)
adjective Not distinguishable; impossible to tell apart. / *Half-Blood Prince,* page 343
Unfortunately, a Flesh-Eating Fern is almost indistinguishable from an ordinary Frondo Fern.

induct (in-**dukt**)
verb To bring in as a member. / *Order of the Phoenix,* page 96
Chuckles, the usually lousy clown, was surprised and thrilled to be inducted as a member of the Order of Wise Crackers.

indulgence (in-**dul**-jence)
noun Lenience or humoring; yielding to the wishes of another. / *Order of the Phoenix,* page 155
Dribbles expected a little indulgence from his Levitation teacher when he hobbled in with a sprained ankle, but she made him levitate, crutches and all.

inept (in-**ept**)
adjective Lacking in skill or aptitude. / *Chamber of Secrets,* page 174
The inept wizard-in-training didn't know one end of his wand from the other.

ineptitude (in-**ep**-tih-tood)
noun Lack of skill. / *Half-Blood Prince,* page 558
His ineptitude—after seven months of wand practice—was hard to understand.

inert (in-**urt**)
adjective Unmoving. / *Half-Blood Prince,* page 612
The Hopeless Shapeless Things were inert, just sitting on the crypt, waiting....

inevitable (in-**ev**-ih-tuh-bul)
adjective Sure to happen; unavoidable. / *Order of the Phoenix,* page 595
It was inevitable that the magical dancing shoes would eventually need new soles.

inexorably (in-**eks**-sur-uh-blee)
adverb Inevitably and unavoidably. / *Half-Blood Prince,* page 566
Inexorably, the molten lava ran down the heaving sides of the volcano, toward the tiny town in the valley below.

inexplicable (in-ek-**splih**-kuh-bul *or* in-ik-**splik**-uh-bul)
adjective Not explainable. / *Half-Blood Prince,* page 409
Bella's failure on the easy math quiz seemed inexplicable unless you knew she'd just broken up with her longtime boyfriend.

inextricably (in-ek-**strik**-uh-blee)
adverb Hopelessly involved or entangled. / *Half-Blood Prince,* page 520
The success of the Flufftones Ball was inextricably linked to how good the music was.

infamous (**in**-fuh-muhs)
adjective Widely and unfavorably known. / *Prisoner of Azkaban,* page 37
Blackpool was the village's most infamous wizard, though that wasn't really much of an honor.

infamy (**in**-fuh-mee)
noun Shameful, outrageous conduct. / *Half-Blood Prince,* page 617
The infamy of the Thieves Guild was well-known throughout the village.

infatuation (in-fach-yoo-**ay**-shun)
noun An absorbing passion or interest. / *Half-Blood Prince,* page 186

Willow's infatuation with the new boy was getting tiresome—she talked about him endlessly.

infectious (in-**fek**-shus)

adjective Catching; easily spread from one person to another. / *Goblet of Fire*, page 95
The sadness over the death of the village mascot was infectious—soon everyone was crying.

infernal (in-**fur**-nul)

adjective Outrageous or damnable. / *Sorcerer's Stone*, page 76
"You and your infernal moat-sweeper," raged the queen. "We still have a dirty moat, and we have this clunker of a non-working, ugly, useless moat-sweeper."

inferno (in-**fur**-no)

noun Hellish fire. / *Deathly Hallows*, page 632
The fire on the edge of the Haunted Forest was an inferno while it lasted, but quick magical work by the village fire wizards eventually put it out.

Inferno

infest (in-**fest**)

verb To invade in great numbers; usually said of vermin (rats) or other unpleasant pests. / *Order of the Phoenix*, page 453
The moldy basement was infested with maggoty grubs and mysterious wriggling purple larva.

infestation (in-fuh-**stay**-shun)

noun A troubling invasion. / *Order of the Phoenix*, page 102
The locust infestation happened every 17 years, and it was nasty.

infiltrate (**in**-fill-trate *or* in-**fill**-trate)

verb To move into, with evil intent. / *Deathly Hallows*, page 33
"Strange celestial forces have infiltrated my cosmic sight," intoned Mrs. Sprocket, the village seer and fortune-teller, "and I am unable to perceive a single thing today. Call back tomorrow."

infinite (**in**-fuh-nit)

adjective Immeasurably boundless and limitless. / *Prisoner of Azkaban*, page 297
With infinite patience, Mrs. Snodgrape went over the potion ingredients for the project one more time.

infinitesimal (in-fin-ih-**tes**-uh-mul)

adjective Immeasurably small. / *Order of the Phoenix*, page 474
There was an infinitesimal pause after the wizard waved his wand, and then BOOM, the lawn was all mowed.

infirmary (in-**fur**-muh-ree)

noun A hospital or a place serving as a hospital. / *Chamber of Secrets*, page 228
Dylan's visit to the school infirmary began shortly after a really unpleasant meal in the cafeteria.

inflection (in-**flek**-shun)

noun A change in the tone of a voice. / *Order of the Phoenix*, page 698
It was that very slight change in inflection in Madam Glinch's voice that indicated she was about to lose her temper.

influential (in-**floo**-en-shul)

adjective Having influence. / *Half-Blood Prince*, page 145
The wandmaker showed his new hybrid wand to the influential investor, who was quite impressed.

infringement (in-**frinj**-munt)

noun A violation or transgression of a rule. / *Order of the Phoenix*, page 417
"Any infringement of these rules about appropriate clothing and there will be trouble," warned the principal.

infusion (in-**fyoo**-shun)

noun A liquid made by steeping or soaking, without boiling; tea, for example, is an infusion. / *Sorcerer's Stone*, page 137
The magical infusion of hay and seaweed helped the baby seahorse fall sleep.

ingenious (in-**jeen**-yus)

adjective Clever and original. / *Goblet of Fire*, page 279
The Royal Plumber had an ingenious suggestion for the moat slime problem—a herd of giant slime-eating slugs!

ingenuity (in-juh-**new**-ih-tee)

noun Cleverness and inventiveness. / *Half-Blood Prince*, page 428
The ingenuity of Bella's solution to the math problem astounded the teacher.

ingrained (in-**graynd**)

adjective Firmly fixed. / *Deathly Hallows*, page 127
One of Wildwood's ingrained habits was coffee at Star Duck's every morning.

ingratiating (in-**gray**-shee-ay-ting)

adjective Charming and pleasing. / *Order of the Phoenix*, page 438
Brilly's ingratiating smile won over many people who otherwise might have dismissed him as an annoying troublemaker.

inhuman (in-**hyoo**-mun)

adjective Not human; cruel, brutal, and lacking all kindness and compassion. / *Half-Blood Prince*, page 604
With an eerie moan, the inhuman Hopeless Shapeless Thing began to wrap itself around the crypt.

inject (in-**jekt**)

verb To introduce or insert. / *Chamber of Secrets*, page 304
The Sea Prom was off to a slow start—time to inject some fun into the proceedings, thought the merpeople.

inkling (**ink**-ling)

noun A hint or indication. / *Chamber of Secrets*, page 289
She had an inkling all was not well when the clamoring bells and blaring sirens began to sound.

inkwell (**ink**-well)

noun A small bottle holding ink. / *Order of the Phoenix*, page 246
The wizard's inkwell magically refilled itself nightly.

inordinate (in-**or**-din-it)

adjective Immoderate and excessive. / *Half-Blood Prince*, page 379
The tent demons spent an inordinate amount of time pulling up tent pegs; it was a very satisfying task.

inquiry (in-**kwir**-ee)

noun An investigation into an incident. / *Chamber of Secrets*, page 88
The investigation into the explosion in the janitor's closet determined that both Brilly (fireworks) and the janitor (illegal flammable materials) were at fault.

inquisitor (in-**kwiz**-ih-tur)

noun An official who asks questions in an unrelenting, harsh manner. / *Order of the Phoenix*, page 306
The inquisitor at the investigation had little patience with the situation.

inquisitorial (in-**kwiz**-ih-**tor**-ee-ul)

adjective Questioning and inquisitive. / *Half-Blood Prince*, page 267
The janitor gave Brilly an inquisitorial look when the school guard ran up to say there was something weird going on with the drinking fountains.

inscrutable (in-**skrew**-tuh-bul)

adjective Mysterious and impossible to comprehend or interpret. / *Half-Blood Prince*, page 139
Rupert's actions seemed inscrutable, but his little brother knew why he was putting an anti-monster spell on the house.

insensible (in-**sen**-suh-bul)

adjective Unconscious; having no senses (hearing, seeing, etc.) because of being knocked out. / *Deathly Hallows*, page 593
Tiny Tinkles, the fairy, crashed into the spider's web and knocked herself insensible, then awoke to find the spider hungrily eyeing her.

insinuation (in-sin-yoo-**ay**-shun)
noun An indirect, sly negative suggestion or hint. / *Order of the Phoenix*, page 365
"I do not appreciate the insinuations you've made about me," sniffed a hurt Willow.

insistence (in-**sis**-tunse)
noun Persistence and firmness about something. / *Goblet of Fire*, page 612
The little girl's insistence about "something strange outside" finally convinced her mother to come see—and it was a huge flock of flying frogs.

insolence (in-suh-luns)
noun Arrogant, rude, and disrespectful behavior. / *Deathly Hallows*, page 130
Blackpool's insolence got him into trouble constantly—like the time he shouted "You udder prat!" at the milkman. He never got his milk delivered again after that.

instability (in-stuh-**bil**-uh-tee)
noun A tendency to be unstable, irresolute, or erratic. / *Half-Blood Prince*, page 212
Mrs. Bird's general instability (particularly her always wearing hats with live parakeets on them) had resulted in her nickname—KooKoo Bird.

instinct (**in**-stinkt)
noun An inborn way of behaving, characteristic of a particular animal; also, a powerful motivation or impulse. / *Chamber of Secrets*, page 278
It was the cat's instinct to chase the mouse. It was the puppy's instinct to chase the cat. And it was Blackpool's instinct to turn the puppy into a rat. We all do what we do.

instinctively (in-**stink**-tiv-lee)
adverb In a way related to instinct; impulsively or unthinking. / *Goblet of Fire*, page 194
Instinctively, Bella knew there was a difference between frog spit and frog slime, but it was difficult—and yucky— to explain.

insubordination (in-suh-bor-dih-**nay**-shun)
noun An act of defiance of authority. / *Order of the Phoenix*, page 473
Brilly didn't think calling the cafeteria manager "a crazed poisoner" was insubordination—he considered it more an honest criticism.

insubstantial (in-sub-**stan**-shul)
adjective Not substantial; weak. / *Order of the Phoenix*, page 60
The light from the flashlight was too insubstantial to show the whole tree monster at once, which was probably a good thing given how terrifying he was.

insufferable (in-**suf**-ur-uh-bul)
adjective Annoying and unbearable. / *Prisoner of Azkaban*, page 172
Parker's insufferable bragging about his new, fast broomstick was especially annoying to his brother, whose broomstick was currently being used to sweep the kitchen floor.

insurmountable (in-sur-**moun**-tuh-bul)
adjective Impossible to surmount or overcome. / *Order of the Phoenix*, page 761
To an ant, a puddle must seem insurmountable.

intelligible (in-**tel**-ih-juh-bul)
adjective Understandable and clear. / *Deathly Hallows*, page 294
Julio thought his dad was the only person who could make chemistry seem intelligible.

intensity (in-**ten**-sih-tee)
noun Intense concentration and focus. / *Order of the Phoenix*, page 588
The intensity of the turtle's glare seemed even more extreme because it took him so long to turn his head.

intent (in-**tent**)
adjective Determined and resolved. / *Half-Blood Prince*, page 436
Dribbles was so intent on getting the potion ingredients just right that he didn't notice when his cauldron started boiling over.

intention (in-**ten**-shun)
noun An action that one intends to follow. / *Goblet of Fire*, page 294
"It's my intention to become a rock drummer whether you like it or not," insisted the prince to his parents.

interference (in-tur-**feer**-unce)
noun The act of interfering or getting

involved, usually in a hindering or obstructive way. / *Prisoner of Azkaban,* page 233

Annie rudely buzzed several pedestrians with her broomstick, an interference that caused several of them to flatten to the ground to avoid her.

interim (in-tur-um)

adjective Temporary or provisional. / *Deathly Hallows,* page 244

"During my extended leave of absence," announced the principal, "Madam Glinch will be in charge as interim principal."

interject (in-tur-jekt)

verb To interrupt, or to insert between two other things. / *Prisoner of Azkaban,* page 215

"May I interject a comment?" Wildwood politely asked, after the mayor and Blackpool had been loudly arguing for 15 minutes.

intermittent (in-tur-**mit**-unt)

adjective Stopping for awhile, then starting again. / *Order of the Phoenix,* page 454

Intermittent boos greeted the long list of homework being assigned for spring vacation.

interrogate (in-**ter**-uh-gate)

verb To formally ask questions of someone. / *Chamber of Secrets,* page 213

The traffic judge interrogated Blackpool about his ticket for "broomstick flying through a stop sign."

interrogation (in-ter-uh-**gay**-shun)

noun The time during which someone is questioned. / *Goblet of Fire,* page 693

Throughout his interrogation, Blackpool maintained he hadn't "run" the stop sign, he had very cautiously, carefully, and slowly drifted through and over it.

interval (in-tur-vul)

noun A space between things. / *Goblet of Fire,* page 493

The knight requested that tiny golden daggers be sewn on his cape at precise intervals of 1.25 inches.

intervene (in-tur-**veen**)

verb To come between two disputing sides; to intercede or mediate. / *Order of the Phoenix,* page 653

When the argument between the two seahorses got too heated, the octopus had to intervene.

intervening (in-tur-**veen**-ing)

adjective Occurring between two events or points in time. / *Deathly Hallows,* page 14

In the intervening months, after the really bad report card and before graduation, Bella realized she'd better think about her schoolwork more and her appearance less.

intestines (in-**tes**-tins)

noun The lower digestive system, specifically the large and small intestines; usually used in the plural. / *Half-Blood Prince,* page 70

His intestines were rumbling and gurgling and complaining—too much fried okra last night.

intimate (in-tuh-mate)

verb To hint, imply, or suggest. / *Deathly Hallows,* page 727

Although Merlin had intimated that he would retire as the Grand Wizard, the official announcement was still a shock.

intimidate (in-tim-ih-date)

verb To fill with fear; to frighten; to compel someone to do something by threats. / *Half-Blood Prince,* page 520

Blackpool knew he couldn't intimidate the judge, and he couldn't enchant him. He'd just have to pay his traffic ticket.

intone (in-**tone**)

verb To say or recite in a monotone. / *Order of the Phoenix,* page 450

"Now we'll jump ahead a few months to April in the year 200 BC…," intoned the lecturer, unaware that every single student was asleep.

intrusion (in-**troo**-zhun)

noun The act of intruding or interrupting suddenly. / *Half-Blood Prince,* page 341

"Forgive my intrusion, but I thought you'd like to know there's a very large carrot sitting on a rock in your garden."

intrusively (in-**troo**-siv-lee)

adverb In an intruding, unwelcome way. / *Deathly Hallows,* page 392

Rupert's little brother was often intrusively annoying; worst of all was when he kept repeating exactly everything Rupert said.

intuitive (in-**too**-ih-tiv)
adjective Understanding immediately and naturally without being taught. / *Half-Blood Prince*, page 378
Annie had an intuitive grasp of broomstick take-offs, but landings were going to take some practice.

invertebrate (in-**vur**-tuh-brit)
noun Animals without a backbone, like insects or mollusks. / *Order of the Phoenix*, page 321
The annual Parade of the Invertebrates took place along the village's Main Street—the snails and slugs came first, then the worms, jellyfish, starfish, and so on, ending with great swarms of various insects.

invincible (in-**vin**-suh-bul)
adjective Unconquerable; unable to be subdued. / *Half-Blood Prince*, page 506
Rupert got a few letters mixed up: The spell that was supposed to make him strong and *invincible* instead made him *invisible*.

involuntary (in-**vol**-un-tare-ee)
adjective Not voluntary; unconscious and unintentional. / *Goblet of Fire*, page 213
She gave an involuntary shudder—just thinking about the bloody-mouthed vulture was terrifying.

irascible (ih-**ras**-uh-bul)
adjective Short-tempered and irritable. / *Order of the Phoenix*, page 730
The irascible witch was known to throw frozen bat wings at passersby if they stopped to ask her directions.

irksome (**urk**-sum)
adjective Annoying, irritating, exasperating. / *Chamber of Secrets*, page 266
The monster chicken found it irksome that everyone expected her to lay a 50-pound egg every single day.

ironclad (**eye**-ern-klad)
adjective Unbreakable, as if encased in iron. / *Half-Blood Prince*, page 616

For once Brilly had an ironclad excuse—he'd been home sick when the school toilets stopped working.

ironic (eye-**ron**-ik)
adjective Meaning the opposite of what is actually said or done. / *Order of the Phoenix*, page 745
"Isn't it ironic that Butch is a famous soccer player but he's happiest taking care of baby giraffes and rhinos?"

irresolute (ih-**rez**-uh-loot)
adjective Not resolute; doubtful or uncertain. / *Chamber of Secrets*, page 255
Facing the giant cockroach, Blackpool's usually unshakable faith in his magical skills was suddenly the tiniest bit irresolute.

irretrievable (ih-ruh-**tree**-vuh-bul)
adjective Not retrievable; impossible to recover or change. / *Order of the Phoenix*, page 821
"Blackpool, I'm afraid my goodwill toward you is gone, irretrievable—how can I ever forgive you turning my puppies into rats?" asked Willow.

irrevocably (ih-**rev**-uh-kuh-blee)
adverb In a way that cannot be revoked or changed; irreversibly. / *Half-Blood Prince*, page 161
"You are irrevocably beyond my forgetting and my forgiving," she shouted.

isolation (eye-suh-**lay**-shun)
noun A separation; being kept apart. / *Goblet of Fire*, page 63
For most villagers, the isolation from the rest of the world made them unaware of things like iPods or video games. The king, however, did love his wide-screen TV.

J

jackal (jak-ul)
noun A wild dog, a little smaller than a wolf; jackals generally hunt in packs. / *Goblet of Fire*, page 664
The vicious jackals growled and drooled as they circled the wounded coyote.

jaunt (rhymes with **haunt**)
noun A short trip, usually for pleasure. / *Order of the Phoenix*, page 520
Brief jaunts away from the castle were okay, but the king really didn't like to travel much.

jauntiness (jawn-tee-ness)
noun A sprightly, easygoing manner. / *Order of the Phoenix*, page 317
Blackpool's usual jauntiness turned cranky when the mayor stopped by to deliver Blackpool's village tax bill.

jaunty (jawn-tee)
adjective Sprightly and perky, with an easy confidence. / *Chamber of Secrets*, page 33
"I'm home, Mom," called Brilly in a jaunty tone, hoping his mother wouldn't ask where he'd been.

javelin (jav-lin *or* jav-uh-lin)
noun A light spear thrown with one hand as a weapon or in a competition. / *Sorcerer's Stone*, page 149
Hassan tossed the javelin farther than anyone else in gym class, but unfortunately it went through the principal's car window and embedded itself in the front seat.

jest (rhymes with **test**)
verb To joke or banter, especially saying things you don't really mean. / *Order of the Phoenix*, page 784
"Surely you jest," said Dr. Greenteeth to the really angry man. "You can't possibly be offering me the opportunity to do that to myself."

jibe (rhymes with **tribe**)
noun An unkind comment or joke. / *Half-Blood Prince*, page 247
"That was a mean jibe, Blackpool. You know Willow doesn't like jokes about turning puppies into rats."

jig (rhymes with **pig**)
noun A lively dance. / *Sorcerer's Stone*, page 241
Tamika was so happy that she danced a jig when she finally finished her paper on "Body Odor in Shaggy-Coated Monsters."

jigger (jig-ur)
adjective Confounded or damned; usually used in a phrase like "I'm jiggered if I know," equivalent to "I'm damned if I know." / *Half-Blood Prince*, page 268
"I'm jiggered if I remember," said Winston honestly when Mrs. Snodgrape asked what the ingredients were for a mini-max size-changing potion.

jinx (rhymes with **links**)
noun A hex; bad luck that seems to have been caused by someone or something. / *Half-Blood Prince*, page 208
Nathan jinxed his skateboard—it was the only way he could keep everyone from borrowing it.

jinx (rhymes with **links**)
verb To place a jinx on someone or something. / *Sorcerer's Stone*, page 190
It was Nathan who'd jinxed his skateboard—it was the only way he could keep everyone from borrowing it.

jocularly (jok-yuh-lur-lee)
adverb In a joking or jesting way. / *Half-Blood Prince*, page 537
The bartender jocularly suggested that a Foaming Dragon's Blood Martini might set Wildwood to breathing fire and flying home.

joint (rhymes with **point**)
noun A large piece of meat with a bone in it. / *Order of the Phoenix*, page 208

At his annual banquet, the king served joints of beef, though a few guests opted for the Tofu Surprise.

jostle (joss-ul)
verb To bump and push while moving. / *Sorcerer's Stone*, page 93
In the elementary school corridors, the sixth graders jostled the fifth graders, the fifth graders jostled the fourth graders, the fourth graders jostled the third graders…and the third graders looked for the second graders, who were hiding under their desks.

jovial (joh-vee-ul)
adjective Friendly, hearty, and happy. / *Goblet of Fire*, page 254
The jovial mayor loved sitting on the park bench on the village green, greeting everyone who passed by.

jowls (rhymes with howls)
noun The lower cheeks, an area that in older or overweight people hangs down a bit; often used in the plural. / *Chamber of Secrets*, page 125
The fleshy jowls on Great Grandfather Brill's face shook with laughter as he recalled some of the mischief he'd gotten into as a kid.

judder (jud-dur)
verb To vibrate or shake violently. / *Order of the Phoenix*, page 130
The elevator in the village hall juddered badly and terrified everyone who used it. Luckily, it only had to go up one floor.

jumper (jum-pur)
noun In British usage, a pullover sweater. / *Order of the Phoenix*, page 502
"Put your jumper on, dear," urged Winston's mum. "It's chilly out today."

junction (junk-shun)
noun An intersection of two roads or paths. / *Goblet of Fire*, page 625
The junction of the Weeping Highway and Sorrow Lane was badly in need of repair.

jut (rhymes with hut)
verb To stick out or to project. / *Chamber of Secrets*, page 191
Blackpool's jaw jutted defiantly when he saw the peculiar beast coming toward him—then he realized it was just Elrod walking backwards.

K

kappa (kah-pah)

noun In Japanese folklore, a water sprite. / *Goblet of Fire*, page 211 / Note: In Potter's world, a kappa is a water-dweller, somewhat like a scaly monkey, that strangles people who wander into the kappa's pond.
Once Elrod heard about kappas, he never went near the lake, though actually he should have worried more about the lake's giant leeches.

keen (rhymes with **lean**)

adjective Eager and enthusiastic. / *Sorcerer's Stone*, page 59
Fiona was really keen to try the new swamp aerobics class.

keening (keen-ing)

adjective Like wailing, usually for someone who has died. / *Deathly Hallows*, page 619
The sound of keening cries echoed through the village when the village mascot—a giant horned toad—suddenly died.

keep your nose to the grindstone

phrase To work really hard and steadily, paying close attention to your task. / *Order of the Phoenix*, page 226
"Just keep your nose to the grindstone, Madam Glinch. This school year will end eventually," counseled the principal.

keepsake (keep-sake)

noun Something given or kept as a token of friendship or remembrance. / *Deathly Hallows*, page 127
The princess gave a keepsake to the cute new Knight of the Hounds—a small framed picture of herself.

kelpie (kel-pee)

noun In Scottish folklore, a water demon shaped like a horse. / *Half-Blood Prince*, page 562
The Loch Ness monster is a kelpie—who knew?

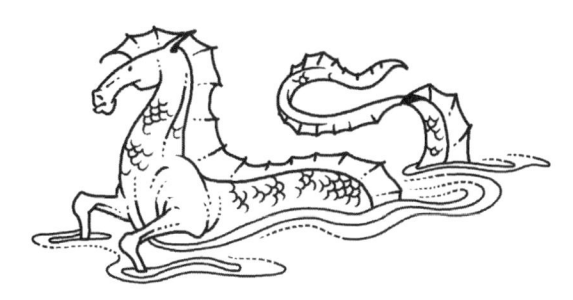

Kelpie

kerfuffle (ker-fuf-ul)

noun A commotion. / *Order of the Phoenix*, page 25
There was quite a kerfuffle at the Castle Regatta—first the prince fell in the moat, two knights in armor almost drowned getting him out, and then three boats rammed the drawbridge.

killjoy (kil-joy)

noun A spoilsport; someone who "kills joy," or ruins things for everyone else. / *Order of the Phoenix*, page 606
Blackpool could be such a killjoy—in the middle of the Parade of the Invertebrates he started hollering about unfair working conditions for worms.

kilt (rhymes with **tilt**)

noun A short, pleated tartan skirt, originally from the Scottish Highlands and generally worn by men. / *Goblet of Fire*, page 75
The king's best kilt was at the cleaners and wouldn't be back in time for the Scottish Games; he'd have to wear one of his old moth-eaten ones.

kindle (kin-dul)

verb To glow or stir up. / *Sorcerer's Stone*, page 247
A mischievous light kindled in Brilly's eyes—if he pretended to have a heart attack, maybe he'd be sent home from school.

kip (rhymes with **nip**)
verb In British slang, to sleep or nap, usually not in one's own bed. / *Sorcerer's Stone*, page 60
"Just kip on the sofa," said Winston. "I'll wake you if anything exciting happens."

kipper (kip-pur)
noun A salted and smoked fish, a favorite British breakfast food. / *Chamber of Secrets*, page 86
Wildwood loved kippers and eggs for Sunday breakfast.

kissing gate (kiss-ing gate)
noun In British usage, a gate in a narrow enclosure that lets only one person pass at a time. / *Deathly Hallows*, page 324
"Look out, gangway, I'm coming through the kissing gate!"

klaxonlike (klak-sun-like)
adjective Sounding like a klaxon, a loud electric horn. / *Order of the Phoenix*, page 353
The klaxonlike sound echoing through the village streets signaled the start of the Castle Regatta.

knack (rhymes with **whack**)
noun A talent or skill. / *Sorcerer's Stone*, page 297
Dribbles had the knack of knowing exactly when it was mealtime.

knave (rhymes with **cave**; sounds exactly like **nave**)
noun An unprincipled or untrustworthy person. / *Prisoner of Azkaban*, page 100
"You rude knave!" the novice jousting knight shouted at his opponent. "You just poked me!"

knead (rhymes with **bead**; sounds exactly like **need**)
verb To press and rub. / *Goblet of Fire*, page 22
Mrs. Snodgrape kneaded her forehead wearily—it was only 10 a.m. and already her Introductory Potions class was driving her crazy.

knickerbocker glory (nik-ur-bok-ur glor-ee)
noun In British usage, an elaborate ice cream sundae made with several scoops of ice cream plus chopped fruit, fruit sauce, whipped cream, nuts, a custardy sauce, and a cherry. / *Sorcerer's Stone*, page 26
"Just one knickerbocker glory a day, that's all I ask," said Winston dreamily.

knickerbockers (nik-ur-bok-urs)
noun Old-fashioned boy's pants, short and loose and gathered in just below the knees; similar to plus-fours, which are somewhat longer and baggier; used in the plural. / *Sorcerer's Stone*, page 32
Winston's mother insisted he wear knickerbockers to his grandfather's birthday party, but he hated them—"I look like an old golfer."

knickers (nik-urs)
noun In British usage, woman's or girl's underpants; used in the plural. (In American usage, "knickers" is a shortened form of knickerbockers, see definition above.) / *Goblet of Fire*, page 122
"Don't get your knickers in a twist!" thought Winston when his mum reminded him about his homework…again.

knobbly (nob-blee)
adjective Bumpy or knobby. / *Sorcerer's Stone*, page 20
The knobbly-headed dwarf usually wore his hat when he went out so people wouldn't stare at his head.

knottiest (not-ee-ust)
adjective Most difficult or involved. / *Chamber of Secrets*, page 250
The knottiest problem for the Royal Plumber was how to clean out the castle moat without actually emptying out all the water.

kumquat (kum-kwat)
noun A small citrus fruit. / *Order of the Phoenix*, page 193
Kumquats are great for pudding or jam, but they're too sour to eat off the tree.

L

laboriously (luh-**bor**-ee-us-lee)
adverb In a way requiring much exertion, work, and perseverance. / *Deathly Hallows,* page 67
The monster chicken laboriously scratched and scraped at the bare dirt, seeking a worm big enough for his teatime snack.

labyrinth (**lab**-uh-rinth)
noun An intricate, complicated, confusing arrangement, as of buildings or streets. / *Half-Blood Prince,* page 21
The village's labyrinth of streets, roads, lanes, and paths confused many visitors.

labyrinthine (lab-uh-**rin**-thin or lab-uh-**rin**-theen)
adjective Like a labyrinth: intricate, complicated, and confusing. / *Chamber of Secrets,* page 219
So many guests got lost in the labyrinthine corridors of the castle that the king started issuing maps to his visitors.

lacewing (**lase**-wing)
noun An insect with lacy gauze-like wings and threadlike antennae. / *Chamber of Secrets,* page 211
The potions master spent Saturday mornings in the meadow catching lacewings to use in upcoming potion assignments.

lacquered (**lak**-urd)
adjective Covered with a varnish that gives a bright, shiny surface. / *Half-Blood Prince,* page 434
Willow's lacquered box held her most prized possessions—the pet rock from her boyfriend, the enchanted locket from Auntie Baba, and her grandmother's mini-wand.

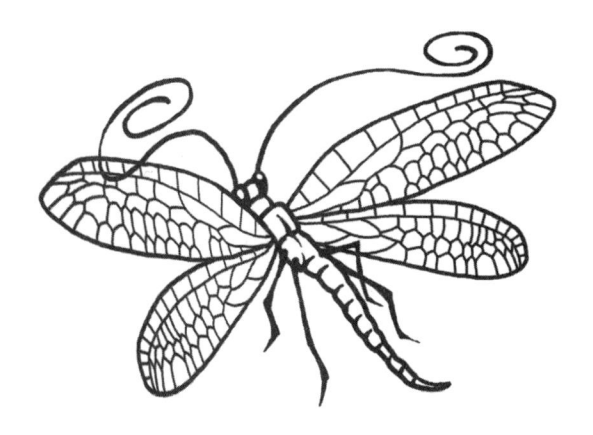

Lacewing

lag (rhymes with **nag**)
verb To fail to keep up; to fall behind. / *Chamber of Secrets,* page 269
Jenn lagged behind the rest of the class as they headed toward the meadow to find botanico-potion ingredients; she was afraid there'd be a snake out there somewhere.

lair (rhymes with **bear**)
noun A den or hiding place of an animal. / *Order of the Phoenix,* page 690
The bear's lair was quite cozy, except for all the gnawed bones on the ground.

lamely (**laym**-lee)
adverb Weakly; without confidence. / *Half-Blood Prince,* page 17
"I guess I shouldn't have done that," said Brilly lamely, after the incident with the food coloring in the hot tub.

lament (luh-**ment**)
noun An expression of sorrow or mourning, especially in song. / *Half-Blood Prince,* page 614
Every time Fiona sang "The Lament of the Lovesick Lizard," she ended up crying.

lament (luh-**ment**)
verb To mourn or express regret or sorrow. / *Half-Blood Prince,* page 367
Blackpool lamented the loss of his favorite racing worm, a victim of wormy diarrhea.

lamentable (luh-men-tuh-bul)
adjective Deplorable and really lousy; deserving of lament or regret. / *Order of the Phoenix*, page 530
Elrod was a lamentable wizard—his wand was held together with tape, his cauldron was scummy (and his potion-work really bad), every herb wilted at the sight of him, and he could remember only a few charms.

lamented (luh-men-tid)
adjective Mourned for. / *Chamber of Secrets*, page 136
The village funeral director asked the zookeeper, "And where would you like the late lamented lizard to be buried?"

lane (rhymes with **mane**)
noun A narrow path or road. / *Sorcerer's Stone*, page 101
The tortoise slowly strolled along the side of the country lane, seeking something for lunch.

languid (lang-gwid)
adjective Without liveliness or energy; lacking spirit or vigor. / *Deathly Hallows*, page 458
Willow dangled her languid fingers in the water as her new boyfriend struggled to row the boat across the lake.

lank (rhymes with **tank**)
adjective Long, straight, limp; said of hair. / *Chamber of Secrets*, page 134
Her lank hair would benefit from a good wash, a good haircut, and a good curling iron.

lanky (lang-kee)
adjective Tall, thin, and gangly. / *Order of the Phoenix*, page 253
The lanky basketball player had grown seven inches in the last year.

lapse (rhymes with **traps**)
noun A failure or error, usually said of memory. / *Half-Blood Prince*, page 410
The elderly wizard described his lapse of memory as a "senior moment," but it was more like a "senior hour"—he'd been forgetting a lot lately.

lapse (rhymes with **traps**)
verb To slip into or to smoothly move into. / *Goblet of Fire*, page 320
The class lapsed into a strained silence when the ticking, rocking parcel was delivered to Mrs. Snodgrape's desk.

lark (rhymes with **dark**)
noun An activity that's a bit of an adventure. / *Order of the Phoenix*, page 276
"This soccer lark has been quite fun," said Butch Thuggins to the reporter after his latest match.

laughingstock (laf-ing-stok)
noun A victim of ridicule. / *Prisoner of Azkaban*, page 420
Dribbles was the laughingstock of the Introductory Potions class when his cauldron tipped over and spilled plain old hot water on him.

lax (rhymes with **max**; sounds exactly like **lacks**)
adjective Careless; not particularly strict. / *Goblet of Fire*, page 78
The village police were quite lax about broomstick parking regulations.

layabout (lay-uh-bowt)
adjective Lazy or idle. / *Deathly Hallows*, page 35
The layabout moat workers were spending more time watching the ducks swimming in the moat than they were doing any moat cleaning.

layabout (lay-uh-bowt)
noun A lazy or idle person. / *Prisoner of Azkaban*, page 17
"Those lousy layabouts will never get the moat clean in time for the Castle Regatta," worried the king.

leaden (led-un)
adjective Dull, spiritless, or gloomy, with much the same feel and look as lead: dark and heavy. / *Chamber of Secrets*, page 167
The leaden sky exactly matched his leaden feelings—gloom and doom all around.

ledger (lej-ur)
noun An old-fashioned account book for keeping track of financial business. / *Sorcerer's Stone*, page 73
Every evening, the elderly woman entered the day's

expenses and expenditure in a giant ledger she stored next to the refrigerator.

leech (rhymes with **screech**)

noun **A bloodsucking worm.** / *Chamber of Secrets*, page 165

Village legend claimed that giant bloodsucking leeches lived at the bottom of the lake, awaiting unwary swimmers.

leech (rhymes with **screech**)

verb **To cling to, to feed upon, to suck or drain.** / *Prisoner of Azkaban*, page 221

A strange pale body lay on the lakeshore—some unidentifiable animal with all its blood gone, leeched out by something…evil…in the lake.

leek (rhymes with **seek**; sounds exactly like **leak**)

noun **An onion-like plant, with long, flat, dark green leaves.** / *Prisoner of Azkaban*, page 301

Wildwood's leeks were doing well—the whole garden looked like it was infested with long, green rabbit ears.

leer (rhymes with **deer**)

verb **To look with a sly or cunning look.** / *Sorcerer's Stone*, page 248

"You have not given everything to me," leered the inexperienced bandit, "so I shall step on your toes until you hand over all your jewels."

legacy (leg-uh-see)

noun **A gift of property left in a will to an heir.** / *Half-Blood Prince*, page 49

The king's legacy to the prince would include two dozen dress suits of armor—made of gold and silver with rubies on every visor.

legion (lee-jun)

noun **A multitude or great number; usually used in the plural.** / *Deathly Hallows*, page 28

Butch's legions of admirers gathered around the stadium exit, hoping to catch a glimpse of their soccer hero after the big match.

leprechauns (lep-ruh-kons)

noun **In Irish folklore, dwarfish bearded elves or "fairie folk" who can reveal hidden treasure to those who catch them; they're known for their mischievousness.** / *Goblet of Fire*, page 104 / Note: In Potter's world, leprechauns are tiny bearded old men who wear red vests and carry small gold or green lamps, flying about and distributing gold coins.

The leprechaun sat exhausted on the ground—lugging around his heavy pot of gold was hard work.

Leprechaun

lest (rhymes with **nest**)

conjunction **For fear that.** / *Goblet of Fire*, page 497

Winston's mum always took a shopping list to the village market lest she'd forget something important.

lethal (lee-thul)

adjective **Deadly, mortal, fatal.** / *Goblet of Fire*, page 198

The lethal blow to Brilly's duct tape scheme was dealt by the principal's latest decree—"No student is allowed to bring duct tape to school for any purpose whatsoever."

lethargy (leth-ur-jee)

noun **The condition of being drowsy, listless, and unenergetic.** / *Order of the Phoenix*, page 44

A mysterious lethargy came over the villagers as the

strange greenish fog drifted through the streets—some people fell asleep where they were, while others just stopped and stared sleepily off into the distance.

letterbox (let-tur-boks)

noun In British usage, a home mailbox. / *Order of the Phoenix*, page 60 / Note: See also **postbox** elsewhere in this dictionary.

"Get the post from the letterbox, would you?" asked Winston's mum.

levitate (lev-ih-tate)

verb To make someone or something rise or float in the air. / *Goblet of Fire*, page 138

The inexperienced wizard levitated his wand, then couldn't get it back down again.

levitating (lev-ih-tayt-ing)

adjective Rising up or floating in air. / *Prisoner of Azkaban*, page 197

The levitating cauldron rose up to the ceiling, circled the room twice, then whizzed out the open window.

liability (lie-uh-bil-ih-tee)

noun A handicap; something that holds one back or is a disadvantage; the opposite of an asset. / *Goblet of Fire*, page 533

Nungie the elf never considered it a liability to have just one leg—he loved his wheelchair and could go faster in it than most other people could run.

liaise (lee-ayz)

verb To work together with another organization or group so both can be more effective. / *Order of the Phoenix*, page 657

The Sisters of Sorcery and the Chamber of Wizards decided to liaise in planning the Day of the Dead festivities.

liberal (lib-ur-ul)

adjective Generous, referring to amounts. / *Goblet of Fire*, page 194

Hassan squeezed a liberal serving of choca-lotta-latté over his ice cream.

license (lie-sunse)

noun Permission to do or not to do something. / *Prisoner of Azkaban*, page 387

"You do not have license to do whatever you want at school," lectured Brilly's father. "You're there to learn."

lichen-spotted (like-un-spot-id)

adjective Spotted with a greenish-gray fungus/algae organism that forms a crusty growth on trees or rocks. / *Deathly Hallows*, page 325

A mysterious lichen-spotted gravestone stood near the church entrance; no matter how many times it was cleaned off, the lichen stubbornly grew back.

lie-in (lie-in)

noun In British usage, an overlong stay in bed in the morning; often used in the phrase "a bit of a lie-in." / *Goblet of Fire*, page 66

Brilly needed a bit of a lie-in after his late-night mischief with Mrs. Snodgrape's spare cauldron.

life buoy (life boy *or* life boo-ee)

noun A flotation device—usually a large circle of cork or hard foam—meant to keep someone afloat until they can be rescued. / *Prisoner of Azkaban*, page 29 / Note: In Potter's world, Aunt Marge swells up, entirely round, "like a vast life buoy," though the description sounds less ring-like (like a life buoy) and more like a giant balloon.

The beach lifeguard tossed the life buoy to the swimmer struggling against the water demons.

lift (rhymes with **gift**)

noun In British usage, an elevator. / *Order of the Phoenix*, page 129

"Hold the lift! Hold the lift! I'm coming," shouted Winston's dad as he ran toward the elevator.

limbo (lim-boh)

noun An in-between, intermediate place or situation. / *Half-Blood Prince*, page 587

Construction on the village archery range was in limbo until more money was raised to complete it.

limelight (lime-light)

noun A situation in which someone is the center of a lot of attention or interest. / *Chamber of Secrets*, page 61

Soccer star Butch Thuggins loved the limelight, the

autograph seekers, the cheers; he was less fond of the aches and pains and the broken noses.

limerick (lim-ur-ik)

noun A humorous short poem with five lines (lines 1, 2, and 5 rhyme with each other, and lines 3 and 4 rhyme with each other). / *Chamber of Secrets,* page 231
Brilly enjoyed writing limericks about himself:
*There once was a boy named Brilly,
Whose errors were more than just silly.
Jellyfish in the pool,
Then blowing up the school—
And that last was one heck of a dilly.*

lingering (ling-gur-ing)

adjective Persisting, over a long period. / *Goblet of Fire,* page 657
The lingering effects of the time-shifting potion meant everyone was starving (for lunch, dinner, breakfast, and lunch again) by the time class was over.

lingo (ling-go)

noun Language or speech, especially if it sounds foreign or different to the hearer. / *Order of the Phoenix,* page 428
Blackpool, ever evil and ever rude, said to Julio, "I don't understand your lingo—speak English to me."

lintel (lin-tl)

noun A beam or piece of stone or wood across the top of a door or window. / *Order of the Phoenix,* page 702
The tall basketball player had learned to duck going through the door of the coach's office—otherwise he banged his head on the door's lintel.

listlessly (list-lis-lee)

adverb In a bored or disinterested way. / *Prisoner of Azkaban,* page 152
Mr. Glinch listlessly trimmed his hedge, first one branch…then another…He wasn't much interested in gardening today.

listlessness (list-lis-ness)

noun The condition of being bored or disinterested in something. / *Deathly Hallows,* page 437

Everyone in the village, it seemed, experienced extreme listlessness that hot summer day.

litany (lit-un-ee)

noun A long, tedious, repeated list or discussion. / *Deathly Hallows,* page 288
Madam Glinch began the parent/teacher meeting with a litany of Brilly's latest misbehavior.

liveried (liv-uh-reed)

adjective Wearing livery, the attire of an official or member of a guild, company, or other group; sometimes livery is the uniform of a servant. / *Deathly Hallows,* page 529
The liveried band director was trying to get the marching band in formation; meanwhile, the trombone players were poking the flute players and the drummers were drumming on the tuba players.

livid (liv-id)

adjective Discolored, a dark grayish-blue, usually said of bruises. / *Prisoner of Azkaban,* page 341 / Note: See the related adjectives **livid** below. Note that livid has several different meanings.
The livid bruises on the gamekeeper's face developed after his confrontation with the stinging nurch babies.

livid (liv-id)

adjective Furiously angry. / *Chamber of Secrets,* page 8 / Note: See the related adjectives **livid** above and below. Note that livid has several different meanings.
Blackpool was livid—someone had stolen his ace racing worm.

livid (liv-id)

adjective Deathly pale or ashen-faced. / *Chamber of Secrets,* page 275 / Note: See the related adjectives **livid** above. Note that livid has several different meanings.
Ravi was livid with terror—the zombie had turned, spotted him, and was slowly walking toward him.

lob (rhymes with **gob**)

verb To toss slowly and with a high curve. / *Chamber of Secrets,* page 187
Brilly lobbed his soda can toward the garbage, prompting a quick reprimand from the cafeteria manager: "No tossing, no lobbing, no throwing."

The Unofficial Harry Potter Vocabulary Builder • 117

loch (rhymes with **block**; sounds exactly like **lock**)
noun A Scottish word for "lake." / *Deathly Hallows*, page 315
Many people believe a huge water horse lives in Scotland's Loch Ness.

lockjaw (lok-jaw)
noun Literally, when the jaw is locked closed in a rigid muscle spasm as a result of the disease tetanus; more generally, saying someone looks like they have lockjaw means they were speechless or unable to utter a word. / *Prisoner of Azkaban*, page 176
After he failed his potions test, his botany test, and his math quiz all in the same day, a stunned Elrod looked like he had lockjaw.

lofty (lof-tee)
adjective Arrogant, haughty, disapproving. / *Prisoner of Azkaban*, page 236
"Well," said Fiona in a lofty voice, "if you want to sit around all day chattering, okay, but I'm going to get something done."

loggerhead (log-ur-hed)
noun Literally, a blockhead or stupid person; more generally—and more usually—used in the phrase "at loggerheads," meaning involved in a dispute or disagreement with someone. / *Order of the Phoenix*, page 452
The two groups were at loggerheads over who would host the annual Day of the Dead festivities.

logic (lodj-ik)
noun Rational and sound reasoning. / *Sorcerer's Stone*, page 285
Logic suggests that bigger animals generally eat smaller animals.

loincloth (loyn-kloth)
noun A short piece of cloth worn by men around the hips, especially in hot countries. / *Order of the Phoenix*, page 107
It was Toga Day at school, but somehow Dribbles got mixed up and appeared at school wearing a loincloth. "Hey Dribbles," cooed all the girls.

loll (rhymes with **doll**)
verb To lounge around in a lazy way. / *Chamber of Secrets*, page 10 / Note: See the related verb **loll** below.
Hassan and Ravi planned to loll around the pool all summer.

loll (rhymes with **doll**)
verb To droop or dangle. / *Goblet of Fire*, page 50 / Note: See the related verb **loll** above.
The ogre's tongue, victim of a really bad bug bite, lolled out of the side of his mouth.

lollop (lol-up)
verb To run with long awkward steps; usually said of dogs. / *Deathly Hallows*, page 619
The puppies loved to lollop across the field, especially when Blackpool—the evil wizard—wasn't chasing them.

loo (rhymes with **zoo**)
noun In British usage, a toilet. / *Order of the Phoenix*, page 458
"Don't start till I get back from the loo," shouted Winston to the rest of the team as he ran off the field.

look a bit peaky
phrase In British usage, to look pale and ill. / *Order of the Phoenix*, page 488 / Note: American usage would more likely be "you look a bit peaked," pronounced **pee-kid**.
"You look a bit peaky today, dear. Did you take your vitamins? Did you sleep well last night?" worried Winston's mum.

look daggers
phrase To glare at angrily. / *Prisoner of Azkaban*, page 149
Bella looked daggers at her father after he refused to let her wear her new fishnet stockings to school.

lookout (look-out)
noun A problem or something to be concerned about; often used in the phrase "that's your lookout." / *Deathly Hallows*, page 569
"If you want to get kicked out of school, well, that's your lookout," said Dribbles. "But I don't."

loom (rhymes with **doom**)

verb To come into view as a large distorted image. / *Goblet of Fire*, page 577

As Butch Thuggins lay groggy on the soccer field, his teammates suddenly loomed over him—they looked huge when you were looking up at them.

loon (rhymes with **soon**)

noun A silly or strange person. / *Prisoner of Azkaban*, page 249

"You loon. No one collects dust bunnies."

loophole (**loop**-hole)

noun A mistake or omission in a law that makes it possible to evade whatever the law is supposed to make you do. / *Chamber of Secrets*, page 39

"I think there's a loophole in the school decree about bringing pets to school," suggested Brilly.

loping (**lohp**-ing)

adjective Moving steadily and easily, with a long stride. / *Half-Blood Prince*, page 16

The loping giant crossed the wide meadow in about ten seconds.

lounge (rhymes with **scrounge**)

noun In British usage, a living room. / *Chamber of Secrets*, page 5

The lounge at Winston's house was so comfortable—except for the enchanted cuckoo clock.

ludicrous (loo-dih-krus)

adjective Ridiculous and laughable. / *Chamber of Secrets*, page 149

"That's the most ludicrous idea I've ever heard. You can't blow up the cafeteria just because the food is terrible."

lull (rhymes with **hull**)

verb To soothe or quiet; often used in the phrase "lulled into a false sense of security," meaning making someone feel safe when they're really not. / *Deathly Hallows*, page 444

The peace treaty between the king and the duke lulled the villagers into a false sense of security—they should have been worrying about the giant blood-thirsty leeches spawning in the lake.

lumbago (lum-**bay**-go)

noun A chronic pain in the lower back area. / *Deathly Hallows*, page 273

"Oh, my lumbago," moaned the piano mover.

lumber (**lum**-bur)

verb To move in an awkward, slow way. / *Chamber of Secrets*, page 187

Merlin lumbered painfully and slowly down the stairs—maybe it was time for a hip replacement.

luminescent (loo-muh-**nes**-unt)

adjective Giving off light but no heat. / *Deathly Hallows*, page 465

The luminescent tip of Wildwood's wand lit his path across the meadow.

luminous (loo-min-us)

adjective Shining or giving off light. / *Sorcerer's Stone*, page 204

The giant moth's luminous glow was almost bright enough to read by.

lunatic (loo-nuh-tik)

noun A demented or insane person. / *Chamber of Secrets*, page 20

"Are you a lunatic or what, Brilly?! It's a crazy idea to put jellyfish in the swimming pool."

lunge (rhymes with **grunge**)

verb To move forward suddenly. / *Chamber of Secrets*, page 338

The giant cockroach lunged at Blackpool—actually, it lunged at the sandwich in Blackpool's hand.

lurch (rhymes with **church**)

noun A sudden unsteady movement. / *Sorcerer's Stone*, page 189

"Urghh." Dylan's stomach gave a lurch when the roller coaster hit the first curve.

lurch (rhymes with **church**)

verb To move with a sudden unsteady movement, often to one side or forward. / *Sorcerer's Stone*, page 111

The monster lurched across the playground, seeking a dodgeball to gnaw on.

lure (rhymes with **pure**)

noun Something that attracts or has the

power to attract. / *Goblet of Fire*, page 312
For Brilly, the lure of mischief was irresistible.

luridly (lur-id-lee)
adverb Garishly, brightly colored. / *Order of the Phoenix*, page 265
Bella's luridly colored hair seemed to throb in the sunlight—was it orange with blue stripes, or blue with orange stripes?

lurk (rhymes with **jerk**)
verb To wait out of view or to lie in wait; also to sneak about. / *Sorcerer's Stone*, page 157
The evil wizard lurked just beyond the boulder, waiting for the negative energy from the spell to gradually leak away.

lurker (lurk-ur)
noun Someone who lurks. / *Deathly Hallows*, page 223
The lurkers kept a watchful eye on everything he did.

lynx (rhymes with **jinx**; sounds exactly like **links**)
noun A large forest-dwelling wildcat. / *Deathly Hallows*, page 159
The lynx was the star attraction in the village zoo, but it would have been much happier running wild in the Haunted Forest.

M

mackintosh (**mak**-in-tosh)
noun A raincoat. / *Order of the Phoenix*, page 521
"Let it rain, let it rain, let it rain," sang Willow, dancing in the spring rain wearing only her mackintosh.

magenta (muh-**jen**-tuh)
adjective Purplish red. / *Half-Blood Prince*, page 117
Their dark magenta graduation robes were impressive, though the students all looked like huge walking eggplants.

maggot (**mag**-ut)
noun A whitish wormlike fly larva. / *Half-Blood Prince*, page 229
Brilly convinced Dribbles that the rice at the bottom of his soup bowl was actually maggots.

maggoty (**mag**-uh-tee)
adjective Infested with maggots. / *Chamber of Secrets*, page 133
The milk cart horse refused to eat the maggoty horse feed so it—the horse feed—got tossed in the compost pile.

magisterially (maj-uh-**steer**-ee-uh-lee)
adverb Imperiously or in a domineering way. / *Order of the Phoenix*, page 818
The queen magisterially ordered the castle kitchen workers to make her a yak butter and nettle jelly sandwich…now!

magnitude (**mag**-nih-tood)
noun Size or importance. / *Order of the Phoenix*, page 545
"An earthquake of such magnitude seldom happens here," mumbled the village mayor, still shaken by the quake's tremors.

magpie-like tendency
noun A tendency to collect and hoard small objects, like the magpie bird. / *Half-Blood Prince*, page 277
Mrs. Snodgrape's magpie-like tendencies made her trips to the village dump difficult for her poor husband—sometimes they brought home more than they took.

mahogany (muh-**hog**-uh-nee)
adjective Made of wood from the mahogany tree, a tropical tree that produces a hard, reddish wood. / *Sorcerer's Stone*, page 166
The mahogany wand was heavier than the beechwood, and not as supple—but oh so beautiful.

maim (rhymes with **blame**)
verb To injure with a disabling wound; to cripple or disfigure. / *Goblet of Fire*, page 438
The tragic accident on the ferryboat had badly maimed the captain—now he generally got around in a wheelchair.

maimed (rhymes with **blamed**)
adjective Injured, crippled, disfigured. / *Prisoner of Azkaban*, page 370
Dr. Greenteeth, the village dentist, had a maimed left hand, injured when a rather large patient had "closed" instead of "opened."

mainland (**main**-land)
noun The principal part of a country, as opposed to islands around it. / *Prisoner of Azkaban*, page 372 / Note: In Potter's world, the mainland is Britain; Azkaban is on an island in the North Sea.
The Sisters of Sorcery took an excursion boat from the mainland to the distant islands.

malady (**mal**-uh-dee)
noun A disorder or disease. Plural: maladies. / *Half-Blood Prince*, page 258
"And what new malady do we have today, sonny?" asked the kindly but annoying village doctor.

malediction (mal-eh-**dik**-shun)
noun A curse. / *Deathly Hallows*, page 380
"A malediction upon you all," shouted the confused priest. He meant to say "A benediction."

malevolent (muh-**lev**-uh-lunt)
adjective Evil. / *Chamber of Secrets, page 193*
The malevolent troll particularly enjoyed summertime, when he could uproot the villagers' gardens nightly.

malfunction (mal-**funk**-shun)
verb To fail to function properly. / *Prisoner of Azkaban, page 347*
Annie's broom malfunctioned again—it swiftly rose three feet off the ground and then just stayed there.

malice (**mal**-is)
noun A desire to injure or harm someone, or to make someone suffer. / *Chamber of Secrets, page 63*
Blackpool's eyes glittered with malice as he considered revenge on those who hadn't supported his bid to be village mayor.

malicious (muh-**lish**-us)
adjective Full of malice, spiteful. / *Prisoner of Azkaban, page 124*
Esmerelda's malicious laughter echoed through the neighborhood; she'd just told Blackpool she wouldn't go out with him, ever.

mallet (**mal**-it)
noun A short-handled hammer with a wood head, good for striking something you don't want to damage, like a tent peg. / *Goblet of Fire, page 79*
Wildwood conjured a mallet to help pound in the tent pegs, but he must have been a little unclear—a croquet mallet appeared by mistake.

manacles (**man**-uh-kuls)
noun Heavy-duty handcuffs, often used to restrain prisoners with their hands up high against a wall. / *Chamber of Secrets, page 125*
The old manacles hanging on the wall were rusty reminders of the dungeon's murderous past.

mandolin (**man**-dih-lin)
noun A musical instrument somewhat like a guitar but with a pear-shaped body. / *Half-Blood Prince, page 315*
"I'd love to take mandolin lessons," enthused Fiona.

"I'm sure 'The Ode to the Living Dead' would sound wonderful on the mandolin."

Manacles

mane (rhymes with **sane**; sounds exactly like **main**)
noun Long, thick, human hair; also the long, heavy hair on a horse's or lion's neck. / *Sorcerer's Stone, page 46*
"What a mane of hair that girl has—six feet long at least."

mangle (**mang**-gul)
noun A wringer, an old-fashioned device to press water out of just-washed clothes. (A more sophisticated mangle was later invented to do ironing.) / *Deathly Hallows, page 87*
"I'll be using the mangle this afternoon, and I want you far, far away," warned Elrod's mother. "Last time you caught your shirt tail in it and I thought you'd get your behind flattened."

mangled (**mang**-guld)
adjective Injured by cutting, tearing, or crushing. / *Sorcerer's Stone, page 182*
The king's badly mangled finger throbbed—next time he would think twice about sticking it anywhere near the moat-sweeper.

mangy (**main**-jee)
adjective Contemptible and grungy. / *Half-*

Blood Prince, page 260
"That mangy thief grabbed the clothes right off the clothesline!" shouted the woman.

manhandle (man-han-dul)

verb To handle roughly. / *Order of the Phoenix*, page 616
"Hey, hey, don't manhandle the merchandise," said Brilly, as the school security guard grabbed his arm and marched him off to the principal's office.

mania (may-nee-uh)

noun An intense, focused interest or enthusiasm. / *Goblet of Fire*, page 530
Collecting model dragons had become a mania for Julio; he was always checking out the Hurly Burly Emporium and local yard sales, hoping to add to his collection.

maniacal (muh-nye-uh-kul)

adjective Wild, insane, and way excessive. / *Order of the Phoenix*, page 541
Blackpool's maniacal laughter—like a gagging hyena—filtered out of the Trolls' Hole pub.

manic (man-ik)

adjective Anxious or excited. / *Prisoner of Azkaban*, page 143
The manic look in the cat's eyes meant only one thing: Bird alert! Bird alert!

manicured (man-ih-kyoord)

adjective Trimmed and neatened. / *Order of the Phoenix*, page 12
The perfectly manicured library lawns looked as if someone had taken a pair of scissors and a ruler to trim every blade of grass exactly the same height.

manifest (man-uh-fest)

verb To show or become evident. / *Half-Blood Prince*, page 90
The stage magician's tremendous skill manifested itself early in his performance—he pulled Rupert out of a hat.

manifesto (man-uh-fes-toh)

noun A public declaration of principles and policies, usually written and political in nature. / *Goblet of Fire*, page 224
Brilly was drafting a manifesto about the lousy cafeteria food, part of his campaign to improve lunchtime offerings.

manky (mang-kee)

adjective In British slang, unattractive, dirty, inferior, rotten, and worthless. / *Goblet of Fire*, page 73
"That manky old coat is disgusting, Blackpool. Don't even come in here with it—toss it in the trash or burn it."

manor (man-ur)

noun A mansion or main house on an estate. / *Chamber of Secrets*, page 29
The duke's manor was not as historic as the king's castle, but it was far more comfortable.

mantelpiece (man-tul-peese)

noun The shelf above a fireplace. / *Sorcerer's Stone*, page 18
The wizard rested his hand on the mantelpiece as he leaned over to toss the spoiled potion in the fireplace.

manticore (man-tuh-kore)

noun A legendary monster with the head of a man, the body of a lion, and the tail of a dragon or scorpion. / *Prisoner of Azkaban*, page 222
Dribbles worried: "Do manticores talk or roar?"

Manticore

mantle (man-tul)

noun Something that covers, conceals, or enfolds. / *Order of the Phoenix*, page 16

A mantle of snow covered the village, turning the houses, streets, and trees into a silent wonderland.

mantra (**man**-truh)

noun Repeated words or sounds, almost like a chant or prayer. / *Half-Blood Prince*, page 636
The princess could often be heard muttering her personal mantra: "I'll shop till I drop, shop till I drop."

manure (muh-**nyoo**-ur)

noun Fertilizer, usually animal dung. / *Chamber of Secrets*, page 10
Mr. Glinch loved the smell of manure in the morning, spread carefully under every shrub and tree in his garden.

marathon (**mare**-uh-thon)

noun A long-distance race, usually a foot race over a 26-mile course. / *Chamber of Secrets*, page 84
The mayor suggested a marathon as a fundraiser but no one in the village seemed interested.

marauder (muh-**raw**-dur)

noun A person who goes in quest of plunder. / *Prisoner of Azkaban*, page 192 / Note: In Potter's world, "marauder" is part of the name of the map of Hogwarts (and its occupants) that Harry uses.
The pirate didn't consider himself a marauder—he was more a nautical Robin Hood.

marauding (muh-**raw**-ding)

adjective Moving around looking for plunder or for something to destroy or kill. / *Prisoner of Azkaban*, page 221
The marauding herd of goats considered all the villagers' gardens, and settled on Wildwood's as the most likely to provide satisfying taste treats.

margin (**mar**-jin)

noun The difference, in points, between winning and losing. / *Prisoner of Azkaban*, page 181
The soccer team lost by a narrow margin—a single goal—but they felt as bad as that time they'd lost by six.

marginally (**mar**-juh-nuh-lee)

adverb Slightly. / *Half-Blood Prince*, page 286
Dylan felt marginally better after two days in the village hospital, but he knew he'd never eat armadillo/possum stew again.

marionette (mar-ee-uh-**net**)

noun A puppet moved by strings held by someone above. / *Goblet of Fire*, page 119
Sometimes Brilly felt like a marionette with someone else pulling his strings—someone who liked to get in trouble.

marks (rhymes with **barks**)

noun A grade given in school to show how good a student's school work is. / *Sorcerer's Stone*, page 49
Brilly got such bad marks last term he was spell-grounded for a month.

marmalade (mar-muh-**laid**)

noun A preserve (like a thick, clumpy jam) made from the pulp and peel of fruits, usually oranges. / *Sorcerer's Stone*, page 41
Merlin was happy—he had tea, he had crumpets, he had butter, and—the best—he had orange marmalade.

maroon (muh-**roon**)

adjective Deep brownish-purple. / *Goblet of Fire*, page 335
Wearing his maroon pants, Flintlock looked like he'd been dipped in grape juice.

marquee (mar-**kee**)

noun In British usage, a tent. / *Half-Blood Prince*, page 643
"My goodness, dear, that dress makes you look like a marquee. Don't you have anything less billowy?"

marshal (**mar**-shul)

verb To gather and arrange clearly. / *Half-Blood Prince*, page 331
Brilly marshaled his thoughts—his scheme to dump jellyfish in the swimming pool demanded careful planning.

mascot (**mas**-kot)

noun An animal, person, or thing that represents a team or organization; thought to bring good luck. / *Goblet of Fire*, page 102
The village mascot—a giant horned toad—was always

available for appearances at village parades, picnics, or other celebrations.

mash (rhymes with **dash**)

noun In British usage, mashed potatoes; often used in the phrase "sausages and mash." / *Order of the Phoenix*, page 388

Winston's favorite dinner was sausages and mash, and he hated sharing any of it with his always-hungry little brother.

masquerade (mas-kuh-**rade**)

verb To go about under false pretenses, pretending to be someone else. / *Half-Blood Prince*, page 42

"Brilly, there must be another way to get better food at school than to masquerade as the cafeteria manager and order 100 pizzas."

massage (muh-**sajh**)

verb To rub with your hands. / *Goblet of Fire*, page 180

Dylan massaged his grumbling stomach—it was time for lunch.

massive (**mas**-iv)

adjective Really big, heavy, and solid. / *Sorcerer's Stone*, page 284

The massive royal dinner table was set for the king's 287 dinner guests.

masterstroke (**mas**-tur-strohk)

noun An extremely skillful and effective action. / *Deathly Hallows*, page 208

Throwing up in the school's third-floor bathroom was a clever masterstroke to decoy the janitor away from his first-floor broom closet, the site of the planned fireworks.

materialize (muh-**teer**-ee-uh-lize)

verb To appear; to take bodily form. / *Prisoner of Azkaban*, page 403

The old wizard suddenly materialized out of the thick fog, paused to ask directions to the castle, and then disappeared again.

matron (**may**-tron)

noun A woman in charge of things at a hospital, orphanage, prison, etc. / *Half-Blood Prince*, page 263

The hospital matron delivered the bad news: the giant horned toad, beloved village mascot, had died.

matte (rhymes with **fat**; sounds exactly like **mat**)

adjective Dull; not shiny. / *Deathly Hallows*, page 545

The matte surface on the painting made all the colors look drab and dull.

matter-of-fact (mah-tur-of-fakt)

adjective Straightforward, commonplace, unemotional, ordinary. / *Prisoner of Azkaban*, page 182

The mayor's matter-of-fact announcement that construction would start soon on the meadow condos caused an uproar among the villagers.

mauve (rhymes with **drove**)

noun A light rose or pinkish-purple color. / *Sorcerer's Stone*, page 76

The soft mauve of Bella's new hair color was lovely, but she'd hoped for fire-dragon red.

mayhem (**may**-hem)

noun Rowdy disorder. / *Chamber of Secrets*, page 186

The mayhem when the pasture poltergeists encountered the barn ghouls terrified the cows—and almost leveled the barn.

mead (rhymes with **bead**)

noun An alcoholic drink made from honey. / *Prisoner of Azkaban*, page 202

Mead was the preferred drink of the Vikings, but it's not as popular now, except at the Trolls' Hole pub, where barrels of it are consumed nightly.

meander (mee-an-dur)

verb To wander or ramble. / *Half-Blood Prince*, page 147

Wildwood meandered into the Trolls' Hole pub, but quickly left when he spotted the bloody handprint on the bar.

meddler (**med**-lur)

noun Someone who meddles, or intrudes into the business of others. / *Goblet of Fire*, page 8

The school secretary was a notorious meddler—not only did she know what every teacher was doing, she knew how they could do it better.

meddlesome (med-ul-sum)
adjective Inclined to interfere in the business of others. / *Chamber of Secrets*, page 338
"You are the most meddlesome, nosy, annoying person I know!" shouted Willow at her former best friend.

medieval (mee-dee-**ee**-vul *or* meed-**ee**-vul)
adjective Having to do with the Middle Ages, the period between 1100 A.D. to 1500 A.D. / *Prisoner of Azkaban*, page 2
"That is such a medieval concept—I am not cooking a whole pig over an open fire for your birthday!"

megaphone (meg-uh-fone)
noun A long cone-shaped device to magnify the voice, often used by cheerleaders. / *Chamber of Secrets*, page 256
"Mpmpfffpm!" Uh-oh, someone slipped a tennis ball down the cheerleader's megaphone.

melodramatic (mel-uh-druh-**mat**-ik)
adjective Very emotional and sentimental. / *Goblet of Fire*, page 287
Bella was so melodramatic—she once started sobbing and banging her fists on the table just because she broke a fingernail. What a drama queen.

memo (mem-oh)
noun Short for memorandum, a written note, and usually a business note. / *Order of the Phoenix*, page 130
The mayor's memo to the village treasurer requested funds to attend the county wizarding fest; he received a one-word memo back: "No."

menagerie (muh-**naj**-ur-ee)
noun A collection of animals. / *Prisoner of Azkaban*, page 58 / Note: In Potter's world, "menagerie" is part of the name of a pet shop.
Since he had such a menagerie of friendly animals hanging around his house, thought Wildwood, maybe he should start a petting zoo.

mental (men-tul)
adjective In British slang, crazy or out of your mind. / *Prisoner of Azkaban*, page 349
"Jeesh, he must be mental to do something that crazy," thought Winston.

mercifully (mur-sih-ful-ee)
adverb Luckily or fortunately. / *Goblet of Fire*, page 346
The explosion was loud but the fire was mercifully brief, so only a few mops in the school janitor's closet were damaged.

meringue (muh-**rang**)
noun A small pastry shell or cake made of beaten and baked egg whites and sugar, and filled with fruit or nuts. / *Sorcerer's Stone*, page 125
Dylan was certain his mother wouldn't notice if he snuck just one meringue off the plate. Dylan was wrong.

mesmerized (mez-muh-rised)
adjective Fascinated, almost as if hypnotized. / *Half-Blood Prince*, page 136
The mesmerized crowd followed every movement of the Rolling Bones as they danced, pranced, and levitated across the stage.

meteoric (mee-tee-**or**-ik)
adjective Sudden and swift, like a meteor. / *Deathly Hallows*, page 17
His meteoric rise to soccer fame still astounded Butch Thuggins, soccer star.

metronome (**meh**-truh-nome)
noun A device used to mark tempo in music; it ticks back and forth in a regular rhythm, much like a clock's pendulum. / *Deathly Hallows*, page 38
Fiona's guitar teacher suggested she use a metronome to keep time, but she preferred just tapping her foot.

mewling (myoo-ling)
noun The cry or whimper of a cat. / *Chamber of Secrets*, page 124
Wildwood heard a faint mewling outside and was surprised to discover a mother cat and six kittens.

midge (rhymes with **ridge**)
noun A small flying insect that bites people. / *Goblet of Fire*, page 92
Wave after wave of midges swarmed over the picnickers, who soon folded their tablecloths and

headed home, swatting at the annoying bugs as they went.

midriff (mid-rif)
noun The part of the body between the chest and waist. / *Goblet of Fire*, page 375
"Pull that shirt down over your midriff before you set foot out of this house!" shouted Bella's father.

miffed (rhymes with **spiffed**)
adjective Offended or annoyed. / *Sorcerer's Stone*, page 124
Hassan was miffed that Bella hadn't met him before class—he really needed help with the math assignment.

mildewed (mil-dood)
adjective Covered in a fungi that grows on damp surfaces. / *Deathly Hallows*, page 732
The mildewed dungeon had been closed and locked for many years.

milk it for all it's worth
phrase To get as many advantages from a situation as possible, often in a somewhat sneaky or dishonest way. / *Prisoner of Azkaban*, page 120
"Flintlock fell and bruised his ribs—now he's home in bed and milking it for all it's worth—meals in bed and everything," complained Klingster.

milkman (milk-man)
noun A person who delivers milk to private home; now considered an old-fashioned service, it was once done daily by a milkman. / *Sorcerer's Stone*, page 40
"Hey Mom, the milkman is here and he wants to know if we need any extra for the baby rhino."

mill (rhymes with **chill**)
verb To move around aimlessly or slowly. / *Goblet of Fire*, page 235
The crowd milled around after the Rolling Bones concert, reliving how exciting it had been.

mime (rhymes with **time**)
verb To act out, with gestures and body movements, to get your meaning across. / *Goblet of Fire*, page 114

Across the classroom, Willow mimed strumming an air guitar—that, plus a questioning look, was enough to inquire about Fiona's new guitar lessons.

mimic (mim-ik)
verb To match or copy. / *Order of the Phoenix*, page 398
Rilda's annoying little sister would follow her everywhere and mimic her every action.

mince pie (mins pie)
noun A pie filled with mincemeat—finely chopped apples, minced meat, raisins, currants, etc. / *Half-Blood Prince*, page 319
Holiday meals at the castle always featured the king's favorite—mince pie.

mingle (ming-gul)
verb To mix or combine with. / *Sorcerer's Stone*, page 149
The frantic music of the Rolling Bones mingled with the excited shouts of the audience to create an unbelievably loud sound.

minimal (min-uh-mul)
adjective Very small and only barely adequate. / *Deathly Hallows*, page 487
"Your chances of passing Introductory Potions are minimal, Brilly, unless you start working harder," lectured Mrs. Snodgrape.

minion (min-yun)
noun A follower of someone, especially a follower who is way too humble, too agreeable, and too deferential. / *Order of the Phoenix*, page 748
Blackpool's minions always did exactly what he said—it was safer that way.

ministration (min-uh-stray-shun)
noun An act of serving or caring for; usually used in the plural. / *Half-Blood Prince*, page 423
The tender ministrations of the local visiting nurse saved many a villager from having to go to the hospital.

minority (mih-nor-ih-tee)
noun The smaller group, as opposed to the majority. / *Goblet of Fire*, page 388
Seven of the Sisters of Sorcery wanted to visit the

Museum of Magic; three—the minority—voted to visit the Dungeons of Doom Amusement Park.

minuscule (**min**-us-kyool)

adjective **Very tiny.** / *Sorcerer's Stone*, page 81
Hassan's chances of winning were minuscule at best, mainly because Blackpool, the evil wizard, had also entered the jinxing contest.

minute (**my**-nyoot)

adjective **Extremely small.** / *Goblet of Fire*, page 104 / Note: Although spelled the same as *minute* (**mih**-nut), this is pronounced differently.
The minute difference in height between the two brothers especially annoyed the older boy.

mirth (rhymes with **birth**)

noun **Laughter or amusement.** / *Deathly Hallows*, page 10
The Royal Jester brought mirth into the cold halls of the castle.

mirthless (**murth**-les)

adjective **Lacking mirth; without gladness or happiness.** / *Goblet of Fire*, page 11
With a mirthless cackle, the old witch put the skull on the shelf—"There now, dearie, you can watch everything I do."

miscarriage of justice

phrase **The failure of a judicial system or court to administer justice fairly.** / *Order of the Phoenix*, page 148
"Your Honor, not prosecuting those who trashed my worms would be a serious miscarriage of justice," said Blackpool to the village judge.

miscreant (**mis**-kree-unt)

noun **An evildoer.** / *Order of the Phoenix*, page 677
Blackpool's father had been a well-known miscreant in the village, at least until he blew up the old library and himself. Then he was…well, a dead miscreant.

misdeed (mis-**deed**)

noun **A wrongdoing; often used in the plural.** / *Half-Blood Prince*, page 532
Brilly's misdeeds ranged from the sort-of-innocent to the brazenly mischievous.

misdemeanor (mis-dih-**mee**-nur)

noun **A wrongdoing or misbehavior.** / *Order of the Phoenix*, page 149
Blackpool was arrested for a broom misdemeanor—he'd run a stop sign out on the Weeping Highway.

misgiving (mis-**giv**-ing)

noun **A feeling of doubt or apprehension; usually used in the plural.** / *Prisoner of Azkaban*, page 115
The king had serious misgivings about the prince and his career hopes—there'd never been a royal prince who played drums in a rock band.

missive (**mis**-iv)

noun **A written message.** / *Half-Blood Prince*, page 44
The missive from Fiona's grandmother invited her to the mountains for a "Ski with the Witches" event.

mistranslation (mis-trans-**lay**-shun)

noun **Something translated incorrectly.** / *Half-Blood Prince*, page 100
An unfortunate mistranslation of an old Saxon will had meant years of servitude for the castle workers.

mitigating (**mit**-ih-gay-ting)

adjective **Excusing or moderating.** / *Order of the Phoenix*, page 659
Perhaps there were mitigating factors in Blackpool's behavior—after all, his father had been a villain and his mother still spoiled him rotten.

mock (rhymes with **lock**)

adjective **Not real, but meant to be similar to something real.** / *Goblet of Fire*, page 567
With a mock farewell salute to his friends standing below, Rupert entered the "Planes of Death" ride at the Dungeons of Doom Amusement Park.

mock (rhymes with **lock**)

verb **To make something seem totally useless and pointless.** / *Half-Blood Prince*, page 634
The inspired guitar playing of the Rolling Bones seemed to mock Fiona's attempts to learn to play the guitar.

modicum (**mod**-ih-kum)

noun **A small or token amount.** / *Deathly Hallows*, page 550

All it took was a modicum of ice cream, and the cranky little boy was smiling again.

moldering (**mole**-dur-ing)

adjective Decaying, or crumbling to dust. / *Deathly Hallows,* page 328
The oldest corner of the graveyard had several moldering wooden tombstones; they'd soon be gone altogether and the graves would go unmarked.

mollified (**mahl**-uh-fied)

adjective Calmed, soothed, pacified. / *Order of the Phoenix,* page 229
Willow was somewhat mollified when Blackpool, the evil wizard, said he'd never enchant her puppies again.

mollycoddling (**mahl**-ee-kod-ih-ling)

noun Overprotectiveness; treating someone almost too carefully and kindly. / *Order of the Phoenix,* page 90
"You know, dear, your mollycoddling isn't really in his best interests," said Winston's father to Winston's mum.

molt (rhymes with **dolt**)

verb To lose feathers so that new ones can grow. / *Goblet of Fire,* page 367
Jake the budgie was molting, and it was not a pretty sight.

molten (**mol**-tn)

adjective Intense, as if glowing from heat. / *Goblet of Fire,* page 319
A molten wave of panic swept over the wandmaker—he was sure he'd put away the samples, but perhaps they were still out on the counter, and who knows what trouble six unattended wands could get into.

momentum (moh-**men**-tum)

noun Impetus; the force that keeps a moving object moving. / *Half-Blood Prince,* page 157
Once the skateboard started down the hill, its momentum kept it going, despite Willow's screams.

mongrel (**mong**-grul)

noun Literally, a dog of mixed breed; more generally, an offensive word for anything or anyone of mixed breed or race. / *Prisoner of Azkaban,* page 216
"You chicken-dung mongrels! You stay out of my yard!" It wasn't clear who or what Blackpool was yelling at, but he was definitely mad.

monitor (**mon**-ih-tur)

verb To watch closely and carefully; to keep under surveillance. / *Prisoner of Azkaban,* page 21
The king closely monitored the Royal Plumber's progress on the moat-cleaning project.

monk (rhymes with **junk**)

noun A member of an all-male religious group; such groups tend to live apart from others. / *Prisoner of Azkaban,* page 101
The monks of the Church of the Retrograde made a silent pilgrimage to the village to honor the grave of the village mascot.

monocle (**mon**-uh-kul)

noun An eyeglass for one eye. / *Order of the Phoenix,* page 138
The Cyclops was thrilled with his new monocle; now he could actually see that trees had leaves.

Monocle

monologue (mon-uh-log)

noun Endless talking by one person who ends up dominating the conversation. / *Half-Blood Prince*, page 132

Blackpool began a lengthy monologue about the excitement of worm racing, but his listeners soon drifted away.

monotonous (muh-**not**-uh-nus)

adjective Droning, with little change in tone; lacking any variety. / *Goblet of Fire*, page 685

The monotonous voice of the village mayor could put anyone to sleep.

monumental (mon-yoo-**men**-tul)

adjective Massive, imposing, and really big. / *Half-Blood Prince*, page 651

The monumental new tomb in the village graveyard overshadowed all the others.

moor (rhymes with **pour**; sounds exactly like **more**)

noun A wild, open area of land, with poor soil and rough grass or heather. / *Chamber of Secrets*, page 72

During the day, the moor was a pleasant spot for hikes or picnics, but at night, when the fog rolled in, it felt eerie and very scary.

morale (muh-**ral**)

noun The emotional condition of a person, organization, or group, based on confidence, cheerfulness, sense of purpose, etc. / *Half-Blood Prince*, page 564

The morale of the villagers had plummeted—first the mayor was pushing for condos in the beloved meadow, then the village mascot died, and finally there were jellyfish in the school swimming pool.

moronic (moh-**ron**-ik)

adjective Stupid. / *Order of the Phoenix*, page 232

"That's a moronic suggestion. We're not closing school in honor of National Knickers Day."

morose (muh-**rohs**)

adjective Sullen, gloomy, and glum. / *Goblet of Fire*, page 462

A morose Blackpool headed home from the worm races—his best worm had come in last.

morsel (mor-sul)

noun A mouthful or a bite. / *Prisoner of Azkaban*, page 94

"Ahh, tender morsels of fried possum, another lunch-time treat," enthused the cafeteria manager.

mortal (mor-tul)

adjective Extreme and dire, even deadly. / *Chamber of Secrets*, page 16

"Anyone who enters here puts their life in mortal danger," warned the mysterious voice booming out of the abandoned cottage.

mortified (mor-tuh-fied)

adjective Humiliated, shamed, and very embarrassed. / *Order of the Phoenix*, page 514

Willow was mortified as she surfaced after her big dive; the top of her swimsuit seemed to be missing.

mossy (moss-ee)

adjective Covered with moss, or with something much like it—soft and green. / *Chamber of Secrets*, page 54

The mossy tree stump provided a comfortable resting place for the exhausted hiker.

moth-eaten (moth-ee-tun)

adjective Tattered and worn-out looking, with lots of small holes. / *Sorcerer's Stone*, page 45

The wizard's old moth-eaten cloak looked like a flock of hungry moths had feasted on it for lunch.

mother-of-pearl (muth-ur-of-purl)

adjective Pearly and iridescent, like the inside of an oyster shell. / *Half-Blood Prince*, page 185

The mist turned the full moon into a mother-of-pearl orb floating over the village.

motley (mot-lee)

adjective Varied; collected together but not really all the same sort of thing. / *Half-Blood Prince*, page 361

The little boy displayed his motley collection of plants—a dandelion, three radish plants, and some moss.

mottled (mot-uld)

adjective Blotched or spotted. / *Chamber of Secrets*, page 93

The dragon's skin had become mottled in the late summer sun.

mournfully (morn-fuh-lee)
adverb Sadly and sorrowfully. / *Goblet of Fire*, page 180
The villagers mournfully said goodbye to the village mascot in a beautiful but sad memorial service at the church.

mousse (rhymes with **goose**)
noun Not a hair gel, but instead a cold sweetened dessert made with flavored whipped cream. / *Prisoner of Azkaban*, page 77
Decisions, decisions…should he have chocolate mousse or strawberry mousse for dessert?

mousy (mous-ee)
adjective Like a mouse in color, behavior, etc. / *Goblet of Fire*, page 176
The mousy-haired girl was one of the shyest kids in school.

muck (rhymes with **yuck**)
noun Mud, filth, dirt, or slime. / *Prisoner of Azkaban*, page 280 / Note: See the related noun **muck** below.
"Don't track that muck in the house," warned Rupert's mother. "Leave your dirty shoes by the door."

muck (rhymes with **yuck**)
noun Something with little value, or something trashy and disgusting. / *Deathly Hallows*, page 299 / Note: See the related noun **muck** above.
The queen was shouting at the king: "Why are my romance novels 'muck,' but your sappy soap operas are 'inspirational stories of human suffering?'"

muck (rhymes with **yuck**)
verb When combined with "out," to clean out, specifically to clean out animal enclosures. / *Deathly Hallows*, page 92
Wildwood mucked out the chicken house, then moved on to the pig pen—another busy day.

mucus (myoo-kus)
noun The thick, gunky fluid from the nose. / *Deathly Hallows*, page 197

"Young man, using your sleeve has only smeared mucus all over your face. Please use a handkerchief."

muffle (muf-ul)
verb To prevent or deaden a sound, usually by wrapping something around the sound producer. / *Goblet of Fire*, page 165
Cloth gags muffled any cries for help from the hostages, but now the novice bank robber had to tie them up.

muffled (muf-uld)
adjective Softer or less loud, because of being muffled. / *Chamber of Secrets*, page 202
The muffled moans seemed to be coming from the attic.

muffler (muf-lur)
noun A heavy scarf. / *Order of the Phoenix*, page 669
Rupert wound his wool muffler around his neck, hoping it would keep out the bitter cold.

mulch (mulch)
noun Literally, a layer or covering of organic matter to help plants grow; more generally, a thick layer of…stuff. / *Deathly Hallows*, pages 14 (stuff) and 292 (organic matter)
His room was knee-deep in treasures when his mother said, "Clear that mulch out today, Brilly, or it's all going in the garbage." Then she headed to the garden to spread mulch under all the camellias.

mulish (myoo-lish)
adjective Like a mule: stubborn. / *Deathly Hallows*, page 401
His mulish insistence on exploring Nightmare Alley would only lead to trouble.

mull (rhymes with **dull**)
verb To carefully think about something; to ponder. / *Order of the Phoenix*, page 101
Brilly mulled over the advantages and disadvantages of putting compost in the school drinking fountains.

mulled (rhymes with **dulled**)
adjective Heated, with sugar and spices. / *Prisoner of Azkaban*, page 202
The most popular winter drink at the Witching Hour

pub was mulled wine; in the Trolls' Hole, mulled mead was preferred.

mullioned window (mul-yund win-doh)

noun A type of window with vertical divisions (stone or wood) between the panes of glass—more a medieval castle-type window as opposed to a double-hung window (one pane of glass over another). / *Chamber of Secrets*, page 265

The castle workers spent all day washing the mullioned windows of the castle's Great Hall—guests were expected.

Mullioned windows

mundane (mun-dane)

adjective Ordinary. / *Prisoner of Azkaban*, page 298

"Such a mundane man," said the queen dismissively. If only she realized just how helpful the Royal Plumber could be.

murky (mur-kee)

adjective Vague or confused; lacking clarity. / *Half-Blood Prince*, page 197

The murky pages of memory are apt to have many erasures, crossings out, and even a few blank pages.

murmur (mur-mur)

noun A low, soft, continuous sound. / *Sorcerer's Stone*, page 187

The murmur of happy cows sounds a lot like the drone of an air conditioner.

murmur (mur-mur)

verb To speak in a low, soft voice. / *Half-Blood Prince*, page 625

In the garden, the giant tomatoes murmured quietly to each other.

musings (myoo-zings)

noun Thoughts; usually used in the plural. / *Order of the Phoenix*, page 10

That afternoon, Dylan's musings focused on how many chocolate frisblots he could sneak out of the kitchen before dinner.

muster (mus-tur)

verb To summon up or to rouse. / *Order of the Phoenix*, page 856

Rupert finally mustered up enough courage to ask out the new girl.

musty (mus-tee)

adjective Stale smelling or moldy. / *Sorcerer's Stone*, page 42

"Yuck," she said, "that towel is so musty. Did you use it to mop up last week when you dropped your aquarium?"

mutant (myoot-unt)

adjective Something really different from the usual; weird. / *Prisoner of Azkaban*, page 9

The mutant mummies were wrapped in colorful yarn.

mutating (myoo-tay-ting)

adjective Changing or altering. / *Half-Blood Prince*, page 177

Every spell he'd ever learned was swirling in his head, mutating and changing, making his attempts to enchant anything totally hopeless.

mutilate (myoo-til-ate)

verb To destroy, injure, or disfigure in a way that can't be repaired. / *Prisoner of Azkaban*, page 124

The wild boars mutilated the tree roots with their endless rooting in the earth.

mutinous (myoot-un-us)
adjective Rebellious, unruly, and uncontrollable. / *Chamber of Secrets*, page 284
The pirates were getting mutinous; it was time to leave the golden beaches behind and do some serious marauding and plundering.

mutter (mut-tur)
verb To speak in low, unclear tones. / *Sorcerer's Stone*, page 42
The old wizard muttered under his breath, trying to remember the spell for filling inkwells.

mystical (mis-tih-kul)
adjective Cryptic, spiritual, and enigmatic. / *Goblet of Fire*, page 201
The mystical mutterings of the sorceress sounded odd, but it was just an old Norse spell to repair a broken toilet.

mystique (mih-steek)
noun An aura of mystery or mystical power. / *Half-Blood Prince*, page 506
Esmerelda's mystique was unexplainable and unmistakable.

N

nag (rhymes with **hag**)
verb To be bothered by a persistent thought or worry. / *Chamber of Secrets*, page 332
The principal finally realized what was nagging at him—no one had complained about anything all day.

naive (nye-eve)
adjective Unsuspecting, innocent, simple; lacking experience or judgment. / *Order of the Phoenix*, page 716 / Note: Can also be spelled "naïve."
Dribbles was a nice guy, but he was so naive about so many things. He actually believed killer tomatoes walked the streets at dawn.

naught (rhymes with **caught**)
noun Zero. / *Order of the Phoenix*, page 170
Annie's old broom went from naught to slow in about ten seconds.

nauseated (naw-zee-ay-tid)
adjective As if something made you sick to your stomach; squeamish and disgusted. / *Half-Blood Prince*, page 166
"Ewww, there's a dead mouse on the floor," said a slightly nauseated Willow. "Mommmm!"

navel (nay-vul)
noun A belly button. / *Goblet of Fire*, page 73
Bella wanted to get her navel pierced but she knew her parents would have fits.

navigate (nav-ih-gate)
verb To find your way in or across. / *Half-Blood Prince*, page 434
The longtime ferryboat captain navigated across the lake by just pointing the boat where he wanted to go.

nearsighted (neer-sigh-tid)
adjective Able to see things well that are near but unable to see things far away. / *Sorcerer's Stone*, page 213
Brilly always sat in front in classes because he was nearsighted, but he insisted he was actually *fear*-sighted.

negligible (neg-lih-juh-bul)
adjective So small or limited as to be insignificant. / *Deathly Hallows*, page 125
Dealings between the duke and the king had been negligible for years, but now they were talking about changing all that.

negotiate (nih-goh-shee-ate)
verb To move around, through, or over. / *Half-Blood Prince*, page 142
It was difficult to negotiate the Big Bog unless you could conjure safe stones to walk on.

negotiation (nih-goh-shee-ay-shun)
noun The process of having mutual discussions and working toward a common goal. / *Goblet of Fire*, page 278
Negotiations between the duke and the king went amazingly well, considering they'd hated each other for the last 20 years.

neighing (nay-ing)
adjective Like the sound a horse makes; a whinny. / *Order of the Phoenix*, page 755
The new girl's neighing laugh and her long narrow face soon earned her the nickname "Happy Horse."

nettle (net-ul)
noun An outdoor plant with small stinging hairs on the leaves. / *Order of the Phoenix*, page 689
Nettles may look innocent but you don't want to grab a bunch of leaves with your bare hand.

nettled (net-uld)
adjective Irritated and annoyed. / *Prisoner of Azkaban*, page 75
"I didn't trample your flowers," said a nettled Brilly. "Everyone blames me for everything."

neutral (noo-trul)
adjective Not siding with or supporting either side in an argument. / *Goblet of Fire*, page 31

Wildwood maintained a neutral position on the mayor's condos-in-the-meadow plan.

newt (rhymes with **hoot**)
noun A type of small salamander. / *Prisoner of Azkaban*, page 58
The entire newt, salamander, and lizard community gathered down by the Big Bog for a moment of silence after the death of Mristle, the Newt King.

Newt

niche (rhymes with **itch**)
noun A segment of a market. / *Goblet of Fire*, page 91 / Note: See also the related noun **niche** below.
The wandmaker believed there was a niche in the wand market for his new invention—a wand/sparkler hybrid.

niche (rhymes with **itch**)
noun A hollow or crevice in a rock. / *Half-Blood Prince*, page 556 / Note: See also the related noun **niche** above.
The giant scrambled over the sharp rocks, seeking a niche to settle in for a few minutes to rest.

nick (rhymes with **pick**)
verb In British slang, to steal something. / *Prisoner of Azkaban*, page 198
Winston nicked the brownie off his brother's plate when he wasn't looking.

nightcap (**nite**-kap)
noun A late-night drink, often enjoyed right before bedtime. / *Goblet of Fire*, page 282 / Note: See also the noun **nightcap** below.
"Care for a nightcap, dear?" asked Wildwood's mother, pouring herself a dandelion wine spritzer.

nightcap, nightclothes, nightdress, nightshirt (**nite**-kap, **nite**-close, **nite**-dres, **nite**-shurt)
nouns Clothing to sleep in. / *Chamber of Secrets*, page 179 (nightcap); *Deathly Hallows*, page 590 (nightclothes), *Chamber of Secrets*, page 179 (nightdress); *Goblet of Fire*, page 470 (nightshirt) / Note: See also the noun **nightcap** above.
Mr. and Mrs. Fracket were in their nightclothes, all ready for bed, she in a nightdress and he in a nightcap and nightshirt.

nimbly (**nim**-blee)
adverb Quickly and easily. / *Chamber of Secrets*, page 18
The giant cockroach nimbly jumped out of Blackpool's reach and headed for the kitchen pantry.

nip (rhymes with **zip**)
verb To go somewhere quickly. / *Goblet of Fire*, page 262
"I'll just nip down to the market for some custard tarts," explained Wildwood to his elderly mother.

nobility (no-**bil**-ih-tee)
noun Nobleness; of a high character. / *Half-Blood Prince*, page 644
"Such nobility of character! Such a gallant, chivalrous man!" The duke was toasting his new best friend, the king.

nonchalantly (non-shuh-**lont**-lee)
adverb Unconcernedly and indifferently. / *Prisoner of Azkaban*, page 99
Blackpool nonchalantly looked up from his knitting and grunted, "What? You got a problem?"

noncommittal (non-kuh-**mit**-ul)
adjective Not committing yourself; being a little vague, evasive, or guarded. / *Deathly Hallows*, page 144
The new boy gave a noncommittal shrug when Willow asked if he liked puppies.

nondescript (non-dih-**skript**)
adjective Ordinary; neither unusual nor interesting. / *Chamber of Secrets*, page 231
The wizard's shoes looked nondescript, but he was the only one who knew they turned into inline skates.

nonentity (non-en-tih-tee)

noun Someone of little or no importance. / *Goblet of Fire*, page 203

Bella looked right through Bubba, as if he were a total nonentity—they were not getting along at all.

nonplussed (non-plusd)

adjective Totally bewildered and puzzled. / *Chamber of Secrets*, page 90

The librarian was completely nonplussed when green smoke started coming out of the library's ornamental fireplace.

nonverbal (non-vur-bul)

adjective Not verbal; not spoken out loud. / *Half-Blood Prince*, page 217

Willow's nonverbal signals indicated she wasn't as happy with the new boyfriend as she had been at first—standing three feet apart is always a clear sign.

nook and cranny

phrase Everywhere in a place, including the tucked-away, hidden places. / *Goblet of Fire*, page 39

Mrs. Snodgrape searched every nook and cranny of her house for her antique teledrone.

nosh (rhymes with **posh**)

noun A light meal, or sometimes, a snack. If someone calls a large meal just "an excellent nosh," they're used to very big meals indeed. / *Prisoner of Azkaban*, page 27

Winston's mum put a tray of crumpets and custard tarts on the table and said, "Time for a nosh, boys."

nostril (nos-trul)

noun A nose opening. / *Sorcerer's Stone*, page 84

It's always embarrassing talking to someone who has…well, something in their nose, but it was really difficult when Elrod had a green bean in his left nostril.

not in the same league

phrase To be not nearly as good as something or someone else. / *Sorcerer's Stone*, page 165

The worm had a crush on the butterfly—but he was gray and slimy and she was so colorful. He just wasn't in the same league.

notch (rhymes with **botch**)

noun A level, step, or degree. / *Goblet of Fire*, page 332

Butch Thuggins was a notch better than the other players on his team.

notes (rhymes with **votes**)

noun Paper currency; bills rather than coins. / *Goblet of Fire*, page 77

Wildwood paid for dinner with some notes he'd found in an old book. Reminder—don't use money for a bookmark.

notoriety (noh-tuh-rye-ih-tee)

noun The condition of being widely known, often for some unfavorable or negative reason. / *Deathly Hallows*, page 16

Blackpool's notoriety as an evil wizard had spread far beyond the village limits.

novelty (nov-ul-tee)

noun A doodad or trinket; a small item with low price, high appeal, and little value. / *Half-Blood Prince*, page 118

Merlin always brought back a novelty or two when he went traveling; he particularly liked snow globes.

novice (nov-is)

noun A newbie; someone new to a situation or activity. / *Half-Blood Prince*, page 178

The novice bank robber forgot his mask, his note saying "This is a holdup," and even the banana he was going to pretend was a gun.

noxious (nok-shus)

adjective Harmful or poisonous. / *Order of the Phoenix*, page 516

"That cheap aftershave is so noxious, it's practically peeling the paint off the walls."

nudge (rhymes with **budge**)

verb To poke someone, usually in the ribs and usually to get their attention. / *Chamber of Secrets*, page 85

The old witch nudged her sister: "Just look at the color of that potion. Have you ever seen anything so pretty?"

nutter (nut-tur)
noun In British slang, an insane person. /
Prisoner of Azkaban, page 75
"Only a nutter would do something like that, son," consoled Winston's dad when Winston's stolen bike turned up on top of the church steeple.

O

oaf (rhymes with **loaf**)
noun A stupid or clumsy person. / *Sorcerer's Stone*, page 249
"You oaf! You dropped an entire tray of donuts," screamed the Royal Baker at his apprentice.

obelisk (ob-uh-lisk)
noun A four-sided shaft of stone, like the Washington Monument (though usually much smaller). / *Deathly Hallows*, page 324
The somber obelisk in the cemetery marked the Tomb of the Unknown Wizard.

obituary (oh-bich-oo-air-ee)
noun A notice of someone's death printed in a newspaper. / *Deathly Hallows*, page 20
The obituary appeared in the local paper: "Our dearly beloved mascot, a fine giant horned toad, passed away at the village hospital yesterday, surrounded by friends and family...."

obligatory (uh-blig-uh-tor-ee)
adjective Required or compulsory. / *Deathly Hallows*, page 210
"Introductory Potions is obligatory before you can even think about taking my advanced class," explained the potions master.

obliquely (uh-bleek-lee)
adverb Not directly; at an angle or from the side. / *Deathly Hallows*, page 457
Ravi stared obliquely at the new boy; he wasn't positive but it looked like he had green freckles.

obliterate (uh-blit-uh-rate)
verb To completely destroy something so nothing is left. / *Goblet of Fire*, page 643
The fire obliterated the garden shed—everything was gone, down to the ground.

oblivious (uh-bliv-ee-us)
adjective Not noticing, unaware, unmindful. / *Goblet of Fire*, page 450
The swimmers were oblivious to their new poolmates—several jellyfish.

obscene (ub-seen)
adjective Offensive, indecent. / *Half-Blood Prince*, page 207
The angry driver's obscene hand gesture *could* have been his pointing out that he was the first to go through the intersection.

obscure (ub-skyoor)
verb To cover or conceal. / *Goblet of Fire*, page 637
The thick clouds completely obscured the solar eclipse.

obsessed (ub-sest)
adjective Totally preoccupied. / *Goblet of Fire*, page 57
Bella is obsessed with her appearance.

obsession (ub-sesh-un)
noun A compulsive preoccupation with something. / *Goblet of Fire*, page 5
Julio's obsession with collecting model dragons was getting out of hand—his latest find was six feet tall.

obsolete (ob-suh-leet)
adjective Out-of-date, outmoded, and over-the-hill. / *Goblet of Fire*, page 307
"Your obsolete theories of fortune-telling are only going to confuse the students," warned the principal.

obtuse (ub-toos)
adjective Not quick on the uptake; dull and not perceptive. / *Order of the Phoenix*, page 658
"Are you just being obtuse on purpose? This is so easy," said Bella, who could do math problems in her sleep. And probably did.

occlude (uh-klood)
verb To close off or block. / *Deathly Hallows*, page 566
"The celestial spirits seem to have occluded my ability to perceive the unknown today," moaned the village fortune-teller.

octave (ok-tiv)

noun In music or sound, a range of eight notes. / *Half-Blood Prince*, page 590

Fiona felt her voice was about an octave too high to sing some songs well, especially "Old Man River."

oddball (od-bawl)

noun Someone unusual, eccentric, and non-conforming. / *Order of the Phoenix*, page 670

Brilly was a troublemaking oddball, Elrod was a clumsy oddball, Winston was a British oddball, Bella was a fashionable oddball. Sometimes Rupert felt like the only normal one in the bunch.

oddity (od-ih-tee)

noun An odd or unusual person or thing. / *Deathly Hallows*, page 302

The green mountain gremlin was an oddity in the village but a very ordinary sight in the mountains.

off-color (off-kul-ur)

adjective Not feeling very well; a little sick. / *Prisoner of Azkaban*, page 58

Dylan felt a bit off-color after lunch; it might have been the cafeteria's new stew recipe.

offhand (off-hand)

adjective Without any preparation or thought. / *Sorcerer's Stone*, page 169

Rupert's offhand report on troll habits sounded like he'd written it at lunchtime.

offspring (off-spring)

noun One's children. / *Half-Blood Prince*, page 368

The king loved his offspring, but the princess was a little flighty and the prince played his drums all day—what would happen to the royal future?

ogle (oh-gul)

verb To stare at or to look at in a flirting way. / *Order of the Phoenix*, page 353

The adoring soccer fans ogled Butch Thuggins and his teammates as they left the locker room for home.

ogre (oh-gur)

noun In folklore, a hideous giant monster who likes to eat people. / *Prisoner of Azkaban*, page 158

The ogres lived high in the foothills and seldom saw anyone from the village.

ointment (oynt-munt)

noun A gooey, spreadable medicine for skin problems or wounds. / *Half-Blood Prince*, page 622

"An ointment of goat bile and essence of eel liver, rubbed on hourly, often clears up problems like that," suggested the dermatolo-witch.

old hat

phrase Old-fashioned; like saying "so yesterday." / *Half-Blood Prince*, page 183

"Dr. Greenteeth, braces are so old hat—my dad can magically straighten my teeth," said the helpful young dental patient.

omen (oh-men)

noun A sign of good luck…or bad. / *Sorcerer's Stone*, page 273

"The omens are good," the ship's captain said. "We'll sail tonight."

ominous (om-uh-nus)

adjective Menacing and threatening. / *Chamber of Secrets*, page 195

Ominous sounds were coming from Blackpool's workshop—what was he building now?

omniscient (om-nish-unt)

adjective All-knowing and infinitely wise. / *Half-Blood Prince*, page 445

"Thanks for thinking I'm omniscient, but I don't know everything; I just know you needed a new dirt bike," said Rupert's kindly dad.

one-off (one-off)

adjective One-shot or one-time. / *Half-Blood Prince*, page 349

The armadillo/possum stew was a one-off lunchtime treat—there just weren't that many armadillos around anymore.

onerous (on-ur-us *or* oh-nur-us)

adjective Burdensome and troublesome. / *Order of the Phoenix*, page 451

The king's duties seemed much more onerous when he had a royal headache.

onslaught (on-slawt)

noun A vigorous attack. / *Deathly Hallows*, page 647

An onslaught of enormous bees successfully chased the picnickers away from the meadow.

opal (oh-pul)

noun A stone used in jewelry, noted for its different colors in different light. / *Goblet of Fire*, page 244

The king and queen gave the princess a lovely opal for her birthday.

opalescent (oh-puh-**les**-unt)

adjective Like an opal, with colors seeming to change. / *Order of the Phoenix*, page 659 / Note: Another related adjective, found in *Prisoner of Azkaban* (page 189), is **opaline**, also meaning "like an opal."

The opalescent fairy lights sparkled over the hillside, a beautiful display of many colors.

opaque (oh-**payk**)

adjective Difficult to see through. / *Goblet of Fire*, page 495

The opaque waters of the lake hid, for a very long time, the giant bloodthirsty leeches living there.

opera glasses (op-ur-uh **gla**-ses)

noun Not glasses to wear to the opera, but small binoculars to get an up-close look at what's going on. / *Order of the Phoenix*, page 705

When Wildwood went to the opera, he took along his opera glasses so he could see the singers close up.

option (op-shun)

noun A choice or possibility. / *Chamber of Secrets*, page 252

"One option, Brilly, is to take summer courses to catch up on your potions work," suggested the school guidance counselor.

orb (orb)

noun A small sphere or globe, like a Christmas ornament. / *Order of the Phoenix*, page 682

Several colorful orbs decorated the holiday wreath on the dwarf's front door.

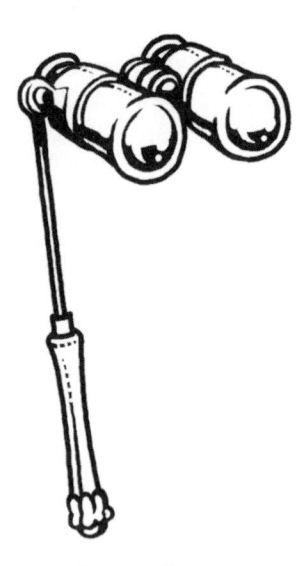

Opera glasses

orifice (or-uh-fis)

noun A bodily opening. / *Deathly Hallows*, page 563

"Brilly, name the body's orifices," said the science teacher, but when Brilly's eyes lit up, she amended her request: "Just the orifices above the waist, please."

originator (uh-**rij**-uh-nay-tur)

noun The original creator of something. / *Prisoner of Azkaban*, page 6

The originator of choco-lotta-latté had made a lot of money with his tasty concoction.

ornament (or-nuh-munt)

noun A decorative object, like a china figure, meant to make a room look more beautiful. / *Goblet of Fire*, page 49

On her coffee table, Mrs. Snodgrape had several china ornaments, including the figure of Rockspurt, the famous wizard, and Mristle, the Newt King.

ornate (or-**nate**)

adjective Fancy and elaborately decorated. / *Sorcerer's Stone*, page 207

The ornate gown had so many decorations sewn on—pearls, gold coins, gilded bat ears—that Bella had a hard time sitting down.

ostentatiously (os-ten-tay-shus-lee)
adverb In a showy, show-off way. / *Order of the Phoenix*, page 369
The queen ostentatiously shook her long string of pearls, then gestured grandly with a hand laden with heavy golden rings.

outcast (out-kast)
noun A homeless wanderer who's been rejected or forced out of his home or society. / *Prisoner of Azkaban*, page 32
Dribbles felt like an outcast—he'd lost his house key and no one was home—maybe he'd have to spend the night in the park.

outcrop (out-krop)
noun A large rock or rocky area sticking up or out from the soil. / *Half-Blood Prince*, page 555
The giant stood on the outcrop high above the village and practiced his yodeling.

outfitter (out-fit-tur)
noun A business that provides equipment or clothing for a specific purpose. / *Goblet of Fire*, page 27
The school outfitters carried every uniform for every school for miles around.

outhouse (out-hows)
noun In British usage, *not* an outdoor toilet, but outbuildings in a yard—like a shed or greenhouse. / *Half-Blood Prince*, page 76
"Put the rake and shovel in the outhouse, please," said Winston's mum.

outmoded (out-moh-did)
adjective Obsolete and out of style; no longer acceptable. / *Order of the Phoenix*, page 213
The outmoded village map was useless—it didn't even have the new library on it, and the Weeping Highway only went part way to the lake.

outrage (out-rayj)
noun Righteous anger. / *Deathly Hallows*, page 41
Wildwood's outrage was justified—someone, or something, had stolen his monster chicken, leaving behind only a few pitiful feathers.

outset (out-set)
noun The beginning. / *Half-Blood Prince*, page 429
From the outset, Wildwood knew he wanted to work with animals.

outskirts (out-skurtz)
noun The area away from the central part of a town or city. / *Sorcerer's Stone*, page 42
The Earl of Silence lived on the outskirts of the city, where it was quieter.

outspoken (out-spoh-kun)
adjective Frank and unreserved in one's speaking; unafraid to speak one's mind. / *Deathly Hallows*, page 574
Brilly had become quite outspoken about the food in the school cafeteria.

outstrip (out-strip)
verb To outdo or surpass. / *Chamber of Secrets*, page 46
Nungie in his wheelchair could outstrip Nathan on his skateboard, and both could outstrip Annie on her old broom.

overcast (oh-vur-kast)
adjective Cloudy. / *Half-Blood Prince*, page 108
Although the overcast skies threatened rain, the Castle Regatta went on as scheduled.

overindulge (oh-vur-in-dulj)
verb To indulge to excess; to eat or drink too much. / *Half-Blood Prince*, page 351
"I believe I have overindulged in the holiday refreshments," said Mr. Fracket, walking home on wobbly legs.

oversee (oh-vur-see)
verb To watch over, and keep an eye on things; to supervise. / *Prisoner of Azkaban*, page 253
Wildwood was willing to oversee the village aquarium until a permanent manager could be hired.

overshadow (oh-vur-shad-oh)
verb To cast a shadow over, or to make someone or something seem insignificant. / *Sorcerer's Stone*, page 213

Her mild dislike for broccoli was overshadowed by her really negative feelings about fried okra.

oversight (oh-vur-site)
noun A failure to notice something. / *Order of the Phoenix*, page 71
By some oversight, no ice cream had been ordered for the school cafeteria.

overt (oh-vurt)
adjective Open and not concealed. / *Goblet of Fire*, page 209
Willow's overt hostility to Blackpool was obvious to everyone.

overtax (oh-vur-taks)
verb To excessively burden or strain someone. / *Prisoner of Azkaban*, page 171
The armadillo/possum stew obviously had overtaxed Dylan's digestive system.

overtime (oh-vur-time)
noun Extra money made by working past the time usually worked. / *Chamber of Secrets*, page 62
He earned overtime teaching extra classes at the Broom Academy.

overwrought (oh-vur-rawt)
adjective Agitated, nervous, and under pressure. / *Order of the Phoenix*, page 682
An overwrought Hassan couldn't sleep the night before the math final.

P

pace (rhymes with **face**)
noun A step or stride. / *Chamber of Secrets*, page 155
According to the map, the treasure was just 100 paces away.

pace (rhymes with **face**)
verb To walk restlessly back and forth. / *Sorcerer's Stone*, page 90
The pack of ghostly hounds paced in the forest, waiting for some word of their missing leader.

pacify (pas-uh-fie)
verb To appease and calm. / *Order of the Phoenix*, page 99
The boy tried to pacify his irate neighbor, but it was difficult when his dog just ate the neighbor's prize begonias.

paddock (pad-uk)
noun An enclosed field. / *Chamber of Secrets*, page 45
Wildwood kept most of his animals in a small paddock behind his house.

painstaking (painz-tay-king)
adjective Careful and diligent; taking pains to do something right and well. / *Half-Blood Prince*, page 363
It took some painstaking research, but the librarian finally determined that the village had been founded 526 years ago by Rockspurt, the famous wizard and alchemist.

paisley (pays-lee)
adjective Patterned with colorful, curved swirls and shapes. / *Sorcerer's Stone*, page 210
Bella's paisley skirt was so beautiful, even her brother complimented her.

pallid (pal-id)
adjective Pale and colorless; usually said of someone's complexion or skin color. / *Prisoner of Azkaban*, page 75
"I don't feel so good," said a pallid Dylan, right before he threw up in his cauldron.

pallor (pal-ur)
noun Unusual or extreme paleness. / *Half-Blood Prince*, page 113
A vampire's pallor is partially caused by his never seeing the sun.

palmistry (pah-muh-stree)
noun The telling of fortunes by looking at the lines on a person's hands. / *Prisoner of Azkaban*, page 53
The lecture on palmistry started badly when the teacher looked at the principal's hand and burst into tears.

palomino (pal-uh-**mee**-no)
noun A horse or pony that's golden, with a white mane and tail. Often "palomino horse" but sometimes just "palomino." / *Order of the Phoenix*, page 598
Katie's new palomino horse was named Butterscotch; she was so pleased the palomino was already well-trained and easy to ride.

palpable (pal-puh-bul)
adjective Tangible; able to be seen or heard. / *Goblet of Fire*, page 92
The excitement was palpable as the villagers eagerly awaited the start of the Castle Regatta.

pandemonium (pan-duh-**moh**-nee-um)
noun Wild uproar and chaos. / *Chamber of Secrets*, page 102
Pandemonium at the Castle Regatta: The raft race ended in a tie, but the king declared the castle entry the winner.

pang (rhymes with **hang**)
noun A sudden feeling of emotional or physical distress. / *Order of the Phoenix*, page 334
Willow was uncertain if it was pangs of hunger or pangs of love she felt when she first saw the new boy in the cafeteria.

The Unofficial Harry Potter Vocabulary Builder • 143

paramount (pare-uh-mount)
adjective Of chief importance. / *Deathly Hallows*, page 56
"It's paramount that you learn proper wand techniques from the beginning so bad habits don't become ingrained," said Madam Glinch.

paranoid (pare-uh-noyd)
adjective Affected with paranoia, an extreme or irrational fear or distrust of others. / *Goblet of Fire*, page 162
The paranoid old witch always locked up her cauldron when she went out.

parapet (pare-uh-pet)
noun A low wall along the edge of a high roof or balcony. / *Order of the Phoenix*, page 718
The castle workers watched the Castle Regatta from the tower's parapet, high above the crowds around the moat.

Parapet

parasite (pare-uh-site)
noun An organism that lives on or in another, feeding on it and giving nothing in return. / *Order of the Phoenix*, page 822
"You're like a sticky parasite. Just leave me alone," Rupert shouted at his little brother, who'd been following him all day.

parasitic (pare-uh-sit-ik)
adjective Like a parasite, especially the characteristic of living on another organism. / *Deathly Hallows*, page 687
The parasitic vines were slowly strangling the willow trees down by the lake.

parcel (par-sul)
noun A wrapped package or bundle, usually one to be mailed. / *Sorcerer's Secret*, page 21
"Could you mail the parcel for your great grand-dad after school, Winston? Next week's his 142nd birthday."

parcel (par-sul)
verb To divide or share something among several others; used with "out." / *Deathly Hallows*, page 545
Brilly parceled out the tasks: Dribbles asks the teacher lots of questions, Elrod flicks the lights, Willow silently opens the storage cabinet door, and Brilly grabs the contents and heads out the classroom door.

parched (rhymes with **arched**)
adjective Very dry. / *Order of the Phoenix*, page 1
The severe drought meant most of the parched lawns in the village were slowly turning brown and dying.

parchment (parch-munt)
noun A paper-like writing material made from sheep or goat skin. / *Sorcerer's Stone*, page 34
The math teacher handed out blank parchments for the quiz: "Please be prepared to show your work—if you need additional parchment, just raise your hand."

parentage (pare-un-tij)
noun Specifically, one's parents; more generally, their origins (social class, country, etc.). / *Half-Blood Prince*, page 637
The parentage of Wildwood's old dog was uncertain—he looked like a wolf-poodle-pug-labrador mix!

parlor (par-lur)
noun A lounge or private room in a bar or club for private meetings. / *Prisoner of Azkaban*, page 43
The Chamber of Wizards met monthly in the back parlor at the Witching Hour pub.

parody (pare-uh-dee)

noun An action that copies something, often in a vaguely humorous way. / *Deathly Hallows*, page 371

Brilly's parody of the teacher's walk had the whole class laughing.

paroxysm (pare-uk-siz-um *or* pah-rocks-siz-um)

noun A sudden violent and uncontrollable emotion or action. / *Order of the Phoenix*, page 595

Paroxysms of laughter greeted an egg-faced Hassan, victim of a reverse-scramble spell.

parrot (pare-ut)

verb To repeat without thought, like a parrot. / *Deathly Hallows*, page 198

The *Repeato* spell worked perfectly—Dylan was parroting the "Allegiance to Wizardry" pledge over and over.

parry (pare-ee)

verb To defend oneself by blocking or deflecting an attack. / *Half-Blood Prince*, page 602

Dylan tried to parry the *Repeato* spell, but he wasn't fast enough.

partisan (par-tuh-zun)

adjective Strongly supporting one side, especially with biased emotional feelings. / *Order of the Phoenix*, page 400

The partisan crowd, opposed to the condos-in-the-meadow idea, booed every pro-condo speaker at the meeting.

pastille (pah-steel)

noun A lozenge, like a cough drop or small hard candy. / *Order of the Phoenix*, page 104

Madam Glinch kept a packet of pastilles in her desk drawer in case a sudden coughing fit occurred.

pasty (pay-stee)

adjective Pale and sickly, usually said of complexions. / *Chamber of Secrets*, page 128 / Note: See also the noun **pasty** below, especially the different pronunciation.

The boy's pasty face suggested he might be having stomach problems—that, plus he'd just burped 26 times in a row.

pasty (past-tee)

noun In British usage, a sort of folded-over meat pie; also made with vegetables or fruits. / *Sorcerer's Stone*, page 101 / Note: Sometimes referred to as **Cornish pasty**, as seen in *Goblet of Fire* (page 618). See also the adjective **pasty** above, especially its different pronunciation.

Winston's mother had put a turnip-and-toad pasty (his least favorite) in his lunch.

patchwork (patch-wurk)

noun A mixture of many pieces or parts, often having the regularity and pattern of sewn pieces of cloth. / *Chamber of Secrets*, page 31

Elrod looked across the patchwork of fields stretching to the horizon and thought it'd be perfect for a giant tic-tac-toe game.

patchwork quilt (patch-wurk kwilt)

noun A bed covering made of cloth pieces of various colors or patterns sewn together. / *Sorcerer's Stone*, page 140

When Willow was sick, she just wanted to stay in bed snuggled under her patchwork quilt.

pate (rhymes with **fate**)

noun The top of the head. / *Order of the Phoenix*, page 57

Katie's dad protected his bald pate from sunburn with a cowboy hat.

patently (pah-tunt-lee *or* pay-tunt-lee)

adverb Obviously; clearly. / *Deathly Hallows*, page 228

The massive cauldron was patently too large to fit through the doorway.

paternal (puh-tur-nul)

adjective Fatherly; caring. / *Goblet of Fire*, page 257

With a paternal air, the king greeted the visiting schoolchildren and even patted one or two on the head.

pattering (pah-tur-ing)

adjective Soft, quick, tapping. / *Deathly Hallows*, page 221

The pattering sounds of little paws coming up the stairs meant Willow's puppies were ready for breakfast.

paunchy (pawn-chee)

adjective Potbellied. / *Goblet of Fire*, page 302
The doctor had a hard time recommending dieting to his overweight patients when he was so paunchy himself.

pavement (payv-munt)

noun In British usage, a sidewalk. / *Sorcerer's Stone*, page 9
Winston stood on the pavement, watching the annual Parade of the Invertebrates.

pay the consequences

phrase To accept and deal with the results of one's actions. / *Order of the Phoenix*, page 757
"Brilly, I hope you're prepared to pay the consequences for your wild behavior," said the principal.

peaky (pee-kee)

adjective In British usage, pale and ill-looking; often used in the phrase "look a bit peaky." / *Order of the Phoenix*, page 488 / Note: American usage would more likely be "You look a bit peaked," pronounced **pee**-kid.
"You look a bit peaky today. Did you take your vitamins? Did you sleep well last night?" worried Winston's mum.

peckish (pek-ish)

adjective A little hungry. / *Goblet of Fire*, page 366
By the time school was over, Winston was feeling peckish.

pedestal (ped-uh-stul)

noun A column or post that supports a table, statue, etc. / *Half-Blood Prince*, page 567
The china figure of Mristle, the Newt King, sat on a small pedestal on Mrs. Snodgrape's coffee table.

peer (rhymes with **ear**)

noun Someone else in the same group as you (same age or same job or same class, etc.). / *Goblet of Fire*, page 176
Brilly's peers thought his antics humorous; his elders did not.

peer (rhymes with **ear**)

verb To look at something intensely. / *Sorcerer's Stone*, page 152
Mother Serpent peered proudly at little Slick, slithering around like he'd never slithered before.

peevishly (pee-vish-lee)

adverb In a cross, cranky, impatient, or annoyed way. / *Goblet of Fire*, page 60
"Stop bothering me," said the old man peevishly.

pell-mell (pell-mell)

adverb In a hasty, uncontrolled way. / *Half-Blood Prince*, page 211
Students ran pell-mell out the door, eager to start the weekend.

pelt (rhymes with **melt**)

verb To throw at again and again. / *Sorcerer's Stone*, page 132 / Note: See the related verb **pelt** below.
Brilly pelted the girls with slimy Algerian puffballs.

pelt (rhymes with **melt**)

verb To move really quickly. / *Sorcerer's Stone*, page 41 / Note: See the related verb **pelt** above.
The girls pelted down the street as fast as they could to avoid Brilly and his Algerian puffballs.

penfriend (pen-frend)

noun In British usage, a pen pal. / *Goblet of Fire*, page 84
Winston's penfriend had just written that she might be able to come visit him someday soon.

penitence (pen-ih-tuns)

noun Regret for a former wrongdoing. / *Deathly Hallows*, page 616
Even evil Blackpool could feel some regret—as penitence for enchanting Willow's puppies, he brought her a huge bag of puppy food.

pensive (pen-siv)

adjective Thoughtful, perhaps even a bit sad. / *Goblet of Fire*, page 219
A pensive Wildwood sat quietly smoking his pipe by the lake.

peony bush (pee-uh-nee bush)

noun An outdoor plant with large showy

flowers. / *Chamber of Secrets,* page 36
The blossoms on the peony bush were as large as saucers.

perchance (pur-**chance**)
adverb Perhaps. / *Prisoner of Azkaban,* page 100
"Perchance you'll find time to do your homework tonight, class?" asked the teacher of her students, with a touch of irony.

perfidy (**pur**-fih-dee)
noun Faithlessness and treachery. / *Deathly Hallows,* page 616
It was Blackpool's perfidy that had turned the villagers against him.

perfunctory (pur-**fungk**-tuh-ree)
adjective Hasty and almost careless or indifferent. / *Deathly Hallows,* page 78
With a perfunctory wave to his mom, the little boy headed off to school.

perilously (**pare**-uh-lus-lee)
adverb Dangerously. / *Order of the Phoenix,* page 286
The giant cockroach was getting perilously close to the kitchen pantry.

perimeter (puh-**rim**-ih-tur)
noun The border around a specific area. / *Goblet of Fire,* page 325
The perimeter of the Haunted Forest was marked with large warning signs—no one could wander in by mistake.

periodic (peer-ee-**od**-ik)
adjective Repeated at irregular intervals. / *Half-Blood Prince,* page 391
Wildwood's periodic absences from the Chamber of Wizards meeting were caused by his caring for his elderly mother.

periwinkle (**pare**-uh-wing-kul)
adjective Blue-violet, like the flower of the periwinkle plant. / *Chamber of Secrets,* page 265
Bella took a periwinkle flower to the hairdresser and said, "*This* is the color I want my hair to be."

permeate (**pur**-mee-ate)
verb To penetrate every part of something or someplace. / *Order of the Phoenix,* page 107

When the prince was practicing his drumming, the banging seemed to permeate every corner of the castle.

perpetrate (pur-**pih**-trayt)
verb To commit or to be responsible for a deed, like a crime or bad joke. / *Order of the Phoenix,* page 100
"Who perpetrated this dastardly act?" shouted Blackpool when he discovered his worm farm overturned and all the worms wiggling away.

perpetrator (pur-**pih**-tray-tor)
noun Someone who commits or is responsible for a deed, like a crime or a bad joke. / *Half-Blood Prince,* page 85
The perpetrators of the worm farm offense were actually some wandering goats.

persecution (pur-sih-**kyoo**-shun)
noun The act of persecuting or treating someone unfairly or cruelly, especially for their beliefs. / *Chamber of Secrets,* page 150
In the early days, many of the villagers feared persecution for their wizardry beliefs, but there never had been any trouble.

perseverance (pur-suh-**veer**-uns)
noun The determination to keep at a task despite difficulties. / *Order of the Phoenix,* page 665
Fiona's perseverance in learning to play the guitar was admirable.

perturbed (pur-**turbd**)
adjective Uneasy or anxious. / *Goblet of Fire,* page 552
Mother Serpent was perturbed—it was late and where were the children? And who were they out slithering around with?

peruse (puh-**rooz**)
verb To read or look at something closely. / *Order of the Phoenix,* page 331
Tamika was perusing her math book, but it was like reading another language—algebra just made no sense to her.

pestilential (pes-tih-**len**-shul)
adjective Likely to cause a nasty disease; more

generally, annoying and troublesome. / *Order of the Phoenix*, page 6
"You pestilential buzzards! Get out of my corn field!"

pestle (pes-uhl)
noun A short rounded stick, used with a small bowl called a mortar, to crush and grind up substances by hand. / *Goblet of Fire*, page 513
The old witch used her mortar and pestle to grind up the dried bat wings.

petrol (peh-trul)
noun In British usage, gasoline. / *Goblet of Fire*, page 195
"We almost ran out of petrol on the way home," said Winston's mum.

petty (pet-ee)
adjective Trivial, unimportant. / *Goblet of Fire*, page 438
"Young man, you may think these are just petty rules, but they're important to a safe educational experience for all," advised the principal.

petulantly (pech-uh-lunt-lee)
adverb In an impatient, irritated way, like a small child. / *Chamber of Secrets*, page 223
"I don't wanna use a bed pan," whined Dylan petulantly.

pewter (pyoo-tur)
adjective Made of pewter, a grayish mix of tin and lead. / *Sorcerer's Stone*, page 67
The king's pewter goblets had to be washed by hand but, unlike the silver goblets, they never got shiny… just sort of dull-looking.

pheasant (fez-unt)
noun A large wild bird. / *Half-Blood Prince*, page 144
The king served pheasant, beef, and tofu at his Friday Feast; most of his guests chose beef.

phial (fie-ul)
noun A small glass or crystal bottle containing a liquid. / *Sorcerer's Stone*, page 67 / Note: The more common **vial**, as seen in *Goblet of Fire* (page 642), is also used.

Merlin emptied one phial after another into the bubbling cauldron.

phlegm (rhymes with **Clem**)
noun The gunky mucus in your throat, especially when you have a cold. / *Half-Blood Prince*, page 93 / Note: In Potter's world, Phlegm is a nickname for the lovely—and very French—Fleur Delacour.
"Phlegm, phlegm, phlegm, I'm drow-dig in phlegm," moaned a stuffed-up, red-nosed, bleary-eyed Dylan.

phoenix (fee-nix)
noun A large mythical bird that lives for centuries, then bursts into flames and dies, but rises renewed from the ashes. It's considered a symbol of immortality. / *Sorcerer's Stone*, page 84 / Note: In Potter's world, the phoenix is also a gentle, faithful bird, whose tears have healing powers.
A large drawing of a phoenix hung on the entrance wall of the library because the new library had risen from the ashes of the old one, after that terrible fire Blackpool's father had set.

Phoenix

phosphorescent (fos-fuh-res-unt)
adjective Glowing without burning or heat. /

Half-Blood Prince, page 567
The phosphorescent light at the tip of Wildwood's wand was blinking—that meant danger ahead.

physique (fih-**zeek**)
noun Body structure or appearance. / *Order of the Phoenix*, page 11
Rupert felt it was time to build up his physique; he was tired of looking and feeling—and being called—wimpy.

pickled (**pik**-uld)
adjective Preserved in a vinegary or briny liquid; done to preserve medical specimens. / *Sorcerer's Stone*, page 136
The village doctor had dozens of pickled medical specimens on the shelves in his waiting room. Funny, nobody ever liked to wait long at the doctor's office.

pigheadedness (**pig**-**hed**-id-ness)
noun Stubbornness and obstinacy. / *Half-Blood Prince*, page 169
Brilly's pigheadedness constantly got him into trouble.

pike (rhymes with **like**)
noun A very bony freshwater fish. / *Deathly Hallows*, page 293
Fishing for pike was much more fun than eating it—too many bones.

pilfer (**pil**-fur)
verb To steal. / *Deathly Hallows*, page 177
Someone had pilfered the newly planted flowers surrounding the village green—it was either the Thieves Guild or a very hungry goat.

pillock (**pih**-lok)
noun A stupid person. / *Goblet of Fire*, page 152
"You pillock," sighed the Royal Plumber as his apprentice dropped his wrench in the castle moat.

pinafore dress (**pin**-uh-for **dress**)
noun In British usage, a sleeveless dress worn over a blouse or sweater. / *Order of the Phoenix*, page 483 / Note: In American usage, this would be called a jumper.
"I'd really like to get that new pinafore dress on sale at the Hurly Burly Emporium," sighed Winston's mum.

pince-nez (**pans**-nay)
noun An old-fashioned pair of glasses that is clipped on the nose with no pieces extending over the ears. / *Chamber of Secrets*, page 51
The old wizard put on his pince-nez and settled down to work on the crossword puzzle.

pincer (**pin**-sur)
noun An animal's claw useful for holding and cutting food or for fighting; usually used in the plural. / *Chamber of Secrets*, page 247
The giant crab snapped its pincers at the swimmers, who quickly decided it was time to go home.

pincushion (**pin**-kush-un)
noun A small cushion that extra sewing pins are stuck into. / *Goblet of Fire*, page 233
Bella's mother put the last pins in the pincushion, turned the dress hem down, and said, "There, that's shorter."

pine (rhymes with **mine**)
verb To yearn for, and to suffer from being apart. / *Prisoner of Azkaban*, page 23
Willow pined for her puppies when she was at school, but they mostly slept the entire time she was gone.

pinion (**pin**-yun)
verb To pin someone's arms so they can't use them or get away. / *Order of the Phoenix*, page 742
Bella and Tamika pinioned Milton's arms to his sides, then frog-marched him out of their very private clubhouse.

pinprick (**pin**-prik)
noun A tiny hole, as if made by a pin. / *Sorcerer's Stone*, page 9
Willow theorized that the nighttime sky was really a magician's giant cloak, and that the stars were just pinpricks in the cloth.

pinstriped (**pin**-striped)
adjective Having a thin, pale line on a darker background; usually refers to cloth or clothing. / *Chamber of Secrets*, page 260
Wildwood looked especially dapper in his pinstriped waistcoat.

The Unofficial Harry Potter Vocabulary Builder • 149

pirouette (peer-oo-et)

noun A whirling about on one foot; if you're a ballet dancer, on your toes. / *Prisoner of Azkaban*, page 281
The lively Whirling Derbies dance group did pirouettes all down the lane.

piston (pis-tun)

noun The part of a train locomotive that looks like a short, solid piece of metal inside a tube. / *Prisoner of Azkaban*, page 81
The locomotive's pistons began to hiss as the train slowly pulled out of the village station.

pitch (rhymes with **itch**)

noun In British usage, the central part of a cricket playing field. / *Chamber of Secrets*, page 107 / Note: In Potter's world, the pitch is the Quidditch field.
"Let's go over to the cricket pitch and practice," suggested Winston.

piteous (pit-ee-us)

adjective Pitiful and pathetic. / *Chamber of Secrets*, page 162
The piteous sounds of baby kittens are hard to resist.

pittance (pit-ns)

noun A small sum; usually refers to a small income or amount paid. / *Half-Blood Prince*, page 437
The king paid a mere pittance to the workers cleaning the slimy castle moat.

pixie (pik-see)

noun A fairylike creature that is elfin and playful, even mischievous. / *Chamber of Secrets*, page 101 / Note: In Potter's world, pixies—specifically Cornish pixies—are small, bright blue, rude, and extremely mischievous.
The pixie enjoyed sitting on the basketball rim and knocking away every ball coming anywhere near it.

placate (play-kate)

verb To appease or pacify. / *Order of the Phoenix*, page 259
The octopus placated the arguing seahorses by suggesting they swim well-separated for a while.

placatory (play-kuh-tor-ee)

adjective Appeasing or placating. / *Order of the Phoenix*, page 705
The mayor's placatory remarks to Blackpool made him feel a little better about receiving only one vote in the election.

placidly (plas-id-lee)

adverb Calmly and quietly. / *Prisoner of Azkaban*, page 103
"I rather enjoy slamming doors," thought the poltergeist placidly.

plague (playg)

verb To bother or torment. / *Order of the Phoenix*, page 7
Rupert had been plagued by his annoying little brother all afternoon.

plaintively (playn-tiv-lee)

adverb Sadly and mournfully. / *Half-Blood Prince*, page 488
Fiona plaintively sang "The Lament of the Lovesick Lizard" and got tears all over her guitar strings.

plait (rhymes with **fate**; sounds exactly like **plate**)

noun Something braided, usually hair. / *Goblet of Fire*, page 241
Esmerelda braided her long black hair into a single plait, hanging down her back almost to her waist.

plane (rhymes with **sane**)

noun A level or standard of understanding. / *Order of the Phoenix*, page 34
"Now class, let's take the time-shifter potion to a different plane altogether—time zones."

plaque (rhymes with **hack**)

noun An inscribed flat sign, usually of metal or stone. / *Chamber of Secrets*, page 40
The plaque on Blackpool's front door read "Abandon hope all ye who enter here."

plaster (plas-tur)

noun In British usage, a band-aid. / *Half-Blood Prince,* page 422

"Put a plaster on that cut or it'll bleed all over your white shirt," warned Winston's mum as they were about to head off to dinner at the fancy Howling Rock restaurant.

plausible (plaw-zuh-bul)

adjective Believable or realistic. / *Order of the Phoenix,* page 576

Brilly was laughing too much to make his fake heart attack seem even the tiniest bit plausible.

pliable (ply-uh-bul)

adjective Flexible or bendable. / *Sorcerer's Stone,* page 82

The new parchment wasn't very pliable yet, and it was hard to roll up into a scroll.

plied

See **ply** elsewhere in this dictionary.

plight (rhymes with **light**)

noun A situation, usually a difficult or unpleasant one. / *Order of the Phoenix,* page 556

Bella's plight was painful—she'd known Bubba since second grade, and he was a nice guy, but they didn't have much in common anymore.

plinth (plinth)

noun A base for a statue, column, etc. / *Prisoner of Azkaban,* page 243

The lengthy inscription on the statue's plinth began "In Honor of Merlin, Wizard Extraordinaire and Great Friend to The Village, Who Has Always...."

plonk (rhymes with **honk**)

verb To sit down heavily. / *Half-Blood Prince,* page 90

Bubba plonked down next to his dad and sadly confided, "I just don't understand girls."

plumage (ploo-mij)

noun The feathers covering a bird's body. / *Chamber of Secrets,* page 207

The plumage of Jake the budgie was mostly green and yellow, except for that one bare spot where he'd pulled out all his feathers.

plumb (rhymes with **dumb**)

verb To examine thoroughly or deeply; to probe. / *Deathly Hallows,* page 550

Mrs. Snodgrape plumbed her memory—hadn't she once had another student as troublesome as Brilly?

plumed (rhymes with **zoomed**)

adjective Having a plume (a feather) or plumes. / *Chamber of Secrets,* page 123

Mrs. Snodgrape selected her plumed hat—the dressiest one—to wear to the memorial service for the village mascot.

plummet (plum-it)

verb To fall or drop rapidly. / *Chamber of Secrets,* page 206

Captain Hummingbird plummeted from the treetop to the most appealing blossom in the garden.

plunderer (plun-dur-ur)

noun Someone who plunders or robs. / *Chamber of Secrets,* page 52

The little boy carefully adjusted his towel cape, jumped out in front of his parents, and shouted, "I am the Masked Plunderer, coming to steal all your jewels and stuff!"

plus-fours (plus-fors)

noun Old-fashioned golfing pants—loose and baggy, gathered a few inches below the knee; used in the plural. / *Goblet of Fire,* page 77

Mr. Glinch took a day off from gardening to play golf; he looked very elegant in his plus-fours, argyle socks, and silk tie.

ply (rhymes with **why**)

verb To offer somewhat insistently. Past tense: plied. / *Half-Blood Prince,* page 106

The king plied his guests with a 17-course meal, plus never-empty goblets of elderberry wine.

pocket watch (pok-it watch)

noun A round watch that fits in a pocket or hangs from a chain worn across a man's waistcoat. / *Prisoner of Azkaban,* page 391

Wildwood checked his pocket watch—yep, the mayor had been speaking for over an hour.

pockmarked (pok-markd)

adjective Marked or scarred with pockmarks, small pits left from smallpox or really bad acne. / *Order of the Phoenix*, page 585
The pockmarked thief should have worn a mask—he'd be easy to identify.

podgy (poj-ee)

adjective Pudgy or plump. / *Deathly Hallows*, page 224
The podgy cauldron salesman was shaped much like the cauldrons he sold.

podium (poh-dee-um)

noun A lectern or stand for a speaker to put his notes on. / *Chamber of Secrets*, page 136
The mayor stepped forward, carefully placed his notes on the podium, and began his annual "State of the Village" speech.

point-blank (point-blank)

adverb Bluntly, frankly, and quickly. / *Goblet of Fire*, page 345
"No, Brilly," refused his father point-blank. "You cannot have a fire extinguisher for your birthday."

poker (poh-kur)

noun A fireplace tool used to stir a fire; a long, straight, metal rod. / *Sorcerer's Stone*, page 48
Chi-Mun used the poker to straighten the logs in the fireplace. They needed to be burning well before the evening's marshmallow-and-jello roast.

polecat (pole-kat)

noun In British usage, a wild animal much like a weasel or ferret that is able to defend itself with a yucky smell. / *Prisoner of Azkaban*, page 98 / Note: In American usage, a polecat is a skunk.
"Jeesh, did you fall in the bog? You smell worse than a polecat."

poltergeist (pole-tur-guyst)

noun A ghost or spirit that makes mysterious noisy disturbances. / *Sorcerer's Stone*, page 129
The poltergeist was slamming doors in the middle of the night…again.

Poltergeist

pompous (pom-pus)

adjective Having exaggerated dignity; speaking or writing with many high-sounding bombastic words. / *Half-Blood Prince*, page 182
The pompous manner of the mayor annoyed many in the village. He never said just "Hello"—it was always "Good day, fellow citizen, and how does this lovely day find one of my dearest constituents?"

poncho (pon-cho)

noun A blanket-like cloak—one large piece of cloth with a hole in the center for one's head; sometimes used as rainwear. / *Goblet of Fire*, page 75
"Brilly, there is no such thing as a prom poncho, so you'll have to wear a suit or rent a tux."

ponder (pon-dur)

verb To consider or think deeply about something. / *Deathly Hallows*, page 181
Mrs. Fracket pondered her great-grandmother's dying words: "Whatever you do, never, ever, go in the—."

popinjay (pop-in-jay)

noun An overly proud, overly talkative person. / *Order of the Phoenix*, page 496

"Listen, popinjay, I'd like to hear nothing but humble silence from you for the rest of the day."

porkpie hat (pork-pie hat)

noun A man's hat made of heavy felt, with a low flat crown and a flexible brim going all the way around. / *Deathly Hallows*, page 151
Mr. Snodgrape preferred his porkpie hat on chilly or rainy days.

portent (pore-tent)

noun An omen or other indication of something soon to happen. / *Goblet of Fire*, page 200
The portents were not all good for a successful Day of the Dead celebration, but the villagers decided to go ahead anyway.

portentously (pore-ten-shus-lee)

adverb Pompously. / *Half-Blood Prince*, page 182
The principal portentously ended his speech to the graduates: "And now, let us raise our voices in glorious harmony, singing together as one united group, our beloved school song."

portly (port-lee)

adjective Stout, even fat. / *Chamber of Secrets*, page 133
The portly wizard was finding it harder and harder to bend over to tie his shoelaces—thank goodness for shoelace magic.

post (rhymes with **ghost**)

noun In British usage, the mail. / *Goblet of Fire*, page 148
"Oh dear, the post still hasn't come and I was hoping my Fears Catalog would arrive today," said Winston's mum.

post (rhymes with **ghost**)

noun A position or office. / *Deathly Hallows*, page 226
Wildwood has just been named to the post of Interim Zoo Director until a new director is found.

postbox (post-box)

noun In British usage, a public mailbox for outgoing mail. / *Order of the Phoenix*, page 132 / Note: See also **letterbox** elsewhere in this dictionary.
"Drop these letters in the postbox on your way to school, would you?" asked Winston's mum.

potter (pot-ur)

verb To putter around; to work on something in a slow, easy way. / *Goblet of Fire*, page 5
Mr. Glinch loved to potter around his garden, weeding, spreading manure, whatever.

pouchy (pow-chee)

adjective Having fleshy little pouches or bags on one's face, like on the cheeks or under the eyes. / *Chamber of Secrets*, page 128
The bags under the eyes of the old man's pouchy face practically hung down over his cheekbones.

pouffe (poof)

noun An upholstered footstool, usually round. / *Half-Blood Prince*, page 369 / Note: This can also be spelled **pouf**, as seen in *Prisoner of Azkaban* (page 102).
"Put your feet up on the pouffe, dear, and I'll bring you a glass of sherry," said Mr. Snodgrape to his tired wife.

pound (rhymes with **mound**)

noun A British unit of money currently worth about 50 cents. / *Sorcerer's Stone*, page 76
Wildwood had to get used to paying with pounds instead of village money every time he visited London.

poxy (poks-ee)

adjective In British slang, either something worthless, or just a word to negatively intensify whatever is being said—for example, saying "those poxy napkin rings" would be much like saying "those darned napkin rings." / *Deathly Hallows*, page 100
"Mum, do I really have to shine these poxy shoes just for graduation?" asked Winston.

pram (rhymes with **bam**)

noun A baby carriage. / *Deathly Hallows*, page 344
Rupert discovered his old pram in the attic. It was dusty and covered in cobwebs, and filled with all his old baby toys.

prat (rhymes with **fat**)

noun In British slang, a stupid fool; it can also mean the buttocks, so saying "You're a

stupid prat" is like saying "You're a stupid ass." / *Goblet of Fire*, page 289
"You prat," said the Royal Cook to the Royal Dishwasher. "You ate the last piece of the king's favorite pie."

prattle (prat-ul)
noun Chatter or babbling. / *Chamber of Secrets*, page 120
The baby's prattle slowed and then faded away completely as he had drifted off to sleep.

preamble (pree-am-bul)
noun An introductory remark or lead-in. / *Goblet of Fire*, page 570
At the staff meeting, and without any preamble, the principal launched into an explanation for his taking a leave of absence, but most of the teachers just looked bored.

precocious (pruh-koh-shus)
adjective Advanced; ahead of normal development. / *Order of the Phoenix*, page 510
"That's precocious broomstick work after only a few months in the air, Annie," complimented Wildwood, as she flew past him upside down and backwards.

predecease (pree-duh-sees)
verb To die first or before someone else. / *Half-Blood Prince*, page 50
"So, should you predecease me, dear," said the queen, "do I get to be queen all by myself?"

predecessor (pred-uh-ses-ur)
noun Someone who came before in a job or position. / *Half-Blood Prince*, page 6
The mayor's predecessor had originated the Day of the Dead festivities, the village's annual fall celebration.

predispose (pree-duh-spoz)
verb To have an inclination or tendency beforehand. / *Half-Blood Prince*, page 439
Blackpool—the evil wizard—was predisposed to dislike people before he even knew them well.

preen (rhymes with **keen**)
verb To primp or groom a little too much or too carefully. / *Goblet of Fire*, page 93
Bella loved walking downtown—she'd stop in front of every shop window to preen.

prefect (pree-fekt)
noun A student monitor, usually in the upper grades in a private school. / *Sorcerer's Stone*, page 96
The headmaster was about to announce the names of the new prefects, but everyone was really more interested in who was going to be on the soccer team.

preferential (pref-uh-ren-shul)
adjective Having preference; being favored. / *Half-Blood Prince*, page 190
"Of course everyone is equal here and no one will get preferential treatment," said the math teacher, but everyone knew he favored Bella, the smartest kid in the class.

pregnant pause
noun A pause when speaking that's full of meaning or emotion. / *Chamber of Secrets*, page 304
The principal began, "I have an important announcement to make," and then there was a long pregnant pause.

prematurely (pree-muh-choor-lee)
adverb Sooner than expected or what's usual. / *Order of the Phoenix*, page 527
Her prematurely lined face made her look old and wizened.

premises (prem-ih-sus)
noun Land or buildings that a shop, restaurant, cabin, etc., are on; used in the plural. / *Order of the Phoenix*, page 105
The wandmaker's premises were right next to the Hurly Burly Emporium and across the street from the premises of the school outfitters.

premonition (preh-muh-nish-un)
noun A strange feeling that something—most likely bad—is going to happen. / *Goblet of Fire*, page 577
Wildwood had a premonition that the Day of the Dead festivities might not go well.

preoccupation (pree-awk-yuh-**pay**-shun)

noun A matter that someone is preoccupied with; something having one's attention. / *Half-Blood Prince*, page 520

The chief preoccupation of the four girls was how to get out of the locked Museum of Magic; then they'd worry about getting home.

prestigious (pres-**tij**-us)

adjective Having a great reputation; being the best or most important. / *Order of the Phoenix*, page 308

Most of the graduates were hoping to go on to a prestigious wizarding college, but Ravi, who never much liked school, was looking around for a job in the village.

presumption (pree-**zump**-shun)

noun Behavior that's rude, too confident, and pushy. / *Deathly Hallows*, page 376

"Your presumption is annoying, young lady. Please try not to be so rude and uppity."

pretense (**pree**-tens)

noun Pretending; make-believe. / *Half-Blood Prince*, page 591 / Note: The British spelling **pretence** also appears in *Goblet of Fire* (page 93).

Under the pretense of a sudden dizzy spell, Wildwood escaped the longest village meeting on record and went home to take his dog for a walk.

pretext (**pree**-tekst)

noun An excuse; a pretended reason or action to hide the real one. / *Goblet of Fire*, page 322

Brilly's pretext to leave class was a desperate need to go to the bathroom, but actually he wanted to see what the cafeteria was serving for lunch.

prey (rhymes with **hey**; sounds exactly like **pray**)

noun Someone or something being hunted or chased; a victim. / *Half-Blood Prince*, page 21

The hungry jackal patiently followed his prey for miles.

prior to

phrase Before or previous. / *Goblet of Fire*, page 24

Prior to his recent lumbago attack, the owl had always found it easy to mouse hunt all day long.

priority (pry-**or**-ih-tee)

noun Something given precedence—the most important and to be dealt with first. / *Goblet of Fire*, page 609

Today, Madam Glinch's priority was to teach 120 students, in six classes, the basics of wandwork. Mr. Glinch's priority was to mow the lawn.

prise

See **prize** elsewhere in this dictionary.

pristine (prih-**steen**)

adjective Spotlessly clean. / *Deathly Hallows*, page 47

The giant cockroach could find fallen crumbs in even the most pristine kitchen.

privates (**pry**-vuhtz)

noun External sexual organs; used in the plural / *Goblet of Fire*, page 84

"Unnggghhh." The soccer ball had landed right in Butch's privates, and he was writhing on the ground.

prize (rhymes with **size**)

verb To move, remove, or lift something by pushing it away with something else; to pry something. / *Order of the Phoenix*, page 158 / Note: The British spelling **prise** also appears in *Goblet of Fire* (page 146).

Rupert prized off the lid of the yak butter container.

problematic (prob-luh-**mat**-ik)

adjective Doubtful, uncertain, unsettled. / *Half-Blood Prince*, page 49

The problematic part of the schedule for the Day of the Dead festivities was the entertainment—the queen of the Day of the Dead festivities had an ugly pimple on the end of her nose.

procession (pruh-**sesh**-un)

noun A somber parade in which participants move along in line, one after the other. / *Prisoner of Azkaban*, page 87

The lifeless zombies moved along in procession, a parade of the past dead.

proclaim (pruh-**klaym**)

verb To announce or indicate. / *Deathly Hallows*, page 365

The Day of the Dead queen's hand covering her face proclaimed the problem—she had had a zits visitation.

procure (pruh-**kyoor**)
verb **To obtain or get.** / *Goblet of Fire*, page 342
The Squirrel Scouts procured a new supply of cookies and went down by the market to sell them to passersby.

prod (rhymes with **odd**)
verb **To poke or jab.** / *Sorcerer's Stone*, page 144
Elrod prodded the unmoving squid, wondering if it was still alive.

prodigious (pruh-**dij**-us)
adjective **Extraordinary; impressively great.** / *Half-Blood Prince*, page 503
The giant's prodigious strength was amazing—he could toss boulders down the hillside like they were pebbles.

profess (pruh-**fess**)
verb **To claim.** / *Deathly Hallows*, page 9
The director of the Museum of Magic professed to know exactly how many wizards lived within a hundred miles of the museum.

proffer (**prof**-ur)
verb **To offer or present for acceptance or rejection.** / *Order of the Phoenix*, page 513
When the duke finally arrived, the princess proffered her hand for him to kiss. The prince just nodded and said, "Dude."

profile (**pro**-file)
noun **A side view of someone's head.** / *Prisoner of Azkaban*, page 75
Esmerelda's profile was quite…unique, what with that chin…and her nose….

prone (rhymes with **drone**)
adjective **Lying flat.** / *Prisoner of Azkaban*, page 377
The prone body of a Hopeless Shapeless Thing was stretched across a tomb in the cemetery…and nobody wanted to even touch it.

pronouncement (pruh-**nowns**-munt)
noun **A formal announcement or statement.** / *Prisoner of Azkaban*, page 103
The principal's extraordinary pronouncement—that he was taking an extended leave of absence—was greeted with delighted (and somewhat rude) cheers from the students.

prop (rhymes with **drop**)
verb **To rest something against a support.** / *Chamber of Secrets*, page 86
Blackpool, lying on the couch, propped the book of ancient secrets against his knees.

propel (pruh-**pel**)
verb **To move forward with some force.** / *Prisoner of Azkaban*, page 59
The giant (and hungry) cockroach propelled himself toward the toaster crumbs.

prophecy (**prof**-uh-see)
noun **A prediction of what will happen in the future.** / *Order of the Phoenix*, page 382
The fortune-teller's prophesy was dire—bad grades next term unless Bella worked harder.

prophet (**prof**-it)
noun **Someone who predicts what will happen in the future. Plural: prophecies.** / *Sorcerer's Stone*, page 64
Dribbles worried: "The prophet suggested I wear clean underwear on my next car ride. Do you think there'll be an accident?"

prophetic (pruh-**fet**-ik)
adjective **Predictive of what will happen in the future.** / *Order of the Phoenix*, page 312
The prophetic signs were ominous—the Day of the Dead might very well be…deadly.

proprietor (pruh-**pry**-ih-tur)
noun **The owner of a business or shop.** / *Prisoner of Azkaban*, page 51
The proprietor of the Wandatorium Shop was pleased to announce he'd soon be carrying a new hybrid line of wands.

prostrate (**prahs**-trayt)
verb **To throw oneself face down on the ground in adoration or submission.** / *Goblet of Fire*, page 138
Brilly, Rupert, Winston, and Elrod prostrated them-

156 • The Unofficial Harry Potter Vocabulary Builder

selves on the ground as Bella walked by in her very short skirt—then they rolled over laughing.

protégée (proh-tuh-zhey)
noun A woman who is taught, helped, or mentored by someone else. / *Deathly Hallows*, page 79 / Note: Protégée is the feminine form of **protégé**, which can mean any person, male of female. Both can be spelled with or without accent marks.
Merlin's protégée thought it was time to be on her own.

prototype (pro-tuh-type)
noun The first or original model of something. / *Prisoner of Azkaban*, page 51
The prototype for the wandmaker's famous hybrid wand was kept in a special display case in the Wandatorium Shop.

protracted (pro-trak-tid)
adjective Lengthy or prolonged. / *Order of the Phoenix*, page 368
Protracted cheers greeted the Rolling Bones on their final musical number, "Jumpin' Jack Bash!"

protrude (pruh-trood)
verb To project or stick out. / *Goblet of Fire*, page 176
Protruding straight out of the Garden of Secrets was what looked from afar like a giant flagpole, but was actually a giant shovel.

protuberance (pro-too-bur-uns)
noun Something that sticks out, like a bulge or projection. / *Order of the Phoenix*, page 85
The enormous protuberance in the middle of the mayor's face had earned him the nickname "Beaky."

proviso (pruh-vy-zo)
noun A condition asked for before a person will agree to something. / *Deathly Hallows*, page 284
"You'll be allowed to go on the field trip, Brilly, with one proviso—no funny business of any kind," cautioned Madam Glinch.

provocation (prov-uh-kay-shun)
noun Something that provokes, angers, incites, or irritates. / *Order of the Phoenix*, page 256

"What provocation will the students come up with today?" wondered the principal as his day began.

prow (rhymes with **cow**)
noun The front part of a boat. / *Half-Blood Prince*, page 563
The prow of the ferryboat rammed the dock—the captain hadn't been paying attention.

proximity (prok-sim-ih-tee)
noun Nearness. / *Order of the Phoenix*, page 659
The proximity of Mother Serpent and her two children, Tweedie and Slick, was enough to totally immobilize the mouse.

prudent (prood-unt)
adjective Wise or smart. / *Chamber of Secrets*, page 50
It would be prudent for the dwarf to hire the Fairy Maids on a regular basis to clean his grotty cottage.

prying (pry-ing)
adjective Unnecessarily curious or inquisitive, especially about and into the business of others. / *Chamber of Secrets*, page 150
Rilda's prying eyes were always alert for anything new or different in the village.

psychedelic (sy-kuh-del-ik)
adjective Wild, bright colors. / *Half-Blood Prince*, page 138
Whoa, those swirling psychedelic colors almost made Willow dizzy.

pterodactyl (ter-uh-dak-til)
noun An extinct flying reptile with a huge wingspan. / *Order of the Phoenix*, page 282
Sometimes when Blackpool, the evil wizard, stormed angrily down the street with his black cloak flying out behind him, he looked just like a pterodactyl.

pub (rhymes with **tub**)
noun Short for "public house," a place—especially in Britain—where alcoholic beverages are served; a bar. / *Sorcerer's Stone*, page 68
Wildwood stopped by the pub on his way home for a quick glass of brewed squakle antlers.

puce (rhymes with **juice**)
noun A tan, brownish-purple color. / *Order of*

the Phoenix, page 149
When Rupert's little brother mixed together prune and grape juice, he couldn't decide between calling the ugly puce beverage "grune juice" or "prape juice."

pudding (puh-ding)
noun In British usage, dessert. / *Chamber of Secrets*, page 10
"There's cake and ice cream for pudding tonight," said Winston's mum.

pudgy (pudj-ee)
adjective Short and thick. / *Chamber of Secrets*, page 268
The witch's pudgy fingers reached across the table for her wand.

pugnacious (pug-nay-shus)
adjective Belligerent or combative. / *Deathly Hallows*, page 147
Blackpool's pugnacious tone of voice annoyed most people even before they heard what he had to say.

pull faces
phrase To make faces. / *Deathly Hallows*, page 293
Willow was shouting at Brilly: "You just sit there and pull faces when I suggest you stop causing so much trouble, but someday you'll do something really dumb, and I just don't want you to get hurt!"

pulsating (pul-say-ting)
adjective Expanding and contracting rhythmically. / *Half-Blood Prince*, page 280
A pulsating floating light flashed across the horizon. A UFO? Or just the mountain gremlins playing lightball tennis?

pulse (puls)
noun The regular throbbing that can be felt as the heart pumps blood; usually checked at the wrist or the side of the neck. / *Prisoner of Azkaban*, page 377
When Dylan passed out in gym class, the P.E. teacher checked his pulse first thing.

pummel (pum-el)
verb To pound with one's fists. / *Chamber of Secrets*, page 70
First the king pummeled the remote control for his widescreen TV, then he threw it across the room. It had failed to respond to his imperious commands.

punch-drunk (punch-drunk)
adjective Dazed and befuddled. / *Half-Blood Prince*, page 93
The merman was practically punch-drunk watching the lovely mermaid dance at the Sea Prom.

punctuality (punk-choo-al-ih-tee)
noun Promptness; being on time. / *Goblet of Fire*, page 42
The village dentist, Mr. Greenteeth, thought punctuality was very important, and he'd charge extra if you were late to an appointment.

pungent (pun-junt)
adjective Sharp, biting, or acrid. / *Order of the Phoenix*, page 58
The pungent smell of baking nettle biscuits woke Dribbles—it was his favorite breakfast.

punt (rhymes with **hunt**)
verb To go on or across a river in a punt, a long flat-bottomed boat that's moved by pushing with a pole against the river bottom. / *Order of the Phoenix*, page 676
Using the metal tub as a boat, the boys tried to punt across the river, but they didn't get very far.

purge (rhymes with **surge**)
noun The elimination or removal of something undesirable. / *Order of the Phoenix*, page 90
Mrs. Snodgrape realized it was time to purge her handbag of unneeded items when she found she couldn't easily lift it anymore—the portable cauldron was the first thing to go.

purge (rhymes with **surge**)
verb To force out people who those in power dislike or think are unworthy. / *Chamber of Secrets*, page 151
The principal wanted to purge the troublesome students, but he realized they were all a little troublesome in one way or another. Such is the life as a school principal.

purification (pyoor-uh-fih-kay-shun)
noun The act of cleansing or purifying,

removing that which is considered unacceptable or impure. / *Order of the Phoenix*, page 112

The purification of the student body—getting rid of anyone who'd ever caused trouble—would leave exactly…well, it wouldn't leave anyone, realized the principal.

pursed (rhymes with **cursed**)

adjective Puckered, usually said of lips and usually a sign of being uptight. / *Sorcerer's Stone*, page 7

The disapproving teacher looked at Brilly with pursed lips and suggested he leave the girls' bathroom immediately.

purveyor (pur-**vay**-ur)

noun A provider or supplier. / *Prisoner of Azkaban*, page 192

The wandmaker, purveyor of wands of many different types, was thinking about branching out and selling cloaks, too.

pustule (**pus**-chool)

noun A pus-filled pimple. / *Order of the Phoenix*, page 612

Yuck. The Day of the Dead queen had an enormous throbbing pustule on the end of her nose.

putrid (**pyoo**-trud)

adjective Bad-smelling, rotten, and very unpleasant. / *Chamber of Secrets*, page 133

That putrid cheese is stinking up the whole house!

pyrotechnical (py-ruh-**tek**-nik-ul)

adjective Pertaining to or resembling fireworks. / *Order of the Phoenix*, page 632

Brilly's pyrotechnical training began at an early age with sparklers.

python

See **snake** elsewhere in this dictionary.

Q

quagmire (kwag-mire)
noun A marshy or boggy area. / *Prisoner of Azkaban,* page 319
The boggy quagmire at the edge of the meadow regularly swallowed up small animals.

quail (rhymes with **pail**)
verb To cower or shrink with fear. / *Sorcerer's Stone,* page 50
Poor Elrod quailed under the principal's disapproving look.

quaking (kwayk-ing)
adjective Shaking. / *Half-Blood Prince,* page 272
The mysterious quaking parcel on Mrs. Snodgrape's desk shook its way over to the desk's edge.

quarry (kwor-ee)
noun Something hunted. / *Prisoner of Azkaban,* page 265
Mother Serpent's quarry, a tiny trembling mouse, was trying to figure out how it was going to escape.

quash (rhymes with **squash**)
verb To suppress or put down. / *Goblet of Fire,* page 147
"It's important to quash rumors before they spread," said Mrs. Snodgrape, "so no, I'm not running off with a handsome stranger."

quaver (kway-vur)
noun A quavering or shaking sound. / *Sorcerer's Stone,* page 146
The reason for the quaver in the terrified monster's voice was clear—he'd just discovered a little boy under his bed.

queasy (kwee-zee)
adjective A little sick to one's stomach; sometimes just troubled or uneasy. / *Sorcerer's Stone,* page 119
Brilly's off-the-wall ideas often made Dribbles feel a little bit queasy.

quell (rhymes with **dwell**)
verb To quiet or suppress. / *Half-Blood Prince,* page 460
The principal quelled the laughter with one imposing look—and the "What the Well-Dressed Wizard Wears" assembly continued.

querulous (kwer-uh-lus)
adjective Complaining, peevish, whining. / *Deathly Hallows,* page 399
The little boy, perched behind his father on the broomstick, made one querulous comment after another: "It isn't very comfortable back here. When will we get there? How much longer?" And finally: "I hafta go to the bathroom!"

quest (rhymes with **nest**)
noun A knight's adventurous expedition; more generally, any search to find something. / *Prisoner of Azkaban,* page 100
"A quest! Oh, I am so excited," enthused the Knight of the Hounds. "I'm off to search for more hunting dogs."

queue (rhymes with **poo**)
noun A line of people waiting for something. / *Goblet of Fire,* page 83
The cafeteria queue moved quickly since most everybody passed on the armadillo/possum stew.

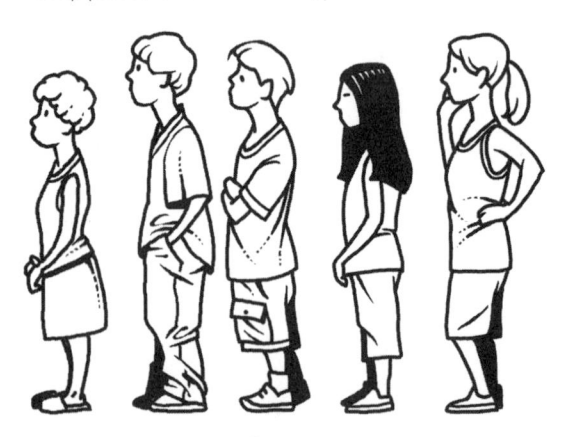

Queue

quibble (kwib-ul)
verb To argue or find fault over small things. / *Goblet of Fire*, page 147
Winston and his brother quibbled over the last brownie on the plate.

quick on the uptake
phrase Quick to understand something, especially something new. / *Order of the Phoenix*, page 621
"Wow, you are so quick on the uptake," said the math teacher to Bella, his star pupil.

quickstep (kwik-step)
noun A lively dance step. / *Chamber of Secrets*, page 192
The king did a happy quickstep when the Royal Plumber announced his solution to the slime problem in the castle moat.

quiescent (kwee-es-unt *or* kwhy-es-unt)
adjective Being quiet and motionless. / *Deathly Hallows*, page 727
A quiescent Brilly stood among the brooms in the janitor's closet, waiting for school to let out so he could get on with his latest scheme.

quill (rhymes with **pill**)
noun A writing pen made from a long feather. / *Sorcerer's Stone*, page 52
Writing quills are elegant-looking but they make a lot of ink blots.

quiver (kwih-vur)
noun A case for carrying arrows, usually slung over the shoulder. / *Sorcerer's Stone*, page 249
The archer's quiver held five arrows and one long baguette.

quiver (kwih-vur)
verb To tremble, vibrate, or move very slightly. / *Sorcerer's Stone*, page 8
The mouse's sensitive whiskers quivered—he sensed cheese, somewhere close by.

R

rack (rhymes with **tack**)
verb To strain to figure out something. / *Half-Blood Prince*, page 167
Tamika racked her memory—what had Wildwood warned her about the Fortress of Solitude?

racking (rak-ing)
adjective Wrenching and painful. / *Chamber of Secrets*, page 141
The pitiful sound of racking sobs lured the boy right into Nightmare Alley.

radiance (ray-dee-unse)
noun A brightness and glow. / *Deathly Hallows*, page 144
The radiance of Fiona's smile as she performed for the school talent show was an indication of how very much she loved to sing.

rafter (raf-tur)
noun One of the sloping timbers of a roof, seen from the inside. / *Goblet of Fire*, page 566
Not a single student remembered the Wing-Binding Spell as the crazed bat dive-bombed them from the gym rafters.

rake (rhymes with **lake**)
verb To go over carefully; to search thoroughly. / *Chamber of Secrets*, page 96
Rilda raked through her drawer of creams and ointments for something that'd help her poison snoak.

rally (rah-lee)
verb To revive or to come back after a setback. / *Half-Blood Prince*, page 445
Down 0-6, the Horrible Hordes rallied as Butch Thuggins scored three quick goals, but, alas, it wasn't enough.

rampage (ram-payj)
verb To act furiously or violently. / *Goblet of Fire*, page 368
The spoiled child rampaged through the candy shop while her indulgent parents just stood by, smiling tolerantly.

rampart (ram-part)
noun The stone fortification atop a high wall or embankment. / *Half-Blood Prince*, page 583
The princess leaned over the castle ramparts to watch the ongoing slime-removal project in the moat far below.

rancid (ran-sid)
adjective Disagreeable and nasty, specifically having the unpleasant taste and smell of decomposing fat. / *Order of the Phoenix*, page 187
Blackpool's favorite racing worm got dreadfully sick after accidentally eating rancid worm food.

rancorous (rang-kur-us)
adjective Full of bitterness and resentment. / *Deathly Hallows*, page 486
Blackpool's rancorous attitude about everything had won him no friends in the village and gained him no votes in the mayoral election.

rangy (rain-jee)
adjective Slender and long-limbed. / *Half-Blood Prince*, page 16
The rangy look of the new teacher reminded Mrs. Snodgrape of Ichabod Crane.

rankle (rang-kul)
verb To cause resentment and bitterness. / *Half-Blood Prince*, page 368
Wildwood's loss at the Crazy Fates Tournament still rankled him.

ransack (ran-sak)
verb To search thoroughly for plunder and, in doing so, to really mess things up. / *Goblet of Fire*, page 282
The kitchen had been ransacked, and the few colorful feathers still floating in the air suggested the parrot had done the evil deed.

rant (rhymes with **ant**)

noun Loud or excessive talking. / *Half-Blood Prince,* page 159

Blackpool's rants about the high price of yak butter were becoming tiresome.

rant (rhymes with **ant**)

verb To speak in a loud angry manner; to go on and on. / *Sorcerer's Stone,* page 53

The Royal Plumber ranted at his apprentice, who had just fallen into the castle moat again.

rap (rhymes with **trap**)

verb To knock. / *Chamber of Secrets,* page 205

When no one responded to the doorbell, Mr. Fracket rapped loudly on the door.

rapt (rhymes with **trapped**; sounds exactly like **wrapped**)

adjective Engrossed and absorbed; really focused on something. / *Chamber of Secrets,* page 100

Rapt attention was essential when Madam Glinch started listing the ingredients for the mini-max potion.

raptor (**rap**-tur)

noun A bird of prey—that is, a bird that eats other animals; eagles, hawks, and owls are all raptors. / *Deathly Hallows,* page 632

A flock of raptors circled high over the meadow, checking out the possibilities for Sunday brunch.

rapturous (**rap**-chur-us)

adjective Ecstatic and delighted. / *Order of the Phoenix,* page 566

Fiona was rapturous when she got a new guitar.

rash (rhymes with **lash**)

adjective Hasty and without thinking it through. / *Chamber of Secrets,* page 131

The evil Draconia Deveel had made a rash mistake—attempting to bewitch Blackpool was not a smart move.

rasp (rhymes with **clasp**)

noun A scraping, grating sound. / *Chamber of Secrets,* page 217

The rasp of a key in the old lock echoed from one damp dungeon wall to another.

Raptor

rasp (rhymes with **clasp**)

verb To speak in a rough, harsh voice. / *Half-Blood Prince,* page 594

Madam Glinch rasped out today's punishment—for poor behavior and inattentive wand work, the entire class would be coming in for extra lessons after school.

rasping (**ras**-ping)

adjective Rough or grating. / *Sorcerer's Stone,* page 47

The rasping sounds of the Shadow Stealer tumbled like prickly burrs down the hallway.

rations (**rash**-uns)

noun Food or a food supply, especially for explorers or soldiers; usually used in the plural. / *Sorcerer's Stone,* page 44

The rations in her backpack wouldn't have kept a hungry bird happy. There were two cans of Jump Juice and a bag of Nutso kernels—for a week!

raucous (**raw**-kus)

adjective Wild and rowdy. / *Chamber of Secrets,* page 251

The fairies' raucous garden party, with hordes of buzzing bees and blinking fireflies, annoyed everyone in the neighborhood.

ravaged (rav-ijd)
adjective Badly damaged or devastated. / *Half-Blood Prince*, page 40
The ravaged trees around the village green had been terribly hurt by the storm. Shattered pine cones, fallen birds' nests, and broken branches littered the ground—and you could almost hear the trees crying.

ravenous (rav-uh-nus)
adjective Famished; really hungry. / *Prisoner of Azkaban*, page 94
The ravenous bear awoke suddenly—his stomach's rumbling and grumbling had ended his hibernation.

raving (ray-ving)
noun Irrational, incoherent talk. / *Goblet of Fire*, page 565
The professor's raving about his right foot turning into a doorbell confirmed what the students already thought about him—he was a ding dong.

realm (rhymes with **elm**)
noun A general area of knowledge or thought where something occurs or dominates. / *Half-Blood Prince*, page 429
Annie's parents were in charge at home, but the world of magic was her realm.

ream (rhymes with **dream**)
noun Literally, a standard quantity of paper (500 sheets); more generally, a large quantity. / *Order of the Phoenix*, page 538
After he finished his reams of homework, Brilly put it all safely in the refrigerator—his fire-breathing salamander was on the loose.

rear guard (reer gard)
noun A part of a force—military or just protective—that stays behind to protect the rest of the group from a surprise attack. / *Order of the Phoenix*, page 55
The Hen Battalion charged the Rooster Brigade, but lost their rear guard to the Army of Nugget Makers.

rebuff (rih-buf)
verb To drive away or, at the very least, to snub. / *Order of the Phoenix*, page 236
The shy Cyclops was rebuffed by the arrogant eight-eyed monster.

recede (rih-seed)
verb To go further away, becoming more distant. / *Chamber of Secrets*, page 229
The sound of Willow's laughter receded as she headed down the hall toward her next class.

reception (rih-sep-shun)
noun A welcome or the act of welcoming or receiving someone. / *Deathly Hallows*, page 1
The mermaid enjoyed the warm reception from the fishermen.

receptivity (rih-sep-tiv-uh-tee)
noun Openness; willingness to receive new ideas or knowledge. / *Prisoner of Azkaban*, page 107
The receptivity of young people makes them the best students of magic.

recess (rih-ses or ree-ses)
noun An alcove or small area set away from the main part of the room. / *Order of the Phoenix*, page 738
"Quick! In here," said Brilly, pulling Dribbles into the recess in the library book stacks. "I need to borrow some money."

recipient (rih-sip-ee-unt)
noun Someone who receives something. / *Order of the Phoenix*, page 578
The octopus was the recipient of a mysterious package addressed to him at "Where the Fourteenth Wave Meets the Riptide."

reciprocal (rih-sip-ruh-kul)
adjective Given in return. / *Order of the Phoenix*, page 415
Their reciprocal agreement meant Katie weeded his entire herb garden and Wildwood took care of her horse when Katie went away for the weekend.

recital (rih-site-ul)
noun An all too-detailed, endless account or description. / *Order of the Phoenix*, page 707
"Blah blah blah blah" was all the bored students heard of the lecturer's endless recital of helpful herbs.

recitation (res-ih-**tay**-shun)

noun A spoken description or recital of an event or series of events. / *Deathly Hallows*, page 157

Winston's recitation of the dramatic events at the Whizzing Fire Ball Tournament had his listeners on the edge of their chairs.

reckon (**rek**-un)

verb To think, assume, or expect. / *Sorcerer's Stone*, page 302

"I reckon we can forget about a picnic in the meadow today," said Hassan. "The fire ants are biting, and the wasps are dive-bombing intruders."

recoil (ree-**koyl**)

verb To draw back in alarm or horror. / *Deathly Hallows*, page 271

The blind slug recoiled from the tree trunk, mistaking it for a disgusting human child.

recollection (ree-kuh-**lek**-shun *or* rek-uh-**lek**-shun)

noun A memory. / *Prisoner of Azkaban*, page 44

Mrs. Birch had no recollection of clucking like a chicken—the hypnotist had been very good.

recommence (ree-kuh-**mens**)

verb To begin again. / *Goblet of Fire*, page 112

After a pause for a rousing chorus of the Magical Anthem, the Whizzing Fire Ball Tournament recommenced.

reconciliation (rek-un-sil-ee-**ay**-shun)

noun An act of reconciling or of returning to friendly relations. / *Deathly Hallows*, page 607

The boys faked reconciliation just to keep the teacher happy, but they were still kicking each other under their cloaks.

reconnaissance (rih-**kon**-uh-suns)

adjective Checking out and getting useful information about the enemy. / *Deathly Hallows*, page 229

Blackpool's late-night reconnaissance mission to check out the worm relay course was successful.

recount (rih-**kownt**)

verb To relate in detail. / *Chamber of Secrets*, page 249

In delicious detail, Winston's mum recounted every bite of the 17-course meal served at the king's grand party.

recruit (rih-**kroot**)

verb To get to enlist or join up. / *Order of the Phoenix*, page 96

Wildwood tried to recruit volunteers to help clean the animal cages at the zoo, but he got no takers.

rectify (**rek**-tuh-fie)

verb To remedy, correct, or put right. / *Order of the Phoenix*, page 239

"We must rectify this situation immediately!" shouted Annie's dad to the principal, shaking his daughter's furry paw to illustrate the point.

recuperate (rih-**koo**-puh-rate)

verb To heal or mend after a sickness or disease. / *Deathly Hallows*, page 364

Dylan recuperated at home after his brief hospital stay.

redolent (**red**-ih-lunt)

adjective Suggestive of or reminiscent of. / *Order of the Phoenix*, page 110

Blackpool's smile was redolent of his true feelings (loathing and disgust) for the wandmaker.

redouble (ree-**dub**-ul)

verb To double or to increase. / *Prisoner of Azkaban*, page 217

Annie's sobs redoubled when she glimpsed her hamster face in the mirror.

reduction (rih-**duk**-shun)

noun The condition of being reduced or made smaller. / *Goblet of Fire*, page 414

Mrs. Snodgrape had promised a reduction in homework over the weekend, but that really meant only a slightly smaller mountain of homework.

reedy (**ree**-dee)

adjective Thin and high sounding, like a reed instrument, if referring to a voice; thin, like a reed, if referring to a person's build. / *Prisoner of Azkaban*, page 401

The werewolf's reedy bark was totally at odds with his hulking, muscular body.

reek (rhymes with **peek**)

verb To give off or to exude a strong, unpleasant smell. / *Half-Blood Prince*, page 640
The witch reeked of mothballs, probably because she'd just pulled her old coat out of storage—she hadn't worn it in over a hundred years.

reel (rhymes with **peel**; sounds exactly like **real**)

verb To stagger. / *Chamber of Secrets*, page 112
The wandering traveler reeled backwards when the stench of the troll drifted down the hillside.

reflex (ree-fleks)

noun An involuntary, instinctive response to a stimulus. When the doctor taps your knee with the little hammer, she's checking your reflexes. / *Half-Blood Prince*, page 594
The older mountain gremlins had a difficult time playing lightball tennis because of their slower reflexes.

refrain (rih-frane)

noun The chorus or other repeated words in a song. / *Half-Blood Prince*, page 487
Fiona sadly sang the refrain of her favorite song, "The Lament of the Lovesick Lizard."

refrain (rih-frane)

verb To hold oneself back from doing something. / *Goblet of Fire*, page 616
Julio refrained from eating his fifth brownie in a row.

refuge (ref-yooj)

noun A place safe from danger or trouble. / *Order of the Phoenix*, page 836
Dribbles' refuge when things weren't going well was under the covers in bed.

regal (ree-gul)

adjective Royal, or at least resembling the expected behavior of a king or queen. / *Half-Blood Prince*, page 244
The king gave a regal nod to start the jousting tournament.

regenerate (rih-jen-uh-rate)

verb To revive or bring into existence again. / *Goblet of Fire*, page 678
"Let us all work together to regenerate a new school spirit," enthused the principal as the school assembly drew to a close.

regeneration (rih-jen-uh-ray-shun)

noun The state of being revived or brought into existence again. / *Goblet of Fire*, page 655
The regeneration of the giant starfish's broken arm had become a popular attraction at the village aquarium.

regime (ruh-zheem)

noun The time when someone is in charge or in power; also a system of government. / *Order of the Phoenix*, page 298
The mayor's regime almost ended at the last election, but in the end he won more votes than his opponents and so will serve another term.

register (rej-uh-stur)

noun An attendance book at school. / *Goblet of Fire*, page 210
Madam Glinch checked her class register and told the boy, "You're in the wrong class, young man!"

regurgitate (ree-gur-jih-tate)

verb Literally, to vomit; more generally, to cast up, eject, or throw back. / *Goblet of Fire*, page 374
The sink's garbage disposal was feeling so cranky that it regurgitated everything put in it since lunch.

regurgitated (ree-gir-jih-tay-tid)

adjective Vomited. / *Goblet of Fire*, page 229 / Note: A related adjective in *Order of the Phoenix* (page 133), **regurgitating** means "vomiting" or (particularly in the case of a regurgitating toilet) "backing up."
The regurgitated gunk from the garbage disposal included smashed snail shells, eel innards, a ground-up plastic spoon, and chudbutt chunks.

reign of terror

phrase A period or situation of brutal oppression. / *Goblet of Fire*, page 439
Brilly felt that serving lousy cafeteria food qualified as a "reign of terror."

rein (rhymes with **stain**; sounds exactly like **rain**)

noun Literally, a strap fastened to a horse's bridle to help the rider (or carriage driver)

control and guide the horse. More generally, used in the phrase "to give free rein," meaning to give someone freedom of action or choice. / *Chamber of Secrets*, page 294 / Note: A related phrase, seen in *Half-Blood Prince* (page 213), is **to give full-rein**.
After much deliberation, the garden gnomes gave the ladybugs free rein of the garden.

reignite (ree-ig-**nite**)
verb To ignite (or light) again. / *Goblet of Fire*, page 277
Wildwood had to reignite the campfire over and over—the tent demons were at work.

reinstated (ree-in-**stay**-tid)
adjective Being put back in a place or a position. / *Order of the Phoenix*, page 846
The reinstated cafeteria manager had outlasted the uproar over the snail/whale sandwiches.

rekindling (ree-**kin**-dling)
verb To revive or renew. / *Deathly Hallows*, page 128
Bella's feelings for Bubba, her old boyfriend, rekindled just a little.

relent (rih-**lent**)
verb To give in or to soften or change an attitude. / *Chamber of Secrets*, page 22
Mrs. Snodgrape would not relent—clean your cauldron after every potion, or sit and watch the class for the rest of the day.

relentless (rih-**lent**-lis)
adjective Not relenting; seemingly unending. / *Order of the Phoenix*, page 51
The relentless march of the Ant Army had begun—ants to the left, ants to the right, and ants down the middle of the kitchen floor.

relevant (**rel**-uh-vunt)
adjective Connected with or having some importance to what's being discussed. / *Prisoner of Azkaban*, page 221
"Bella, is your new hair color really relevant to our discussion of useful charms for dangerous situations?"

reliance (rih-**lie**-uns)
noun Trust, confidence, and faith in someone or something. / *Deathly Hallows*, page 158
Blackpool had always placed a great deal of reliance in his wand—at least until it shattered when he pointed it at the giant cockroach.

relic (**rel**-ik)
noun Something that has survived from a previous experience or a past time. / *Goblet of Fire*, page 611
Brilly had a small scar on his backside, a relic of the unsuccessful firecracker-in-the-toilet experiment.

relinquish (rih-**ling**-kwish)
verb To give up or let go of something. / *Order of the Phoenix*, page 367
The wind talker sadly relinquished the tree's secrets.

reminisce (rem-uh-**nis**)
verb To remember and share past experiences. / *Goblet of Fire*, page 617
Ethelbell and the Sisters of Sorcery loved to reminisce about the good old days when they were in school together.

reminiscent (rem-uh-**nis**-unt)
adjective Remembering or looking back. / *Half-Blood Prince*, page 326
With a reminiscent smile, Brilly thought back to kindergarten and the day he'd surprised his teacher with the spider-in-the-thermos trick.

remnant (**rem**-nunt)
noun A remaining or leftover part or quantity. / *Order of the Phoenix*, page 813
The last remnants of the meal disappeared down the sink's garbage disposal, which could be heard belching and burping happily.

remonstrance (rih-**mon**-struns)
noun A complaint or protest. / *Order of the Phoenix*, page 857 / Note: **Remonstration**, a related noun seen in *Half-Blood Prince* (page 172), also means "a complaint or protest."
The principal's usual remonstrance about students wearing polka-dotted clothing had not been successful—perhaps he needed a better line than "Dots... Nots."

remorse (ree-morse)

noun Regret or guilt for having done something wrong. / *Sorcerer's Stone*, page 303
Brilly's remorse over the jellyfish-in-the-pool scheme was mostly because he felt sorry for the jellyfish.

rend (rhymes with **bend**)

verb Literally, to split or tear something apart violently; more generally, to disturb (or "split") the air with a loud sound. Past tense: rent. / *Goblet of Fire*, page 71
Mysterious screams from the Fortress of Solitude rent the morning silence.

render (ren-dur)

verb To do or perform. / *Order of the Phoenix*, page 604
"As cafeteria manager, you've rendered a great service to our school," congratulated the principal. Well, thought Dylan, except for that armadillo/possum stew and the snail/whale sandwiches.

renege (rih-**nig**)

verb To go back on one's word; to fail to carry out a promise or obligation. / *Deathly Hallows*, page 517
Blackpool reneged on his agreement with Klingster about collecting unicorn hair.

renown (rih-noun)

noun Fame. / *Order of the Phoenix*, page 469
The renown of soccer star Butch Thuggins had brought him a huge salary and many girlfriends.

rent

See **rend** elsewhere in this dictionary.

repellent (rih-**pel**-unt)

adjective Repulsive and hateful. / *Deathly Hallows*, page 503
The repellent Blackpool decided to soften his image, so he started knitting. But then he was just a repellent knitter.

repentance (rih-**pen**-tuns)

noun A feeling of sorrow, remorse, and regret for something done in the past. / *Half-Blood Prince*, page 616
Looking back, Brilly had felt repentance for only one thing all year—those poor jellyfish.

repercussion (ree-pur-**kush**-un)

noun An effect or result, especially one that's indirect or unexpected. / *Order of the Phoenix*, page 355
The major repercussion of Brilly's latest scheme was being spell-grounded for a month.

repetitive (rih-**pet**-ih-tive)

adjective Repeating; saying much the same thing over and over. / *Deathly Hallows*, page 288
The repetitive warnings from the principal featured overuse of the phrases "Do not ever…" and "It is not allowed…."

replenish (rih-**plen**-ish)

verb To fill and make complete again. / *Order of the Phoenix*, page 212
With a wave of her wand, Mrs. Snodgrape replenished her kitchen shelves with her favorite snack—Squirrel Scout cookies.

replete (rih-**pleet**)

adjective Satisfied; well-filled with food and drink. / *Order of the Phoenix*, page 87
The boys were feeling particularly replete after their mid-day snack at the soccer game—hot frogs and fries, and plenty of Jump Juice.

replicating (rep-lih-**kayt**-ing)

adjective Duplicating or reproducing. / *Deathly Hallows*, page 541
Wildwood's replicating rabbits were soon going to overrun his garden.

repose (rih-**pohz**)

verb To put confidence or trust in. / *Order of the Phoenix*, page 308 / Note: See also the related verb **repose** below.
"Despite all the problems, I continue to repose all my confidence in the principal and his staff," announced the president of the PWA (Parents-Wizards Association).

repose (rih-**pohz**)

verb To lie or rest on something. / *Deathly Hallows*, page 368 / Note: See also the related verb **repose** above.
Dylan lazily reposed beside the swimming pool, enjoying the sun and idly counting how many jellyfish Brilly had snuck in.

repository (ree-**poz**-ih-tor-ee)

noun A place where stored things are kept safe, like a storehouse, bank, warehouse, etc. / *Deathly Hallows*, page 530
Mrs. Snodgrape's repository for her special treasures was her locked curio cabinet.

representative (rep-rih-**zen**-tuh-tive)

noun Someone who represents others. / *Goblet of Fire*, page 85
The mayor asked that a representative of each of the village's neighborhoods come to a town meeting.

repress (ree-**pres**)

verb To keep under control or to suppress. / *Order of the Phoenix*, page 3
The girls who were locked in the Museum of Magic overnight repressed their fears and decided to look for something to eat.

repressive (rih-**pres**-iv)

adjective Severe or harsh. / *Goblet of Fire*, page 264
The repressive clothing restrictions at school were restricting Bella's fashion choices.

reprieve (rih-**preev**)

verb To delay impending punishment. / *Deathly Hallows*, page 656
Whew, Brilly'd been momentarily reprieved—no one knew about the food coloring in the hot tub. Yet.

reprimand (**rep**-ruh-mand)

noun A severe criticism or rebuke, especially from someone in authority. / *Goblet of Fire*, page 599
The principal's reprimand about blowing up the janitor's closet wasn't nearly as unpleasant as what Brilly's father had to say about it.

reprimand (**rep**-ruh-mand)

verb To speak severely to someone because he or she has done something wrong. / *Half-Blood Prince*, page 62
Being reprimanded for his bad behavior wasn't as much fun as the bad behavior had been.

reproach (rih-**prohch**)

noun An expression of blame or fault. / *Deathly Hallows*, page 216
Willow's silent reproaches—plus her not-so-silent ones—convinced Blackpool to un-enchant her puppies.

reproving (ree-**proov**-ing)

adjective Reproachful or reprimanding. / *Chamber of Secrets*, page 200
Mother Serpent gave Tweedie a reproving look when the little snake tried rolling over and over down the hill.

reptilian (rep-**til**-ee-un *or* rep-**til**-yun)

adjective Resembling or like a reptile. / *Order of the Phoenix*, page 282
The reptilian look of the substitute botany teacher—plus her snaky voice—gave Dribbles nightmares for weeks.

Reptilian-looking substitute teacher

repugnant (rih-**pug**-nunt)

adjective Distasteful, offensive, and repulsive. / *Half-Blood Prince*, page 52
"Blackpool, that's a really repugnant idea," said Wildwood. "Keep the glue away from my rabbits."

repulse (rih-**puls**)

verb To cause feelings of revulsion. / *Half-Blood Prince*, page 571

Wildwood was repulsed by Blackpool's attitude toward his racing worms: Don't feed them unless they win.

repulsion (rih-**pul**-shun)

noun A feeling of extreme distaste, aversion, and repugnance. / *Deathly Hallows*, page 565
The repulsion Wildwood felt over Blackpool's worm-raising techniques made Wildwood want to avoid Blackpool completely.

repulsive (rih-**pul**-sive)

adjective Disgusting, hideous, horrible. / *Goblet of Fire*, page 368
The repulsive mask on the wall never much bothered Rupert until the day it winked at him.

reputation (rep-yoo-**tay**-shun)

noun The general opinion that others have about someone. / *Goblet of Fire*, page 139
The wizard's reputation as a public speaker was well-earned—his talk on "Dark Deeds, Frog Slime, and Horse Leeches: My Life as a Wizard" had gone over very well.

residue (**rez**-ih-doo or **rez**-ih-dyoo)

noun The remains or the leftovers. / *Half-Blood Prince*, page 41
The gunky residue at the bottom of Nathan's cauldron was actually moaning.

resignation (rez-ig-**nay**-shun)

noun The act of resigning, or leaving, a job permanently; also, the actual document giving notice of the resignation. / *Prisoner of Azkaban*, page 429 / Note: See also the related noun **resignation** below.
When the cafeteria manager's resignation was announced, shouts of joy came from every classroom.

resignation (rez-ig-**nay**-shun)

noun An unresisting, accepting attitude. / *Goblet of Fire*, page 350 / Note: See also the related noun **resignation** above.
With resignation, Brilly made the familiar "Walk of Blame" into the principal's office.

resign (ree-**zyne**)

verb To formally give up or leave a job. / *Prisoner of Azkaban*, page 422
"I am resigning as president of the Chamber of Wizards," announced the wizard, "to devote my time to a new magazine, *Village Spillage—The News Run-off*."

resilience (rih-**zil**-yuns)

noun The ability to recover quickly and easily from adversity or hardship. / *Deathly Hallows*, page 257
The resilience of the clumsy, trouble-prone Elrod was admirable.

resilient (rih-**zil**-yunt)

adjective Elastic; able to spring back to its normal shape. / *Half-Blood Prince*, page 282
The resilient soccer ball survived the monster's gnawing.

resolutely (**rez**-uh-**loot**-lee)

adverb In a resolved, firm, and determined way. / *Goblet of Fire*, page 288
Brilly walked resolutely into the principal's office—this time he knew he hadn't caused the problem.

resolution (rez-uh-**loo**-shun)

noun The condition of being determined and resolute. / *Goblet of Fire*, page 634
It took more resolution than he thought he had, but Dylan went bungee jumping.

resolve (rih-**zolv**)

noun Resolution or determination. / *Chamber of Secrets*, page 270
Nungie's resolve to start a dessert restaurant was shaken when a new Hastee Breeze ice cream parlor opened in the village.

resonance (**rez**-uh-nuns)

noun A reverberation or vibration. / *Prisoner of Azkaban*, page 107
"I am getting odd cosmic resonances that indicate… uh…is someone kicking the table?" asked the village fortune-teller.

respite (**res**-pit)

noun A delay or postponement; a temporary period of relief. / *Order of the Phoenix*, page 378
The respite during the storm was brief, and soon the

meadow mice were back to dodging and scampering away from hungry owls.

resplendent (rih-**splen**-dunt)
adjective Splendid or dazzling in appearance. / *Chamber of Secrets*, page 189
Bella was resplendent at graduation—her dress lilac, her robes magenta, and her hair lavender.

restive (**res**-tiv)
adjective Restless, impatient, uneasy, even difficult to control. / *Half-Blood Prince*, page 231
The substitute teacher dealt with the restive class by getting her parrot to sing old Tomb Tones songs.

restorative (rih-**store**-uh-tiv)
noun Something that restores or renews health or strength. / *Chamber of Secrets*, page 92
Essence of emu is an excellent restorative after a loss of vigor from enchantment or overwork.

resume (rih-**zoom**)
verb To continue after an interruption; to go on with. / *Chamber of Secrets*, page 170
The match resumed after the wandering ostrich was removed from the field.

resurgence (rih-**sur**-juns)
noun The return or revival of something; the bringing of something back into activity. / *Order of the Phoenix*, page 748
With a resurgence of energy, the Old Hags Choir belted out their final song, "Amazing Curse."

resurrected (rez-uh-**rek**-tid)
adjective Brought back to life. / *Goblet of Fire*, page 246
The resurrected mummy staggered through the village, trailing loose pieces of his wrappings.

retaliation (rih-tal-ee-**ay**-shun)
noun The act of retaliating or getting back at someone, like for like. / *Prisoner of Azkaban*, page 309
The garden gnome's retaliation for being sprayed with the garden hose involved dumping mulch on the kitchen elf's head.

retaliatory (rih-**tal**-ee-uh-tore-ee)
adjective Having the nature of retribution, of paying back like for like. / *Order of the Phoenix*, page 260
In a retaliatory move, the kitchen elf poured ice water down the back of the garden gnome.

retch (rhymes with **fetch**)
verb To gag or vomit. / *Chamber of Secrets*, page 116
Dylan retched as he got off Annie's broomstick—after dozens of loops, swoops, and dives, he never wanted to ride the "vomit comet" again.

retina (**ret**-nuh *or* **ret**-in-uh)
noun The delicate membrane lining the eyeball, connected by the optic nerve to the brain. / *Deathly Hallows*, page 367
The fireworks display seemed to be still pulsating on Elrod's retinas.

retirement (rih-**tire**-munt)
noun The state of being retired or of having withdrawn from one's occupation or business. / *Half-Blood Prince*, page 74
Mr. Fracket's retirement didn't last long—he got bored and decided he'd work part-time at the school cafeteria.

retort (rih-**tort**)
noun A quick, sharp, sometimes witty reply. / *Order of the Phoenix*, page 453
"Brilly, it is not an appropriate retort to say 'If you don't like my peaches, don't shake my tree.'"

retribution (reh-truh-**byoo**-shun)
noun Something given in repayment, especially punishment. / *Half-Blood Prince*, page 125
"There will be retribution," said the principal ominously, after the water fountains mysteriously became vinegar fountains.

reunion (ree-**yoon**-yun)
noun A time of getting together or uniting again. / *Goblet of Fire*, page 143
The reunion of the lost miniature dragon with its mother was heartwarming to see.

revel (**rev**-ul)
verb To take great pleasure or delight in something. / *Deathly Hallows*, page 113

The prince reveled in playing his drums, long and loud, from atop the castle tower.

revelation (rev-uh-lay-shun)
noun Something not revealed, disclosed, or understood before that is now clearer. / *Goblet of Fire*, page 429
It was a revelation to the mayor that Blackpool had actually expected to win the election.

reveler (rev-ul-ur)
noun A person making merry and sharing in a noisy party. / *Deathly Hallows*, page 161
The revelers at the Groundhog Day Festival were drinking Shadow Shakes and dancing the Groundhog Jig.

revelry (rev-ul-ree)
noun Boisterous merrymaking. / *Deathly Hallows*, page 151
The revelry at the Castle Regatta went on far into the night.

reverberate (rih-vur-buh-rate)
verb To echo and re-echo, bouncing back and forth. / *Order of the Phoenix*, page 468
The shouts of the mountain gremlins reverberated from peak to peak.

reverence (rev-ur-uns)
noun Honor, esteem, and veneration; deep respect tinged with awe. / *Prisoner of Azkaban*, page 142
The villagers had great reverence for Merlin, a direct descendant of Rockspurt, the village's founder.

reverently (rev-ur-unt-lee)
adverb In a deeply respectful way. / *Chamber of Secrets*, page 15
"We shall now sing the school song," said the principal reverently.

reverie (rev-uh-ree)
noun A state of dreamy thought or daydreaming. / *Goblet of Fire*, page 280
Bella's blissful reverie was interrupted by Bubba, who rudely sat down next to her and asked, "What's up?"

revision (rih-vizh-un)
noun A rewriting or alteration. / *Half-Blood Prince*, page 238
Mrs. Fracket's tattered recipe card for glazed-doughnut-and-fish-stick stew had had so many revisions over the years that she could barely read it.

revival (rih-vy-vul)
noun The act or state of being revived, or brought back to consciousness. / *Goblet of Fire*, page 109
Dylan's revival, after fainting while bungee jumping, was helped immeasurably by a bit of Wildwood's magic.

revive (rih-vive)
verb To restore to consciousness. / *Chamber of Secrets*, page 251
Dylan groggily revived after passing out and was really embarrassed, but Wildwood said it was no big deal.

revolting (rih-vol-ting)
adjective Disgusting. / *Sorcerer's Stone*, page 24
Blackpool wore the same revolting shirt again, for the seventh day in a row.

revulsion (rih-vul-shun)
noun A feeling of dislike and loathing. / *Prisoner of Azkaban*, page 373
The ogre stared at the troll with utter revulsion.

rhapsodize (rap-suh-dize)
verb To speak in an extremely enthusiastic manner. / *Order of the Phoenix*, page 170
Fiona rhapsodized about the new song she'd learned—"The Tadpole Blues."

rheumatism (roo-muh-tiz-um)
noun A painful stiffening disorder of the joints. / *Order of the Phoenix*, page 629
Auntie Baba's rheumatism was acting up, so she skipped the dancing at the Groundhog Day Festival.

rhododendron (roh-duh-den-drun)
noun An evergreen shrub with big, showy flowers. / *Half-Blood Prince*, page 344
Mr. Glinch's rhododendron won the blue ribbon at the village fair for "Biggest Brightest Blooms."

rickety (rik-ih-tee)
adjective Shaky; ready to fall apart. / *Sorcerer's Stone*, page 131

The rickety raft almost sank when the water horse slammed into it.

ricochet (rik-uh-shay)
verb To hit something and rebound at an angle. / *Goblet of Fire*, page 58
Rupert hadn't planned on the mashed potatoes ricocheting and coming back to hit him in the face.

riddle (rid-ul)
verb To spread throughout. / *Chamber of Secrets*, page 172
The fangs on the fangbark tree were riddled with decay—the tree dentist was going to have a big job fixing them.

riffle (rif-ul)
verb To quickly turn or flip through pieces of paper or pages of a book. / *Deathly Hallows*, page 352
The old hag riffled through the pages of her potions journal, seeking that wonderful Dranksgiving potion.

riffraff (riff-raff)
noun Disreputable or worthless people. / *Sorcerer's Stone*, page 109
Cliques exist even on the farm: sheep stick together, chickens keep to themselves, and horses think any animal without a mane is riffraff.

rifle (rye-ful)
verb To search quickly when looking for something. / *Chamber of Secrets*, page 100
Esmerelda rifled through her old journals looking for the one describing her first meeting with Blackpool.

rift (rhymes with **drift**)
noun A break in friendly relations. / *Half-Blood Prince*, page 40
The current rift between Blackpool and Wildwood—they hadn't spoken for three days—had a lot to do with Blackpool's bulldozing Wildwood's troll fence.

rigging (rig-ing)
noun The ropes, chains, etc., that work the sails on a ship. / *Goblet of Fire*, page 404
The ship's rigging tugged and pulled as the pirate ship sailed through the Straits of Dismay.

rigidity (rih-jid-uh-tee)
noun The condition of being rigid, or stiff and unbending. / *Order of the Phoenix*, page 293
With a certain regal rigidity, the queen rode the Royal Stallion at the head of the Castle Regatta parade.

rigorous (rig-ur-us)
adjective Really hard and demanding. / *Goblet of Fire*, page 547
It had been a rigorous workout, especially since Brilly liked to jog and practice wandwork at the same time.

rile (rhymes with **style**)
verb To irritate. / *Order of the Phoenix*, page 686
Blackpool riled Wildwood so much they may never speak again.

ringlet (ring-lit)
noun A long curl of hair. / *Goblet of Fire*, page 487
The ship's captain had long black ringlets that kept getting caught in the ship's wheel.

roan (rhymes with **tone**)
adjective Having a brownish color, often sprinkled with white or gray; usually referring to the color of a horse. / *Prisoner of Azkaban*, page 114 / Note: In Potter's world, it's a hippogriff that's a pinkish roan color.
Though Katie had really liked the roan horse at first, she eventually decided she wanted a palomino, not a roan.

robustly (roh-bust-lee)
adverb Strongly and vigorously. / *Half-Blood Prince*, page 241
"My goodness, that's *quite* an outfit, dear," said Bella's mother robustly. "But perhaps your father might find it a little…revealing."

rock cake (rok-kake)
noun In British usage, a kind of fruitcake that has a hard surface, like a rock. / *Sorcerer's Stone*, page 140
"Eating too much rock cake isn't good for your teeth," cautioned Dr. Greenteeth, the village dentist.

rogue (rhymes with **vogue**)
adjective Unpredictable, uncontrollable, destructive. / *Chamber of Secrets*, page 170
The rogue mummy escaped the village museum and wandered down the Weeping Highway.

rogue (rhymes with **vogue**)
noun A scoundrel or rascal. / *Prisoner of Azkaban*, page 100
"Oh Brilly, you rogue!" said Willow.

roguish (**roh**-gish)
adjective Playfully mischievous. / *Chamber of Secrets*, page 100
With a roguish smile, Wildwood bowed and asked his elderly mother for the next dance.

rook (rhymes with **crook**)
noun A chess piece shaped like a castle. / *Deathly Hallows*, page 397 / Note: In Potter's world, "rook" is first misunderstood to refer to a large, black crow-like bird.
Wildwood was carving a new chess set, but the rook was causing trouble—it was difficult to get the battlements right.

rosette (roh-**zet**)
noun A badge made of ribbon or silk that's pleated so that it looks like a small rose. / *Prisoner of Azkaban*, page 305
The fans of the Horrible Hordes wore green rosettes, while fans of the Terrible Trolls wore orange rosettes.

rotund (roh-**tund**)
adjective Round, plump, fat. / *Half-Blood Prince*, page 369
The rotund wizard, in his scarlet dress robes, looked like a large walking apple.

rouge (roozh)
noun A red cosmetic to make cheeks look rosier. / *Half-Blood Prince*, page 433
Brilly put a little of his mother's rouge on his nose—maybe he could convince her he had a terrible cold and couldn't go to school

round the twist
See **go round the twist** elsewhere in this dictionary.

rouse (rhymes with **cows**)
verb To waken. / *Goblet of Fire*, page 2
Dylan roused his mother early Sunday morning and said, "I don't feel so good."

Rotund wizard

rove (rhymes with **drove**)
verb To wander at random. / *Chamber of Secrets*, page 311
Butch's eyes roved over the crowd—now where was his new girlfriend sitting?

row (rhymes with **cow**)
noun In British usage, an argument or quarrel. / *Order of the Phoenix*, page 70
Blackpool and Wildwood were having a row over what was the best potion for worm cramps.

row (rhymes with **cow**)
verb In British usage, to argue or quarrel noisily. / *Order of the Phoenix*, page 70
The two wizards rowed noisily for most of the afternoon.

rubbish (**rub**-ish)
noun Nonsense; foolish talk. / *Prisoner of Azkaban*, page 78 / Note: **Rubbish!**, a related exclamation seen in *Order of the Phoenix* (page 253), is similar to saying "Nonsense!"
"That's just rubbish, Esmerelda. I never said that about you," asserted Blackpool.

rubble (rub-ul)

noun Broken bits and pieces of stone, brick, etc. / *Goblet of Fire*, page 44
The Royal Plumber found piles of rubble at the bottom of the castle moat, probably dumped by the Royal Bricklayer after the castle renovation.

ruby (roo-bee)

noun A gem, usually with a deep reddish color. Plural: rubies. / *Sorcerer's Stone*, page 73 / Note: In Potter's world, rubies are used to measure House points in the Gryffindor hourglass.
Given the choice between an opal ring and a ruby one, the princess chose opal—she'd never liked red much.

rucksack (ruk-sak)

noun A sturdy backpack used by hikers and campers. / *Goblet of Fire*, page 69
The campers struggled into their overloaded rucksacks and headed off to the village campground.

ruckus (ruk-us)

noun A disturbance or commotion. / *Half-Blood Prince*, page 4
Uh-oh, there's a ruckus in the kindergarten—the chairs in Musical Chairs are enchanted, and someone just sat on an octopus.

ruddy (rud-ee)

adjective In British slang, damned; not quite as bad as saying "bloody." / *Order of the Phoenix*, page 29 / Note: In Potter's world, "ruddy" is one of Uncle Vernon's favorite words.
"Get your ruddy hands off my wand," shouted Winston at his little brother.

ruddy-faced (rud-ee-fayst)

adjective Having a reddish complexion, sometimes naturally, sometimes from excessive exertion. / *Goblet of Fire*, page 71
The ruddy-faced hikers who just walked 26 miles were hot, worn out, and ready for a refreshing dandelion wine spritzer.

rudimentary (roo-duh-men-tuh-ree)

adjective Imperfect or undeveloped. / *Goblet of Fire*, page 656
"The rudimentary structure of the troll's brain explains many of its patterns of violent behavior," lectured the visiting professor.

rue (rhymes with **dew**)

noun An herb with a strong smell and bitter taste, used in various concoctions. / *Half-Blood Prince*, page 400
Both witches had grown rue for their potions, but Esmerelda was sure hers was going to be the strongest and most effective.

rue the day

phrase To regret something done. / *Chamber of Secrets*, page 167
"You'll rue the day you ordered 100 pizzas for the cafeteria," shouted the cafeteria manager at Brilly.

ruefully (roo-ful-ee)

adverb Sorrowfully, regretfully, remorsefully. / *Order of the Phoenix*, page 394
"I guess the third and fourth rides on the Tilt-a-Whirl were probably a mistake," said Dylan ruefully.

ruff (rhymes with **puff**)

noun An old-fashioned neck ruffle, with pleats and folds, covering the entire neck; a popular style in the 16th century. / *Sorcerer's Stone*, page 115
The duke's costume party might have been more fun if he hadn't insisted every guy dress in linen shirts with ruffs, doublets and leather jerkins, and even hose—the 16th century wasn't much fun, fashion-wise.

ruffle (ruf-ful)

adjective Vexed or aggravated. / *Sorcerer's Stone*, page 9
She looked very ruffled when he guessed who it was behind the mask.

ruffle (ruf-ful)

verb To rumple or mess up; usually said of hair. / *Sorcerer's Stone*, page 22
Rupert didn't much like his great aunt—she always ruffled his hair, saying over and over how much he'd grown. Plus she smelled like lizard's breath.

rumble (rum-bul)

verb In British slang, to discover or find out something. / *Half-Blood Prince*, page 127

"Did you rumble why the Horrible Hordes lost their match last week?" asked Winston.

rummage (rum-ij)
verb To search through, looking for something. / *Sorcerer's Stone*, page 9
Dribbles rummaged through his Halloween bag for one of his favorites—a box of grasshoppers dipped in liver oil.

rumormongering (roo-mur-mon-gur-ing)
noun The spreading of rumors. / *Order of the Phoenix*, page 94
Because of Rilda's constant rumormongering, most villagers tried to avoid her.

run amok
See **amok** elsewhere in this dictionary.

rune (rhymes with **June**)
noun The characters of an ancient alphabet used by Germanic people in the third to thirteenth centuries. / *Order of the Phoenix*, page 190
The village café had part of its menu written in runes.

runic (roo-nik)
adjective Consisting of or written in runes. / *Deathly Hallows*, page 662
The worn runic markings on the tombstone were a hint that the grave had been there a long time.

runty (run-tee)
adjective Small or stunted. / *Order of the Phoenix*, page 691
Whenever the height-challenged Butch Thuggins scored a goal, the fans of the opposing team would chant "Runty stunty, you're no funty."

run-up (run-up)
noun The preliminaries; the time before something starts. / *Half-Blood Prince*, page 520
During the run-up to the curtain rising for the school play, students sold crayfish-icles and Jump Juice in the theater lobby.

rupture (rup-chur)
verb To break or burst. / *Order of the Phoenix*, page 380
"I thought my dad was going to rupture a blood vessel when he found out about the jellyfish in the swimming pool," said Brilly.

ruse (rhymes with **twos**)
noun A clever, crafty trick or plan. / *Half-Blood Prince*, page 414
The mouse's ruse worked well—the cat went scampering after the catnip mouse while the real mouse snuck past.

S

sabotage (sab-uh-tahj)
noun A sneaky or underhanded interference with or destruction of something. / *Prisoner of Azkaban*, page 257
The sabotage against Annie's broom was hard to understand since everyone liked her.

sabotage (sab-uh-tahj)
verb To hinder the normal workings of something, or to sneakily destroy property. / *Deathly Hallows*, page 602
Brilly sabotaged the cafeteria one more time by gluing the ketchup and mustard containers to the tables… and on hot frogs day, too.

sack (rhymes with **back**)
verb To fire from a job. / *Sorcerer's Stone*, page 247
The school's astrology teacher was sacked—sadly, she had no idea she'd get fired.

sacrifice (sak-ruh-fise)
noun Something important that you give up. / *Sorcerer's Stone*, page 283
It wasn't much of a sacrifice for Annie to give up her after-school time to teach Hassan some new, intricate broomstick maneuvers.

sagely (sayj-lee)
adverb In a wise way. / *Chamber of Secrets*, page 83
"Running a village of wizards is like herding bees," said the mayor sagely.

saliva (suh-lie-vuh)
noun The clear watery stuff in the mouth. / *Deathly Hallows*, page 140
"Ogre saliva? Gnome saliva? Salamander saliva? Oh dear, I should have labeled these bottles," worried Mrs. Snodgrape, the Introductory Potions teacher.

sallow (sal-oh)
adjective A sickly yellow complexion. / *Sorcerer's Stone*, page 126
Dylan was downright sallow after his fourth ride on the Tilt-a-Whirl.

salt cellar (salt sel-ur)
noun A small dish that holds salt. / *Order of the Phoenix*, page 711
The salt cellar was nearly empty, prompting the queen to ring for the cook to complain.

salver (sal-vur)
noun A tray for serving food or beverages. / *Chamber of Secrets*, page 133
The café waiters didn't like using salvers to bring food to the table—they thought levitating the plates was more dramatic.

sanctimonious (sank-tuh-**moh**-nee-us)
adjective Excessively, hypocritically goody-goody; smarmily trying to appear good and right. / *Order of the Phoenix*, page 141
The cafeteria manager gave a sanctimonious smile after being awarded the "Most Interesting Recipe" award for his armadillo/possum stew.

sanction (sank-shun)
noun A penalty that works to ensure compliance with the rules. / *Order of the Phoenix*, page 416
"New sanctions will be imposed after spring vacation, including increased penalties for troublemaking," warned the principal.

sanctuary (sank-choo-air-ee)
noun A place of refuge, immunity, and shelter. / *Prisoner of Azkaban*, page 429
The bear frantically sought the sanctuary of his cave—the ogres were out bear hunting.

sanguine (san-gwin)
adjective Optimistic, hopeful, confident, cheerful. / *Deathly Hallows*, page 331
The king was more sanguine than he'd been in months—the prince's rock band had broken up.

sanity (san-ih-tee)
noun The condition of being sane. / *Order of the Phoenix*, page 255

Mrs. Snodgrape began to doubt her own sanity. No one had stolen her antique teledrone—she'd just loaned it to the library for a display.

sap (rhymes with **tap**)

verb To gradually drain, undermine, or weaken. / *Half-Blood Prince*, page 262
Weeding Wildwood's herb garden for six hours had sapped Katie of all her gardening interest and most of her energy.

sapling (sap-ling)

noun A young tree. / *Order of the Phoenix*, page 753
It was the custom in the village to plant a sapling in the front yard when a baby was born.

sapphire (saf-ire)

noun A gem, usually with a bluish color. / *Sorcerer's Stone*, page 256 / Note: In Potter's world, sapphires are used to measure House points in the Ravenclaw hourglass.
The giant gecko loved the sapphire earrings, but she had nowhere to wear them.

sardonic (sar-don-ik)

adjective Scornful, mocking, sneering, cynical. / *Goblet of Fire*, page 588
Blackpool's sardonic laugh echoed through the Trolls' Hole pub, where he'd just won the Crazy Fates Tournament for the fourth year in a row.

satsuma (sat-soo-muh)

noun A kind of mandarin orange. / *Half-Blood Prince*, page 330
The juicy satsuma Wildwood ate tasted like liquid sunshine.

saturated (sach-uh-ray-tid)

adjective Drenched or soaked. / *Order of the Phoenix*, page 682
Thanks to Brilly, Willow's backpack was saturated with frog slime.

savage (sah-vage)

adjective Fierce, enraged, furious. / *Order of the Phoenix*, page 833
Blackpool took savage delight in beating everyone at Crazy Fates.

savage (sah-vage)

verb To attack wildly. / *Sorcerer's Stone*, page 62

The dog, enraged by the loud fireworks, savaged her rag doll.

savagery (sahv-ij-ree)

noun Savage and cruel actions. / *Deathly Hallows*, page 447
The savagery of the hounds in the Haunted Forest was well-known. Just last week they attacked a poor zebra that had escaped from the visiting circus.

savior (save-yur)

noun A person who saves or rescues someone else. / *Deathly Hallows*, page 370
"Oh, my savior," cried the girl as Wildwood pulled her out of the Big Bog.

savor (save-ur)

verb To enjoy or appreciate. / *Order of the Phoenix*, page 704
The vampire savored the last dregs of the Bite Wine.

scabbard (skab-urd)

noun A sheath or case for the blade of a sword. / *Prisoner of Azkaban*, page 100
The knight had mislaid his scabbard. How could he ride into battle without a scabbard for his sword?

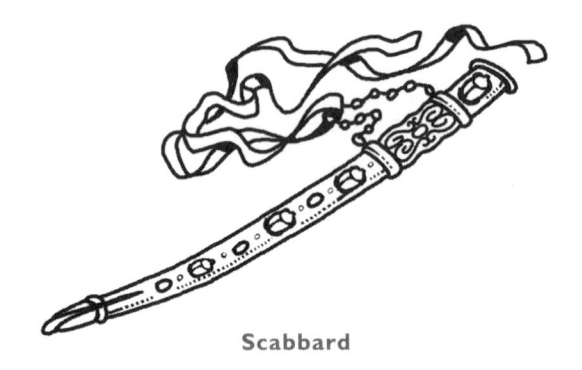

Scabbard

scalawag (skal-uh-wag)

noun A scamp or rascal. / *Chamber of Secrets*, page 119
"You scalawag," said the wandmaker to the little boy. "Get out of here—you're too young for a wand."

scalpel (skal-pul)

noun A very sharp surgical instrument, much like a small, straight knife. / *Order of the Phoenix*, page 267

The doctor used his sharpest scalpel to carefully cut through the skin of the miniature dragon. Who knew dragons could get appendicitis?

scandal (skan-dil)
noun A disgraceful or shocking incident or event. / *Deathly Hallows*, page 157
The latest scandal in the village was the newspaper editor running off with the librarian.

scandalized (skan-dil-ized)
adjective Shocked and horrified, usually by something considered immoral or improper. / *Order of the Phoenix*, page 314
The scandalized villagers couldn't believe the old witch had gone shopping with nothing on under her cloak.

scapegoat (skape-goht)
noun Someone made to bear the blame of others. / *Half-Blood Prince*, page 346
Elrod was so trouble-prone that he became the scapegoat whenever anything went wrong.

scarab beetle (skare-ub beet-ul)
noun A largish beetle with a hard shell, considered sacred in ancient Egypt. Its image is often used in jewelry. / *Goblet of Fire*, page 513 / Note: In Potter's world, scarab beetles are also crushed for use in potions.
Esmerelda's ring, shaped like a scarab beetle, looked both beautiful and creepy.

scarlet (skar-let)
adjective Bright red. / *Sorcerer's Stone*, page 93
Elrod's face turned scarlet when he dropped his wand in the toilet by accident.

scarlet woman (skar-let woom-un)
noun An old-fashioned term for a sexually promiscuous woman. / *Goblet of Fire*, page 513
The queen said the librarian had acted "just like a scarlet woman" when she ran off with the newspaper editor, not realizing they'd been secretly married for months.

scarper (skarp-ur)
verb To escape hurriedly. / *Deathly Hallows*, page 507
Brilly scarpered right before Mrs. Snodgrape stormed into the cafeteria.

scratch
See **up to scratch** elsewhere in this dictionary.

scathing (skay-thing)
adjective Critical. / *Half-Blood Prince*, page 31
Bella's father's scathing remark about her short skirt hurt her feelings.

scavenge (skav-inj)
verb To gather or take something usable from discarded things. / *Order of the Phoenix*, page 3
Wildwood scavenged through the dumpster outside the greengrocer's, hoping for some additions for his compost pile.

scavenger (skav-in-jur)
noun Someone who scavenges, or collects things discarded by others. / *Deathly Hallows*, page 461
The scavenger looked for old bottles discarded along the road.

sceptical (British spelling)
See **skeptical** elsewhere in this dictionary.

scheme (rhymes with **team**)
noun A plan or project, usually a secret or devious one. / *Chamber of Secrets*, page 288
Brilly's latest scheme was putting goldfish in the school toilets.

scoff (rhymes with **off**)
verb To mock something. / *Prisoner of Azkaban*, page 184
Madam Glinch scoffed at the suggestion to use the *Denturamus* spell to keep her dentures in.

scope (rhymes with **dope**)
noun The extent or range of actions or thoughts. / *Half-Blood Prince*, page 122
The scope of Brilly's mayhem was only limited by his imagination…and his allowance.

scorn (rhymes with **horn**)
noun Contempt, disdain, disgust. / *Deathly Hallows*, page 156

With a look of scorn, Blackpool stalked out of the Wandatorium Shop—*such* high prices.

scorpion (skor-pee-un)
noun An arachnid with a segmented body and a curled-upwards tail that has a stinger on the end. / *Goblet of Fire*, page 295
The scorpion practically wagged its tail when it spied the slipper under the bed, a perfect spot for a nighttime snooze.

scraggy (skrag-ee)
adjective Bony, thin, and lean. / *Deathly Hallows*, page 121
The scraggy traveler hunched in a corner of the village café, eating one hot bowl of soup after another.

scramble (skram-bul)
verb To move quickly. / *Sorcerer's Stone*, page 157
Rupert and Dribbles scrambled down the hill, feeling the hot breath of the wild boar right behind them.

scrawny (skraw-nee)
adjective Skinny and bony. / *Sorcerer's Stone*, page 132
He had gotten awfully scrawny ever since he started the bug juice and fish eyes diet.

screw (rhymes with **crew**)
verb To twist one's face out of shape. / *Sorcerer's Stone*, page 23
Nathan screwed up his face when he heard what was for dinner—he hated fried newt.

scroll (rhymes with **troll**)
noun A roll of parchment. / *Sorcerer's Stone*, page 122
Willow unrolled the just-delivered scroll—at last, an invitation to the Groundhog Day Festival.

scrounge (rhymes with **lounge**)
verb To seek out or gather something in an effort to get it with no cost. / *Goblet of Fire*, page 534
The panhandler tried to scrounge enough money for a cup of coffee at Star Ducks.

scrounger (skroun-jur)
noun Someone who scrounges or begs. / *Prisoner of Azkaban*, page 28
Some people thought the panhandler was a lazy scrounger, but he worked hard at what he did.

scrubby (skrub-ee)
adjective Undersized, stunted; not much to it. / *Goblet of Fire*, page 71
The few scrubby bushes around the library barely came up to the bottom of the windows.

scruff (rhymes with **buff**)
noun The back of the neck. / *Sorcerer's Stone*, page 36
The huge winged lizard swooped down, grabbed the gecko leader by the scruff of its neck, and flew off toward the mountain.

Gecko held by scruff of neck

scrum (rhymes with **drum**)
noun Literally, a beginning play in rugby when everyone crowds around the ball and struggles to gain possession of it; more generally, and especially in British usage, a hubbub or confused situation involving many people and much noise. / *Order of the Phoenix*, page 608
"Look at that scrum outside the Emporium," said Winston's mum. "Must be a sale on cauldrons."

scruples (skroo-puls)
noun A moral or ethical principle that keeps someone from doing something bad;

usually used in the plural. / *Deathly Hallows*, page 716
Even Blackpool, the evil wizard, had *some* scruples. He'd never enchant his mother, for example.

scrupulously (**skroo**-pyuh-lus-lee)
adverb Precisely or exactly. / *Order of the Phoenix*, page 25
Mrs. Fracket's bathroom was scrupulously clean—even the rubber duckie got scrubbed regularly.

scrutiny (**skroot**-un-ee)
noun A close and searching look or examination of something or someone. / *Deathly Hallows*, page 563
The intense scrutiny from the king's Royal Ripsnorter dog was making the castle visitors a little uneasy.

scrutinize (**skroot**-un-ize)
verb To look at or examine very carefully. / *Half-Blood Prince*, page 89
The Royal Plumber scrutinized the slimy castle moat, trying to figure out how to clean it without emptying it.

scud (rhymes with **mud**)
verb To move quickly and easily; often said of clouds. / *Sorcerer's Stone*, page 248
The clouds scudded across the sky so fast it looked like a time-lapse video.

scullery (**skul**-uh-ree)
noun A small room off the kitchen where various kitchen-related things, like dishwashing, cleaning pots, storing utensils, etc., are done. / *Deathly Hallows*, page 87
Wildwood was in the scullery scrubbing the pan he'd burned while making dinner.

scum (rhymes with **bum**)
noun A slang word, and a derogatory one, for a person considered low, worthless, even evil. / *Order of the Phoenix*, page 107
"Dear," began the king, "I don't think it's appropriate for you to refer to the hardworking kitchen help as 'scum.'"

scumbag (**skum**-bag)
noun A slang word, and a derogatory one, for a person considered despicable, objectionable, even sleazy. / *Order of the Phoenix*, page 851
"You scumbag, Klingster. You're as sleazy as they come," said the wandmaker.

scummy (**skum**-ee)
adjective Despicable, contemptible, worthless. / *Goblet of Fire*, page 205
"Blackpool, dear, enchanting those sweet little puppies was really a scummy thing to do," reprimanded the evil wizard's elderly mother.

scupper (**skup**-ur)
verb To ruin. / *Deathly Hallows*, page 49
Madam Glinch scuppered Brilly's plan when she suddenly appeared in the hallway.

scurry (**skur**-ee)
verb To run quickly and lightly; to scamper. / *Sorcerer's Stone*, page 158
The mouse scurried under the cottage, followed by the cat softly calling, "Here mousie mousie."

scurvy (**skur**-vee)
adjective An old-fashioned word for despicable and mean. / *Prisoner of Azkaban*, page 100
The pirate taught his parrot to say, "You scurvy bum—to the poop deck with you!"

scuttle (**skut**-ul)
verb To run or move quickly, especially in a secretive, furtive way. / *Sorcerer's Stone*, page 53
The scorpion scuttled across the bedroom floor, looking for a hiding place.

seamless (**seem**-les)
adjective Smooth-working and consistent. / *Goblet of Fire*, page 107
With seamless precision, the raiders of the supply closet worked together to distract the teacher.

searing (**seer**-ing)
adjective Burning. / *Chamber of Secrets*, page 171
The searing heat from the pizza oven nearly curled the cook's eyelashes.

secateurs (**sek**-uh-turs)
noun In British usage, pruning shears; used in the plural. / *Half-Blood Prince*, page 281

"Could you bring me the secateurs, please?" asked Winston's mum. "These bushes need pruning."

seclusion (sih-**kloo**-zhun)
noun The state of being secluded, isolated, apart, or away from others. / *Deathly Hallows,* page 117
The king sought the seclusion of the tower's secret hideaway; he needed a little time to himself.

second (**sek**-und)
noun The helper or attendant for each duelist in a duel. / *Sorcerer's Stone,* page 153
"Okay, Ravi, you're my second," said Wildwood. "Sharpen my sword, bring me my best boots, and—sigh—be prepared to carry my wounded body home."

secretion (sih-**kree**-shun)
noun Any substance secreted or discharged, like mucus, tears, etc. / *Goblet of Fire,* page 632
The gunky secretions from the ogre's nose were dripping into a puddle at his feet.

sedately (sih-**date**-lee)
adverb Calmly, quietly, deliberately, and in a composed way. / *Order of the Phoenix,* page 710
The participants in the Parade of the Invertebrates sedately moved past the crowds along the sidewalk.

seedy-looking (**see-dee-look**-ing)
adjective Looking worn, shabby, unkempt, and a little disreputable. / *Half-Blood Prince,* page 111
The seedy-looking cat was missing most of her fur, had one ear bent and battered, and lost part of her tail during a run-in with a miniature dragon.

seep (rhymes with **beep**)
verb To slowly leak. / *Sorcerer's Stone,* page 139
What was that red liquid seeping out of his locker? It was too thick to be cherry vitamin water, too thin to be ketchup….

seer (rhymes with **beer**)
noun A person who prophesies events in the future; an oracle or soothsayer. / *Prisoner of Azkaban,* page 109
Mrs. Sprocket, the village seer and fortune-teller, had found celestial influences and astrological indications particularly weak on three-day weekends.

seethe (seeth)
verb To be in a state of excitement and agitation. / *Goblet of Fire,* page 2
The evil Draconia Deveel seethed with anger—someone had cut off all her tulips and spread them on her doorstep.

seize (rhymes with **peas**)
verb Together with "up," to get stuck and stop working; applies to bodies as well as machinery. / *Goblet of Fire,* page 70
"Oh dear, my back's seized up," moaned the old sorceress, standing up after a long afternoon watching the levitating contest.

seizure (**see**-zhur)
noun A sudden attack, spasm, or convulsion. / *Half-Blood Prince,* page 308
The principal was so angry that the school secretary feared he might have a seizure.

self-
This prefix suggests "self-ness," that is, "to, with, for, of, on, or in oneself."
   self-absorption
   noun Preoccupation with one's self. / *Deathly Hallows,* page 436
   self-pity
   noun Pity for oneself. / *Order of the Phoenix,* page 823
   self-restraint
   noun Restraint of one's self. / *Order of the Phoenix,* page 680

senile (**see**-nile)
adjective Related to problems of old age, especially memory loss, dementia, etc. / *Half-Blood Prince,* page 150
"Is the mayor going senile? He just poured prune juice all over Merlin's statue."

sentient (**sen**-shunt)
adjective Conscious; experiencing feeling. / *Deathly Hallows,* page 632
The sink's garbage disposal acted much like a sentient

being—it burped, it sang, it moaned, it gnashed its gears.

sentinel (**sen**-tin-el)
noun Someone or something that watches or guards. / *Deathly Hallows*, page 258
Standing like proud sentinels, the king's security forces watched the approach of the duke and his men.

sepulchral (suh-**pul**-krul)
adjective Gloomy and deep. (FYI: A sepulchre is a tomb.) / *Order of the Phoenix*, page 135
His sepulchral tones suggested he had bad news to deliver.

serenely (suh-**reen**-lee)
adverb Happily, calmly, peacefully. / *Deathly Hallows*, page 217
The Shadow Stealer smiled serenely at the group of boys—they'd be back for their shadows shortly.

serpentine (**sur**-pen-teen)
adjective Serpent-like, especially in appearance and shape: winding, sinuous, and looping. / *Half-Blood Prince*, page 437
Flying along the serpentine road, Annie actually began to get a little broomsick.

serried (**sare**-eed)
adjective Packed closely together. / *Goblet of Fire*, page 586
The serried lines of students waited to get into the auditorium.

servility (sur-**vil**-uh-tee)
noun The condition of being servile (or slavishly submissive), especially in a cringing, fawning way. / *Order of the Phoenix*, page 156
Caught trying to steal the wandmaker's secrets, Klingster adopted a tone of servility that was totally disgusting.

servitude (**sur**-vih-tood)
noun Slavery or bondage. / *Order of the Phoenix*, page 698
Essentially, the castle chambermaids were in servitude to the Royal Family.

sever (**sev**-ur)
verb To cut off a part of something. / *Goblet of Fire*, page 386
The novice bank robber threatened to sever the bank manager's head, but he only had fingernail clippers with him.

severity (suh-**var**-ih-tee)
noun Sternness and harshness. / *Goblet of Fire*, page 592
The king's tone of severity suggested that he was not happy.

shabbiness (**shab**-ee-ness)
noun The condition of being shabby, worn, and threadbare. / *Goblet of Fire*, page 40
The dwarf offset the shabbiness of his small house with dozens of potted geraniums.

sham (rhymes with **dam**)
verb To pretend. / *Order of the Phoenix*, page 610
Dylan shammed sleep, hoping his mother wouldn't realize he was still awake.

shamrock (**sham**-rok)
noun A type of clover; Ireland's national emblem. / *Goblet of Fire*, page 93
"I'm looking over… a four-leafed shamrock…." Somehow the song lyrics didn't sound quite right.

shard (rhymes with **hard**)
noun A fragment or broken piece, especially of glass or pottery. / *Prisoner of Azkaban*, page 25
The miniature dragon knocked the glass to the floor, and shards of glass flew everywhere.

sheaf (rhymes with **leaf**)
noun A bundle or collection, gathered together, of paper, tickets, etc. / *Goblet of Fire*, page 65
The thick sheaf of papers meant a long night of grading essays for Madam Glinch.

sheen (rhymes with **keen**)
noun A gleaming luster. / *Half-Blood Prince*, page 185
Annie used broomstick polish to put a glowing sheen on her broomstick handle.

sheepish (sheep-ish)

adjective Embarrassed. / *Half-Blood Prince*, page 283
"I guess goldfish in the toilets was a bad idea," said a sheepish Brilly.

shepherd (shep-urd)

verb To watch, guard, or tend. / *Chamber of Secrets*, page 266
The wizarding preschool teacher shepherded her young students along on their first "World of Wonder" field trip.

shepherd's pie (shep-urds pie)

noun A baked meaty stew with a crust of mashed potatoes. / *Order of the Phoenix*, page 235
After his third helping of shepherd's pie, Dylan skipped dessert.

sherry (share-ee)

noun An alcoholic wine. / *Sorcerer's Stone*, page 68
"I think that's enough sherry for you," advised the bartender. The old witch was starting to slide off her bar stool.

shifty (shif-tee)

adjective Tricky, evasive, untrustworthy. / *Sorcerer's Stone*, page 229
"I really don't like Blackpool—he has shifty eyes," said Mrs. Birch.

shifty *or* **shufti**, as in **have a shifty** *or* **have a shufti**

phrases In British slang, both phrases mean to have a quick look around. / *Order of the Phoenix*, page 102 (shifty); *Half-Blood Prince*, page 460 (shufti)
The Royal Plumber had a shifty around the slime-filled castle moat. Later, the king came along and had a shufti himself.

shirty (sure-tee)

adjective In British slang, rude and ill-tempered, annoyed and angry. / *Prisoner of Azkaban*, page 244
"No need to get shirty with me, Blackpool. I merely pointed out that your wand seems a bit… undersized," said Madam Glinch.

shock (rhymes with **mock**)

noun A thick mass of bushy or shaggy hair. / *Prisoner of Azkaban*, page 90
Blackpool and his shock of black hair had been evading his mother's magical hair clippers for months.

shoddy (shod-ee)

adjective Of poor quality. / *Order of the Phoenix*, page 393
The shoddy quill left ink blots every other word.

short-listed (short-lis-tid)

adjective Being on a short list of the top or best. / *Goblet of Fire*, page 187
The Horrible Hordes were short-listed for the league championship.

shortsighted (short-sye-tid)

adjective Lacking foresight; with little regard for the future. / *Goblet of Fire*, page 711
Brilly's shortsighted plan to duct-tape the cafeteria manager to his refrigerator overlooked the expense of the duct tape…and the expanse of the refrigerator.

shot (rhymes with **hot**)

noun A small quantity—about an ounce—of hard liquor. / *Goblet of Fire*, page 147
"Just a quick shot," said Wildwood to the bartender. "No time to linger—the chickens need feeding."

shot *or* **shut**, as in **shot of him** *or* **shut of him**

phrases In British slang, both phrases mean to be rid of someone or something. / *Half-Blood Prince*, page 411 (shot of); *Order of the Phoenix*, page 70 (shut of)
"You may be shot of him, and I may be shut of him—whatever, he's finally gone."

shot-putter (shot-put-ur)

noun A competitor in an athletic event who heaves a heavy metal ball (the shot) as far as possible. / *Goblet of Fire*, page 260
The burly shot-putter easily tossed the shot halfway across the meadow.

show your true colors
phrase To do something that clearly shows what your real attitudes and beliefs are, especially when they're bad. / *Order of the Phoenix*, page 112
Blackpool, the evil wizard, showed his true colors when he bulldozed Wildwood's new troll fence.

shrapnel (shrap-nul)
noun Literally, artillery shell fragments; more generally, any projectiles like artillery shell fragments. / *Deathly Hallows*, page 621
The exploding pine cones spewed pine cone shrapnel everywhere.

shriek (rhymes with **peak**)
noun A loud, shrill cry. / *Sorcerer's Stone*, page 206
Madam Glinch, the wand teacher, let out a joyful shriek when every student successfully turned a mouse into a mouseburger.

shriek (rhymes with **peak**)
verb To cry out loudly and shrilly. / *Sorcerer's Stone*, page 224
Madam Glinch shrieked unhappily when she realized every enchanted mouseburger had ears, whiskers, and a tail.

shrill (rhymes with **still**)
adjective High and piercing; usually said of a voice or sound. / *Sorcerer's Stone*, page 19
Her shrill tones sounded like a fire engine's siren.

shriveled (shriv-uld)
adjective Shrunken or crumpled. / *Sorcerer's Stone*, page 48
The last shriveled apple in the bowl looked remarkably like the head of the old witch up the street.

shudder (shud-dur)
noun A sudden tremor or shaking movement. / *Goblet of Fire*, page 213
She gave a shivery shudder as she opened the pantry door—there, on the shelf…was it a dead mouse or a very old banana?

shudder (shud-dur)
verb To tremble or shake with a sudden movement, from fear, cold, horror, or revulsion. / *Sorcerer's Stone*, page 2
Willow shuddered just thinking what might happen if she got lost wandering on the Isle of Weird Creatures.

shuffle (shuf-ul)
verb To move one's feet without lifting them off the floor. / *Chamber of Secrets*, page 18
The students shuffled into the auditorium, grumbling about having to sit through another boring assembly on "The Dangers of Smoking, Drinking, and Hanging Out with the Wrong Type of Wizard."

shufti
See **shifty** elsewhere in this dictionary.

shun (rhymes with **bun**)
verb To avoid, evade, and keep away from. / *Prisoner of Azkaban*, page 356
It seemed that Blackpool, the evil wizard, generally shunned anyone decent.

shunt (rhymes with **stunt**)
verb To move along onto another path; to turn aside. / *Chamber of Secrets*, page 153
Mrs. Birch was shunted right past the tea pots and tea cozies by the eager crowd heading to the cauldron sale in the Emporium.

shut, as in **shut of him**
See **shot or shut** elsewhere in this dictionary.

sibilant (sib-uh-lunt)
adjective Hissing; like the sounds for "s" and "sh." / *Deathly Hallows*, page 653
The frog wished he could say sibilant sounds the way Mother Serpent could.

sick (rhymes with **ick**)
noun In British usage, vomit or throw-up. Cat sick, for example, would be cat vomit. / *Deathly Hallows*, page 239
The virulent vio-blatt flu caught the villagers by surprise, and the hospital's emergency room floor was soon slick with sick.

sickle (sik-ul)
adjective Crescent-shaped, like a sickle tool. / *Order of the Phoenix*, page 58 / Note: In Potter's world, another more unusual sickle also appears. In

The Unofficial Harry Potter Vocabulary Builder • 185

Sorcerer's Stone (page 203), Percy nearly broke his teeth on a tiny silver sickle in the Christmas pudding; it's a British custom to hide small coins or toys in Christmas puddings.

The slender sickle moon provided just enough light for the ghostly hounds to see their prey.

sideboard (side-bord)

noun A piece of dining room furniture with drawers and shelves to hold plates, glasses, silverware, etc. / *Deathly Hallows*, page 79

It was convenient having the sideboard so near the dinner table, but Winston still disliked setting the table.

sidekick (side-kik)

noun A buddy or close friend. / *Chamber of Secrets*, page 78

"Hey, who's your sidekick?" Wildwood asked Brilly as he passed Brilly and Hassan on the village green.

sidelong (side-long)

adjective Directed to one side; sideways. / *Prisoner of Azkaban*, page 171

Dribbles' lingering sidelong glance suggested he had a crush on the new girl.

sidesaddle (side-sad-ul)

adverb An old-fashioned way for a woman to ride a horse: seated on the horse's back, usually on a special saddle, with both legs on one side of the horse. / *Order of the Phoenix*, page 764 / Note: In Potter's world, the sitting was done on a thestral and without a saddle. It's the same idea, though—on the animal's back with both legs to one side, rather than one on each side.

The princess always rode sidesaddle but the queen never did.

sideshow (side-shoh)

noun Literally, a minor show at the circus (not the dramatic doings in the big tent); more generally, a minor or subordinate event. / *Deathly Hallows*, page 436

The compost in the drinking fountains was only a sideshow to the week's big event—the mysterious explosion in the janitor's closet.

Woman riding sidesaddle under a sickle moon

sidestep (side-step)

verb To step to one side or around something. / *Goblet of Fire*, page 558

The passersby carefully sidestepped the pile of purple animal droppings in the middle of the sidewalk.

sidle (side-ul)

verb To move or edge along sideways, often in an unobtrusive or furtive way. / *Chamber of Secrets*, page 60

The crab sidled over to the lobster to check out how his sore claw was feeling.

signature move (sig-nuh-chur move)

noun An action so associated with someone that the action alone distinguishes that person. / *Deathly Hallows*, page 71

Annie's signature broomstick move—the one that won the Broomstick Olympics—was a reverse half-tuck upper-body kick-out flutter.

silhouette (sil-oo-et)

noun A dark image outlined against a lighter background. / *Prisoner of Azkaban*, page 178

The silhouette of a huge one-eyed rabbit slowly moved across the wall. Wildwood had mastered the perfect hand shadow.

silkily (silk-uh-lee)
adverb Smoothly, softly, ingratiating. / *Half-Blood Prince*, page 24
"Why, yes, I also raise racing worms. Care to have a little race?" asked Blackpool silkily as the worm dealer peered over the fence at Blackpool's worm farm.

sill (rhymes with **pill**)
noun The horizontal piece beneath a window or door. / *Deathly Hallows*, page 743
The princess sat, elbows on the sill, staring gloomily out the castle window. When would the handsome Keeper of the Hounds return?

silt (rhymes with **tilt**)
noun Fine sand and mud; a gummy, gooey, slimy mixture. / *Goblet of Fire*, page 494
The river had deposited a thick layer of silt along the shore, making it hard to find a good place to go skinny-dipping.

simmering (sim-ur-ing)
adjective Cooking liquids at a temperature just below boiling. Simmering liquids are usually just steaming, with small bubbles rising. / *Sorcerer's Stone*, page 137
The simmering cauldron held no magical potions—just hot chocolate.

simper (sim-pur)
noun A silly self-conscious smile. / *Order of the Phoenix*, page 147
Rilda's annoying simper meant she thought she knew something no one else did.

simper (sim-pur)
verb To smile or act in a silly, self-conscious, affected way. / *Half-Blood Prince*, page 435
"Why, hello, Mr. Blackpool," simpered Miss Pandora, the owner of the worm race track.

sinew (sin-yoo)
noun A tendon, the inelastic tissue that connects muscles with bones. / *Chamber of Secrets*, page 124
When Nathan really messed up a landing, his skateboard slammed down on top of him, badly bruising the sinews and calf muscles in his leg.

sinewy (sin-yoo-ee)
adjective Lean, muscular, strong, and tough, like sinews. / *Goblet of Fire*, page 327
The sinewy boarhound loped quickly along the street, carrying his master's groceries home from the market.

singe (rhymes with **hinge**)
verb To burn or scorch slightly. / *Goblet of Fire*, page 393
The cat singed her whiskers sitting too close to the fire.

singed (rhymes with **hinged**)
adjective Slightly scorched or burned. / *Half-Blood Prince*, page 388
The cat's singed whiskers were shorter now, with little curls on the end.

singsong (sing-song)
adjective Having a monotonous voice that rises then falls. / *Sorcerer's Stone*, page 160
The singsong voice of the principal came over the PA system: "Students, students, students! You **must not** practice magic while playing soccer or while walking in the halls or while...."

singularly (sing-gyuh-lur-lee)
adverb Remarkably, extraordinarily, extremely; in a singular way (think "one of a kind"). / *Order of the Phoenix*, page 596
In his singularly rude way, Blackpool pushed to the front of the line.

sinuously (sin-yoo-us-lee)
adverb In a winding, bending, curving, supple, or smooth way. / *Order of the Phoenix*, page 769
Rupert watched the circus bellydancer sinuously moving her hips (and most everything else, too) and decided he'd fallen in love.

siphon (sigh-fun)
verb To convey, draw off, or empty, as if with a siphon. / *Half-Blood Prince*, page 454
In science class, Dribbles siphoned water from one glass to the next, wishing it was as easy to siphon off worry and dread—math class was next hour.

skein (rhymes with **rein**)

noun A length of hair, thread, yarn, etc., wound in a loose, long coil. / *Half-Blood Prince*, page 486

Mrs. Blackpool bought several skeins of yarn to make a sweater for her dear son, but her knitting needles got cramps and refused to do any knitting.

skeletal (skel-ih-tul)

adjective Like a skeleton. / *Chamber of Secrets*, page 124

Beneath his wrappings, the mummy was practically skeletal.

skeptical (skep-tih-kul)

adjective Doubtful. / *Goblet of Fire*, page 568 / Note: The British spelling **sceptical** also appears in *Goblet of Fire* (page 287).

Brilly's friends were totally skeptical—stay out of trouble for a week? He would never be able to do it.

skepticism (skep-tuh-siz-um)

noun A feeling of doubt or questioning. / *Half-Blood Prince*, page 146

Blackpool's skepticism about the effectiveness of his new Big Bug Trappah didn't stop him from plugging it in and eagerly awaiting a visit from the giant cockroach.

skim (rhymes with **dim**)

verb To go over or read very quickly. / *Sorcerer's Stone*, page 271

Mrs. Birch skimmed the recipe and realized she'd have to do a bit more shopping before starting her Eggs Croco-mander.

skint (rhymes with **hint**)

adjective In British slang, being poor or having no money. / *Deathly Hallows*, page 588

"I am so skint," said Winston. "Can I borrow money for lunch?"

skirt (rhymes with **hurt**)

verb To move around the edges, rather than pass close by. / *Goblet of Fire*, page 717

The mouse skirted the sleeping cat and headed to the kitchen for teatime.

skitter (skit-ur)

verb To run or move quickly and lightly. / *Chamber of Secrets*, page 192

Tiny Tinkles the fairy skittered through the cloud of moths, looking much like a moth herself.

skittle (skit-il)

noun A wooden pin, somewhat like a bowling pin, used in the game of skittles. / *Deathly Hallows*, page 542

"He went over like a skittle," said Winston, describing the way he'd tackled someone in the Whizzing Fire Ball Tournament.

skulk (rhymes with **bulk**)

verb To lurk in a sneaky or sinister way. / *Sorcerer's Stone*, page 274

Blackpool skulked outside the pub, hoping to confront the mayor about the problem of the visiting circus.

skullduggery (skul-dug-uh-ree)

noun Deception or trickery. / *Deathly Hallows*, page 79

Some skullduggery had happened—Blackpool's ace racing worm had been kidnapped.

slack (rhymes with **back**)

adjective Loose; not tense or taut. / *Goblet of Fire*, page 126

"Keep the reins just a little slack," instructed Wildwood as Katie practiced cantering.

slacken (slak-un)

verb To become looser and less tight or taut. / *Half-Blood Prince*, page 571

As Brady's broom twirled out of control, he felt his grip on the handle slacken.

slavish (slay-vish)

adjective Like a slave; submissive, subservient. / *Deathly Hallows*, page 53

Poor Bubba—his slavish look at Bella said it all: he wasn't at all happy with the break-up of their relationship.

sledge (rhymes with **hedge**)

noun In British usage, a sled. / *Order of the Phoenix*, page 693

The giant cockroach, as big as a sledge, scurried from corner to corner of the kitchen, seeking fallen crumbs.

sleek (rhymes with **peek**)

adjective Smooth and glossy. / *Chamber of Secrets*, page 287
Mother Serpent's skin had been especially sleek lately, ever since she'd discovered Urping Elmer's Mud Bath.

sleet (rhymes with **fleet**)

noun A mixture of rain and snow. / *Half-Blood Prince*, page 243
The wintry sleet pounded against the windows.

slide rule (**slide** rool)

noun An old-fashioned device for making mathematical calculations. / *Goblet of Fire*, page 90
Great Uncle Clem's slide rule was one of Bella's most prized possessions. It made math so much easier.

slipstream (**slip**-streem)

noun The turbulent air that slips around the sides of something—a train, a plane, a large animal—moving very fast. / *Prisoner of Azkaban*, page 431
Captain Hummingbird flew along in the slipstream behind Annie's broom.

slither (**slith**-ur)

verb To slide along like a snake. / *Sorcerer's Stone*, page 26
Mother Serpent and her children, Slick and Tweedie, slithered along the park's nature trail.

slog (rhymes with **bog**)

noun Literally, a long, tiring walk; more generally, long, laborious work. / *Chamber of Secrets*, page 298
It had been quite a slog pulling the little witch out of the Big Bog and getting her home.

slope (rhymes with **hope**)

verb To move off in a somewhat sneaky way. / *Sorcerer's Stone*, page 145
The suspicious trio sloped off down the street.

sloping (**sloh**-ping)

adjective On an angle. / *Sorcerer's Stone*, page 145
The sloping castle walls came down to the very edge of the moat.

sloth (rhymes with **moth**)

noun A very slow-moving mammal from South America known for hanging from tree branches upside down. / *Goblet of Fire*, page 261
"A sloth could do the dishes faster than you," complained Elrod's mother.

sludge (rhymes with **drudge**)

noun Soft, squishy, slushy mud. / *Prisoner of Azkaban*, page 280
Wildwood was certain a little sludge mixed in with the mulch would please his leek plants.

slump (rhymes with **dump**)

verb To sit slouched or hunched. / *Chamber of Secrets*, page 38
Madam Glinch slumped in the armchair, her eyes drooping—it'd been a hard day at school.

slur (rhymes with **blur**)

noun An insulting remark. / *Order of the Phoenix*, page 257
"One more slur from you about our singing," said the angry Old Hags Choir leader to the fisherman, "and your bass is grass."

slurred (rhymes with **blurred**)

adjective Indistinct or run together; usually refers to a voice or words. / *Half-Blood Prince*, page 578
The Royal Plumber was so exhausted his slurred words could hardly be understood.

slut (rhymes with **hut**)

noun A derogatory word for a prostitute or a sexually promiscuous female. / *Half-Blood Prince*, page 365
"I am furious with that little slut!" shouted the irate villager, upset with her long-missing cat who'd just reappeared with six kittens.

small consolation

phrase An ironic phrase meaning "not much help." *Consolation* means "comfort or solace"; just a little bit of it isn't that helpful. / *Order of the Phoenix*, page 637
It was small consolation that the goo on the gym floor

hadn't really hurt anything—it was still yucky to clean up.

smarmiest (smar-mee-ust)

adjective Affected, insincere, overly deferential and ingratiating, excessively flattering—in short, oily. / *Chamber of Secrets*, page 228
The Master of the Knights was sometimes the smarmiest, two-faced, most fawning knight in the realm.

smarten (smar-ten)

verb To spruce up or improve one's appearance. / *Sorcerer's Stone*, page 114
Every weekend, Blackpool smartened up for the worm races—you never know who you might meet there.

smirk (rhymes with **jerk**)

verb To smile in an annoying, self-satisfied way. / *Sorcerer's Stone*, page 196
The math teacher smirked at the class. "I bet you all think you got As on that easy test, don't you?"

smithereens (smith-uh-reenz)

noun Small fragments or pieces; used in the plural. / *Chamber of Secrets*, page 199
Uh-oh. One big firecracker + one toilet = smithereens.

smock (rhymes with **clock**)

noun A long, loose, shirt-like garment. / *Order of the Phoenix*, page 693
The kindergartners dressed in matching smocks for their field trip.

smolder (smol-dur)

verb To burn with little smoke and no flame. / *Order of the Phoenix*, page 40
The tired hikers' campfire smoldered and almost went out as they dozed.

smother (smuth-ur)

verb To hide or conceal. / *Sorcerer's Stone*, page 165
Tamika and Emily smothered their giggles as Elrod tripped over his shoelaces.

smug (rhymes with **bug**)

adjective Well-satisfied with oneself—perhaps a little too well-satisfied. / *Prisoner of Azkaban*, page 10
The boy's smug look meant he'd beaten Blackpool at chess—again.

snake (rhymes with **rake**)

noun Okay, okay, "snake" is a pretty common word, but there are many types of snakes, including adders (*Half-Blood Prince*, page 204), boa constrictors (*Sorcerer's Stone*, page 28), cobras (*Sorcerer's Stone*, page 27), and pythons (*Chamber of Secrets*, page 75). This last snake is big (20 feet long, more or less) and coils around and suffocates its prey. /
Jenn wasn't a big fan of snakes, but it was pythons that really gave her the whim-whams. Imagine being squeezed to death!

Snakes

sneak thief (sneek theef)

noun A burglar who sneaks in an open door or window to do his thievery. / *Deathly Hallows*, page 192
The alleged sneak thief had done more sneaking than thieving—Elrod had just snuck in for a nap.

sneer (rhymes with **fear**)

noun A mocking, scornful look done by raising one corner of the upper lip a little. / *Sorcerer's Stone*, page 78
With a sneer, Blackpool played the winning card and snarled, "You'll never beat me at Crazy Fates—you can't play your way out of a bowl of pigeon poop!"

sneer (rhymes with **fear**)
verb To smile in a mocking, scornful way. / *Prisoner of Azkaban*, page 20
Blackpool sneered at the ostrich's futile attempt to escape.

snide (rhymes with **wide**)
adjective Critical in a sly and nasty but not open way. / *Half-Blood Prince*, page 161
His snide compliments always sounded a little false.

snigger (snig-gur)
noun A barely stifled laugh. / *Sorcerer's Stone*, page 108
The snigger escaped before he could stop it—it's not a good idea to laugh in front of a herd of centaurs.

snigger (snig-gur)
verb To laugh a barely stifled laugh. / *Chamber of Secrets*, page 341
The whole class sniggered when Elrod tripped over his backpack and fell flat on the floor.

snippet (snip-it)
noun A small piece, scrap, or fragment. / *Order of the Phoenix*, page 865
Rilda wandered the aisles of the village market, hoping to hear some fresh snippets of gossip.

snivel (sniv-ul)
verb To whine or complain tearfully. / *Sorcerer's Stone*, page 43
The baby gecko sniveled at first, but eventually fell asleep.

snog (rhymes with **bog**)
verb In British slang, to make out, or kiss a lot. / *Order of the Phoenix*, page 117
"Oh look, dear, at that sweet couple snogging in the corner....Wait a minute, that's our son!"

snout (rhymes with **out**)
noun The lower part of the face; primarily the nose but also the jaws. Usually used in reference to animals. / *Sorcerer's Stone*, page 175
"Keep your snout out of my business," snorted the wild boar to the boarhound.

snuff (rhymes with **stuff**)
verb To die. / *Prisoner of Azkaban*, page 253
Blackpool was in mourning—his ace racing worm had snuffed it over the weekend.

snuffbox (snuf-box)
noun A small container for snuff (ground tobacco). / *Sorcerer's Stone*, page 262
Bella's Great Uncle Clem left his jeweled snuffbox to her when he died; she kept her purple spangles in it.

snuffling (snuf-ling)
noun The sound made when sniffling or snoring. / *Sorcerer's Stone*, page 156
That loud snuffling was either a troll asleep under the bridge or Dylan with a really bad cold.

soberly (soh-bur-lee)
adverb Seriously, solemnly, in a subdued way. / *Prisoner of Azkaban*, page 425
The manager of the visiting circus soberly explained the situation to Chuckles—the circus just didn't have enough money to hire another clown.

socket (sok-it)
noun A hollow part or cavity into which another part fits—an eye socket or a candlestick socket, for example. / *Deathly Hallows*, page 178
The king went through the entire castle putting energy-saving light bulbs in all the light sockets.

sodden (sod-en)
adjective Soaked and saturated. / *Prisoner of Azkaban*, page 178
Merlin tossed his sodden cloak on the hat rack—it was pouring outside.

sojourn (soh-jurn)
noun A temporary visit or stay. / *Order of the Phoenix*, page 678
Wildwood's sojourn to London was brief, and he was soon back in the village tending his garden and chickens.

solace (sol-is)
noun Comfort and consolation. / *Half-Blood Prince*, page 485
It was no solace to Blackpool that his ace racing worm had died a quick death. He was still dead.

sole (rhymes with **mole**; sounds exactly like **soul**)

adjective The only one. / *Order of the Phoenix,* page 625

The sole "A" in the math quiz was Bella's, the math whiz; everyone else barely passed.

sole (rhymes with **mole**; sounds exactly like **soul**)

noun The bottom of the foot. / *Goblet of Fire,* page 248

The old wizard massaged the soles of his feet—the long walk home from the library had them aching.

solemnly (sol-um-lee)

adverb In a serious, dignified, earnest way. / *Prisoner of Azkaban,* page 62

The school band solemnly played at the village mascot's funeral.

solicitous (suh-**lis**-ih-tus)

adjective Anxious or concerned. / *Deathly Hallows,* page 724

The solicitous cards and notes Dylan received while in the hospital buoyed his spirits.

solicitousness (suh-**lis**-ih-tus-ness)

noun The act of being anxious and concerned about someone in a kindly way. / *Deathly Hallows,* page 364

When Dribbles broke his nose on someone's fist, the school nurse's solicitousness helped him feel a little better.

solidarity (sol-ih-**dare**-uh-tee)

noun The uniting of purpose, interests, or actions. / *Order of the Phoenix,* page 737

The members of the Thieves Guild had great solidarity of purpose (thievery), of interest (thievery), and of actions (thievery).

solidify (suh-**lid**-uh-fie)

verb To make or become solid. / *Deathly Hallows,* page 173

The gooey potion slowly solidified and became a solid mass that couldn't even be stirred.

solstice (**sol**-stis)

noun The time when the sun is at the greatest distance from the equator—about June 21 (summer solstice) and about December 21 (winter solstice). The summer solstice is the longest day of the year, the winter solstice the shortest. / *Order of the Phoenix,* page 785

School wasn't out until the summer solstice, and the days just got longer and longer.

somber (**som**-bur)

adjective Serious, even melancholy. / *Chamber of Secrets,* page 208

His somber expression suggested it was time for a serious father-son discussion.

sonorous (**sohn**-ur-us)

adjective Deep, loud, and resonant; usually said of sound. / *Deathly Hallows,* page 228

The sonorous sound of the ferryboat horn alerted the villagers to the boat's arrival at the lake dock.

soot (rhymes with **foot**)

noun The fine, black, sticky powder left in the fireplace, especially after the burning of coal. / *Chamber of Secrets,* page 48

The chimney sweep tracked soot all over the castle's Great Hall.

sophisticated (suh-**fis**-tih-kay-tid)

adjective Complex; reflecting educated taste and worldly knowledge. / *Half-Blood Prince,* page 460

The sophisticated singing group sang madrigals and medieval tone poems in Latin. "Gee," said Fiona afterwards, "that sure wasn't 'The Tadpole Blues.'"

soporific (sop-uh-**rif**-ik)

adjective Tending to cause drowsiness or sleepiness. / *Order of the Phoenix,* page 229

The soporific tone of the lecturer's voice put even the fly in the room to sleep.

soppy (**sop**-ee)

adjective Overly sentimental. / *Deathly Hallows,* page 53

The king loved watching soppy soap operas on his widescreen TV—especially *The Young and the Rustless.*

sorcerer (**sore**-sir-er)

noun A wizard. / *Sorcerer's Stone,* page 57

Every sorcerer from miles around had come to the

village's Annual Magical Fair to show off the latest spells and enchantments.

sorceress (**sore**-sir-us)

noun A woman who practices magic. / *Chamber of Secrets*, page 34
Bella's mother was a sorceress, which meant Bella never had to fold the clean laundry.

sordid (**sore**-did)

adjective Morally degraded; trashy. / *Order of the Phoenix*, page 4
"Did you hear those sordid rumors about Willow and the new boy? They actually… whoops! Here comes Madam Glinch. I'll tell you later."

souvenir (soo-vuh-**neer**)

noun A small reminder or memento of a place or an experience. / *Prisoner of Azkaban*, page 6
As a souvenir of his London trip, Merlin brought home a snow globe with a tiny castle tower inside.

sow (rhymes with **grow**; sounds exactly like **sew**)

verb Literally, to spread or plant seeds; more generally, to spread or plant ideas. Past tense: sown. / *Deathly Hallows*, page 208
Blackpool the evil wizard had sown suspicion and disbelief among the villagers over the election results.

sown

See **sow** above.

spangled (**spang**-guld)

adjective Decorated with spangles—small, round, bright, sequin-like decorations. / *Prisoner of Azkaban*, page 102
Bella and Bubba dressed up for the party—Bella in a slinky spangled dress and Bubba in his spangled cloak.

spasm (**spaz**-um)

noun Literally, a sudden involuntary muscle contraction; more generally, a sudden brief emotion, feeling, or reaction. / *Sorcerer's Stone*, page 290
Bubba experienced a stabbing spasm of pain when Bella suggested they break up.

spat

See **spit** elsewhere in this dictionary.

spate (rhymes with **fate**)

noun A large amount or number of something. / *Chamber of Secrets*, page 122
There had been a sudden spate of feather mold among Wildwood's chickens, a result of a leak in the chicken coop.

spats (rhymes with **rats**)

noun An old-fashioned shoe covering for the ankle and instep, now often worn by marching bands. Used in the plural. / *Half-Blood Prince*, page 199
The school marching band wore shiny red coats with brass buttons, fancy trousers, and black shoes with white spats.

spawn (rhymes with **dawn**)

noun The eggs or young of fish, mollusks, amphibians, etc. Frog spawn, for example, would be a bunch of tadpoles. / *Sorcerer's Stone*, page 53
"Teddy, what did you have in your dirty jeans pockets? There's frog spawn in the washing machine."

spawn (rhymes with **dawn**)

verb To produce or give rise to. / *Half-Blood Prince*, page 443
Blackpool's rude behavior at the worm races spawned a lot of angry looks and mutterings among the crowd.

specky (**spek**-ee)

adjective In British slang, covered with pimples. / *Deathly Hallows*, page 49
"Ewww, the May Fete queen looks all specky—how embarrassing," thought Winston.

spectacles (**spek**-tuh-kuls)

noun Eyeglasses. / *Sorcerer's Stone*, page 8 / Note: In Potter's world, several types of spectacles are worn: wire-rimmed (*Half-Blood Prince*, page 348), half-moon (*Sorcerer's Stone*, page 8), horn-rimmed (*Deathly Hallows*, page 605), and the more ordinary square (*Sorcerer's Stone*, page 9) and round (*Sorcerer's Stone*, page 20).

"I've lost my spectacles," complained the king. "How can I do the crossword puzzle?"

specter (**spek**-tur)

noun A phantom or ghostly apparition. / *Goblet of Fire*, page 181
The specter of Blackpool's father was sometimes seen in the library—not unusual as he was the one who burned down the old library.

spectral (**spek**-trul)

adjective Ghostly. / *Prisoner of Azkaban*, page 107
The mysterious spectral figure seemed to float across the meadow.

speculate (**spek**-yoo-late)

verb To imagine or discuss the possibilities, usually with insufficient information. / *Goblet of Fire*, page 265
The boys speculated on what life after school would be like.

speculation (spek-yuh-**lay**-shun)

noun Wonderings and guesses, usually based on incomplete information. / *Half-Blood Prince*, page 257
Among the castle staff, there was lots of speculation about what would happen to the Royal Plumber if he *couldn't* get the castle moat cleaned out.

spell (rhymes with **yell**)

noun A word—or words—believed to have magical powers. / *Sorcerer's Stone*, page 64
The old wizard was having a senior moment—he couldn't remember the spell for changing hedgehogs into soup tureens.

spew (rhymes with **brew**)

verb To vomit. / *Goblet of Fire*, page 224 / Note: In Potter's world, "spew" is also the acronym for the Society for the Promotion of Elfish Welfare.
A very sick Dylan spewed in his cauldron, on his cloak, and all over Madam Glinch's desk.

sphere (rhymes with **beer**)

noun A round, ball-shaped object. / *Order of the Phoenix*, page 635
The full moon—an astoundingly perfect bright sphere—rose over the mountains.

sphinx (rhymes with **stinks**)

noun In mythology, a monster with the body of a huge lion, clawed paws, a long tail, the wings of an eagle, and the head of a woman. / *Goblet of Fire*, page 628
Dribbles wondered: Did the sphinx mostly prowl, its tail swishing, or did it fly?

Sphinx

spiffing (**spif**-ing)

adjective Excellent or splendid. / *Prisoner of Azkaban*, page 62
"What a spiffing idea. I'd love to go out for Chinese food."

spike (rhymes with **bike**)

verb To add something (a poison or some chemical) to a beverage. / *Half-Blood Prince*, page 393
"This tastes terrible. I think someone spiked it with squakle juice."

spill the beans

phrase To disclose a secret accidentally or thoughtlessly; to tell all. / *Goblet of Fire*, page 445
Rilda spilled the beans about Willow's new crush.

spindly (**spin**-dlee)

adjective When said about a person or a body part: thin and weak. When said about furniture: rounded legs or arms on chairs or

tables. / *Sorcerer's Stone*, page 82
Luckily, it was the spindly boy who sat on the very delicate spindly chair.

spiraling (spy-rul-ing)
adjective Resembling a spiral; circling around a center. / *Prisoner of Azkaban*, page 416
The prince was counting the tower's spiraling steps—he got to 265 before he got too dizzy and lost count.

spit (rhymes with **twit**)
verb To eject saliva from the mouth; when done *at* someone, it's a rude gesture of anger or contempt. "To spit out" means to speak so angrily that spit is (almost) flying. Past tense: spat. / *Half-Blood Prince*, page 208
Blackpool rudely spat on the pub floor and shouted, "You know nothing—NOTHING—about it!" The bartender tried to spit out an angry reply, but Blackpool had already stormed out.

spite (rhymes with **might**)
noun A malicious feeling of ill will toward someone, and a desire to harm, annoy, or humiliate that person. / *Half-Blood Prince*, page 443
Blackpool bulldozed Wildwood's troll fence out of spite—the two had argued for months about where it should go, and Blackpool hadn't liked the decision.

spittle (spit-il)
noun Saliva or spit. / *Goblet of Fire*, page 555
"You may call it spittle, but I call it drool, and I say it's disgusting."

splayed (rhymes with **blade**)
adjective Spread out, or turned outward. / *Goblet of Fire*, page 127
Elrod's splayed feet meant he walked a little like a duck.

spleen (rhymes with **keen**)
noun A body organ located near the stomach. / *Sorcerer's Stone*, page 72
"Eye of newt and toe of frog, spleen of goat and…. Jeesh, it's going to be hard to get all these potion ingredients," worried the witch.

splint (rhymes with **glint**)
noun A thin piece of wood or metal used to keep a broken bone from moving. / *Prisoner of Azkaban*, page 377
A splint for a broken elbow is tricky to create.

splotched (rhymes with **botched**)
adjective Stained or spotted. / *Chamber of Secrets*, page 215
The splotched tablecloth was covered with the remains of the fairies' picnic—beetle juice, gob-hobs, froglette candy, and naughter melons.

splutter (splut-ur)
verb To speak rapidly and incoherently because of confusion, anger, or embarrassment. / *Half-Blood Prince*, page 246
Blackpool began to splutter when the giant cockroach opened the refrigerator and looked inside.

sponge cake (spunj kake)
noun A light, sweet cake with a spongy texture and appearance. / *Goblet of Fire*, page 511
A slice of sponge cake was the perfect conclusion to Mrs. Birch's birthday celebration.

sporadic (spuh-rad-ik)
adjective Infrequent and at irregular intervals. / *Goblet of Fire*, page 154
Brilly's sporadic attempts to improve his behavior were ultimately unsuccessful.

sport (rhymes with **port**)
verb To display or show off. / *Half-Blood Prince*, page 98
The Princess of the Deep sported a new seashell necklace.

spot (rhymes with **hot**)
noun A small quantity; used in phrases like "do a spot more" (do a little bit more) or "a spot of bother" (a bit of trouble.) / *Goblet of Fire*, page 615 (spot more); *Half-Blood Prince*, page 9 (spot of bother)
"I'll have a spot more tea," said Mrs. Snodgrape, "if that isn't a spot of bother."

spread-eagled (spred-ee-guld)
adjective Lying flat with arms and legs outstretched. / *Half-Blood Prince*, page 608

The mouse lay spread-eagled on the floor, crushed to death when Blinky, the enormous cat, sat on it.

springboard (spring-bord)
noun Another word for diving board, the springing board at the swimming pool that one dives from. / *Goblet of Fire*, page 103
Brilly made a dramatic dive off the springboard. Well, actually, it was a dramatic cannonball jump.

sprite (rhymes with **light**)
noun An elf or pixie. / *Half-Blood Prince*, page 562
A lake sprite floated by on a lily pad.

spur (rhymes with **purr**)
verb To incite or stimulate. / *Order of the Phoenix*, page 553
Fiona's love of singing spurred her to learn the guitar so she could accompany herself.

spurn (rhymes with **turn**)
verb To reject something disdainfully or with contempt. / *Deathly Hallows*, page 616
Esmerelda spurned Blackpool's attempts to ask her out.

squally (skwah-lee)
adjective Stormy, on and off. / *Order of the Phoenix*, page 605
The squally weather varied between brilliant sunshine and gloomy rain.

squalor (skwah-lur)
noun Wretchedness, filth, and misery. / *Half-Blood Prince*, page 212
The old man lived in squalor in a shack down by the railroad tracks.

squander (skwon-dur)
verb To spend wastefully. / *Half-Blood Prince*, page 212
Brilly squandered all his money on the rides at the Dungeons of Doom Amusement Park.

squat (rhymes with **hot**)
adjective Short and broad. / *Sorcerer's Stone*, page 76
The squat hedgehog sat on the hilltop, thinking about breakfast. And lunch. And dinner.

squeamish (skwee-mish)
adjective Easily made to feel sick or offended; on the fastidious side. / *Order of the Phoenix*, page 431
"Ewwww." It was only a dead moth, but Willow was a little squeamish.

squelch (rhymes with **belch**)
verb To walk heavily in mud or water, making a "squelch" sound. / *Chamber of Secrets*, page 123
Wildwood squelched his way through the mud to feed the chickens.

squid (rhymes with **hid**)
noun A sea creature with ten tentacles and a long, tapered body. / *Prisoner of Azkaban*, page 421
"Ten's best." "No, eight." "No, ten!" The squid and the octopus were arguing over whether it was better to have eight or ten tentacles.

squit (rhymes with **quit**)
noun In British usage, an insulting term for someone considered of low status or little importance. / *Deathly Hallows*, page 95
"That ruddy squit, he's done it again," said an angry Blackpool.

staff (rhymes with **laugh**)
noun A large walking stick, more a stick or pole rather than a cane. / *Goblet of Fire*, page 184
The wizard used his staff to help him maneuver across the stepping stones in the stream.

staggered (stag-gurd)
adjective Shocked or astounded. / *Prisoner of Azkaban*, page 375
The king was staggered when he realized he didn't remember why he and the duke had become enemies.

stagnation (stag-**nay**-shun)
noun A lack of activity and growth. / *Order of the Phoenix*, page 213
Economic stagnation had hit the village—maybe it wasn't the best time to open a restaurant, thought Nungie.

staking out

phrase To watch for someone continuously from a hidden place; detectives are always "staking out" suspects. / *Deathly Hallows*, page 204

The policeman staking out the pub had heard the unsuccessful bank robber might be inside, drowning his sorrows.

stalactite (stah-lak-tite)

noun In a cave, an icicle-shaped mineral deposit that sticks downward from the cave roof. / *Sorcerer's Stone*, page 74

Elrod was uneasy standing under the cave's pointy stalactites.

stalagmite (stah-lag-mite)

noun In a cave, an upside-down icicle-shaped mineral deposit that sticks upward from the cave floor. / *Sorcerer's Stone*, page 74

Rupert hung his hat on a stalagmite near the cave entrance.

Stalactites and stalagmites

stalk (rhymes with **hawk**)

verb To walk in a proud, haughty, even stiff manner. / *Chamber of Secrets*, page 164

Bella stalked over to Bubba, her longtime boyfriend, and announced, "I think it's time we had a long talk."

stampede (stam-peed)

verb To rush or scatter, like a herd of frightened horses. / *Chamber of Secrets*, page 62

The shoppers stampeded into the Hurly Burly Emporium on half-price day.

stark (rhymes with **bark**)

adjective Complete or extreme. / *Half-Blood Prince*, page 545

"Class, please list at least five stark differences between the spell for poltergeists in the attic and the spell for poltergeists in the barn."

state of disrepair

See **disrepair** elsewhere in this dictionary.

state of siege

phrase A situation in which attacking forces surround a place and either try to gain control of it or force people out of it. / *Deathly Hallows*, page 596

The castle knights were practicing how to handle a state of siege.

stationary (stay-shuh-nar-ee)

adjective Unmoving; standing still. / *Order of the Phoenix*, page 171

The giant cockroach was perfectly stationary, listening to see if that mysterious hum from the refrigerator meant trouble.

station (stay-shun)

verb To put someone in a place or position to perform some duty. / *Prisoner of Azkaban*, page 66

During the practice state of siege, the knights were stationed along the castle walls, ready to pour boiling oil on invaders.

statute (stach-oot)

noun A law, decree, or edict. / *Order of the Phoenix*, page 27

According to village statute, it was unlawful to drop anything from a broom flying higher than ten feet.

staunch (rhymes with **launch**)

verb To stop the flow of something, like tears or blood. / *Deathly Hallows*, page 73

The soccer doctor staunched the bleeding from Butch Thuggins' broken nose.

staunchly (stonch-lee)

adverb In a firm, strong way. / *Half-Blood Prince*, page 146

"I don't care if I get in trouble," said Brilly staunchly. "It isn't fair that we have to eat such terrible cafeteria food, and I'm going to do something about it."

stave (rhymes with **grave**)

verb To keep off or away by force. / *Goblet of Fire*, page 355

"We'll easily stave off all attackers with our many defensive techniques," declared the Master of the Knights.

stealth (rhymes with **health**)

noun Sneakiness, especially secret, dishonest, and furtive sneakiness. / *Order of the Phoenix*, page 96

Klingster planned on getting the wandmaker's secrets by stealth.

steed (rhymes with **feed**)

noun A horse, especially a frisky, lively one. / *Goblet of Fire*, page 245

"My valiant steed," shouted the Master of the Knights. "Together we shall ride in pursuit of the elusive fox!"

steely (stee-lee)

adjective Tough and determined. / *Chamber of Secrets*, page 213

With a steely look in his eyes, Blackpool stared down the ogre.

steep (rhymes with **sleep**)

verb Literally, to soak; more generally, to be immersed, saturated, or "soaked" in a concept or influence. Something "steeped in history," for example, would be "soaked" with history. / *Half-Blood Prince*, page 440

The librarian, steeped in village history, was hoping Rockspurt, the village founder, could be honored with a statue.

stench (rhymes with **wrench**)

noun A strong, unpleasant smell. / *Sorcerer's Stone*, page 174

"Yuck, what a stench—your shaving lotion smells like octopus poop."

stifle (sty-ful)

verb To suppress or bottle up. / *Prisoner of Azkaban*, page 105

The girls tried to stifle their giggles when Elrod walked by with his backpack on upside down.

stifling (sty-fling)

adjective Really hot and stuffy. / *Sorcerer's Stone*, page 231

It was stifling in the castle; the royal air conditioner wasn't working.

stigma (stig-muh)

noun A mark of disgrace or social unacceptability. / *Order of the Phoenix*, page 298

The stigma of attending the very ordinary Cauldron College—instead of the prestigious university—always bothered Ethelbell.

stile (rhymes with **mile**; sounds exactly like **style**)

noun A series of steps up and over a fence that people can handle but cows and horses cannot. / *Goblet of Fire*, page 510

Elrod sat atop the stile, watching the frustrated cows trying to figure out how to climb it.

stimulant (stim-yuh-lent)

noun A substance (drug, food, beverage) that stimulates or makes a person more alert, focused, and full of energy. / *Half-Blood Prince*, page 582

The Jump Juice acted as quite a stimulant on the young boys since they were unused to potent energy drinks.

stoat (rhymes with **float**)

noun An ermine or weasel, a small wild animal prized for its fur (white in winter, brown in summer). / *Sorcerer's Stone*, page 231 / Note: In Potter's world, stoat sandwiches are served. Actually, the meat of a stoat isn't particularly edible—consider it an only-in-Potter's-world food. Stoats make great fur coats (though not so great for the stoat).

stock-still (stok-stil)

adverb Not moving at all. / *Half-Blood Prince*, page 157

The terrified mouse stood stock-still—a cat behind

him, a snake ahead, and a hawk overhead. This was no time for moving.

stoically (stow-ih-klee)
adverb In a calm, unaffected way. / *Half-Blood Prince*, page 518
Wildwood stoically rebuilt his troll fence after Blackpool spitefully bulldozed a big hole in it.

stoke (rhymes with **poke**)
verb To stir up and add fuel to a fire. / *Order of the Phoenix*, page 660
Parker stoked the campfire—the water in the kettle wasn't nearly hot enough for tea yet.

stone-flagged
See **flagged stone** elsewhere in this dictionary.

stooge (rhymes with **scrooge**)
noun An assistant, accomplice, or flunky; used in a disapproving way. / *Half-Blood Prince*, page 28
"Blackpool, your stooge Klingster tried to pass off horsehair as unicorn hair," complained the wandmaker.

stooping (stewp-ing)
adjective Having the back and shoulders rounded. / *Chamber of Secrets*, page 51
The stooping, misshapen old witch stumbled out of her cottage shouting "Fire!"

stores (rhymes with **bores**)
noun A supply of something saved for future use; used in the plural. / *Chamber of Secrets*, page 186
The cafeteria manager was sure he'd laid in sufficient stores of possum meat and chudbutts, but he worried that he might not have enough eel meat.

stout (rhymes with **out**)
adjective Chunky, heavy, even fat. / *Chamber of Secrets*, page 198
The stout knight had a difficult time finding armor that fit.

stoutly (stout-lee)
adverb Bravely and in a determined way. / *Goblet of Fire*, page 370
"I know I can do this," said Dribbles stoutly as he tried to levitate his pencil.

stow (rhymes with **slow**)
verb To put or pack something away until it's needed; to stash something. / *Chamber of Secrets*, page 214
Brilly stowed the fireworks in the back of his closet.

straggling (strag-ling)
adjective Spread out in a scattered way. / *Chamber of Secrets*, page 37
A straggling row of sing-out bushes grew along the edge of the Haunted Forest; together with all the signs, they warned of the dangers ahead.

straightaway (strayt-uh-way)
adverb At once; immediately. / *Deathly Hallows*, page 482
"Wands down, class, straightaway, then you may be excused."

straitjacket (strayt-jak-it)
noun Literally, a piece of clothing that keeps the wearer from moving; used to restrain someone violent or who might hurt themselves. More generally, a feeling of being constrained, restrained, or immobilized. / *Goblet of Fire*, page 504
Bella felt like she was in a straitjacket—she cared for Bubba but she wanted her freedom.

Straitjacket

strand (rhymes with **brand**)
verb To be helpless, left in a difficult, lonely place. / *Sorcerer's Stone*, page 91
Esmerelda was stranded in the Fortress of Solitude after her broomstick caught on fire.

strangled (**strang**-guld)

adjective Unclear or muffled. / *Sorcerer's Stone*, page 38
In a strangled voice, Bella muttered, "I think this particular yoga position is not my favorite."

strapping (**strap**-ing)

adjective Strong, powerful, healthy. / *Prisoner of Azkaban*, page 320
O'Harris, the Scottish elf, was about as strapping as an elf could get.

strategic (struh-**tee**-jik)

adjective Important or essential to a strategy, plan, or action. / *Goblet of Fire*, page 459
The king realized the strategic importance of having a variety of castle defenses.

strategy (**strat**-ih-jee)

noun A plan of action. / *Half-Blood Prince*, page 374
Strategy in lightball tennis involved plenty of overhead lobs, steaming smashes as needed, and hitting the lightball where your opponent wasn't.

stream (rhymes with **beam**)

verb To move or flow steadily. / *Sorcerer's Stone*, page 135
The students streamed into the auditorium, eager for the afternoon program on "Invisibility Issues for Growing Wizards."

streaming (**streem**-ing)

adjective Flowing; in the case of eyes, flowing with tears. / *Sorcerer's Stone*, page 16
Chi-Mun's streaming eyes were relieved when he finished peeling the last of the three dozen onions.

strew (rhymes with **brew**)

verb To scatter. Past tense: strewn. / *Chamber of Secrets*, page 253
The contents of Elrod's closet were strewn all over his room, but that was the only way he could find anything.

strewn

See **strew** above.

stricken (**strik**-un)

adjective Affected by emotion, like fear, grief, or sadness. / *Prisoner of Azkaban*, page 214
A stricken Fiona slowly sat down—she'd just heard her grandmother had died.

stricture (**strik**-chur)

noun A negative remark or criticism. / *Deathly Hallows*, page 674
"Your strictures about my son are neither accurate nor welcome," said Brilly's father to the principal. "He *has* caused a few problems, but he's basically a well-meaning boy."

stride (rhymes with **wide**)

verb To walk with long steps. Past tense: strode. / *Prisoner of Azkaban*, page 418
The giant strode past the waterfall, and was next seen striding along the river's edge.

stringent (**strin**-junt)

adjective Strict; with great attention to rules and procedures. / *Half-Blood Prince*, page 41
The school instituted stringent new security rules after the little problem with the naked visitor.

strode

See **stride** elsewhere in this dictionary.

strut (rhymes with **butt**)

verb To walk in a self-important, vain way. / *Chamber of Secrets*, page 191
Blackpool strutted into the Trolls' Hole pub and announced, "I'm going to run for mayor!"

stub (rhymes with **tub**)

noun The short part left over after something has broken off or been used up. / *Sorcerer's Stone*, page 235
The witch collected the candle stubs left over from the party. They were an essential ingredient for her Glowing Potion.

stubbly (**stub**-lee)

adjective Having a short growth of whiskers. / *Goblet of Fire*, page 571
Wildwood's stubbly whiskers and uncombed hair meant he'd stayed up all night trying to catch the monster chicken thief.

stubby (**stub**-ee)

adjective Like a stub: short and thick. / *Order*

of the Phoenix, page 665
The ogre had surprisingly stubby toes and fingers.

stump (rhymes with **hump**)
verb To walk with a heavy clumping, thumping step. / *Sorcerer's Stone*, page 150
The angry peg-legged pirate stumped from one end of the ship's deck to the other.

stupefied (**stoo**-puh-fied)
adjective Amazed, astonished, or silent because of surprise. / *Chamber of Secrets*, page 213
The stupefied ogre just stared at the flock of students practicing broomstick maneuvers overhead.

stupor (**stoo**-pur)
noun A state of mental numbness or of being zoned out in a self-induced daze. / *Chamber of Secrets*, page 108
Bella was in a shopping stupor after spending the day roaming the aisles of the Hurly Burly Emporium.

stutter (**stut**-ur)
verb When referring to candles or lights, to flicker or to move unpredictably and unsmoothly. / *Sorcerer's Stone*, page 172
The candles in the castle grotto stuttered in the slight draft.

stymie (**sty**-mee)
verb To prevent someone from doing what they'd planned to do. / *Half-Blood Prince*, page 235
The monster chicken was stymied in its desire for mega-worms. The ground was just too hard.

subdue (sub-**doo**)
verb To overpower and bring under control. / *Goblet of Fire*, page 356
The Witching Hour bartender subdued the tipsy patron with a *Skrewski Brewski* spell.

subjugate (**sub**-juh-gate)
verb To bring someone else under complete control; to conquer and master someone. / *Deathly Hallows*, page 6
The duke had spent 20 years wanting to subjugate

the king, and now everything had changed and they were becoming best friends.

submerge (sub-**murj**)
verb To immerse oneself below the surface of the water. / *Deathly Hallows*, page 369
The snake submerged itself in the lake waters, except for its eyes, which were watching Rupert on the shore.

submission (sub-**mish**-un)
noun The act of submitting, of being totally controlled by someone and accepting that. / *Goblet of Fire*, page 509
Dribbles worried: What if invaders surrounded the castle and tried to starve the Royal Family into submission?

subnormal (sub-**nor**-mul)
adjective Below the normal. / *Prisoner of Azkaban*, page 26
For the past week, subnormal temperatures had plagued the villagers. Where was global warming when you needed it?

subsequent (**sub**-sih-kwent)
adjective Following or coming later. / *Deathly Hallows*, page 17
In the subsequent weeks after the huge flood, a million mosquitoes and midges descended on the villagers.

subservience (sub-**sur**-vee-unce)
noun The condition of being in a subservient state, or being powerless and weak. / *Deathly Hallows*, page 716
The monster chicken felt certain it would never be in subservience to anyone or anything.

subside (sub-**side**)
verb To become quieter, less active, calmer. / *Chamber of Secrets*, page 285
The terrible storm finally subsided, and the villagers could start cleaning up their yards.

substandard (sub-**stan**-durd)
adjective Below the usual standard; less than adequate and acceptable. / *Goblet of Fire*, page 540
The substandard service at the Trolls' Hole ever since

the waitress left was a problem—one night Blackpool waited half an hour for a flagon refill.

subsume (sub-soom)
verb To include or incorporate into something larger. / *Deathly Hallows*, page 478
You know it's going to be a boring announcement when it begins, "These new rules subsume the previous rules in this area…."

subtle (suht-il)
adjective Difficult to describe, explain, or understand because something is so mysterious, complex, or delicate in meaning. / *Sorcerer's Stone*, page 136
The subtle art of magical wandwork had always intrigued Madam Glinch.

subtlety (suht-il-tee)
noun Fine distinctions, with careful attention to small details. / *Order of the Phoenix*, page 530
"A great deal of subtlety is involved in wand work," advised Madam Glinch. "You don't just wave and wish."

suburban (suh-bur-bun)
adjective Relating to the suburbs of a city, away from the center; neither rural nor urban. / *Goblet of Fire*, page 18
Luckily, the village was far from the tacky suburban developments around the city.

subversive (sub-vur-sive)
adjective Likely to destroy or overthrow a government or other authority. / *Order of the Phoenix*, page 308
Brilly's endless pranks had convinced his classmates that he was involved in a subversive plot to overthrow the school's administrator.

succession (suk-sesh-un)
noun Something happening in order, one after another. / *Order of the Phoenix*, page 4
The Royal Archer shot eight arrows in quick succession, and each one hit the target.

successive (suk-ses-ive)
adjective Consecutive, in uninterrupted order; characterized by succession. / *Goblet of Fire*, page 429
Blackpool's string of four successive victories at Crazy Fates was a new record.

successor (suk-ses-ur)
noun A person who follows another in a specific office or position. / *Chamber of Secrets*, page 264
Overheard in the halls: "His successor will have a challenging task." Were they talking about the principal or Brilly?

succinct (suh-singkt)
adjective Concise, brief, and terse. / *Half-Blood Prince*, page 507
"Class, please compose a succinct, one-page report on the eating habits of mountain gremlins as compared to garden gnomes."

succulent (suk-yuh-lunt)
adjective Tasty and juicy. / *Half-Blood Prince*, page 145
The succulent Tofu Surprise was, nevertheless, not everyone's favorite at the king's dinner party.

succumb (suh-kum)
verb To yield or give in to, especially to disease, wounds, or old age; to die. / *Half-Blood Prince*, page 363
The village mascot—a giant horned toad—succumbed suddenly while hospitalized.

suffice (suh-fise)
verb To be enough. / *Order of the Phoenix*, page 618
"That will suffice, Dribbles. It isn't necessary to sing the Wizarding Anthem every day at noon. Please sit down."

suffuse (suh-fyooz)
verb To be covered with a warmth, liquid, or light. / *Goblet of Fire*, page 96
The Tomb of the Unknown Wizard was always suffused with an eternal glowing light.

sugar tongs (shoog-ur tongs)
noun Small two-pronged device used for serving sugar cubes; used in the plural. / *Chamber of Secrets*, page 31

The queen was so mad at the prince's rudeness at dinner that she pinched his ear with the sugar tongs.

sullen (**sul**-un)
adjective Ill-humored and morose; when speaking of weather, gloomy and dismal. / *Prisoner of Azkaban*, page 171
The sullen gray weather had turned everyone's mood sullen and gray, too.

sullenness (**sul**-un-ness)
noun An irritated, bad-tempered, gloomy, unsociable tone. / *Goblet of Fire*, page 10
"Now, just get that sullenness out of your voice, young man, if you expect to go out with your friends tonight."

sultry (**sul**-tree)
adjective Very hot; usually said of weather. / *Order of the Phoenix*, page 10
The day of the Castle Regatta was so sultry, half the crowd ended up jumping in the castle moat to cool off.

sumptuous (**sump**-choo-us)
adjective Luxurious, lavish, and splendid. / *Chamber of Secrets*, page 65
The king's dinner party had been sumptuous: golden plates, goblets of pure silver, and unbelievably tasty food.

sundry (**sun**-dree)
adjective Various and miscellaneous. / *Deathly Hallows*, page 179
The old witch displayed sundry magical items for sale at her garage sale.

sunken (**sung**-kun)
adjective Having sunk or fallen inwards, especially because of illness, stress, or age. / *Prisoner of Azkaban*, page 365
The wizard's sunken cheeks and bloodshot eyes reflected the stress he'd been under lately.

supercilious (soo-pur-**sil**-ee-us)
adjective Disdainful, contemptuous, self-importantly disapproving. / *Order of the Phoenix*, page 142
Bella always felt the supercilious waiters at the village café were making fun of her—she never was sure how to pronounce "blancmange."

superiority (suh-peer-ee-**or**-ih-tee)
noun The condition of being superior. / *Prisoner of Azkaban*, page 236
The horses felt their superiority should be obvious to the mules and donkeys, and certainly to the cows.

supine (soo-**pine**)
adjective Lying face-up on your back. / *Order of the Phoenix*, page 21
Auntie Baba, supine on the lawn, tried to entice a flock of fireflies to land on her nose.

supple (**sup**-ul)
adjective Moving or bending easily. / *Sorcerer's Stone*, page 84
Blackpool's wand was almost as supple as a stalk of cooked asparagus—but much more powerful.

supplication (sup-lih-**kay**-shun)
noun A humble request for help made to someone in authority. / *Deathly Hallows*, page 476
The village mascot, fading fast, stared at the doctor with a look of supplication.

suppress (suh-**pres**)
verb To hold back, repress, or keep in. / *Chamber of Secrets*, page 267
Ravi could hardly suppress his pride—he'd actually repaired Annie's malfunctioning broom.

surfeit (**sur**-fit)
noun An excess or overabundance; almost too much. / *Deathly Hallows*, page 561
The Royal Table was covered with a surfeit of the king's favorite desserts—treacle tarts, tapioca pudding, and mince pie.

surly (**sur**-lee)
adjective Rude, bad-tempered, unfriendly, and hostile. / *Prisoner of Azkaban*, page 269 / **Note: Surlier**, a related adjective found in *Goblet of Fire* (page 114), means "in comparison even more rude, bad-tempered, unfriendly, and hostile."
The guards and sentries at the castle had a reputation for being needlessly surly.

surmise (sur-mize)

verb To think or guess, usually based on incomplete information. / *Goblet of Fire*, page 452

"I can surmise that you're up to something, Brilly, just by the devious look on your face."

surname (sir-name)

noun A last name or family name. / *Sorcerer's Stone*, page 78

It wasn't easy having Dribbles for a surname, but it was better than his first name, which he tried never to use.

surreptitiously (sur-rup-tish-us-lee)

adverb In a secretive way, without others seeing. / *Goblet of Fire*, page 309

The dog surreptitiously surveyed the kitchen pantry. Somebody better conjure some dog food soon because the cupboard was bare.

surrogate (sur-uh-gate or sur-uh-git)

adjective Acting as a substitute, taking the place of someone else. / *Order of the Phoenix*, page 836

Wildwood had become a surrogate big brother to Brilly.

survey (sur-vay)

verb To take a general, comprehensive look at a situation. / *Chamber of Secrets*, page 203

The cafeteria manager surveyed the lunchroom right after lunch and it was not a pretty sight.

susceptible (suh-sep-tuh-bul)

adjective Likely to be easily influenced or affected. / *Deathly Hallows*, page 4

O'Harris, the Scottish elf, was particularly susceptible to poison snoak. It didn't make him itch—it made him sneeze.

suspend (suh-spend)

verb To hang or float motionless in a liquid or gas. / *Chamber of Secrets*, page 79

Odd unidentifiable body parts were suspended in giant glass containers in the doctor's waiting room.

suspension bridge (suh-spen-shun brij)

noun A bridge hung from cables strung from bridge towers. / *Sorcerer's Stone*, page 43

The huge locomotive roared across the suspension bridge, setting the cables to humming.

Suspension bridge

sustain (suh-stain)

verb To experience or undergo injuries, loss, etc. / *Order of the Phoenix*, page 436

Brady sustained only slight injuries when his broomstick stalled since he was just a few feet off the ground.

sustenance (sus-tuh-nunse)

noun Something, like food and drink, that sustains or supports life. / *Deathly Hallows*, page 285

Finding sufficient sustenance was an ongoing challenge for the monster chicken.

swagger (swag-ur)

noun A strutting, defiant, insolent manner or walk. / *Prisoner of Azkaban*, page 316

With his usual confident swagger, Blackpool strode into the Trolls' Hole to announce his recent triumphs at the worm races.

swarthy (swor-thee)

adjective Dark-complexioned. / *Sorcerer's Stone*, page 72

The swarthy ogre clumped across the pasture, looking a lot like a dark cloud.

swathe (swoth)

verb To wrap or enfold. / *Chamber of Secrets*, page 262

Swathed in his wrappings, the escaped mummy sat on the park bench observing passersby.

sweet (rhymes with **feet**)
noun In British usage, a small piece of candy, like a lemon drop. / *Sorcerer's Stone*, page 10
Dr. Greenteeth, the village dentist, liked to remind his patients that sticky sweets were the worst kind for wizard teeth.

sweltering (**swel**-tur-ing)
adjective Very hot and humid. / *Sorcerer's Stone*, page 262
Everyone was sweating in the sweltering castle because the king had insisted on turning off the air conditioner to save energy.

swig (rhymes with **pig**)
noun A mouthful or swallow of a liquid. / *Chamber of Secrets*, page 187
One swig was enough for Dylan: "Blehh. I'm never taking that medicine again!"

swig (rhymes with **pig**)
verb To drink in large and hurried gulps. / *Order of the Phoenix*, page 49
Blackpool swigged a large glass of brewed squakle antlers, his favorite.

swill (rhymes with **pill**)
verb To swirl or cause a liquid to flow around. / *Half-Blood Prince*, page 261
As the water swilled around the bottom of the canoe, Willow shouted to her new boyfriend, "Stop paddling and start bailing!"

swivel (**swiv**-ul)
verb To turn around or pivot quickly. / *Chamber of Secrets*, page 88
The queen loved riding down the street and seeing heads swivel as she passed by.

swooning (**swoon**-ing)
adjective So ecstatic and filled with rapture as to be feeling faint. / *Half-Blood Prince*, page 117
A swooning Bella almost fainted when her favorite author walked into the village café.

swoop (rhymes with **poop**)
noun A sudden swift instance of an emotion, as if it had suddenly descended on someone. / *Goblet of Fire*, page 722
With a swoop of delight, Brilly poured the red food coloring into the hot tub.

swoop (rhymes with **poop**)
verb To sweep through the air; birds and bats are particularly good at swooping. / *Sorcerer's Stone*, page 167
Annie swooped around Brilly and Dribbles as they walked home from school, relishing how responsive her new broomstick was.

sycophantically (sik-uh-**funt**-uh-kuh-lee)
adverb In a fawning, flattering, self-serving way. / *Goblet of Fire*, page 294
The janitor and the cafeteria manager laughed sycophantically at the principal's bad jokes.

syllabary (**sil**-uh-bare-ee)
noun A set of written symbols, each one being a syllable, used to translate another language. / *Deathly Hallows*, page 94 / Note: In Potter's world, the syllabary is used to translate runes.
The wizard used the old syllabary to translate the writing on the mysterious stone plaque.

syllabus (**sil**-uh-bis)
noun A plan of study, usually written, setting out what students are expected to learn in a particular subject. / *Order of the Phoenix*, page 363
The teachers realized the syllabus, especially for the magical arts, needed an extensive update.

T

tabby cat (tab-ee kat)
noun A dark-striped cat. / *Sorcerer's Stone*, page 2 / Note: Sometimes a tabby cat is simply called a tabby.
The mysterious tabby cat jumped up on the table, carefully washed both pointy ears, and then actually smiled.

taciturn (tas-ih-turn)
adjective Silent, stern, and dour. / *Order of the Phoenix*, page 516
The taciturn school secretary, who had never been known to smile, grimaced at Elrod's latest joke.

tack (rhymes with **black**)
noun A way of doing something. Often used in the phrase "take a different tack." / *Chamber of Secrets*, page 250
"Perhaps it's time I tried a different tack with Brilly," thought his dad.

tact (rhymes with **fact**)
noun The ability to be careful about what you say or do so as not to hurt someone's feelings or embarrass or upset them. / *Deathly Hallows*, page 97
Willow's kindness and tact were two of the most appealing things about her.

tactless (takt-lis)
adjective Lacking tact; likely to upset or embarrass someone, even if you don't really mean to. / *Half-Blood Prince*, page 347
"That was a tactless thing to say, Brilly. I'm sure Madam Glinch was already aware her dentures were chattering across the floor."

tad (rhymes with **bad**)
adjective A little bit. / *Goblet of Fire*, page 152
It's a tad unwise to attempt enchanting ogres until you're really good at spells.

tail (rhymes with **mail**)
verb To follow someone closely and observe what they do. / *Prisoner of Azkaban*, page 261
The policeman tailed the suspected bank robber to the pub.

tailcoat (tale-koht)
noun A man's dress coat, usually black, with two long tapering tails at the back, worn with a dress shirt and trousers. / *Sorcerer's Stone*, page 32 / Note: Also sometimes called just **tails**, as in *Goblet of Fire* (page 387).
Rupert's dad wore his tailcoat to the fancy dress ball, but he forgot to change out of his sneakers.

taint (rhymes with **paint**)
noun A trace of something, usually offensive or dishonorable, like corruption, disgrace, evil, shame, etc. / *Deathly Hallows*, page 171
The taint of failure haunted poor Milton.

taken aback
phrase To be surprised and unsure how to react. / *Half-Blood Prince*, page 73
Tamika was totally taken aback when Winston asked her out.

talisman (tal-is-mun)
noun An object (stone, ring, etc.) believed to have magical powers; worn as a charm or amulet. / *Chamber of Secrets*, page 185
Willow touched the talisman (a small carved griffin) on her necklace whenever she got worried or frightened.

tally (tal-ee)
verb To match up or agree. / *Prisoner of Azkaban*, page 45
Brilly's recent behavior certainly didn't tally with his previous behavior—something had changed.

talon (tal-un)
noun A claw. / *Prisoner of Azkaban*, page 114
The owl's talons gripped the branch tightly—when would this windy storm end?

tamper (tam-pur)

verb To make changes to something without permission; to interfere or change something in a harmful way. / *Half-Blood Prince*, page 439

Someone tampered with the gravestones, and now the cemetery caretaker can't figure out who's buried where.

tankard (tang-kurd)

noun A large drinking container with a handle and hinged cover; usually made of pewter or silver. / *Prisoner of Azkaban*, page 120

Regular customers of the Witching Hour pub keep their personal tankards on the back wall.

tantamount (tan-tuh-mownt)

adjective Equivalent or equal to in effect or value. / *Deathly Hallows*, page 159

"Brilly, not paying back money you owe is tantamount to theft," advised Willow.

tapestry (tap-us-tree)

noun Very heavy cloth with designs, pattern, or pictures woven in. / *Sorcerer's Stone*, page 128

The tapestry hanging in the throne room depicted the king's ancestors winning the famous Battle of the Golden Isle.

taradiddle (tare-uh-did-ul)

noun A small lie, or pretentious nonsense. / *Order of the Phoenix*, page 142

"I've had enough of your taradiddle, young man. Tell me what really happened."

tarantula (tuh-ran-choo-luh)

noun A type of large, hairy spider with a painful but not deadly bite. / *Goblet of Fire*, page 214

The tarantula couldn't understand why everyone ran when she entered a room.

tarnish (tar-nish)

verb To dull or diminish. / *Deathly Hallows*, page 152

Fiona's hopes for a singing career were tarnished a little when she didn't win the school talent contest.

Tarantula

tarred with the same brush

phrase To have the same faults and bad habits as someone else. / *Order of the Phoenix*, page 297

Brilly was tarred with the same brush as his grandfather and great-grandfather—they were troublemakers, too.

tarry (tare-ee)

verb To linger, wait, or remain in place. / *Goblet of Fire*, page 497

Parker didn't want to tarry anywhere near the huge web of the sucking spider.

tartan (tar-tn)

adjective A type of plaid used especially for Scottish kilts and cloth. / *Sorcerer's Stone*, page 240

O'Harris, the Scottish elf, always wore tartan socks.

tartly (tart-lee)

adverb In a sharp, cutting way. / *Prisoner of Azkaban*, page 229

"Put that wand down, young man. You're done for the day," said Madam Glinch tartly.

tassel (tas-ul)

noun Short threads or cords tied together at one end; used as a decoration on clothes, curtains, printed programs, etc. / *Deathly Hallows*, page 139

At graduation, the students wore magenta robes and witch's hats with black tassels at the top.

tattoo (Nope, not what you think.)
See **beat a tattoo** elsewhere in this dictionary.

tatty (tat-ee)
adjective Tight, tense, strained. / *Prisoner of Azkaban*, page 130
Wildwood's tatty cloak had seen better days.

adjective Shabby, run-down, worn-out. / *Prisoner of Azkaban*, page 130
Wildwood's tatty cloak had seen better days.

taut (rhymes with **fought**; sounds exactly like **taught**)
adjective Tight, tense, strained. / *Half-Blood Prince*, page 444
A taut silence followed Blackpool's challenge. Would anyone take him on?

tauten (tawt-en)
verb To become taut or tight. / *Order of the Phoenix*, page 230
The skin around her eyes tautened as she shouted, "You did what!?"

tawdry (taw-dree)
adjective Gaudy, showy, and cheap. / *Deathly Hallows*, page 342
"Oh, son, the tawdry trappings of the big city.... Why do you ever want to go there?" asked Wildwood's elderly mother.

tea cozy (tee koh-zee)
noun A padded cover that's put over a teapot to keep the tea warm. / *Sorcerer's Stone*, page 141
The tea cozy looked more like a teapot parka.

tease (rhymes with **peas**)
verb To backcomb the hair; to comb hair in the opposite direction of how it grows so it looks thicker and more dramatic. / *Deathly Hallows*, page 254
The fashion consultant's hair was so teased it looked like a beehive, and she wore a pink plaid skirt with ugly green sandals. Who could pay attention to this person?

technicality (tek-nih-kal-ih-tee)
noun A small, insignificant detail. / *Order of the Phoenix*, page 297
Blackpool evaded a traffic ticket on a technicality; he'd been flying 20 feet high when he ran the stop sign, and the law covered only up to 20 feet.

technicolor (tek-nih-kul-ur)
adjective Lurid and over bright. / *Order of the Phoenix*, page 265
The technicolor fireworks hurt Elrod's eyes.

tedious (tee-dee-us)
adjective Long, tiresome, and boring. / *Order of the Phoenix*, page 241
The tedious report comparing lake spirits to river spirits and river spirits to creek spirits seemed endless.

teem (rhymes with **seem**; sounds exactly like **team**)
verb To be full of creatures, people, or things. / *Order of the Phoenix*, page 442
The village sidewalks teemed with people watching the Parade of the Invertebrates.

teeter (tee-tur)
verb To tip up and down (or back and forth) unsteadily. / *Chamber of Secrets*, page 285
The laughing dwarf teetered on top of the fence.

temperamental (tem-pur-uh-**men**-tul)
adjective Sensitive, erratic, unpredictable. / *Goblet of Fire*, page 308
The lead singer for the Tomb Tones was very temperamental, and it was always difficult to predict what would set him off.

temple (tem-pul)
noun The flattened areas on either side of a person's forehead. / *Order of the Phoenix*, page 29
Poor Wildwood—he had a bad headache, and his temples were throbbing.

temptress (temp-tris)
noun A woman who tempts or beckons seductively. / *Half-Blood Prince*, page 56
The wailing temptress on the ghost ship lured the sailors to their deaths.

tendril (ten-dril)
noun On a climbing plant, the long, slender, coiling parts holding the plant to a support. / *Sorcerer's Stone*, page 277
The long tendrils of the Puff Bluster vine held it securely to the garden wall.

tentacle (ten-tuh-cul)

noun The long slender "arms" of invertebrates, like on squid and octopuses. / *Sorcerer's Stone*, page 263
The argument between the squid and the octopus was still going on: "Ten tentacles are better than eight!" "No, eight are better than ten!"

tentative (ten-tuh-tive)

adjective Uncertain, unsure, hesitant. / *Chamber of Secrets*, page 96
A tentative hand was raised in the back of the room: "Uh, I'm not sure I'm in the right class."

tenterhooks, as used in **on tenterhooks**

phrase To be in a state of uneasy suspense or anxiety. / *Chamber of Secrets*, page 130
The wizard was on tenterhooks, wondering if his protective shield charm would be powerful enough.

term (rhymes with **germ**)

noun The time when school is in session, like a semester or a quarter. / *Sorcerer's Stone*, page 96
The school term had just started, and already Elrod had lost his potions book, dropped his new backpack in the toilet, and broken two quills.

terse (rhymes with **purse**)

adjective Brief and to the point. / *Goblet of Fire*, page 42
His terse reply: "No."

testily (tes-tuh-lee)

adverb In an impatient, irritated way. / *Prisoner of Azkaban*, page 42
Blackpool testily replied, "Mother, I'm not going to get my hair cut. It's my hair and I like it like this."

testimony (tes-tuh-moh-nee)

noun A statement made by a witness in a court of law. / *Goblet of Fire*, page 592
The witness's testimony seemed to verify that the broom collision had been an accident.

testy (tes-tee)

adjective Irritable, impatient, touchy, short-tempered. / *Order of the Phoenix*, page 616
Julio's testy mood was the direct result of too little sleep, too much Jump Juice, and too many exams.

tetchy (tech-ee)

adjective Touchy, irritated, annoyed, easily upset. / *Goblet of Fire*, page 510
Madam Glinch was tetchy. It had been a long day.

tether (teth-ur)

verb To tie to a post; usually said of animals. / *Prisoner of Azkaban*, page 114 / Note: *Chamber of Secrets* (page 75) also features the phrase "at the end of one's tether," similar to "at the end of one's rope," meaning "so worried or tired that one can no longer deal with a situation."
Wildwood tethered the lost miniature dragon in the paddock and wondered what he was going to do with it.

thatch (rhymes with **hatch**)

noun A thick pile of hair on someone's head, resembling a thatched roof. / *Half-Blood Prince*, page 261
The ogre's thatch of hair looked like birds had been nesting in it.

thatched (rhymes with **hatched**)

adjective Covered with a thick layer of dried straw or reeds; usually said of a cottage roof. / *Prisoner of Azkaban*, page 200
The thatched roof of the dwarf's cottage was badly in need of repair; it was starting to leak.

theoretical (thee-uh-**ret**-ih-kul)

adjective In theory; speculative and not practical. / *Order of the Phoenix*, page 243
Theoretical knowledge is useful, but knowing how a broomstick works is rarely as important as being able to do a reverted back flip out of danger.

theoretician (thee-ur-ih-**tish**-un)

noun A person skilled in the theoretical side of a subject. / *Deathly Hallows*, page 17
The slime theoretician examined the castle's slime-filled moat and declared it…a victim of slime!

thick (rhymes with **tick**)

adjective Stupid and dumb; also used in the phrase "thick enough to…." / *Goblet of Fire*, pages 507 and 633
"Elrod is so thick! In fact, he's thick enough to think he isn't thick."

thicket (thik-it)

noun Literally, a dense growth of trees; more generally, anything like a dense growth of trees. / *Chamber of Secrets*, page 172
A thicket of hands went up when Mrs. Snodgrape asked how many students wanted to go on the Museum of Magic field trip.

thickset (thik-set)

adjective Solid or stocky. / *Sorcerer's Stone*, page 108
The thickset troll easily tossed the tree trunk out of his way.

thin on the ground

phrase Not much of something. / *Prisoner of Azkaban*, page 227
School spirit was definitely thin on the ground after the 26-page "Code of Acceptable Behavior and Clothing" was distributed.

thoroughfare (thur-oh-fair)

noun A road, street, path, or passageway. / *Goblet of Fire*, page 85
The Weeping Highway was the fastest thoroughfare to the lake.

threadbare (thred-bair)

adjective Worn and shabby, especially a rug or garment so worn that the nap is gone and the underlying threads show. / *Order of the Phoenix*, page 300
Wildwood's threadbare flying carpet could still get off the ground.

threshold (thresh-old)

noun Literally, the sill of a doorway; more generally, the entire entrance or doorway. / *Prisoner of Azkaban*, page 22
Ruffles, the Royal Ripsnorter, stood at the threshold of the castle's Great Hall and barked loudly at the king's visitors.

thrice (rhymes with **mice**)

adverb Three times. / *Deathly Hallows*, page 408
The magical shroud spun thrice, and then settled slowly over the tomb of the three unknown travelers.

throng (rhymes with **strong**)

noun A crowd. / *Chamber of Secrets*, page 153
The throng ran onto the soccer field to celebrate the stunning upset victory of the Horrible Hordes.

throng (rhymes with **strong**)

verb To gather together, move, or press along in a crowd. / *Sorcerer's Stone*, page 111
The students thronged the school candy counter, eager to buy Now-and-Thens, chocolate frisblots, and sprinkle-covered skorpo-bits.

throw caution to the winds

phrase To stop worrying and just go ahead and take a risk. / *Sorcerer's Stone*, page 267
"I decided to throw caution to the winds and expand the Wandatorium Shop," said the wandmaker.

thuggish (thug-gish)

adjective Like a thug—mean and violent. / *Chamber of Secrets*, page 97
"Dear, I really don't approve of your thuggish friends," said Blackpool's elderly mother.

thunderous (thun-dur-us)

adjective Thunder-like. / *Sorcerer's Stone*, page 161
In a thunderous voice, the giant asked his son just exactly what he was doing sitting on the compost pile.

thunderstruck (thun-dur-struk)

adjective Extremely shocked and surprised. / *Prisoner of Azkaban*, page 257
Mrs. Fracket was thunderstruck when she won first prize at the village fair for her nettle jam.

thwart (rhymes with **wart**)

verb To prevent someone from doing something they want to do. / *Goblet of Fire*, page 654
Brilly's plan was thwarted when the new rule against duct tape at school was issued.

tiara (tee-are-uh *or* tee-air-uh)

noun A small crown-like semi-circle that a woman wears during formal or important occasions. / *Half-Blood Prince*, page 527
The princess carefully placed her tiara on her head and headed to the Great Hall for the Castle Regatta dinner.

tic (rhymes with **quick**)

noun A sudden uncontrollable muscle

movement in the face. / *Chamber of Secrets*, page 128
A tic started throbbing, right below the pirate's eye, as he realized he had inadvertently sailed into Bone Crushers Cove.

ticket, as in **that's the ticket**
phrase An old-fashioned phrase meaning "that's exactly what's needed." / *Prisoner of Azkaban*, page 27
"That's the ticket, young man. A little of that spirit and you'll soon be feeling as right as brains," said the kindly but annoying village doctor.

ticket barrier (tik-et bare-ee-ur)
noun Where tickets are collected, either by a person or a machine. / *Sorcerer's Stone*, page 67
The ticket barrier wouldn't let Elrod through when he used his school ID instead of a ticket.

tidal wave (tide-ul wave)
noun Literally, an enormous ocean wave caused by an earthquake; more generally, an overwhelming feeling. / *Chamber of Secrets*, page 128
A tidal wave of anger washed over Wildwood when he saw his troll fence being bulldozed into rubble.

tier (rhymes with **deer**; sounds exactly like **tear**)
noun One of a series of levels or layers rising one above the other. / *Order of the Phoenix*, page 773
The arrangement of seating tiers in the auditorium meant that the older students were always closer to the principal's wrath.

till (rhymes with **chill**)
noun In British usage, a cash register; older wooden tills were more like cash drawers. / *Order of the Phoenix*, page 337
The wandmaker decided to replace his old wooden till with something more modern once the expanded Wandatorium Shop opened.

tinge (rhymes with **hinge**)
noun A small amount, even just a hint, of color. / *Sorcerer's Stone*, page 109
That slight tinge of pink in the east meant another new day, and Willow seriously wished she hadn't stayed up all night to write her botany essay.

tinker (ting-kur)
verb To work on a project—inventing, repairing, improving—but without useful results. / *Chamber of Secrets*, page 39
Mr. Glinch loved to tinker. His current project was to try to make a flying lawnmower.

tinned (rhymes with **pinned**)
adjective In British usage, canned. / *Sorcerer's Stone*, page 42
"Open the tinned peas, will you? The opener is in the drawer," said Winston's mum.

tinny (tin-ee)
adjective High, metallic, and thin; usually said of sounds. / *Prisoner of Azkaban*, page 76
The village's dragon-warning siren needed to be replaced; it was sounding more tinny and less siren-like all the time.

tinsel (tin-sul)
noun Thin strings of shiny paper (like very thin strips of aluminum foil) used as decorations, generally on Christmas trees. / *Prisoner of Azkaban*, page 224
Ravi couldn't understand the allure of tinsel—it looked like rain to him. Who wants a Christmas tree covered in rain?

tipsily (tip-suh-lee)
adverb In an unsteady, slightly drunken way. / *Prisoner of Azkaban*, page 405
The very strong medicine had Dylan acting tipsily, but at least he wasn't coughing anymore.

tipsy (tip-see)
adjective Slightly drunk. / *Goblet of Fire*, page 411
The two tipsy witches had only one drink, but those Magic Mojitos packed a punch.

titter (tit-ur)
noun A tittering giggle—self-conscious and nervous. / *Goblet of Fire*, page 593
Rilda's titter could clearly be heard over the general hum of sound in the school auditorium.

titter (tit-ur)

verb To laugh or giggle in a nervous, self-conscious, and affected way. / *Half-Blood Prince*, page 370
"Oh, Mr. Blackpool, you are so funny," tittered Miss Pandora.

to the hilt

See **hilt** elsewhere in this dictionary.

toadishly (tohd-ish-lee)

adverb Like a toad. / *Order of the Phoenix*, page 744
"I beat Blackpool in chess," bragged the boy, his chest swelling up toadishly.

toffee (taw-fee)

noun A hard sticky candy, like taffy. / *Chamber of Secrets*, page 71
The Emporium candy counter featured Pirate Toffee, "guaranteed to shiver your timbers" and probably pull out a filling, too.

toga (toh-guh)

noun A long, loose garment worn by the ancient Romans. / *Goblet of Fire*, page 97
It was Toga Day at school and almost everyone was draped in old sheets. They looked less like ancient Romans and more like Roman ghosts.

token (toh-kin)

noun A round metal piece, like a coin, used instead of money in machines. / *Deathly Hallows*, page 237 / Note: In Potter's world, gold tokens were used to get into public toilet cubicles that are really the gateway to the Ministry of Magic. Many of the games at the Dungeons of Doom Amusement Park took tokens instead of coins; you could change money for tokens near the Urpsy Daisy Roller Coaster.

tonic (ton-ik)

noun A drink that, taken as medicine, makes one feel stronger and more energetic. / *Prisoner of Azkaban*, page 59
Spa-zam, a new energy tonic, was selling out at the village market.

took a different tack

See **tack** elsewhere in this dictionary.

Man wearing a toga and a top hat

top hat (top hat)

noun A man's tall hat, usually black or gray, worn on formal occasions; the kind of hat Abraham Lincoln wore. / *Sorcerer's Stone*, page 117
Poor Rupert—he had to wear a top hat, frock coat, *and* spats in the school play. "I feel like an old man!"

topple (top-ul)

verb To fall over or into, especially from somewhere high. / *Sorcerer's Stone*, page 217
The giant toppled off the cliff's edge, bounced several times on the way down, landed, then dusted himself off and walked away.

torpid (tore-pid)

adjective Sluggish, slow, and dull. / *Order of the Phoenix*, page 725
It was so hot, a dragon's egg would fry on the sidewalk, and the villagers were all in a torpid haze of summer boredom.

torpor (tore-pur)

noun Sluggish inactivity and apathy. / *Chamber of Secrets*, page 152

Ever since the break-up with Bella, Bubba had sunk into a state of torpor. He felt like hibernating.

torso (**tore**-soh)
noun The central part of the body (minus arms, legs, and head). / *Order of the Phoenix*, page 697
False alarm: Tamika thought she saw a human torso floating in the lake, but it turned out to be an old pillow.

tosh (rhymes with **posh**)
noun In British slang, nonsense. / *Sorcerer's Stone*, page 56
"That's just ridiculous tosh," said Winston's mum.

totter (**tot**-ur)
verb To walk or move unsteadily. / *Prisoner of Azkaban*, page 36
The frail wizard, carrying his library books, tottered down the street.

touched in the head
phrase A little bit crazy. / *Order of the Phoenix*, page 159
The old witch was a little touched in the head. She was taking a bath in her cauldron in the front yard.

tousle-haired (**tou**-sul-haird)
adjective Disheveled and disordered; rumpled, especially one's hair. / *Chamber of Secrets*, page 107
Tousle-haired Wildwood looked like he'd just gotten up, but actually he'd never gone to bed.

toxic (**tox**-ik)
adjective Poisonous, or containing poison. / *Half-Blood Prince*, page 187
Blackpool dumped the toxic potion in a corner of the yard, where it immediately killed all the grass, two worms, fourteen slugs, and a spider.

traffic (**traf**-ik)
verb To trade in illegal goods; in British usage, also appears as **traffick**. / *Deathly Hallows*, page 558
Klingster hoped to start trafficking in unicorn hair as soon as he'd collected enough.

traffick
See **traffic** above.

trainers (**tray**-nurs)
noun In British usage, tennis shoes, gym shoes, or sneakers. / *Order of the Phoenix*, page 1
"Those trainers are filthy—toss them in the washing machine," said Winston's mum.

traipse (rhymes with **grapes**)
verb To walk or tramp about. / *Chamber of Secrets*, page 94
The entire class traipsed off to the cafeteria for the monthly program on "Nutrition for Young Wizards."

traitorous (**tray**-tur-us)
adjective Treacherous and disloyal, like a traitor. / *Goblet of Fire*, page 649
"Klingster, you traitorous scum, I thought we had a deal," raged Blackpool.

trance (rhymes with **dance**)
noun A dazed or bewildered condition, almost as if hypnotized. / *Sorcerer's Stone*, page 57
The cat curled up in front of the fireplace and fell into a deep trance, failing to notice the demon hound sneaking up on her.

transaction (tran-**zak**-shun)
noun Something transacted, that is, some exchange or negotiation made. / *Order of the Phoenix*, page 124
The transactions at Broomsticks Aplenty had gotten complicated: trade-ins, exchanges, returns, short-term loaners, trial rides, and plain old sales.

transfiguration (trans-fig-yuh-**ray**-shun)
noun A change in appearance, usually moving toward something more beautiful. / *Sorcerers Stone*, page 66 / Note: In Potter's world, Transfiguration is a class focused on magic that changes one object into another object.
Elrod's transfiguration began after he saw himself in a full-length mirror—he looked like a slob.

transfigured (trans-**fig**-yurd)
adjective Changed completely in appearance; transformed. / *Half-Blood Prince*, page 271

Blackpool was transfigured when he got his hair cut—he looked like a different person.

transfix (trans-**fiks**)

adjective Motionless from terror or fear. / *Sorcerer's Stone*, page 210
Dribbles was suddenly transfixed by a singing shark that leapt out of the swimming pool and twirled three times in the air before disappearing.

transformation (trans-for-**may**-shun)

noun A change in form, appearance, or character. / *Order of the Phoenix*, page 791
Elrod made quite a transformation for the dance—his suit was pressed, his shirt was clean, his hair was combed…and he didn't trip once.

translucent (trans-**loo**-sunt)

adjective Letting light through, but not quite transparent. / *Order of the Phoenix*, page 859
"Translucent glass is a nice feature, especially in bathrooms," advised the Royal Decorator.

transpire (tran-**spire**)

verb To happen or take place. / *Deathly Hallows*, page 108
Brilly, it transpired, had a crush on someone, but he wasn't talking about it much.

transplant (trans-**plant**)

verb To move something—generally a plant—from one place to another. / *Goblet of Fire*, page 237
Wildwood transplanted leeks from the garden into old cauldrons that he could keep on the back porch.

trauma (**traw**-muh)

noun An experience that causes injury or emotional pain. / *Goblet of Fire*, page 306
The trauma of getting lost in Skeleton Valley haunted the little boy for months.

travesty (**trav**-uh-stee)

noun A grotesque or distorted imitation or version of something. / *Goblet of Fire*, page 14
"In London," said Wildwood, "I saw a woman pushing a pram, and in it was a dog, not a baby. What a travesty!"

treachery (**trech**-uh-ree)

noun A betrayal of trust; disloyalty. / *Half-Blood Prince*, page 519
Brilly worried that Bella would consider it treachery if he asked her friend out.

treacle tart (**tree**-kul tart)

noun In British usage, a traditional dessert—a very sweet pie, with no top crust, made of pastry crumbs, golden syrup, and lemon juice. Treacle tart can refer to a full-sized pie or small individual pies. It's usually served warm, but it's tasty cold, too. / *Sorcerer's Stone*, page 125 / Note: Treacle is another word for molasses, but treacle tarts are usually made with a British honey-like syrup called golden syrup.
Given the choice between treacle tarts with clotted cream and a piece of rock cake, just about anyone would choose the treacle tarts.

tread (rhymes with **bread**)

verb To step or walk on. Past tense: trod; past participle: trodden. / *Sorcerer's Stone*, page 47
"Tread on a crack, break a wizard's back—is that how it goes?" asked Willow, who had accidentally trodden on a crack earlier that day and was feeling extremely guilty.

tremor (**trem**-ur)

noun An uncontrollable shaking or quivering of the body. / *Order of the Phoenix*, page 37
Tremors shook the tiny body of Tinkles, the fairy. A giant hawk had just tried to pluck her out of the sky.

tremulous (**trem**-yuh-lus)

adjective Trembling, shaking, quivering; often said of the voice. / *Goblet of Fire*, page 26
The little girl's tremulous voice explained: "And then I ran down the Far Hills with the…the…the big monster ogre right behind me!"

trepidation (trep-ih-**day**-shun)

noun Fear, alarm, anxiety, and agitation. / *Goblet of Fire*, page 156
With great trepidation, the boy pushed open the door of the abandoned cottage. A strange rotten smell drifted out.

trestle bench, trestle table (tres-ul bench, tres-ul tay-bul)
noun A kind of furniture, usually temporary in nature, with a rigid top across two end supports. Think about a door resting on two sawhorses for the general concept. / *Chamber of Secrets*, page 91 (bench); *Goblet of Fire*, page 390 (table)
The picnickers pulled the trestle benches up to the trestle table and started eating.

trice (rhymes with **mice**)
noun A really short time; a moment. / *Deathly Hallows*, page 108
"Be with you in a trice," the wandmaker called from the back of the shop.

trifle (try-ful)
noun A small, unimportant matter. / *Prisoner of Azkaban*, page 174 / Note: See the related noun **trifle** below.
"Ah, 'tis but a trifle," said the doctor. "Everyone breaks an elbow sooner or later."

trifle (try-ful)
noun In British usage, a cold dessert of sponge cake, jam, a custardy sauce, and whipped cream. / *Sorcerer's Stone*, page 125 / Note: See the related noun **trifle** above.
The guard savored the delicious trifle, a momentary distraction that was just long enough for his prisoner to escape.

trill (rhymes with **drill**)
verb To sing or speak with a high-pitched, quivering effect. / *Goblet of Fire*, page 398
Fiona trilled the final chorus of "The Lament of the Lovesick Lizard."

tripe (rhymes with **pipe**)
noun The lining of the stomach of a cow, sometimes cooked and eaten as food. / *Sorcerer's Stone*, page 104 / Note: See the related noun **tripe** below.
"Tripe? I thought I wouldn't like it when I saw it, and I really don't like it now that I know what it is."

tripe (rhymes with **pipe**)
noun Something worthless; rubbish. / *Half-Blood Prince*, page 459 / Note: See the related noun **tripe** above.
"That is a load of tripe, Elrod—no one can get their butt stuck in a toilet."

trivial (triv-ee-ul)
adjective Something insignificant or of little importance. / *Order of the Phoenix*, page 603
"Those are trivial problems," said Blackpool. "We can figure out a buyer for the unicorn hair once we have enough to sell."

trod
See **tread** elsewhere in this dictionary.

troll (rhymes with **roll**)
noun A really ugly mythical creature, human-like but huge (though in some stories, small and dwarfish), that lives under a bridge or in a cave; trolls have really bad tempers and they don't like humans. / *Sorcerer's Stone*, page 172 / Note: In Potters world, trolls are huge (12 feet tall), with bald heads, short thick legs, long arms, and a horrible smell.
Village parents warned their children that the best ways to avoid trolls were to not play under the bridge and never, ever go in the mountain caves.

Troll sitting on a trestle bench

trollish (trohl-ish)

adjective Like a troll. / *Chamber of Secrets*, page 110
Hanging out under a bridge is such a trollish thing to do.

trolley (trol-ee)

noun In British usage, a cart of some sort, for luggage at a train station or for food served on a train. / *Chamber of Secrets*, page 67 (luggage trolley); *Goblet of Fire*, page 167 (lunch trolley); *Order of the Phoenix*, page 188 (food trolley)
On the Frackets' train trip, the station luggage trolleys were helpful, but the family really liked the food trolleys on the train. There's nothing like having hot chudbutt sandwiches delivered right to your seat.

troop (rhymes with **loop**)

verb To walk or march; to go. / *Goblet of Fire*, page 582
Mrs. Birch trooped all over the village looking for Urping Elmer's Magic Dust, but every shop was out of it.

troupe (rhymes with **loop**)

noun A performing group that travels about. / *Chamber of Secrets*, page 131
The Whirling Derbies troupe of dancers performed Saturday night at the village auditorium, then headed on to the next village.

trousers (trow-surs)

noun Men's pants; used in the plural. / *Sorcerer's Stone*, page 265
Mr. Glinch wore his favorite old trousers when he gardened—they were a little short, well-patched, and severely grass-stained.

trove (rhymes with **rove**)

noun A collection of valuable objects. / *Deathly Hallows*, page 530
The trove of treasure in the temple was so well-hidden, no one would ever find it.

trowel (trow-ul)

noun A gardening tool with a small curved metal blade. / *Sorcerer's Stone*, page 234
The grave robber lost his shovel and had to do all his digging with a small trowel.

truculent (truk-yuh-lent)

adjective Hostile, belligerent, and ready to argue. / *Deathly Hallows*, page 485
Truculent Blackpool was always willing to argue over just about anything.

trudge (rhymes with **budge**)

verb To walk slowly; to plod along. / *Sorcerer's Stone*, page 170
The young witch trudged home after school, dreading telling her parents what she'd accidentally done to the crossing guard.

true colors

See **show your true colors** elsewhere in this dictionary

trundle (trun-dul)

verb To travel or move in a wheeled vehicle. / *Chamber of Secrets*, page 66
The milk cart slowly trundled down the street.

truss (rhymes with **fuss**)

verb To tie up someone so they can't move at all. / *Deathly Hallows*, page 703
The bank robber trussed up the bank manager and sat him on a stool in the bank vault.

tub (rhymes with **rub**)

noun A small container, usually round. / *Half-Blood Prince*, page 118
The empty yak butter tub meant someone had been making a lot of yak butter and nettle jam sandwiches.

tuber (too-bur)

noun A botanical word meaning a thickening on the root of a plant—think potato. / *Half-Blood Prince*, page 229
"Are we having mashed or roasted tubers for dinner?" asked the botany teacher, annoying his wife no end.

tuck in

phrase In British usage, to start eating. / *Goblet of Fire*, page 180
"Tuck in, son, the food's getting cold," urged Winston's dad.

tuffet (tuf-ut)

noun A clump or tuft of grass. / *Goblet of Fire*, page 70

"Hello, little girl," said the spider to the young lady eating a snack on a lovely green tuffet. "Wait, don't run away."

tuft (rhymes with **huffed**)

noun A clump of small things, like hairs, grass, feathers, etc. / *Sorcerer's Stone*, page 15 / Note: **Tufted**, a related adjective found in *Order of the Phoenix* (page 643), means "with a tuft or tufts." **Tufty**, another adjective found in *Chamber of Secrets* (page 92), means "abounding in tufts."
The potion was supposed to encourage hair growth but, unfortunately, a tuft of hair grew on the bald man's nose, not his head.

tumbledown (tum-bul-down)

adjective Ruined, run down, and falling down. / *Chamber of Secrets*, page 32
The old man's tumbledown shack was disgusting inside and out.

tumult (too-mult)

noun A confused and noisy commotion. / *Goblet of Fire*, page 112
The tumult at the end of the graduation ceremonies was incredible—hats thrown in the air, everyone hugging everyone else, parents clapping (and crying a little, too), everyone cheering….

tumultuous (too-mult-choo-us)

adjective Very loud, noisy, and boisterous. / *Chamber of Secrets*, page 255
Tumultuous cheers greeted the Horrible Hordes as they came on the field.

tunic (too-nik)

noun A loose, sleeveless garment that reaches anywhere from the hips down to the ankles. / *Half-Blood Prince*, page 268
The tunic was not a fashion that the very fashionable Bella was going to adopt; it seemed to her like a glorified sack, or like something little poor children in a Charles Dickens novel would wear.

turban (tur-bun)

noun A scarf-like cloth wound around the head. / *Sorcerer's Stone*, page 122
One nice thing about school, thought Ravi, was that no one had ever given him a hard time about wearing a turban.

turbulent (tur-byuh-lunt)

adjective Fast-moving and agitated. / *Prisoner of Azkaban*, page 177
"I would have been here sooner," explained Annie, "but we ran into some turbulent headwinds as we flew through the valley."

tureen (tur-een)

noun A serving dish, usually for soup or stews. / *Sorcerer's Stone*, page 203
The tureen refilled itself as quickly as the guests served themselves.

turncoat (turn-koht)

noun A traitor; someone who abandons one side or group and starts supporting the other side. / *Prisoner of Azkaban*, page 206
"You turncoat!" shouted Duke Fresser at his former spy, Marmaduke. "I thought you were on my side."

turquoise (tur-koyz)

adjective Greenish-blue or bluish-green. / *Chamber of Secrets*, page 24
Her overuse of turquoise eye shadow made her look like an unsuccessful boxer.

turret (tur-it)

noun A small tower in a castle, usually part of a larger tower. / *Sorcerer's Stone*, page 111
The prince set up a practice room for his band in one of the castle turrets. His father was grateful that he chose a room far from the throne room.

tussle (tus-ul)

noun A scuffle or struggle. / *Goblet of Fire*, page 203
After quite a tussle, Wildwood pinned the unruly stoat to the ground.

tut (rhymes with **but**)

verb To show disapproval, impatience, or annoyance by making a "tut" or "tsk" sound. / *Prisoner of Azkaban*, page 59
The school secretary tutted dismissively when Elrod tried to get her to smile at his jokes.

tutu (too-too)

noun A short skirt, with many folds of a stiff net material, worn by ballet dancers. / *Half-*

Blood Prince, page 330
The lead dancer of the Whirling Derbies donned a rainbow-colored tutu for her final dance.

tweed (rhymes with **weed**)
adjective A rough woolen cloth used to make jackets, coats, etc. / *Order of the Phoenix*, page 414
Wildwood saved his tweed robes for extremely cold situations.

twiddle (twid-ul)
verb To turn about or play with lightly; to fiddle, generally because one is bored or nervous. Usually thumbs are twiddled. / *Half-Blood Prince*, page 73 / Note: One might also twiddle necklaces or rings or even knobs, as in *Goblet of Fire* (page 99).
Klingster was late, and Blackpool was tired of just sitting and twiddling his thumbs.

twilit (twhy-lit)
adjective Lit by twilight, the time of day (usually early morning or early evening) when the light is soft outside. / *Half-Blood Prince*, page 211
The twilit street was dusky gray; all the color seemed to have gone out of it.

twinge (rhymes with **hinge**)
noun A sudden slight feeling (of regret, sadness, etc.). / *Half-Blood Prince*, page 103
Eventually Bella felt only a twinge of sadness when she thought about Bubba. That relationship was *so* over.

twist
See **go round the twist** elsewhere in this dictionary.

twitch (rhymes with **itch**)
noun A sudden quick movement of a muscle, especially one you can't control; somewhat larger than a tic. / *Deathly Hallows*, page 164
The twitch in the gravedigger's shoulder was a painful reminder of the time he was carrying a casket on his shoulder and a knock came from inside.

twitch (rhymes with **itch**)
verb To move suddenly with a jerk or spasm. / *Sorcerer's Stone*, page 218
His right eye twitched slightly as the monster chicken came waddling toward him.

twitter (twit-ur)
verb To make a lot of short, high-pitched sounds; usually said of a bird. / *Goblet of Fire*, page 36
"Life is good," twittered the robin. "Easy for you to say," cawed the crow. "You just found a boxful of worms."

tyke (rhymes with **bike**)
noun A young child. / *Sorcerer's Stone*, page 2
"Sweet little tyke," thought the mama rhino, looking lovingly at her baby daughter.

U

umpteenth (ump-teenth)
adjective A large but unspecified number. / *Order of the Phoenix*, page 584
"For the umpteenth time, you cannot have another chocolate chip frisblot," the mother reminded the little boy.

un-
This prefix adds the concept of *a lack, a negative, or an opposite* to many ordinary words. Most are easy to figure out (and their root word is defined elsewhere in this dictionary).

> **unabashed = not abashed**
> *adjective* / *Half-Blood Prince*, page 64
>
> **unbiased = not biased**
> *adjective* / *Order of the Phoenix*, page 442
>
> **unencumbered = not encumbered**
> *adjective* / *Deathly Hallows*, page 118
>
> **unhampered = not hampered**
> *adjective* / *Deathly Hallows*, page 322
>
> **unimpeded = not impeded**
> *adjective* / *Half-Blood Prince*, page 122
>
> **unintelligible = not intelligible**
> *adjective* / *Half-Blood Prince*, page 14
>
> **unobscured = not obscured**
> *adjective* / *Order of the Phoenix*, page 425
>
> **unperturbed = not perturbed**
> *adjective* / *Goblet of Fire*, page 125
>
> **untarnished = not tarnished**
> *adjective* / *Half-Blood Prince*, page 65
>
> **unwary = not wary**
> *adjective* / *Half-Blood Prince*, page 117

unabashed
See **unabashed** in the list above.

unaccountably (un-uh-**kown**-tuh-blee)
adverb In an inexplicable, unexplained way. / *Chamber of Secrets*, page 332
Unaccountably, the shadows of the two boys disappeared and they both began to sob.

unassailable (un-uh-**say**-luh-bul)
adjective Not assailable; not open to attack, denial, or dispute. / *Order of the Phoenix*, page 36
The pots of boiling oil, the archers with flaming arrows, and the moat all meant the castle was essentially unassailable.

unauthorized (un-**aw**-thuh-ryezd)
adjective Not authorized; not having official permission. / *Order of the Phoenix*, page 51
The unauthorized use of love potions had caused trouble before.

unbalanced (un-**bal**-unst)
adjective Not balanced; mentally disordered or deranged. / *Deathly Hallows*, page 564
She was sure that the man walking down the street in a pink tutu and singing "Frosty the No-Man" was seriously unbalanced.

unbecoming (un-bih-**kum**-ing)
adjective Not becoming; unsuitable and detracting from one's appearance, behavior, or character. / *Goblet of Fire*, page 98
"Dear, your behavior last night at the party was most unbecoming," reprimanded Blackpool's elderly mother.

unbiased
See **unbiased** in the list above.

unbidden (un-**bid**-en)
adjective Not asked, not summoned, not invited. / *Half-Blood Prince*, page 601
Unbidden, the golden orb floated in the window and began to hum and spin over the witch's chair.

unblemished (un-**blem**-isht)
adjective Not blemished or marked in any way. / *Goblet of Fire*, page 216
The unblemished skull gave no hints as to how the man had died.

uncanny (un-**kan**-ee)
adjective Extraordinary, even difficult to explain. / *Prisoner of Azkaban*, page 194
Brilly did an uncanny imitation of Mrs. Snodgrape's walk, but he'd learned the hard way not to show it off in school.

unceremoniously (un-ser-uh-**moh**-nee-us-lee)
adverb In a discourteous, hasty, rude way, without ceremony or formalities. / *Half-Blood Prince*, page 426
Bubba felt that Bella had unceremoniously dumped him.

uncharacteristic (un-kare-uk-tuh-**ris**-tic)
adjective Not characteristic; unusual / *Order of the Phoenix*, page 834
The laughing dwarf's behavior was very uncharacteristic—no laughing, and not even a smile.

uncivilized (un-**siv**-uh-lyezd)
adjective Not civilized; rude and socially unacceptable. / *Goblet of Fire*, page 181
"Slow down, young man, There's no need to eat in such an uncivilized manner."

unclench (un-**klench**)
verb To open or to stop being clenched; to relax. / *Order of the Phoenix*, page 3
The falconer unclenched his fist, releasing the leather strap holding the hawk, and the bird soared into the sky.

uncomprehending (un-com-prih-**hend**-ing)
adjective Not comprehending, not understanding. / *Half-Blood Prince*, page 606
The young girl's face was uncomprehending—how could a unicorn be walking along the side of the Weeping Highway?

unconscious (un-**kon**-shus)
adjective Not conscious; passed out. / *Prisoner of Azkaban*, page 408
The two jousting knights slammed into each other at full speed, and the novice jouster fell from his horse, unconscious.

uncouth (un-**kooth**)
adjective Awkward, clumsy, rude, socially unacceptable. / *Half-Blood Prince*, page 545
The uncouth man eating at the village café had burped loudly, picked his nose, and was now licking his plate.

unctuous (**uhngk**-choo-us)
adjective Insincere, oily, affected, and way too smooth. / *Goblet of Fire*, page 247
The unctuous sword salesman promised to sharpen the blade monthly, to rub the knight's tired shoulders weekly, and, especially, that every duel would be won once the knight bought the "Super Deluxe Rough Rider Sword."

undaunted (un-**dawn**-tid)
adjective Not daunted, not dismayed, and not discouraged. / *Prisoner of Azkaban*, page 168
"I remain undaunted by your disbelief in crystal-gazing as a tool to examine the future," sniffed Mrs. Sprocket, village fortune-teller.

Underground (un-dur-ground)
noun London's transportation system, with most trains running underground like a subway. / *Sorcerer's Stone*, page 15 / Note: In London, many people refer to the Underground as "the Tube."
"We took the Underground," said Winston, "and the trains were incredibly noisy, especially in the tunnels."

underhanded (un-dur-**han**-did)
adjective Dishonest, sneaky, secretive, devious, and sly. / *Deathly Hallows*, page 506
In his usual underhanded way, Blackpool fooled everyone in the village pub into thinking he'd never played Crazy Fates before.

undermine (un-dur-**mine**)
verb To weaken or destroy something by malicious actions. / *Goblet of Fire*, page 53
Wildwood didn't realize Blackpool was undermining his credibility in the Chamber of Wizards by claiming Wildwood couldn't enchant his way out of a paper bag.

undertone (un-dur-tone)
noun A quiet tone of voice. / *Chamber of Secrets*, page 35
"Uh, are you sure you want to make that move?" Rupert's dad asked in an undertone, as his chess-playing son almost made an illegal move.

undetected (un-dee-tek-tid)
adjective Not detected; not noticed by anyone. / *Half-Blood Prince*, page 628 / Note: **Undetectable**, a related adjective found in *Order of the Phoenix* (page 49), means "not detectable or noticeable by anyone."
The old tramp had been living undetected in the abandoned warehouse for months.

undeterred (un-dih-turd)
adjective Not deterred; not letting anything stop or get in the way of an action. / *Order of the Phoenix*, page 660
Though already muddy and badly bruised, the goalie was undeterred as she raced to grab the ball heading toward her.

undulate (un-juh-late)
verb To move in a smooth, wavelike motion. / *Deathly Hallows*, page 697
"My goodness," thought Mrs. Birch, "that bellydancer certainly can undulate."

undulating (un-juh-lay-ting)
adjective Having a wavy, rippling form or movement. / *Goblet of Fire*, page 12
The undulating bellydancer totally entranced Rupert.

unearthly (un-urth-lee)
adjective Seemingly not of this world; strange and unnatural; weird. / *Chamber of Secrets*, page 315
The unearthly sound of sobbing ogres echoed through the hills.

unease (un-eez)
noun Not easy in mind or body; restless or perturbed about something. / *Goblet of Fire*, page 625
Even knowing that the hideous giant leech was securely encased in gluco-ment didn't reduce Dribbles' unease.

unencumbered
See **unencumbered** in the list above.

unfazed (un-fayzd)
adjective Not fazed, not dismayed, not disconcerted, not shocked. / *Half-Blood Prince*, page 3
Julia, the Royal Cook, was unfazed when the roasted chicken fell on the floor; she just picked it up, put it on the platter, and sent in out to be served.

unfounded (un-fown-did)
adjective With no foundation; not based on fact. / *Goblet of Fire*, page 153
"Your theories of planet movement and celestial inclinations are totally unfounded," she said.

unfurl (un-furl)
verb To unfold or shake out from a furled state. / *Goblet of Fire*, page 355
Father Goose unfurled the morning paper and settled down to read the village news.

unhampered
See **unhampered** in the list above.

unhinge (un-hinj)
verb To upset, unbalance, or disorient. / *Prisoner of Azkaban*, page 209
The sight of pointed hats and bubbling cauldrons unhinged the terrified wizard.

unhinged (un-hinjd)
adjective Distraught or disordered, even emotionally unstable. / *Order of the Phoenix*, page 220
Clearly, the unhinged wizard might benefit from a short stay in the Asylum for the Deranged.

unicorn (yoo-nuh-korn)
noun A legendary one-horned, horse-like animal that has a large horn protruding from its forehead. Usually white, the unicorn is a symbol of purity and chastity. / *Sorcerer's Stone*, page 84 / Note: In Potter's world, unicorn horns and tail hairs are used in potions, and the tail hair is also used in some wands.
Most villagers had never seen a unicorn; they tended

to be very elusive, staying deep within the Haunted Forest.

Unicorn

unimpaired (un-im-paird)

adjective Not impaired; not damaged. / *Order of the Phoenix*, page 613
"My eyesight isn't impaired, just my hearing," said the old man, "and I saw you put that in your pocket without paying, Klingster."

unimpeded

See **unimpeded** in the list above.

unison

See **in unison** elsewhere in this dictionary.

unintelligible

See **unintelligible** in the list above.

unkempt (un-kempt)

adjective Not kempt; not combed, not cared for; messy and disheveled. / *Prisoner of Azkaban*, page 366
Blackpool's elderly mother disliked his unkempt hair and was always trying to sneak up on him with her magical hair clippers.

unmelodious (un-muh-loh-dee-us)

adjective Not melodious; not pleasant-sounding. / *Deathly Hallows*, page 294
"Madam, the dragon-warning siren is *meant* to be unmelodious—it's important to take heed and not just sing along!" asserted the mayor.

unnerved (un-nurvd)

adjective Nervous, upset, unconfident. / *Half-Blood Prince*, page 272 / Note: In *Order of the Phoenix* (page 592), the related adjective **unnerving** means "inspiring fear," or "making someone nervous and upset."
Julio was unnerved when Mrs. Snodgrape suggested he share the contents of the note Tamika had just passed him with the entire class.

unobscured

See **unobscured** in the list above.

unobtrusive (un-ub-troo-sive)

adjective Not obtrusive; inconspicuous and not obvious. / *Goblet of Fire*, page 70
The king requested that his security guards be available but unobtrusive when he welcomed the duke into the castle's Great Hall.

unperturbed

See **unperturbed** in the list above.

unplumbed (un-plumd)

adjective Not plumbed, that is, not yet fully measured or examined. / *Half-Blood Prince*, page 428
"You have unplumbed depths of compassion and kindness," predicted Mrs. Sprocket as she looked deep into Blackpool's eyes. As usual, she was very wrong.

unprecedented (un-pres-ih-den-tid)

adjective Without precedent; not having happened before. / *Order of the Phoenix*, page 306
Winston's win at the Whizzing Fireball Tournament was unprecedented; no one from the village had ever won before.

unravel (un-rav-ul)

verb To unwind or undo; to untangle. / *Sorcerer's Stone*, page 278
Blackpool unraveled the sweater he'd been knitting—he must have misread the directions since it now had three arms.

unrequited (un-rih-kwhy-tid)

adjective Not requited; not returned or reciprocated. / *Half-Blood Prince*, page 262

Willow's feelings for the new boy were obviously unrequited; perhaps it was time to move on.

unscathed (un-**skaythd**)

adjective Not scathed; not harmed or injured in any way. / *Order of the Phoenix*, page 849

Amazingly, Brilly survived the explosion unscathed.

unstable (un-**stay**-bul)

adjective Not emotionally stable; apt to behave so suddenly and randomly that no one can predict what will happen. / *Goblet of Fire*, page 611

The terrified wizard had become emotionally unstable; he needed real help, more than just a magical time-out.

unsullied (un-**sul**-eed)

adjective Not spoiled by anything. / *Deathly Hallows*, page 726

Wildwood's reputation was unsullied by scandal, rumors, or mistakes in behavior…unlike Blackpool.

untarnished

See **untarnished** in the list above.

unwary

See **unwary** in the list above.

unwonted (un-**wawn**-tid *or* un-**wohn**-tid)

adjective Unusual, unexpected, out of the ordinary. / *Half-Blood Prince*, page 640

Her unwonted kindness, when he was feeling so blue, would always be appreciated.

up to scratch

phrase Meeting requirements. / *Order of the Phoenix*, page 307

"Young man, this essay on the foods favored by centaurs and unicorns is too short and too vague—it's just not up to scratch," complained the teacher.

upshot (**up**-shot)

noun The final result of a situation. / *Order of the Phoenix*, page 633

The upshot of Bella and Bubba's long discussion was a decision to be just good friends.

upsurge (**up**-surj)

noun An increase; a surging up. / *Order of the Phoenix*, page 83

The Master of the Knights felt an upsurge of pride as his team was awarded the jousting trophy.

upswing (**up**-swing)

noun An increase in the level of something. / *Half-Blood Prince*, page 136

There'd been an upswing in the number of bats in the village, and no one seemed able to explain it.

usher (**ush**-ur)

verb To escort someone. / *Sorcerer's Stone*, page 234

The mother slug ushered her baby slugs toward daycare, but it took a long, long, long time—they'd never make it before lunch.

usurp (yoo-**surp**)

verb To seize and hold someone else's position, office, or authority when you don't have a right to it. / *Deathly Hallows*, page 682

The cafeteria manager felt the principal was usurping his role as nutritional provider and dietetic decision-maker for the school.

usurper (yoo-**surp**-ur)

noun A person who usurps, or seizes another's position, office, or authority. / *Deathly Hallows*, page 209

The king never worried about usurpers to the throne. Who'd want to live in the drafty castle anyway?

utmost (**ut**-most)

adjective Of the greatest or highest degree. / *Prisoner of Azkaban*, page 263

"I will apply my utmost efforts to ensure you do well on your final exams, class, but you need to do the same."

utter (**ut**-ur)

adjective Complete and total. / *Chamber of Secrets*, page 300

The draft blew out the candles, and there was utter darkness in the Royal Grotto.

utter (**ut**-ur)

verb To say or speak. / *Order of the Phoenix*, page 83

Bella was so happy with her math scholarship that she couldn't utter a word.

uvula (yoo-vyuh-luh)
noun The small piece of flesh that hangs down in the back of the throat. / *Deathly Hallows,* page 99
Dylan had the flu so badly that every part of his body seemed to hurt, including his fingernails, his uvula, and even his hair.

V

vacate (vay-kate)
verb **To leave or go away.** / *Half-Blood Prince*, page 441
The wizard vacated his position as president of the Chamber of Wizards to work on a new local magazine.

vagrant (vay-grunt)
noun **A homeless beggar or tramp who wanders about idly.** / *Goblet of Fire*, page 554
The tired vagrant, having walked all over town, sat down to rest on the park bench.

vain (rhymes with **main**; sounds exactly like **vane**)
adjective **Conceited and way too proud.** / *Half-Blood Prince*, page 74
Blackpool was awfully vain about his looks, especially his long black hair and his goatee.

valiant (val-yunt)
adjective **Courageous and brave.** / *Chamber of Secrets*, page 179
Wildwood's valiant efforts to pull the girl from the Big Bog won him the village's Hero of the Year award.

vampire (vam-pire)
noun **In folklore, a corpse that sucks human blood from sleeping people.** / *Sorcerer's Stone*, page 70
The vampire cackled at the foolish attempt to trick him. Ketchup? Ketchup!

vandal (van-dul)
noun **A person who willfully destroys property.** / *Order of the Phoenix*, page 125
Vandals broke every window in the abandoned warehouse.

vandalize (van-dil-ize)
verb **To maliciously destroy or deface property.** / *Order of the Phoenix*, page 3
Someone vandalized the basketball court last night—all the nets were cut off and the poles bent.

vanquish (van-kwish)
verb **To conquer or defeat.** / *Order of the Phoenix*, page 835
Winston vanquished his opponent in the Whizzing Fireball Tournament.

vapid (vap-id)
adjective **Dull and lifeless.** / *Order of the Phoenix*, page 156
The vapid conversation between the two was so boring they both fell asleep.

vapor (vay-pur)
noun **Fog, mist, steam, or smoke.** / *Sorcerer's Stone*, page 293
The vapor on the ocean's surface swirled into the form of a giant salmon that glared at the terrified fishermen, then slowly faded away in the darkness.

varieties (vuh-rye-ih-tees)
noun **Types or sorts of a thing. Singular: variety.** / *Goblet of Fire*, page 349
The potions counter at the Hurly Burly Emporium offered 14 varieties of goat spleen, 4 varieties of bat wings, and 16 varieties of fairy dust.

vast (rhymes with **last**)
adjective **Big in size or extent.** / *Deathly Hallows*, page 241
A vast area of the village would be affected by a new highway, and most of the villagers were against the idea.

vastness (vast-ness)
noun **Largeness in size or extent.** / *Half-Blood Prince*, page 402
The vastness of the overweight wizard made it difficult for him to get through the doorway.

vat (rhymes with **bat**)
noun **A large container to hold or store a liquid.** / *Half-Blood Prince*, page 454
The old witch kept a large vat of pesko-potion in her

basement; spread on her doorstep, it kept everyone away, especially small children and lost rabbits.

vault (rhymes with **halt**)

noun A strengthened storage room for valuables. / *Sorcerer's Stone*, page 64
You can keep little treasures under the bed, but for real security, hide your important ones in a vault.

vault (rhymes with **halt**)

verb To jump over or into something. / *Order of the Phoenix*, page 219
Brilly vaulted the bench and ran down to the lakeside—the giant leech was moving closer to Willow and she didn't even see it.

vaulted (vawl-tid)

adjective Arched; usually said of a ceiling. / *Chamber of Secrets*, page 315
The village's new library had vaulted ceilings.

veer (rhymes with **seer**)

verb To turn or change direction suddenly. / *Prisoner of Azkaban*, page 260
Annie veered to the right to avoid a witch who'd suddenly slowed her broomstick.

vehement (vee-uh-munt)

adjective Impassioned, emotional. / *Goblet of Fire*, page 695
Blackpool's vehement denial of wrongdoing fooled no one.

veiled (rhymes with **mailed**)

adjective Hidden, unknown, obscure. / *Prisoner of Azkaban*, page 103
"Ah yes, the veiled unknown, the strange secrets of life, the ambiguous mysteries beyond human understanding…." The village fortune-teller certainly could go on and on.

velvet (vel-vit)

noun A soft, thick, dense fabric. / *Chamber of Secrets*, page 85
Bella's new floor-length gown was made of an expensive velvet.

vendetta (ven-det-uh)

noun A long and bitter feud or grudge. / *Goblet of Fire*, page 548
It was time for the vendetta between Blackpool and Wildwood to end, thought Merlin.

venerable (ven-ur-uh-bul)

adjective Worthy of respect because of age, wisdom, or achievements. / *Deathly Hallows*, page 21
The venerable wizard Merlin was honored with a statue on the village green.

venerate (ven-ur-ate)

verb To respect and honor. / *Deathly Hallows*, page 314
Everyone in the village venerated Merlin.

venom (ven-um)

noun The poisonous fluid a snake (or some other poisonous animal) injects into something or someone when it bites. / *Goblet of Fire*, page 656 / Note: See also the related noun **venom** below.
Cobra venom is extremely powerful; most bitten animals die within minutes.

venom (ven-um)

noun Malice, spite, or mean hostility. / *Chamber of Secrets*, page 82 / Note: See also the related noun **venom** above.
Blackpool spoke with such venom; it was hard to understand how someone could be so bitter and mean.

venomous (ven-uh-mus)

adjective Full of or containing venom; poisonous. / *Chamber of Secrets*, page 320
The snake sank its venomous fangs into the black boot that had disturbed its territory, but luckily the venom didn't reach the man's leg.

vent (rhymes with **bent**)

verb To relieve strong feelings. / *Deathly Hallows*, page 757
Milton vented his rage over his failing grade in potions by stomping on every flower he passed between school and his home.

vent one's spleen

phrase To vent or express one's anger. / *Order of the Phoenix*, page 716
Butch Thuggins vented his spleen over his latest

broken nose by tossing the locker room garbage can out on the lawn.

ventriloquist (ven-**tril**-uh-kwist)

noun A person who "throws" his voice, speaking so that it seems his voice is coming from somewhere or someone else. / *Goblet of Fire*, page 518
The ventriloquist made it sound like the soccer ball was talking: "Don't kick me! Don't kick me!"

verbal (**vur**-bul)

adjective Out loud, using words; oral rather than written. / *Goblet of Fire*, page 118
The very verbal little girl was speaking clearly by the time she was a year old.

verdict (**vur**-dikt)

noun A decision or judgment in a court case. / *Prisoner of Azkaban*, page 292
The jury's decision was "guilty" in the dispute between Blackpool and Wildwood and the troll fence.

verge (rhymes with **merge**)

noun A point beyond which something is going to happen; an edge or brink. / *Half-Blood Prince*, page 446 / Note: See the related noun **verge** below.
Poor Bella was on the verge of tears as she argued with Bubba about their relationship.

verge (rhymes with **merge**)

noun In British use, the grassy area between the road and the sidewalk. / *Order of the Phoenix*, page 526 / Note: See the related noun **verge** above.
Mrs. Birch planted wildflowers in the verges near her house; the flowers certainly brightened up the roadway.

veritable (**ver**-ih-tuh-bul)

adjective Actual and absolute; used to intensify what you're saying. / *Goblet of Fire*, page 655
"Brilly, you are a veritable wizard at troublemaking."

vermin (**vur**-min)

noun A collective word to suggest a whole bunch of disgusting, objectionable, icky animals: rats, cockroaches, lice, flies, etc. / *Chamber of Secrets*, page 178
Blackpool thought that besides the Parade of the Invertebrates, the village should sponsor a Parade of Vermin.

vestige (**ves**-tij)

noun A mark or trace or some visible evidence of something. / *Goblet of Fire*, page 93
The last vestiges of the burned-down library were finally gone.

viaduct (**vie**-uh-dukt)

noun A series of spans or arches that, bridge-like, carry a road or a railroad over a valley. / *Order of the Phoenix*, page 526
The locomotive steamed over the viaduct, heading for the big city.

vial (**vie**-ul)

noun A small glass or crystal bottle usually containing a liquid; in British usage, often called a **phial**. / *Goblet of Fire*, page 642
Merlin emptied one vial after another into the bubbling cauldron.

vicelike (British spelling)

See **viselike** elsewhere in this dictionary.

vicinity (vih-**sin**-ih-tee)

noun The surrounding area. / *Order of the Phoenix*, page 403
The explosion in the janitor's closet made everyone in the vicinity jump.

vigil (**vij**-ul)

noun A period of watchful attention or wakefulness, waiting for someone or something. / *Deathly Hallows*, page 75
Merlin and Wildwood joined the silent vigil at the bedside of the village mascot.

vigilance (**vij**-uh-luns)

noun Watchfulness. / *Goblet of Fire*, page 217
The vigilance of the wandmaker paid off; he caught Klingster red-handed, trying to steal wand secrets.

vilify (**vil**-uh-fie)

verb To slander, defame, or say nasty untrue things about someone. / *Half-Blood Prince*, page 529

The election got pretty nasty, with Blackpool constantly vilifying the mayor.

vindictive (vin-**dik**-tive)

adjective Revengeful or vengeful; out to get someone. / *Prisoner of Azkaban*, page 142
Rilda had been spreading vindictive rumors about Brilly and Willow.

vindictiveness (vin-**dik**-tiv-ness)

noun A malevolent and mean desire for revenge. / *Goblet of Fire*, page 209
The vindictiveness of the poltergeist caused endless problems in the house; his latest trick involved putting giant slugs on the stairs.

visage (**viz**-ij)

noun The face. / *Order of the Phoenix*, page 508
The visage of the May Fete queen was still specky, but at least the worst of the pimples had disappeared.

vicelike (**vise**-like)

adjective A British spelling of "viselike," meaning like a vise, a device that holds an object very firmly. / *Order of the Phoenix*, page 609
The hawk's talons held the struggling rat in its viselike grip.

visibility (viz-uh-**bil**-ih-tee)

noun The ability to get a clear view. / *Order of the Phoenix*, page 51
The visibility from the Far Hills was amazing.

visor (**vie**-zur)

noun On a suit of armor, a hinged piece that comes down over the eyes, but with slits or holes so the wearer can see out. / *Prisoner of Azkaban*, page 100
The prince was certain there were really people in the empty suits of armor, and kept peering in the visors to see who was there.

visualize (**visz**-oo-uh-lize)

verb To make a mental image of; to imagine visually. / *Deathly Hallows*, page 65
"I just can't visualize myself at school today," explained Brilly. "Tough," said his mother. "Get up and go to school."

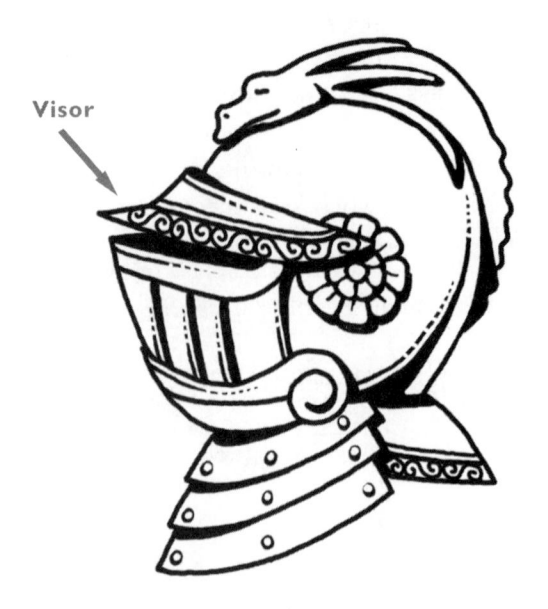

Visor

vivacious (vih-**vay**-shus)

adjective Lively, animated, and high-spirited. / *Half-Blood Prince*, page 70
The vivacious Willow charmed everyone at the dance, but she only had eyes for a certain someone.

vociferous (voh-**sif**-ur-us)

adjective Noisy and talkative in an intent and determined way. / *Goblet of Fire*, page 239
Blackpool's vociferous arguments were getting tiresome.

void (rhymes with 'droid)

noun An empty space. / *Deathly Hallows*, page 260
Dylan, about to bungee jump, looked down into the void and wondered if he'd lost his mind.

vol-au-vents (voh-lo-**vuhn**)

noun A small, light pastry shell filled with meat (or fish or chicken) and sauce, served as an appetizer or a main course. / *Deathly Hallows*, page 89
The king preferred a joint of beef to more delicate foods such as vol-au-vents.

volition (voh-**lish**-un)
noun An act of one's own choosing or willing. / *Half-Blood Prince*, page 435
The Hopeless Shapeless Things drifted down Nightmare Alley, moving seemingly of their own volition (but perhaps it was the wind).

volley (**vol**-ee)
noun A bursting forth of many things together, usually noisily. / *Chamber of Secrets*, page 95
The volley of crashes suggested the Royal Cook's apprentice had dropped the doughnut pans again.

voluble (**vol**-yuh-bul)
adjective Talking a lot or quickly. / *Deathly Hallows*, page 516
The voluble concert crowd made it difficult to hear the man sitting behind her, but he seemed to want her to remove her witch's hat.

voluminous (vol-**loo**-muh-nus)
adjective Ample, even very big. / *Goblet of Fire*, page 120
The old witch's voluminous cloak held many ancient secrets.

Witch with voluminous cloak

vouch (rhymes with **pouch**)
verb To attest or guarantee. / *Goblet of Fire*, page 590
"I wasn't at school that day," explained Brilly, "so I couldn't have done it. My mom'll vouch that I was home in bed."

vouchsafe (vowch-**safe**)
verb To promise something as a privilege or special favor. / *Half-Blood Prince*, page 541
Merlin vouchsafed the exiled wizard's return.

vulture (**vul**-chur)
noun A large, creepy bird of prey with dark feathers and a featherless head that usually eats dead bodies. / *Chamber of Secrets*, page 163
The flock of vultures enjoyed lunch on the Weeping Highway, devouring a possum that had misjudged the milk cart's wheels.

W

waddle (whad-ul)
verb To take short steps that sort of tilt the body from side to side. / *Sorcerer's Stone*, page 28
Father Goose waddled into the Fowl Weather Friends meeting, late again.

waft (rhymes with **boffed**)
verb To float along easily; to drift. / *Sorcerer's Stone*, page 170
The potion's smell wafted through the air, convincing everyone in the neighborhood that someone somewhere was baking an apple pie.

wail (rhymes with **mail**)
verb To express pain or grief with long, loud cries. / *Sorcerer's Stone*, page 23
The giant let out a wail of surprise and pain when the tree he was sitting under suddenly fell over on him.

waistcoat (wayst-koht)
noun A vest—sleeveless, buttons down the front, worn over a shirt and, sometimes, under a jacket. / *Order of the Phoenix*, page 437
Wildwood's waistcoat had a small pocket for his pocket watch and a larger pocket for treats for any passing animals.

wake (rhymes with **make**)
noun The path behind someone or something that's passed. / *Half-Blood Prince*, page 341
Tiny Tinkles, the fairy, flew through the crowd in Wildwood's wake—it was so nice to have someone open a path ahead.

walking stick (walk-ing stik)
noun In British usage, a cane. / *Sorcerer's Stone*, page 129
Winston's grandfather used a walking stick to help him walk, and to wave whenever he got mad.

wallop (wol-up)
verb To really hit someone hard. / *Chamber of Secrets*, page 79
"Unghhnh." The soccer penalty kick walloped Butch in the stomach, and he crumpled to his knees.

wallow (wol-oh)
verb To indulge or revel in a feeling, like sadness or self-pity. / *Order of the Phoenix*, page 536
Milton wallowed in self-pity when he failed two classes last year.

wan (rhymes with **don**)
adjective Pale and weak. / *Chamber of Secrets*, page 286
Wildwood was so tired and wan after the Day of the Dead excitement that he went home and slept 14 hours straight.

wane (rhymes with **bane**; sounds exactly like **Wayne**)
verb To decline in strength or importance. / *Order of the Phoenix*, page 699 / Note: See also the related verb **wane** below.
The later it got, the more the ogre's energy waned.

wane (rhymes with **bane**; sounds exactly like **Wayne**)
verb To move from the full moon to the new moon, as gradually less and less of the moon is visible. / *Prisoner of Azkaban*, page 353 / Note: See also the related verb **wane** above.
The moon waned slowly every night. Soon, the bright mystery of the full moon became the stumbling darkness of the new moon.

wardrobe (war-drohb)
noun A large piece of furniture to hang clothes in. / *Chamber of Secrets*, page 292
Wildwood decided to clean out his wardrobe when it became so crowded he couldn't hang another thing in there.

warlock (war-lok)
noun A male witch or sorcerer. / *Chamber of Secrets*, page 31
The visiting warlock spoke at the school assembly on "Chills and Thrills—Freezing Spells and How to Use Them."

warming pan (war-ming pan)

noun A long-handled, covered pan, usually brass, that's filled with hot coals then slid between the bed sheets and moved around to warm the bed. / *Goblet of Fire*, page 191
A bed warmed by a warming pan—a wonderful treat on a cold winter night.

wary (ware-ee)

adjective Watchful and a little cautious. / *Half-Blood Prince*, page 120 / Note: **Warier**, a related adjective found in *Half-Blood Prince* (page 270), means "even more watchful and cautious."
The owl gave the hawk a wary look—who exactly was going to use this corner of the meadow to find lunch?

waspish (wos-pish)

adjective Spiteful and resentful. / *Chamber of Secrets*, page 186
Blackpool's waspish comments about Willow and her "insignificant little whelps" were needlessly cruel.

wasted (way-sted)

adjective Thin, weak, frail. / *Prisoner of Azkaban*, page 340
When the cast finally came off the boy's broken arm, his muscles were wasted from disuse.

wastrel (way-strul)

noun A lazy idler or good-for-nothing person. / *Prisoner of Azkaban*, page 28
Milton was getting a reputation as a wastrel—he didn't want to go to school or do much of anything.

waterlogged (wah-tur-lawgd)

adjective Saturated with water. / *Half-Blood Prince*, page 575
The pieces of wood washed up on the lake shore looked like they'd make good firewood, but actually they were so waterlogged they'd probably never burn.

watermark (wah-tur-mark)

noun A design that's pressed into paper when it's made; it can only be seen by holding the paper up to the light. / *Order of the Phoenix*, page 161
"This is practically scratch paper," said the annoyed shop owner. "There's no watermark and it's as light as newsprint—I want some *real* paper."

waxen (wak-sun)

adjective Looking like wax—pale, smooth, unmoving. / *Deathly Hallows*, page 461
His waxen face stared back at him in the bathroom mirror—he was so tired he could hardly lift an eyebrow.

waxwork (waks-work)

noun A wax model of someone. / *Half-Blood Prince*, page 597
Brilly took a huge fat candle, sat in the hot sun, and tried to carve a waxwork of his dog.

waylay (way-lay)

verb To intercept someone unexpectedly. / *Goblet of Fire*, page 285
Wildwood tried to waylay Ethelbell on her way to the Day of the Dead festivities, but he missed her.

wayside (way-side)

adjective Located along the side of a road or path. / *Goblet of Fire*, page 11
The little boy's wayside lemonade stand wasn't getting much business, so he relocated to the village green.

weal (rhymes with **zeal**; sounds exactly like **wheel**)

noun A painful mark on the skin raised by a blow; a welt. / *Order of the Phoenix*, page 534
The vine snapped back and whipped across Wildwood's forearm, leaving a nasty weal.

weasel (wee-zul)

verb To evade an obligation; usually used with the word "out." / *Order of the Phoenix*, page 343
Rupert weaseled out of babysitting his little brother on Friday night.

weather vane (weth-ur vain)

noun A device on a rooftop that indicates which way the wind is blowing. / *Goblet of Fire*, page 78
The weather vane on Blackpool's house was in the shape of a broom-riding wizard.

The server at the Trolls' Hole pub wended her way between the tightly packed tables, carrying brimming flagons of mead.

werewolf (where-wulf)

noun In folklore, someone who assumes the form of a wolf when the moon is full; generally considered an evil being. / *Chamber of Secrets*, page 161 / Note: In Potter's world, there are both very good and very evil people who change into werewolves.

The curious werewolf checked the almanac to see the coming year's schedule of full moons.

wheedle (weed-ul)

verb To persuade or try to persuade with flattery or deceit. / *Half-Blood Prince*, page 497

"Please please please, I'll be good," wheedled the little boy, hoping to stay up late to watch the gecko races.

whelp (rhymes with **help**)

noun A young dog or lion; can be used in a derogatory way meaning a young person, especially a despised one. / *Deathly Hallows*, page 592

"Those little whelps trashed my garden!" raged Blackpool.

whey-faced (way-faysd)

adjective Having a pale face, especially from fright. / *Order of the Phoenix*, page 468

The whey-faced Dribbles worried: Ahead in the field was a very mad cow, and might that mean it had mad cow disease?

wholeheartedly (hole-har-tud-lee)

adverb Completely, sincerely, unreservedly. / *Chamber of Secrets*, page 287

The Sisters of Sorcery threw themselves wholeheartedly into the Day of the Dead preparations.

wickerwork (wik-ur-work)

adjective Made of interlaced twigs or twig-like material called wicker. / *Prisoner of Azkaban*, page 70

The wickerwork basket on Blackpool's bike held a book on worm diseases, a thermos of hot bipple juice, his wand, and a skull.

Werewolf in winged armchair

weedy-looking (wee-dee-look-ing)

adjective Scrawny or ungainly looking. / *Order of the Phoenix*, page 583

"That's one weedy-looking giraffe," said Ravi, leaning on the zoo fence.

Wellington boots (wel-ing-ton boots)

noun High (almost to the knees) rubber or leather boots meant to keep feet dry; named after the Duke of Wellington, a famous general. / *Deathly Hallows*, page 106

"Have you seen your dad's Wellington boots?" asked Winston's mum. "He's going newt hunting in the Big Bog."

welt (rhymes with **melt**)

noun A painful mark on the skin raised by a blow; a weal. / *Order of the Phoenix*, page 847

The enchanted rope whipped out of control and hit Tamika's arm, raising a nasty welt.

wend (rhymes with **mend**)

verb To move or go slowly from one point to another. / *Order of the Phoenix*, page 236

wide berth, as in **to give someone a wide berth**

phrase To avoid or stay away from someone or something. / *Chamber of Secrets*, page 132
The feuding ogres gave each other a wide berth as they passed in the mountains.

wind me up

phrase In British slang, to say or do something to make someone else angry or worried, as a joke. / *Prisoner of Azkaban*, page 192
"You're just winding me up, aren't you?" said Winston's dad. "You didn't really get suspended…did you?"

windpipe (wind-pipe)

noun The trachea, the tube-like body part that carries air to the lungs. / *Order of the Phoenix*, page 802
"Ackkhhhk." Something had gone down the boy's windpipe and he was choking, but with a deft wave of her wand, Mrs. Snodgrape popped it out. That move became known as the Snodgrape Maneuver.

wing mirror (wing-mir-ur)

noun In British usage, the side mirror on a car or truck. / *Deathly Hallows*, page 755
Whenever Merlin visited London, he loved to stop and look at himself in the wing mirror of every car on the street. He seemed to see something different in every mirror.

winged armchair (wingd arm-chair)

noun A large upholstered chair with a high back and large side pieces to rest your head against. / *Half-Blood Prince*, page 494
Wildwood's winged armchair was the perfect place for an afternoon nap.

wireless set (why-ur-less set)

noun An old-fashioned word for a radio; sometimes called just a wireless. / *Half-Blood Prince*, page 330
The king tuned his wireless set to the local station every evening at 6 p.m. for the news.

wistfully (wist-ful-ee)

adverb In a wishful, yearning, sad way. / *Goblet of Fire*, page 164
The Princess of the Deep waved wistfully as the herd of seahorses waggled a goodbye back—they were off to find warmer water, and she'd really miss them.

wither (with-ur)

verb To rapidly grow older, shriveling and wrinkling quickly. / *Prisoner of Azkaban*, page 320
The enchanted sorceress started the day as a young girl, but by evening she had withered into an old woman.

without further ado

phrase Without delaying or wasting any more time. / *Order of the Phoenix*, page 503
"And now without further ado, here are the Tomb Tones to open our annual Day of the Dead celebration, with your favorite songs of death and decay."

wizened (wiz-und)

adjective Small, thin, withered, and wrinkled. / *Prisoner of Azkaban*, page 42
Dribbles worried: Why isn't a wizened person really wise instead of just old and wrinkled?

woe betide

phrase To be in trouble unless one does some task or action. / *Chamber of Secrets*, page 36
"Woe betide anyone who keeps me from watching the Super Bowl on TV today," warned the king.

woebegone (woh-bih-gawn)

adjective Showing or indicating woe and sadness. / *Prisoner of Azkaban*, page 59
The woebegone little boy was crying—a demented wasp had just popped his balloon.

wolf down (wulf down)

verb To eat as fast and greedily as possible, like a hungry wolf. / *Sorcerer's Stone*, page 21
Hassan was so hungry he wolfed down the gummy bear salad in about 30 seconds.

wolfhound (wulf-hound)

noun A large dog used for hunting wolves. / *Order of the Phoenix*, page 236
The huge wolfhound bounded across the village green, chasing down any passing Frisbee.

wolverine (wool-vuh-reen)

noun A very fierce, stocky, shaggy mammal. /

Goblet of Fire, page 43
The wolverines didn't attack the mountain gremlins, but they were quick to attack anything else that wandered into their territory.

woolly (wool-ee)
adjective Mentally disorganized; not showing clear thinking. / *Prisoner of Azkaban*, page 111 / Note: In *Order of the Phoenix* (page 255), a related adjective **woolly** means "fuzzy or made of wool."
"Your plan seems pretty woolly to me, Brilly. Jellyfish in the swimming pool? Where will you get them? And why in the world would you do it?"

worm (rhymes with **germ**)
verb To get or obtain something by persistent efforts. / *Chamber of Secrets*, page 185
Rilda badgered Willow until she finally wormed the secret out of her.

wrack (rhymes with **brack**; sounds exactly like **rack**)
verb To try very hard to remember something or to figure out something. / *Half-Blood Prince*, page 447
Elrod wracked his memory—was it feed the mold, starve a beaver, or feed a beaver, starve the mold?

wrathful (rath-ful)
adjective Very angry. / *Chamber of Secrets*, page 82
The wrathful owl, upset that the hawk had beaten him to a mouse snack, flew through the Haunted Forest hooting "Yoooo! Yoooo!

wreak (rhymes with **tweak**; sounds exactly like **reek**)
verb To inflict or bring about something. / *Half-Blood Prince*, page 12
The poltergeist wreaked more damage that night than ever before—something must have really annoyed him.

wrench (rhymes with **bench**)
noun A sharp distressing strain or feeling of sadness. / *Prisoner of Azkaban*, page 191
It was a wrench to leave the village, even for a few days, but Wildwood had business in London, so off he went.

wrench (rhymes with **bench**)
verb To pull or twist with sudden force. /

Sorcerer's Stone, page 41
An angry Wildwood wrenched open Blackpool's front door and shouted, "What did you do to my fence?!"

wrest (rhymes with **best**; sounds exactly like **rest**)
verb To take something from someone, especially with some effort. / *Half-Blood Prince*, page 372
The old witch wrested her wand from the curious little boy. "Now give that back, dearie, RIGHT NOW!"

writhe (ryeth)
verb To twist and turn the body, or to struggle, usually in great pain or discomfort. / *Deathly Hallows*, page 85
The Royal Sentry writhed in pain when the chain broke and the castle drawbridge fell on his foot.

wrong-foot (rong-foot)
verb To get someone to lead with or to use the wrong foot. / *Prisoner of Azkaban*, page 169
"If you wrong-foot yourself with the first step, you'll never get back in time with the music," advised the dance teacher.

wrought (rhymes with **got**)
verb To make, especially metal articles that are shaped by beating with a hammer. / *Deathly Hallows*, page 490
The metal lampshade had been wrought by the talented elves at the Light & Power factory.

wrought-iron (rawt-eye-urn)
adjective A form of iron that can be easily shaped, forged, or welded. / *Sorcerer's Stone*, page 93
The wrought-iron fence around the witch's cottage was very effective. Despite the thorny roses that grew on it, it looked like prison bars and kept everyone away.

wry (rhymes with **why**; sounds exactly like **rye**)
adjective Ironically humorous or amusing. / *Deathly Hallows*, page 518
A wry idea came to Brilly: What if he went a whole month without breaking a single rule? That'd confuse them all.

Y

Y fronts (why frunts)
noun In British usage, men's underwear or briefs. / *Deathly Hallows*, page 227
"Keep your Y fronts on, Winston. I'll be right there."

yearn (rhymes with **turn**)
verb To long extremely for something or someone, or to do something. / *Chamber of Secrets*, page 270
Annie yearned for a newer, faster broomstick.

yeoman (yoh-mun)
noun In British usage, an old-fashioned word for a farmer who owned and worked on his own land. Plural: yeomen. / *Prisoner of Azkaban*, page 249
The king greeted the yeomen working in the cornfield next to the castle—it's always best to stay on good terms with one's neighbors.

yeti (yet-ee)
noun A legendary large, hairy, manlike creature that many believe really lives in the Himalayan Mountains; also known as the Abominable Snowman. / *Chamber of Secrets*, page 161
Dribbles worried: Are there any women yeti? Is there an Abominable Snowwoman?

Yorkshire pudding (york-shur puh-ding)
noun A British food, like a popover or very light puffy biscuit, baked in the pan with the drippings from roast beef. / *Sorcerer's Stone*, page 123
The Yorkshire pudding wasn't really a pudding at all—maybe it should be called a Yorkshire popover.

The Unofficial Harry Potter Vocabulary Builder • 235

Z

zombie (zom-bee)
noun A corpse revived by a magic spell or by a supernatural power. / *Sorcerer's Stone*, page 134 / Note: In Potter's world, the zombie-like beings are called Inferi.
The zombies walk at midnight, so it's best to be home safe in bed well before then.

Zombie

zoological (zoo-uh-**lodj**-uh-kul)
adjective Having to do with zoology, the study of animals. / *Goblet of Fire*, page 370
The zoological expert enjoyed lecturing about animals at the school—today's topic was "Raising a Rhino at Home for Fun and Profit."

Epilogue

Brilly, amazingly, calmed down eventually. He's doing very well in college and would one day like to be a school principal himself.

Willow and **Brilly** have been going together for a long time. It looks serious. She still has four of her puppies. They've grown into sizable dogs, so they'll need a big place to live.

Dylan, sadly, died before graduating—apparently he had real stomach problems. Fiona sang at his funeral and everyone still misses him.

Dribbles, who always wondered and always worried, is studying linguistics and philosophy. He'll be a university professor some day.

Bella wants to be a math teacher—she'll certainly be the best-dressed one ever. She still changes her hair color regularly.

Fiona got on *American Idol* and did well, but it was her single, "The Lament of the Lovesick Lizard," that really boosted her career.

Annie has won every broomstick award there is. She loves—and lives—to fly.

Milton, a lost soul, dropped out of school, and no one knows what's happened to him. Sad.

Ravi never much liked school. He opened a broomstick repair shop and is doing well.

Chi-Mun started a health food restaurant in the village. Armadillo/possum stew is not on the menu.

Rilda writes a gossip column for the local paper.

The rest of the kids—**Rupert, Elrod, Winston, Brady, Parker, Tamika, Nathan, Hassan, Julio, Jenn,** and **Daniel**—have all gone on to college. Nathan also won the National Skateboarders Cup just last year, and Brady is writing a fantasy novel.

Butch Thuggins retired from soccer after his fourth broken nose and first broken leg. He works at the village zoo now and is very happy.

Esmerelda is rapidly becoming a lonely old witch.

Nungie and **Tinkles** became best friends. Tinkles often perches on Nungie's lap as he wheels about the village.

Blackpool ran for mayor again and got two votes. This time his mother voted for him, too. He remains as creatively evil as ever.

Wildwood still sits quietly by the lake and smokes his pipe. He's helping Butch at the zoo, and his leek crop this year was the best ever. His old dog died, but now he's raising one of Willow's puppies.

Madam Glinch, Mrs. Snodgrape, and the **potions master** are still teaching. The **principal** and the **cafeteria manager** have gone on to other jobs.

The **mayor** is still in office. Both of his dream plans—condos in the meadows and a highway through town—were not successful.

The **Rolling Bones** decided not to retire and are still performing sold-out concerts. The **Tomb Tones** broke up just last year, and their lead singer is trying a career on his own.

As for the **Royal Family**, the king continues to rule imperiously and kindly, both at the same time. The queen is as uppity as ever. The princess and the Knight of the Hounds almost got married, but it turned out he really *did* think more of his hounds than of her. The prince plays drums in Fiona's back-up band.

The **Royal Plumber** cleaned the castle moat successfully and was knighted by the king. He travels a lot now, making speeches on "Slime—How It Changed My Life."

W

About the Author

Sayre Van Young, reference librarian and editor, knows a difficult word when she sees it. She brings her British background, her library skills, and her quirky imagination—honed during many long hours in the library—to this vocabulary builder "story." Her previous books include *London's War: A Traveler's Guide to World War II* and *MicroSource: Where to Find Answers to Questions about Microcomputers*. Van Young lives in Berkeley, California, where she seldom has the opportunity to use "pince-nez" or "basilisk," but is happy she can pronounce them and use them appropriately if needed.